The Flowers of the Forest

Scotland and the First World War

Trevor Royle

BIRLINN

This corrected edition first published in 2007 by
Birlinn Limited
West Newington House
10 Newington Road
Edinburgh
EH9 1QS

www.birlinn.co.uk

3

First published in 2006 by Birlinn Limited

ISBN: 978 1 84341 040 9

British Library Cataloguing-in-Publication Data
A catalogue record for this book is available from the British Library

Designed and typeset by Iolaire Typesetting, Newtonmore
Printed and bound by Grafica Veneta
www.graficaveneta.com

Dedicated to the memory of a much-loved son,
PATRICK EVANS ROYLE
1975–2006

Contents

List of Illustrations

Preface and Acknowledgements

On 15 January 1917 Captain J. C. Black, the convener of the British Services Committee of the St Andrew Society of Glasgow wrote a long and impassioned letter to the Scottish secretary, Robert Munro. His message was clear and simple. Reminding Munro that his society contained some of the greatest names in Scottish public life, Black got straight to the point. He understood that an official history of the war was being planned by the Historical Branch of the Committee of Imperial Defence, and, that being so, the St ·Andrew Society of Glasgow wanted to ascertain that great care would be taken to ensure 'that correct national names and terms be used throughout in these histories and to ask your valuable assistance in obtaining this most desirable result'. Lest anyone should have thought that this was a case of being over-sensitive, Black hoped that Munro would 'not view this letter as a premature protest, but as an earnest appeal on behalf of the Scottish nation to make certain that, in the forthcoming histories, justice will be accorded, and due credit given to Scotland for the part which she has, and is, so nobly playing in this great war'. In other words Black and his committee did not want to see Scotland's contribution to the war being under-played nor did they want 'English' to be used in place of 'British' as a generic national description.

It was not the first letter that Black had produced on the subject. Three months earlier, on 14 October 1916, he had written in similar vein to the Hon. John Fortescue, the Royal Librarian at Windsor, who had been engaged as the first official historian in February that year. Whatever else it did, Black's letter clearly nettled Fortescue, a patrician military historian who was the author of a number of highly rated titles, including a monumental *History of the British Army*. His reply was short and to the point: 'Will you kindly ask your committee if it has ever heard the story of the grandmother and the eggs?' Taking that as a slight, as indeed it was, Black wrote again, this time to the Secretary of the Historical Section, Committee of Imperial Defence, complaining about Fortescue's rudeness and forcibly stating the case for Scotland's contribution to be emphasised in the official history. Once again the correspondence managed to cause offence. On 3 November the secretary sent a tart reply, stating that he could not intervene and indicating that Black was being too prickly in his approach: 'Being entirely in sympathy with your complaint I may perhaps suggest that a different tone in your appeals would be more likely to carry conviction on this side of the border.' The matter was eventually resolved to Black's satisfaction on 22 January 1917 when James M. Dodds of the Scottish Office replied on behalf of the Scottish Secretary. Having discussed the matter with the official historians he informed Black that the Scottish Secretary was 'satisfied that they are quite alive to the importance of the point on which your Society lays stress'.[1]

It would take until 1925 before the first of the fourteen volumes of the official history of the First World War on the Western Front was produced, under the title *History of the Great War Based on Official Documents by Direction of the Historical Section of the Committee of Imperial Defence, Military Operations, France and Belgium*. By then the compilation had passed into the hands of Brigadier-General J. E. Edmonds, a career soldier who had served on Haig's staff on the Western Front. It was a huge achievement, involving a team of writers and researchers who based their evidence on 25,000 boxes of wartime papers and all the campaign maps produced during the war. Other official histories were published for the war's main fronts and also for naval and air force operations. By the time they appeared Fortescue had long since relinquished any role in their compilation. From the outset he had been reluctant to accept the task and by 1919 he had taken the history as far as May 1915. Even though he had written 1,800 pages he was increasingly frustrated by the absence of key documents and by a growing suspicion that they would never be produced. Matters came to a head when Field Marshal Sir John French published *1914*, his account of the first months of the war: Fortescue produced such a highly critical review ('one of the most unfortunate books ever to be written') that he was asked to stand down as official historian, a decision he did not question as by then his heart was not in the task.[2]

Any reading of the Official History (as it is generally known) would show that Black and his fellow St Andrew Society members need not have been concerned about nomenclature. The authors make scrupulous use of the term 'British', and although they did not single out Scottish regiments or names, other than as a matter of record, it is possible to understand the role, say, of the 9th and 15th Scottish Divisions at the Battle of Loos in 1915 or the part played by Scottish contingents at Gallipoli. Quite rightly, this is a British reading of a British military experience and, while they have been criticised for their interpretation of events, the volumes did succeed in achieving the aims of the Historical Section of the Committee of Imperial Defence, namely, to produce a reasonably impartial narrative based on primary sources. However, that thorough approach means that with the notable exception of Catriona M. M. Macdonald and E. W. McFarland's collection of essays, *Scotland and the Great War,* based on a conference held in November 1997, Scotland's history of the First World War remains largely unwritten. In the field of oral history both Ian MacDougall, *Voices from War*, and Derek Young, *Forgotten Scottish Voices from the Great War*, have done sterling work in recording and memorialising the testimony of individual Scots and making sure that their contribution has not been overlooked. There have also been sizable examinations of the period in recent histories of twentieth-century Scotland, most recently by Richard Finlay and Christopher Harvie, but, ninety years after the Battle of the Somme in which so many Scottish soldiers lost their lives, the time might be ripe for some deeper digging and reassessment.

First things first: this is not a history of the First World War as seen through Scottish eyes or an attempt to wrap the home front and the main battle-fronts in a kilt. Rather, it is the story of the role played by Scotland and Scots in influencing the British management of the war and of how the country was changed irrevocably as a result of the experience of over four years of warfare. Within the United Kingdom Scotland supplied a greater proportion per head of population of the assault troops that engaged in the great battles of attrition in 1915 and

1916; half of Scotland's male population aged between eighteen and forty-five was in uniform. Casualties were correspondingly high and consequently disproportionate. Industry too suffered. From being the workshop of the British war effort Scotland's heavy industries went into decline and while there were innovations in the workplace, such as the rise of trade union influence and the employment of women, these turned out not to be the breakthrough hoped for by many idealists and dreamers. Home rule was also a casualty: it was almost on the statute books in August 1914 but disappeared as a result of the collapse of its sponsors, the Liberals, and the failure of Labour to offer it any realistic support.

No book of this kind could have been attempted without a thorough reading of the many works that have helped to inform my thinking. The titles are listed in the bibliography but I would like to place on record the following authors' names in thanks for the keen insights provided by their work: Jack Alexander, John Baynes, Eileen Crofton, Tom Devine, Richard Finlay, Christopher Harvie, Diana Henderson, I. G. C. Hutchison, Billy Kay, William Kenefick, Clive H. Lee, Leah Leneman, Catriona M. M. Macdonald, Ian MacDougall, Arthur McIvor, Iain McLean, Hugh Peebles, Gary Sheffield, T. C. Smout, Hew Strachan, John Terraine, Ian S. Wood and Derek Young. I am particularly grateful to Ian S. Wood for lending me material on Scottish labour history and to Lindy Ogilvy Maclean for guiding me through Glen Prosen's muster roll.

For permission to quote copyright material I would like to thank the following: Elizabeth Hamilton Lauder for *Minstrel in France* by Harry Lauder (Andrew Melrose), Ian Macdougall for the use of extracts from *Voices from War* (Mercat Press), Mainstream Publishing for *McCrae's Battalion* by Jack Alexander, Penguin Books Ltd for Lyn Macdonald, *Voices and Images of the Great War* (Michael Joseph), Regimental Headquarters Royal Scots for *Pontius Pilate's Bodyguard: The History of the Royal Scots* vol. i by Robert Paterson. Every attempt has been made to contact copyright holders and any omissions will be made good in future editions.

For their customary help and courtesy I would also like to thank the staff of the National Library of Scotland and the staffs of the National Archives at Kew and the National Archives of Scotland in Edinburgh.

My final thanks are to my publisher Hugh Andrew, who suggested the book in the first place. He and the Scottish Arts Council made sure that it saw the light of day. Little did he know at the time that it was a book that I was waiting to write.

Trevor Royle
Edinburgh/Angus
August 2005

Prologue
The Braes of Angus 1914

Take a look at the horizon in any part of Scotland and the hills are never far away. They are constant companions, unchanging and unchangeable, part of a familiar landscape. Turn from the wider picture and focus on the particular; drive up one of the roads on the coastal littoral between Dundee and Aberdeen and to the west the hills appear as a purple line, pencilled from late autumn to spring with unmistakable streaks of snow. Beyond, out of sight, rise the peaks of the Grampian massif, the high heart of Scotland with its austere tracks leading to distant lonely places. Here lie the Angus glens, or the Braes of Angus as they are also known, Highland by reason of rising on the north side of the fault line, yet less than an hour away from the city of Dundee and then another hour from the Central Belt. The hills are softer and more rounded than anything found further west towards the Atlantic coastline; the main glens – Isla, Prosen, Clova, Lethnot and Esk – stretch like fingers into the upper reaches where the bottomland along the burns and rivers gives way to the high heather-clad moors; farms dot the landscape, with blackface sheep and beef-rich cattle never far away. The number of people who live in the glens is not huge, their numbers are declining and that has been the way for at least two centuries, but one thing binds them to the Braes of Angus. They are in league with a land that for most of them has been home for generations. Not that the relationship has always been easy: for the most part their home is best described as 'marginal land' whose economic viability has always been fragile and perhaps always will be.

For the romantic, though, these are the hills of home, scattered with Munros and sufficiently uninhabited to turn a day's ridge-walk into an adventure, an open-air playground with soaring eagles and far-off deer for company. To the north, up Jock's Road and into the Mounth, Glen Doll is the entrance to the sterner values of the Cairngorms, irresistible to hill-walkers and climbers who want to test themselves against the harsher conditions of the high ground. Beyond beckons the huge bulk of dark Lochnagar, the mountain that dominates the eastern Grampian skyline. However, locals pay less attention to the scenery for they have to work in it in all weathers. Most make their living from sheep-farming and the shepherding that goes with it. Others are gamekeepers or provide the agricultural services that keep a small country farming community in business. Tourism is also important and there is an ever-changing succession of other smaller concerns, the kind found in any rural locality in Scotland. Big estates are still the focus of much employment and provide the bulk of the housing, just as they have done for centuries.

In a sense the Braes of Angus offer a microcosm of rural Scotland. Although they are made up largely of marginal land and the numbers of people living there have never been populous, they are not so far away from urban life as to be considered overly remote. Dundee, Perth and Aberdeen are less than fifty miles away and towns like Forfar, Brechin, Montrose and Kirriemuir are civic centres in their own right, with steady populations and economies. At the beginning of the twenty-first century the essential character of the Braes of Angus has altered little from what it was a hundred years ago in the period before the world went to war in August 1914. Of course there have been changes; no community ever stands still. Farming no longer offers employment to the army of horsemen, grieves, orra men and loons who once ran the big ferm-touns and won their work at the annual feeing markets; the heavy horse has disappeared to be replaced by the tractor and nowadays the farming is wholly mechanised; steam trains no longer puff along sleepy country branch lines, everywhere the car is king and in the glens themselves the numbers are declining. Take Glen Prosen, which has been in Ogilvy hands for over five hundred years since one Thomas Ogilvy bought 'the lands of Clova, Kyrktone of Clova, Arnitybbyr, Clauchleich and Balinharde'. It is a pleasant, rolling glen which benefits from having no through road as it runs its way from Dykehead to the upper reaches at Kilbo; there is a church but no village worth the name; the bottomland along the Prosen Water was once used for cropping and the high moors are home to sturdy upland blackface sheep. As is the case in most other rural areas, employment opportunities are limited and with only tourism to add to the local agricultural and sporting economy the glen's story has been one of steady if gentle decline over the past hundred years. The school was closed in the 1980s, attempts at running a shop or tearoom regularly come to grief, the congregation in the white-washed church is shrinking and there are few young heads to be seen amongst the greying ones of those who worship there of a Sunday.

Today there are only a score of households in the glen yet on the eve of war in 1914 there were forty-eight. Thanks to the presence of the Ogilvys' estate at Balnaboth, at the beginning of the twentieth century there was a sawmill, a blacksmith and a forge; each farm had its own corn mill and the estate employed a sizable workforce of gamekeepers, estate workers, shepherds and foresters, as well as domestic help in the 'big house'.[1] It was a thriving, self-contained community in which men had employment and families lived in their tenanted cottages, maintaining a thrifty domestic economy. Not that people living in Scotland's rural areas always enjoyed an easy life. The toil on the land was hard, the working day was long, there was no electricity and few cottages had running water or proper sanitation. In 1917 a Royal Commission on Housing in Scotland remarked that the average farm worker's house 'has too often been selected not for its suitability as a site but for economy of land and the convenience of the farm worker. The result is that the site is often a contributing factor in the prevailing dampness of the houses, and aggravates the difficulties of water supply and drainage.'[2] The pay was poor, too, with men on the land being paid an average of £20 a year, and although the Agriculture (Scotland) Act of 1911 had extended the rights of security and tenure it was still easy enough for landowners to evict tenants from their cottages. It would be convenient to sentimentalise that way of life and to make legends of the people who lived on the land but, as one of the chroniclers of rural life in Angus and the Mearns has pointed out, the area bred 'dour folk; strange folk often droll to the point of eccentricity; folk with a humour so dry sometimes that it was just this side of maliciousness; folk whose pleasures were mainly simple and not infrequently carnal. They were people of a special strain, resilient and enduring; in another context their men became the backbone of regiments and their loyalty was heavily traded in the discreet corridors of Whitehall.'[3]

The First World War was the first great challenge to this frequently precarious way of life. As happened in other parts of the country the young men of the glen joined up in 1914 with the same sense of enthusiasm and urgency that took thousands of other volunteers into the colours. David Archer, a blacksmith, was already a member of the Territorial Force when he went off to war with the 1/5th (Angus) Battalion of the Black Watch, which landed at Le Havre on 13 November 1914 and was soon in action as part of 24th Brigade in the British Army's 8th Division. David Shaw, the under-keeper at Craig Lodge, joined up as soon as he was eighteen and enlisted on 6 October with 9th Seaforth Highlanders at Fort George near Inverness. Harry Volume, the son of the schoolmaster at Wateresk, was working in Glasgow as a clerk when the war broke out but he was in uniform by the end of August as a private in the 9th Cameronians, one of the army's special service battalions which had been formed at Hamilton to train the growing numbers of volunteers. By coincidence, across the Atlantic in Montreal his brother Edward joined up at the same time in the Montreal Highlanders. Others were already in the armed forces, notably members of the glen's landed families. From Balnaboth John Ogilvy served in the Indian Army (1st Gurkha Rifles) as did his kinsman Alastair Fitzhugh MacLean (33rd Punjabis), while John Stormonth-Darling of neighbouring Lednathie was a career soldier in the Cameronians, having served in the Boer War with the regiment's 2nd battalion, which was designated 2nd Scottish Rifles, but in 1914 he was with the 1st battalion when it crossed over to France on 22 August. Stormonth-Darling was described by a regimental historian as being 'a big man physically, and a powerful heavyweight horseman. He was strict with junior officers and other ranks alike, and demanded very high standards. He was not particularly clever, but full of common sense and blunt and forthright in his speech. There was a definite type like him found in the Services in those days.'[4]

As the war progressed and it became obvious that it was going to be a long and drawn-out business other men from the glen followed them, first as volunteers and then as conscripts after the passing of the National Military Service Act at the beginning of 1916. William Lindsay, the shepherd at Spott farm, joined The Black Watch as soon as he was of age on 28 May 1915. George Howe, the under-gardener at Balnaboth, was called up in July 1916 at the age of twenty-six. He served with 9th Black Watch and was wounded while fighting with them as part of 15th Scottish Division during the Battle of Arras a year later. One young man, Edward McPherson, who was born in the glen at Pitcarity in 1897, was under-age when he joined the Mercantile Marine to serve on the fleet auxiliary *Moorfoot*. Another man of the glen, James Melville, a ploughman, was only four days past his eighteenth birthday when he was called up into 1/6th Black Watch on 31 May 1918 even though agricultural workers had been ex-empted from the call-up in 1917. His father, David Melville, the glen's blacksmith, had been a soldier with The Gordon Highlanders for seventeen years and had fought with them in the Egyptian campaigns and in the Boer War.

The names of the glen men involved range from the Earl of Airlie, one of the leading landowners in the area, who served in France as a captain with the 10th Hussars, to Geordie McIntosh, the gamekeeper at Craig Lodge (the glen's shooting lodge), who served as a lance-corporal with 1/5th Black Watch and was wounded in action three times during his service in France. Both men were roughly the same age, having been born in 1893 and 1892 respectively, and both came from well-established Angus families. The Ogilvys, the family name of the Airlie earldom, are central to the history of the area. Their seat is at Cortachy Castle at the foot of Glen Clova, and it has been their main residence since 1642 following the destruction of Airlie Castle ('The Bonny Hoose o' Airlie') by the Argyllshire Campbells during the Wars of the Three Kingdoms. Prominent supporters of the Stewart cause in the seventeenth and eighteenth centuries, the Ogilvys inter-married with the English aristocracy to become prominent members of the British establishment. David Lyulph Gore Wolseley's father, the 6th earl, had been killed commanding the 12th Lancers at Diamond Hill during the Boer War. (According to local legend, his last words were hopelessly optimistic 'Moderate your language, sergeant!') Geordie McIntosh also came from a family with a long history in the area, his Stewart forebears having farmed at Presnerb in neighbouring Glen Isla before becoming established at Cormuir in Glen Prosen. Both men survived the war and continued their connection with the Braes of Angus, becoming in their time and in their different ways well-known and well-liked local personalities.

Once the war was over, in common with other rural communities, the people of Glen Prosen produced their own muster roll of men from the area who had left the Braes of Angus to fight in the country's armed forces, as a means of commemorating their service and recording their sacrifice. Altogether fifty-nine names were listed in the document and of that number eleven were killed in action or died later from their wounds. The names of these men are also listed on a simple tablet in the nave of the glen's small church:

Lieutenant-Colonel John Collier Stormonth-Darling, DSO, Lednathie, 9th Highland Light Infantry (Glasgow Highlanders), France 1916

Captain Alastair Fitzhugh Maclean, Balnaboth, 33rd Punjabis (attached 14th Sikhs), Gallipoli 1915

Lieutenant William Whyte, Spott, 5th Black Watch, France 1918

2nd Lieutenant Robert Hamilton Maclagan-Wedderburn, Corriehead, 1st Cameronians, France 1915

Lance-Corporal Duncan Campbell, Cramie, 5th Ox and Bucks Light Infantry, France 1916

Private James Campbell Davidson, Dalinch, 113th Infantry, 29th Division, US Army, France 1918

Private David Young Davidson, Dalinch, 2nd Scots Guards, France 1916

Private John Henry Charles Leighton, Balnaboth, 6th King's Own Scottish Borderers, Germany 1918

Private Allan Macpherson, Pitcarity, 8/10th Gordon Highlanders, France 1917

Private Charles Peters, Braeshalloch, 9th Black Watch, France 1918

Private George Stormont, Corriehead, 6th Canadian Highlanders, France 1917

Three other names not listed in the glen's muster roll also appear on the war memorial, bringing the glen's total war dead to fourteen: Corporal W. Addison, Black Watch, Tombeth; Private W. Leighton, Black Watch, Clova and Sapper W. T. White, Royal Engineers, Inchmill. A further twenty men of the glen were wounded or suffered from shellshock and two became prisoners of war. Of those who went off to war between 1914 and 1918, thirty-two were living in the glen at the beginning of the conflict or had close connections with households in the glen: twenty-two of their number were born in the glen and five were born elsewhere but had parents in the glen. Of the latter two groups, sixteen left to live elsewhere in Scotland at the end of the war and nine had already emigrated – five to Canada, two each to the United States and Australia.

In many respects Glen Prosen's example typifies the Scottish experience of the First World War as far as the countryside is concerned. The majority of the men who went off to fight far away from home were infantry privates. Excluding three who served in the Royal Navy, the Merchant Marine and the Royal Flying Corps the number amounted to forty-four, and there were slightly higher casualties in this group including the two Campbell brothers from Dalinch. At just over 16 per cent of the total, the glen's casualty rate was higher than the Scottish national figure, which has been estimated at around 100,000, although the figure has been computed to be as low as 74,000 and as high as 148,000. As with all statistics, Glen Prosen's figures have to be put into local context. Three of those killed belonged to the landowning families and had no direct links with the glen, in that they did not live there all the time, and three were already serving abroad, in India. Twice as many were wounded or went into captivity; David Shaw, the Craig Lodge shepherd, had the misfortune to be wounded four times between 1914 and 1918 and David Volume, a student in 1916, was shellshocked at Arras and turned up later in a German prison camp. The biggest loss to the glens came from those twenty-five young men who left the glen to live in other parts of Scotland or continued living abroad once the war was over; at almost 40 per cent of the glen's muster roll, this figure mirrors the depopulation of rural Scotland after the war.

The war did not completely change Glen Prosen. It would take another world conflict to complete the steady decline as men moved off the land to escape the tedium and drudgery of rural labour and seek work in the towns, but because the Scottish war losses in rural areas were disproportionately high it did alter the complexion of the glen. In 1914 about 250,000 of Scotland's population of 4.8 million lived in rural areas such as the Braes of Angus. As a result the loss of so many young lives was more marked than in the larger and more densely populated towns and cities, not least because one in three country men had volunteered (most being members of the Territorial Force) and because losses were difficult to make good. Between 1921 and 1931 the size of Scotland's agricultural workforce was reduced by some 16 per cent and the output fell proportionately: returning soldiers did not always want to go back to the long hours and isolation of a life which held few attractions in the bothies and chaumers of the ferm-touns. However, for the survivors who came back to Prosen life went on much as before, if on a reduced scale. After the First World War both the glen's main estates remained in the hands of the Ogilvys and the Stormonth-Darlings, and, although there were cutbacks and economies in the local community, the grouse moors provided ample employment and stability at a time when those virtues were lacking elsewhere in Scotland, where one in five estates were put on the market between 1918 and 1921. The changes were more subtle and longer lasting. By the 1930s only one in five Scots were living in settlements numbering fewer than a thousand people, and the housing stock was poor, with a 1937 Report on Rural Housing in Scotland revealing that the bulk of agricultural homes were unfit for human habitation. There had been a steady exodus away from the land with numbers regularly exceeding the 60,000 who emigrated each year in the run-up to 1914. Ahead, too, lay the great depression and economic collapse of the 1920s, which plunged the country into crisis and made a mockery of the government's claims that it was creating 'a land fit for heroes'.

For the glen and for the wider Scottish rural community the years of the First World War proved to be a bleak punctuation mark, but as with every account of warfare there were moments when the conflict seemed to be a distant drum. The poet Helen Burness Cruickshank worked as post girl to Glen Prosen in the summer of 1918 and she found that although most of the menfolk were away on the business of war, life went on much as it always had done in the upper reaches of the glen.

How lovely the glen was that summer. How sweet the birches smelt after rain! The cuckoos were still calling from rowan and gean trees that held scattering sprays of white blossom; but before I left the glen the cuckoos were silent and the corncrakes, the invisible context of early summer, had taken up their craiking in the hay.

By some miracle no news of casualties came to the glen folk during my period of service. The outstanding event was assurance of the safety of one man, a favourite of all the neighbours, who had long been posted as 'missing'. The whole glen seemed to smile that day when his wife learned he was a prisoner-of-war, and with her I drank his health in yellow, lumpy buttermilk.★ Twice a week his wife kirned. And twice weekly after that, a glass of milk was set aside for 'postie'.[5]

After the war Cruickshank, a native of Angus, became a close friend and confidante of the writers Lewis Grassic Gibbon and Hugh MacDiarmid and with them was one of the instigators of the later Scottish literary renaissance. By then her account of Glen Prosen in that last summer of the war was already passing into history, but at the time it was written the area was about to join the rest of Scotland in mourning the country's sacrifice and the loss of so many young lives. They were remembered in families' hearts and in the many monuments and crosses which were thrown up all over the country to commemorate those who were known simply as 'the fallen'.

The majority of the men from the glen enlisted in, or were conscripted into, The Black Watch (Royal Highland Regiment), the local regiment whose traditional recruiting grounds were (and remain) in the counties of Angus, Fife and Perthshire. Founded in 1725 as an internal security force of 'independent companies' to 'watch' or guard the entries to the Highlands, the regiment came into being as a Regular formation in 1739 and owed its name, in Gaelic *Am Freiceadan Dubh*, to the dark green and black government tartan used for its kilts. The senior Highland regiment in the British Army, The Black Watch comprised two earlier numbered regiments, the 42nd and 73rd Highlanders, and like every other Scottish, English, Irish and Welsh infantry regiment it expanded rapidly in the years of the First World War, drawing most of its support from the local area.

★ He was John Leighton, forester at Balnaboth, who served in the 1/6th King's Own Scottish Borderers and was listed in the muster roll as being a prisoner-of-war. Later it was learned that he died while in confinement and he is listed on the war memorial.

In 1914, in addition to the two Regular battalions (1st and 2nd) there was a Special Reserve battalion (3rd) and four Territorial Force battalions made up of part-time soldiers and representing the breadth of the regiment's area: 4th (City of Dundee), 5th (Angus), 6th (Perthshire) and 7th (Fife). As the war progressed second- and third-line Territorial battalions were raised for training purposes and a further five Service battalions (8th, 9th, 10th, 11th and 12th) were raised for the thousands of recruits who flocked to the colours following the request for manpower made by the Secretary for War, Field Marshal Lord Kitchener of Khartoum in August and September 1914. Later in the war, as the demands increased due to the high casualties and the changing nature of the conflict, two Scottish yeomanry regiments were dismounted and re-badged as infantry, serving as 13th Black Watch (Scottish Horse) and 14th Black Watch (Fife and Forfar Yeomanry). All eleven service battalions served in France and Flanders while others fought in Mesopotamia (2nd), Salonika (10th and 13th) and Palestine (2nd and 14th). In that sense, too, the Black Watch mirrored what was happening elsewhere in Scotland and the rest of the United Kingdom, and the many war memorials scattered throughout the regimental area provide mute witness to the sacrifice of some 10,000 Black Watch soldiers who left quiet places like the Braes of Angus, never to return.

1 Your King and Country Need You: August 1914

In 1914 Scotland's summer broke as it usually does in the northern parts of the British archipelago. July and August, the traditional holiday months, are often wet and windy, with few days of prolonged sunshine, and the fourteenth year of the new century was no exception. Later, people would remember the summer months of 1914 as representing a long hot interlude before the onset of war, the last golden age before the world was plunged into the horrors of global conflict, but the weather records of the period show a somewhat different picture. While there were days of sunshine, the polar opposite also prevailed: the Clyde Corinthian Yacht Club regatta, held on 9 July, was plagued by what the organisers called 'fluky weather', which made for difficult sailing on the rain-soaked Clyde estuary, while two days later on the same west coast the Turnberry Amateur Golfing tournament took place in 'brilliant sunshine and exuberating [sic] heat'. A royal visit by King George V and his wife, Queen Mary, in the first half of the month also met with mixed conditions. It rained in Edinburgh for much of the visit, but the royal couple visited Lanarkshire on 12 July in 'beautiful weather' and the *Scotsman* reported that the visit had been a great success, underlining the importance of the monarchy to the country and its people. The only setbacks had the been enforced cancellation of a visit to Falkirk because striking joiners had refused to erect the necessary barricades and stands, and a potentially damaging incident in Dundee when an English suffragette called Olive Walton, the local organiser of the Women's Social and Political Union, threw a missile at the royal carriage while the king and queen were visiting the Dens Flax Works in Victoria Street.

Scotland's holidaymakers were apparently not downhearted by the prospect of the season's frequent cold spells and showers. The previous year had seen a boom in Scotland's popular holiday resorts and 1914 followed that pattern. The *Glasgow Herald* reported that record crowds had flocked to fashionable destinations such as North Berwick and Elie and the city's trades' fair fortnight had seen large numbers of day trippers and holidaymakers taking the traditional voyage 'doon the watter' from the Broomielaw in Glasgow to the resorts on the Clyde estuary. Special trains were run to resorts in England, Blackpool being a popular destination, while other holidaymakers took steamers to the Isle of Man and further afield to resorts in Northern Ireland. The trades' holidays in Aberdeen and Edinburgh were equally busy with visitors flocking to the seaside towns on the Fife, East Lothian and Ayrshire coasts. Over 1,200 US visitors made the pilgrimage to Sir Walter Scott's home at Abbotsford in the Border country, and higher numbers of Americans than ever before were reported to be visiting Scotland. For the Scottish tourist trade, which had faced a long period of economic uncertainty at the end of the nineteenth century, business was booming and record takings looked possible.[1] The mood was briskly self-confident and the tourist advertising brochures made most of the pleasures that awaited anyone wanting to visit Scotland:

> Stress and strain, which are in these busy days the inevitable accompaniment of works, have made those breaks in the ordinary routine which we term 'holidays' almost as essential to existence as are food and raiment. More especially is this case with those whose lot is cast where the exercise of brain and intellect, rather than those of muscle, brings them the means of comfortable living . . . why not fall back on our own resources and, for this year's holiday at least, in a voyage which shall have all the charm of novelty, moderate expense and comfort combined make the acquaintance of beautiful Britain under the auspices of the Clyde Shipping Company.[2]

It was not just in the market for tourism that things were improving. There was also the prospect that a parliament would be restored to Scotland with the advent of political devolution. In May 1914 a Home Rule Bill had passed its second reading in the House of Commons, mainly as a result of the promptings of the Scottish Home Rule Association and the Young Scots Society, a radical-minded grouping within the ruling Liberal Party who were in favour of free trade, social reform and what they called 'the unquenchable and indefinable spirit of nationalism'. Introducing the bill, J. I. Macpherson, the Liberal member for Ross and Cromarty, argued that the measure had the backing of a party that had won 80 per cent of Scotland's seventy-two seats at the last general election in 1910, and that it deserved to succeed on those grounds alone. The bill envisaged the creation of a devolved Scotland within the framework of a new federal structure for the United Kingdom, or, as Prime Minister H. H. Asquith put it, the new union would have a peculiarity in that 'while for common purposes all its constituent members can deliberate and act together, none of them is at liberty to deal with those matters which are specially appropriate and necessary for itself without the common consent of all.'

The Liberals had supported home rule since the 1880s when it seemed that Ireland would be granted a measure of independence as part of Gladstone's desire to settle the 'great moral issue of Ireland' and that in the process Scotland would lose out. In 1894 and 1895 Scottish home rule bills had gained parliamentary majorities but had not been passed due to lack of parliamentary time. The Liberals had also been responsible for the creation in 1885 of the Scottish Office under the leadership of a secretary for Scotland who had specific responsibilities in a number of areas including education, agriculture and fisheries. (It was, in fact, a restitution: the office of secretary for Scotland dated back to the period before the Act of Union of 1707.) The Liberals' home rule initiative had the support of the Conservatives, who had introduced the post of Scottish Secretary after the Marquis of Salisbury succeeded Gladstone as prime minister following the split in the Liberal Party over Irish home rule. While the Conservatives, were not overly enthusiastic about devolution they reasoned that the union was best preserved by making concessions of this kind, or, as Salisbury expressed it in his invitation to the Duke of Richmond and Gordon to accept the post, the move would 'redress the wounded dignities of the Scottish people – or a section of them – who think enough is not made of Scotland'.[3]

By 1914 the Liberal Party was still a mighty institution which permeated all levels of the country's life although it had lost the over-arching influence that had seen it become Scotland's political powerhouse in the years following the passing of the Reform Act in 1832. The enfranchisement of working men in 1884 had eroded its support amongst the growing working class and had encouraged the emergence of newer socialist factions, and there was dissent within the party over the question of the disestablishment of the Church of Scotland. However, despite the formation of the Liberal Unionist party to oppose home rule for Ireland in the general election of 1885, the party still enjoyed a hegemony that was seemingly proof against Labour and/or Conservative* incursions. It was the party of reform and innovation. After winning a landslide election in 1906 with fifty-eight seats being won in Scotland, it set about reforming health care and introduced old age pensions and unemployment benefit.

By 1914 the Liberals enjoyed their greatest support in Scotland in rural areas outside the Central Belt, where the Conservatives had gained ground largely as a result of their opposition to home rule for Ireland and Scotland. Even so, in successive elections the Liberals had still managed to consolidate their power. Asquith sat for a Scottish constituency, East Fife, and had married into a powerful Scottish manufacturing family, the Tennants, who held the British patent rights for producing dynamite; nearly a third of his cabinet were Scots or sat for Scottish seats; and Scots warmed to the party's policies or 'tribal incantations', as the novelist John Buchan called them, of free trade, religious equality and land reform. Scottish Liberals espoused the issue of home rule with enthusiasm, candidates were obliged to embrace it, and even though the measure did not enjoy widespread support across Scotland, political change was in the air and in the early summer of 1914 Scottish Liberals were confident that their bill would eventually reach the statute books.[4]

The economy was also in reasonable fettle thanks mainly to the enduring strength of the heavy industries of the west of Scotland, which produced ships, locomotives and heavy engineering plant for the international markets. In 1913 the Clyde shipyards, the motor of Scotland's economy, had produced a record tonnage of ships: at 757,000 tons it was a third of the British total and superior to the

---

* In 1912 the breakaway Scottish Liberal Unionists joined forces with the Scottish Conservatives to create the Scottish Unionist Party to oppose the granting of home rule to Ireland. While both names were used in Scotland the party will be referred to throughout as Conservative.

646,000 tons of ships produced in German yards. Some of the most successful engineering and manufacturing enterprises were Scottish-owned or based in Scotland. Railway locomotives built by the North British Locomotive Company were sold all over the empire and accounted for half of Britain's total production, the engineering industry employed 78,000 workers who produced an output worth £16 million in 1913 and in Clydebank the US-owned Singer Sewing Machine Company employed 10,000 workers with an output of 13,000 machines per week. Coal was still king: although seams were becoming exhausted in the Ayrshire and Lanarkshire fields this was balanced by new exploitation in Fife and the Lothians. With a skilled and specialised workforce at the disposal of the foundries and work-shops of the heavy industries, Scotland's manufacturing might seemed to be built on firm foundations. 'Clyde-built' was a byword for shipbuilding quality around the world, and as many of the less skilled workers were paid significantly lower wages than other parts of the United Kingdom this gave Scottish firms a distinct advantage in the marketplace. Add on other successful industries such as jute produc-tion in Dundee, the cotton factories of Paisley, the fishing industry, which employed 35,000 men and 50,000 women in seasonal work, and innovations such as the Albion motor-car company, and Scotland seemed to be in a strong economic position, largely as a result of its achievements during the Victorian period.[5]

Not that everything was rosy however: there is compelling evi-dence to suggest that in the run-up to the outbreak of war in 1914 Scotland's industrial economy was facing a gentle decline that would accelerate in the post-war years.[6] Scotland's industrial success was built largely on heavy industries that supplied a specialised range of products and depended on selling them to the international market, one result being that there was little diversification. On the Clyde, for example, the shipyards owed much of their success to building warships for both the Royal and other navies. Profits also depended on keeping wages low for unskilled workers. Not only did this spread resentment, it meant that the domestic economy stagnated as low wages did not encourage consumer demand. On the first score wages had not kept pace with rises in the cost of living and this factor encouraged outbreaks of labour unrest and unofficial strike action on Clydeside in the period before the war. A Board of Trade Inquiry into the Cost of Living, Earnings in Hours, published in 1913, revealed that food prices had increased by 25 per cent since the beginning of the new century and that wages had fallen behind, and in the same year the Scottish Trades Union Congress (STUC), founded in 1897, concluded that 'the basic cause of labour unrest is poverty'. The Glasgow Labour History Workshop found that a rash of strikes and sporadic discontent on Clydeside in the four years before the war were created by 'a combination of real wage erosion and high levels of under-employment and insecurity in the 1900s, with tightening labour market conditions from c1910 and an all-pervasive process of work intensification'.[7]

Low wages also meant that, on the whole, living conditions in the industrial areas were not of the best. Victorian wealth had changed the complexion of the big cities by allowing those who created the prosperity to benefit from it. Glasgow's city centre was adorned with ostentatious office buildings and its west end contained fine family houses and terraces designed by architects such as Alexander 'Greek' Thomson and John Burnett. In Edinburgh the aspiring middle classes were moving out of the confines of the city centre to new villas and terraced houses in the south-side suburbs of Newington and Morningside, which were served by an equally new suburban railway. Dundee's wealth was reflected in the big rentier houses built by the jute barons along the Perth Road and these were replicated further north in the 'Granite City' of Aberdeen. For those who did the hard grinding work that allowed the wealth to be produced in the first place, life was a lot less agreeable. Due to a mixture of laissez-faire attitudes, indifference to the plight of working people, the ignorance of the scientific community and primitive approaches to sanitation, the four main cities all contained areas that were contaminated by disease and crime and in which people lived lives of abject poverty in desperate surroundings. Visitors to Victorian Scotland marvelled at the country's growing wealth, but they were also appalled by the physical conditions and high mortality rates endured by the workers.

True, in the latter half of the century, there had been improvements in the provision of public health. Water supplies were modernised, sewage systems were brought into use and strides were made in combating epidemic diseases and introducing new standards in antisepsis, but the housing stock remained poor, with crowded tenement buildings offering little in the way of even elementary standards of hygiene. Water supplies were confined to single taps and there was little provision for basic lavatories; these were usually communal privies, but over-crowding was the eternal and most serious problem: most families lived one to a single room. In that environment men turned to alcohol for escape, thereby exacerbating the problem, women endured downtrodden lives trying to make ends meet and children were brought up believing that their lot in life was normal, perhaps even expected. Even at the beginning of the twentieth century there was a hangover from the Victorian mindset that insisted that the people in the slums had brought their misfortune on their own heads by leading lives that were irresponsible and that they were incapable of prudence or forethought. In 1912 O. H. Mavor, an alumnus of Glasgow Academy and Glasgow University, was beginning his career as a medical practitioner and was only too aware of his native city's shortcomings and the ways in which his patients in the poorer areas attempted to address them: 'The badge of rank was cleanliness, and cleanliness was preserved in bug-infested houses with one tap in a kitchen sink as its only instrument.'[8] During the war Mavor served as a military doctor in France, Mesopotamia and central Asia and emerged as Scotland's leading playwright in the post-war period, writing under the name of James Bridie.

Despite the wretched conditions endured by the majority of the working-class population and the potential for instability in the industrial heartlands there were signs which suggested that Scotland, or at least Lowland Scotland, was enjoying one of its periods of economic success and social well-being. In 1911 Glasgow had mounted its third international trade exhibition, its object being to endow a chair of Scottish History and Literature at Glasgow University. Its aims might have been limited and even parochial but the exhibition raised £143,000 and attracted 9.4 million visitors to its site at Kelvingrove, where the inquisitive and the curious found 'an old-world Scottish "toonie", a Highland Village, a Pavilion on Old Glasgow, an Aerial Railway, a Mountain Slide, a West African Village and various side-shows.'[9] The same city also gave birth to a Scottish National Theatre Society and in 1907 the final wing was added to Charles Rennie Mackintosh's School of Art, a pioneering example of functional architecture that explored the architect's belief that all aspects of a building are part of a single artistic unity. Mackintosh synthesised a new kind of Scottish architecture, and from the school he created artists such as S. J. Peploe, J. D. Fergusson, F. C. B. Cadell and Leslie Hunter, who produced works that presaged the Modernist movement. Later they would be known as the Scottish Colourists. The Arts and Crafts movement also flourished in Scotland, building on traditional respect for individual craftsmanship.

Literature was going through one of its periodic troughs and, indeed, there were question marks over whether Scotland had a distinctive literature at all. Robert Louis Stevenson had died in 1894 and his early death had removed a writer who spoke with a distinctively Scottish voice that was understood and loved all over the world. Adventure novels such as *Treasure Island* and *Kidnapped* enjoyed a wide readership and in works of the calibre of *The Master of Ballantrae* and *The Strange Case of Dr Jekyll and Mr Hyde* he explored an age-old schism in the Scottish psyche: the split between heart and mind, emotion and intellect. His loss meant that Scotland no longer had a world-class writer, but that did not lessen the appeal of best-selling contemporaries such as Margaret Oliphant, the author of over a hundred novels, or George Macdonald, whose fantasy novels later influenced J. R. R. Tolkien in the writing of *The Lord of the Rings*. Unfortunately for the reputations of the practitioners, the most popular writers before the First World War belonged to a school which was later denigrated as the 'Kailyard', the catch-all phrase used by the critic J. H. Millar in the April 1895 issue of the *New Review* to describe the novels of J. M. Barrie, S. R. Crockett and Ian Maclaren (the pen-name of John Watson). In their work is a well-defined Arcadia of rural sentimentality peopled by characters who represent solid virtues: the minister or the village worthies who voice pastoral morality, the industrious son who rises by dint of hard work and his own endeavours, the honest tenant farmers who give of their best for no other reward than their families' improvement and sickly virginal heroines who are not long for the world. Behind them are stock rapacious landlords, self-satisfied incomers and the ever-present figures of death and disease. The city only appears as a distant rumour, a place to be avoided; instead, the virtues of village life are emphasised, and in that sense the world created by the Kailyard novelists is little more than a projection of eighteenth-century Romantic views about nature and its beneficial effects on humankind. In that respect the Kailyard writers were only pandering to the popular taste of a public who preferred the sentimentality of an imagined past, when life was sweet and worry-free, to the harsher realities of their own lives.

At the same time that they were being devoured in numbers by a largely non-conformist middle-class British audience, they were balanced by novels such as George Douglas Brown's *The House with the Green Shutters* (1901) and John Macdougall Hay's *Gillespie* (1914), which borrowed many of the features of the Kailyard school but put them in a more brutal and realistic setting. And as the literary critic William Donaldson has revealed in recent studies, the excesses of the Kailyard were balanced by a wide range of novels and short stories whose authors were prepared to tackle robustly contemporary themes and to question cosy assumptions about the country and its people. Donaldson also found that many nineteenth-century news-papers were not shy about publishing work in vernacular Scots and that its tone was 'intensely anti-imperialist, routinely anti-clerical, [and] fundamentally egalitarian in its hatred of hypocrisy'.[10] This contradicts a contemporary belief that English was the only tongue for a serious Scottish writer and that the use of Scots was only suited for pawky sentiments.

This subculture ran contrary to what has come to be the received opinion about the period, namely that Scottish literature before the First World War was merely nostalgic and provincial and that it awaited a spring awakening. While it is true that the Kailyard fiction was dominant there was also a confidence to the nation's cultural life that transcended the banalities of Thrums and Drumtochty. Political agitation for home rule was mirrored by a new sense of pride in nationhood that spilled over into art and literature and from there into everyday lives. Some of the smug self-satisfaction in defining Scottishness was bogus and rooted in the past but the creation of national cultural institutions such as the national galleries and museum in Edinburgh and the establishment of learned societies underlined a willingness to preserve the national identity against encroaching anglicisation. In his magazine *The Ever-green* the writer and social reformer Patrick Geddes spoke of the arrival of a Scottish renaissance and, more recently, the period between 1890 to the outbreak of the First World War has been described as 'the high summer of a confident, renewed sense of national consciousness, at its strongest amongst the middle and working classes'.[11]

Only for those who cared to watch the distant horizon were there clouds of a different kind ready to spoil that high summer content-ment. On 28 June came news that the heir to the throne of Austria-Hungary, Archduke Franz Ferdinand, had been shot to death with his wife in Sarajevo, the capital of the province of Bosnia-Herzegovina. Initially the incident seemed to be an isolated though shocking terrorist attack, and the first reaction was that the perpetrators would be caught and punished by the imperial authorities. Certainly, in the British press the news from Serbia had to take second place to the crisis in Ulster caused by Unionist opposition to the imminent passing of the Irish Home Rule Bill that would establish an autonomous parliament in Dublin. At that stage there was no hint that the assassination would endanger the peace that had held in Europe since the end of the Napoleonic wars in 1815. Even when it was reported that the blame for the outrage was being shifted on to neighbouring Serbia, the first of the Slav states to gain independence and a source of constant irritation in Vienna, there was no reason to believe that the task of hunting down those responsible would precipitate a crisis. During their annual summer camp at Machrihanish in the Mull of Kintyre a Territorial Force officer astonished the rest of the mess by reading aloud a story about 'trouble in the Near East' and musing that their battalion, 6th Argyll and Sutherland Highlanders, could soon be at their war station at Auchterarder in Perthshire. Those listening gave him short shrift: 'This remark was greeted with a round of incredulous laughter, but he only miscalculated the date by about a week.'[12] The general opinion was that even if there was a war it would only be a local affair involving the two countries. However, the assassination had lit a slow-burning fuse: the assassin, Gabriele Princip, had links to a Serbian nationalist group called the Black Hand, which in turn was supported by Serbian military intelligence, and it did not take long for anti-Serb sentiment to sweep through Austria-Hungary, creating a mood for revenge.

What followed next was the well-documented progression towards a global confrontation with demands being issued, threats being made and positions becoming entrenched as Europe marched inexorably towards confrontation. Britain, which had wanted to remain aloof from the crisis and was not formally in alliance with any of the main participants, was now about to be pressed into the conflict through a treaty of 1839 that guaranteed Belgium's neutrality. On 4 August, no answer having been received to an ultimatum that there must be no attack on Belgium, Britain declared war on Germany. For the Scottish poet Charles Murray, a native of Aberdeenshire, it seemed that the distant 'sough' (rustle) of the summer wind was about to turn into a harvest tempest that could not be stopped:

> The corn was turnin', hairst was near,
> But lang afore the scythes could start
> A sough o' war gaed through the land
> An' stirred it to its benmost heart.
> Nae ours the blame, but when it came
> We couldna pass the challenge by,
> For credit o' our honest name
> There could be but the ae reply.[13]

In the next quatrain Murray promised that the challenge would be met by 'buirdly [sturdy] men fae strath and glen' and he was not far wrong in making that bold assertion. As the news from Europe worsened and it became clear that the rumours of war were slowly becoming reality the British government had already begun taking precautionary steps. At the end of its summer manoeuvres on 29 July the Royal Navy's Grand Fleet was ordered to sail from Portland through the Dover Straits north to its war station at Scapa Flow in the Orkney Islands, where it was put on a war footing. Part-time soldiers of the Royal Garrison Artillery (Orkney Territorial Force) were called out to man emergency gun positions alongside Royal Marines, and notices to shipping were posted indicating that harbour navigation lights would be extinguished. In the waters of the huge natural harbour the naval crews started clearing their ships for war, stripping from them wooden and unnecessary fittings and surplus ships' boats, anything that would burn if the ship were hit in battle. For the remainder of the war this distant and Spartan anchorage would be the main base for the ships of the Grand Fleet, and for the crews it would prove to be a mixed blessing. In the long days of the summer months the Flow had an austere beauty but the short stormy daylight hours of

winter when 'everything – sea, sky, land and ships – is a dull grey and
that only from 10 to 3' could be a purgatory. One sailor's letter home
summed up what most of the crews felt about Scapa Flow: 'Dear
Mum, I cannot tell you where I am. I don't know where I am. But
where I am there is miles and miles of bugger all. Love Ted.'[14] Scapa
might have been a key base for the navy's command of the North Sea
but it was clearly an unloved posting.

The army, too, was on the move. As part of the 'Precautionary
Period' of the Defence Plan Prior to Mobilisation, formations of the
Regular Army based in Britain were told to return to their depots on
29 July. Most were on their annual summer camps or undergoing live
firing exercises, but even so, war seems to have been far from their
thoughts. The 1st Cameronians were at camp near Blair Atholl and
one of their officers, Captain James Jack, noted that the regiment had
not been in that part of Scotland since 1689 'when, under Colonel
Cleland, who was killed, they defeated a large body of Highlanders at
Dunkeld [in the aftermath of the Battle of Killiecrankie]'. He also
noted almost by way of an after-thought, that tensions in Europe had
been increasing ever since Austria declared war on Serbia.[15] Jack, a
veteran of the Boer War, had just finished playing tennis at Blair Castle
when the telegram arrived ordering his battalion to return to Glasgow.
Further nòrth, at Tain, on the shores of the Dornoch Firth, another
kind of military exercise was coming to an end as U Company of the
1/4th (City of Aberdeen) Battalion Gordon Highlanders ended their
annual camp with 'a huge bonfire around which the volunteer soldiers
held a sing-song fuelled by some bottles of beer'.[16] The following day,
30 July, came news of the general mobilisation and the 132 soldiers of
U Company, all students or graduates of Aberdeen University, found
themselves on the verge of going off to war. To make matters worse it
began raining and the special train taking them home had to be
cancelled.

The men of U Company were part-time soldiers in the Territorial
Force, which had been formed in 1908 as a second line for home
defence and provided one of the eight (later four) rifle companies of
the local Territorial battalion, 1/4th Gordon Highlanders. As their
historian has recorded, their association with Aberdeen University
meant that they were very much the Scottish nation in uniform:
'although the majority of its members were from Aberdeen and the

North-East, students from Caithness and the Lothians served in the ranks with Gaelic speakers from the Hebrides and the Western Isles'.[17] One of their number, Alexander Rule, remembered that they were happy enough to embrace mobilisation provided that they could retain 'the original title of a University Unit which, even after months of heavy trench warfare in the Ypres salient, sang Gaudeamus to the end'.[18] Before it left for France U Company was designated D Company, 1/4th Gordon Highlanders when the battalion's companies were regrouped as double companies to meet army requirements, but within the battalion and amongst its own members it kept its old title.

Away from the world of the armed forces the countdown to war was followed with keen interest throughout Scotland and the announcement of the declaration of war was accompanied by a mixture of relief, anticipation and excitement. All over Europe there were huge public rallies in the main cities as the belligerent countries began their preparations. In Paris crowds voiced their encouragement and the first regiments began marching off to war with shouts of 'À Berlin!' (To Berlin!) ringing in their ears. The carriages of German military trains taking soldiers to the front for the invasion of France were chalked with the confident slogan 'Ausflug nach Paris' (Excursion to Paris). In Munich a contemporary photograph captured cheering crowds in the Odeonsplatz welcoming the prospect of war; amongst their number was a young painter called Adolf Hitler, who was trying to earn a living by selling his poorly executed watercolours. In London, 3 August was Bank Holiday Monday and the weather was surprisingly good, with unbroken sunshine, and amidst the heightened tensions people wanted to make the most of the balmy weather. As all special excursion trains to the Channel coast had been cancelled most people took to the streets or visited attractions such as the Anglo–American exhibition at the White City. Scotland, too, was agog at the turn of events in Europe. No sooner had war been declared on 4 August than the *Scotsman* declared in its leader that this was a decisive moment and that the country had to meet it with all seriousness and resolution:

Belgium has resolved to stand by her liberties at all risks and she will not stand less firmly knowing that she has Britain in the array behind her. This attitude on our part is dictated by the considerations of duty and of statesmanship. For if, as Sir Edward Grey [the British foreign secretary] points out, we allow Belgian rights to be forcibly over-ridden at this time, and if Germany succeeds in her schemes of 'beating France down into the dust', the independence of the smaller States that stand in the path of Teutonic aggression could never be preserved or recovered. Holland and Denmark would also be swallowed up before Germany could obtain that 'place in the sun' that accords with the aspirations of those who guide her destinies. In time, and probably no long time, it would be our turn to fall victims to the greed and ambition of a Power which, to judge by the latest development in its policy, is prepared to go to any lengths of force and cunning to attain its ends and that regards no rights as sacred except its own.[19]

Elsewhere, the paper recorded that the declaration had been greeted with enthusiasm and that an anti-war demonstration mounted in Edinburgh city centre on the Mound had been broken up by 'an antagonistic element in the large crowd'. Quiet satisfaction was also expressed at the alert reaction of the sentries on the Forth Railway Bridge when they chased two men who seemed to be making drawings of the defences at the Rosyth naval base. The two men jumped on an Edinburgh-bound train at Dalmeny and were not apprehended: they were to be the first participants in a succession of 'spy scares' reported by the *Scotsman* and other papers in those initial uneasy weeks. Another 'first' reported widely and enthusiastically in the Scottish press was the landing at Scapa pier of thirteen German fishermen who had been apprehended at sea on the first day of war. This was followed on 7 August by equally gratifying reports that German vessels had been detained in the ports of Leith, Grangemouth, Burntisland and Wick,[20] and all Scottish papers carried warnings that the registration of aliens was about to begin.

There was no danger that Britain would be invaded, but self-defence also provided an impulse for the displays of public patriotism that were common to all the nations about to face the unknown horrors of modern industrialised warfare. (Of the European powers only Holland, Switzerland, Spain, Denmark, Norway and Sweden remained outside the conflict.) Contemporary evidence shows that thousands of Scottish people were prepared to voice their support for war and found themselves taking part in demonstrations of national pride and patriotism which often bordered on hysteria. Even realists who should have had their feet on the ground were caught up in the excitement. After war had been declared the novelist and journalist Neil Munro travelled by train to Glasgow from his home in Inveraray and later shamefacedly admitted, 'what silly patriotic and romantic elations were stirred in me when I found that already there were armed guards on every railway viaduct, on reservoirs, and the Loch Long torpedo testing station. All along the Callendar-and-Oban and West Highland Railways, the fiendish ubiquity of German spies, and their readiness to start immediately blowing up culverts and railway bridges, or poisoning us at our kitchen-taps, were already taken for granted!'[21] By that time Munro was fifty and a successful novelist – his latest novel, *The New Road*, an adventure in the tradition of Stevenson, had just been published – but even he was caught up in the excitement of the hour and wanted to do something. That sense of enthusiastic conviction was shared by many others and gave the early days of the war an unreal quality, creating a feeling that war was a great adventure and that man had been transformed and liberated from the doldrums of a humdrum existence.

Chivalry, self-sacrifice and heroism were the catchwords of those early days of the war and there were very few people who did not respond to their call. Artless verses flooded by the thousand into local papers speaking of the noble necessity of doing one's duty; everywhere tub-thumping patriotism was rife; and the elation even found its way into mainstream literature. Two years later, in 1916, long after the initial enthusiasm had waned, Neil Munro produced a series of poems under the collective title of 'Bagpipe Ballads' that were published in *Blackwood's Magazine*. By then his son Hugh had been killed in action while serving with 1/8th Argylls at the Battle of Loos and he himself had visited the Western Front as a correspondent, but, as he told his publisher George Blackwood, the poems were a compensation of sorts, having been 'suggested by the names of bagpipe airs, so that some of them take on that spirit of braggadocio which comes so natural to youth: and to races like the Gaels who loiter so much in their past that they are always the youngest and most ardent when it comes to sentiment – the first and last excuse for poetry'.[22] One of them, 'Hey, Jock, are ye glad ye "listed"?', caught the exhilaration of those first days of the war:

> Come awa, Jock, and cock your bonnet,
> Swing your kilt as best ye can;
> Auld Dumbarton's Drums are dirlin'
> Come awa, Jock, and kill your man![23]

Not everyone was caught up in the Gadarene rush to hate the Hun and to turn war into a great adventure. Five days after the declaration 5,000 protesters attended a large anti-war rally in Glasgow featuring speakers from the Independent Labour Party (ILP), the Scottish branch of the British Socialist Party and the Glasgow branch of the Peace Society. Amongst those who addressed the demonstration were Patrick Dollan, a prominent city councillor representing the ILP, and a young militant socialist called James McDougall, who had already been sacked by the Clydesdale Bank for participating in socialist political activities. To McDougall the war was not only unnecessary but a capitalist adventure that would benefit the profiteers and damage the working class, and according to contemporary newspaper reports the crowd appeared to agree with him. Initial panic in some sections of the industrial sector seemed to suggest that the first victims of the war might indeed be the workers. In Ayrshire a number of textile factories decided to cut back on their output and issued short-time notices to their workforces. As a result of cancelled orders one firm, Morton Sundour Fabrics Ltd, decided to introduce half-day working on Thursdays along with a curtailed working day on Saturdays until further notice. The directors also warned the workforces not to panic and that they should 'try to LIVE ON LESS', keep their money in the bank and refuse the temptation to lay in large supplies of food and other requisites.[24]

On the political left, though, there was some confusion about how best to respond. Although the chairman of the Labour Party, Ramsay MacDonald, resigned in protest on 6 August (for which offence he was expelled from the Moray Golf Club), the party itself decided to support the government and they were followed by other labour movements such as the Trades Union Congress and the Co-op movement. At that stage the ILP also kept to a pacifist line, a stance which it maintained throughout the conflict, but it was left to men like McDougall, Tom Bell and above all John Maclean, a remarkable socialist teacher and Marxist agitator, to lead the most sustained opposition to the war in Scotland. In a letter to the radical newspaper *Forward*, Maclean claimed that the war was essentially a confrontation between two rival capitalist ideologies and that the question of Belgium's neutrality was a smokescreen to wage a decisive war against Germany: 'In view of the eventualities like these indicated, it is our business as Socialists to develop a class patriotism, refusing to murder one another for a sordid world capitalism.'[25] Similar views were being put forward in Germany by socialists such as Karl Liebknecht, who spoke out against the war, claiming that 'the chief enemy is at home' and founded the anti-war newspaper the *Internationale*. His agitation proved that socialist opposition was not an irrelevant minority on either side of the battle-lines, and in Scotland, as we shall see, the anti-war sentiments voiced by Maclean and his colleagues were to grow in strength and significance as the conflict progressed. When conscription was introduced in 1916 some men would go to prison rather than compromise deeply held religious, ethical or political beliefs about the conflict.

Others, too, were repelled by the cheering crowds and the widespread fervour for the unknown war that lay ahead. Charles Hamilton Sorley was born in 1895 in Aberdeen, where his father had been professor of moral philosophy, but the family had moved to England five years later when Professor Sorley was appointed to a chair at Cambridge. Educated at Marlborough, an English private school, Charles Hamilton Sorley spent some time in Germany before taking up a place at University College, Oxford, and was attending the University of Jena when war broke out. With a friend he managed to get back to Britain, travelling by train and a specially commandeered ferry from Antwerp. Having spent seven enjoyable months in Germany he was disposed to be understanding about the country he had just visited, telling an old school friend in a letter, 'They are a splendid lot, and I wish the silly papers would realise that they are fighting for a principle just as much as we are.' But what took him aback was the hysteria and unthinking patriotism. A letter to another friend, Alan Hutchinson, reflected his exasperation with the mood he found on his return: 'But isn't all this bloody? I am full of mute and burning

rage and annoyance and sulkiness about it. I could wager that out of
twelve million eventual combatants there aren't twelve who really
want it. And "serving one's country" is so unpicturesque and unheroic
when it comes to the point. Spending a year in a beastly Territorial
camp guarding telegraph wires has nothing poetical about it: nor very
useful as far as I can see.'[26] Even so, and despite his cynicism about
patriotic impulses, like thousands of others of his class, Sorley soon
joined up as a volunteer and was gazetted a second lieutenant in the
7th Suffolk Regiment.

Enthusiasm for the war was one thing, finding the soldiers to fight it
was another. As yet Britain had no troops in continental Europe, and it
would take another fortnight before the four (later six) divisions of the
British Expeditionary Force (BEF) crossed over to France to take their
prearranged place on the left of the French Army. Even at that stage
some members of the government thought that such a deployment
might not be necessary; Foreign Secretary Sir Edward Grey assured
the House of Commons that there was no definite military commitment. A feeling grew that the war might be over quickly, perhaps
before Christmas, and that the main weight of the fighting would fall
on the Royal Navy and the continental armies. One man thought
otherwise and his pronouncements on the matter were to lay the
foundation for the creation of Britain's volunteer army: Field Marshal
Horatio Herbert Kitchener, the hero of the Victorian wars in the
Sudan and the later Boer War and generally considered to be the
greatest British soldier of the period.

Against his better instincts Kitchener accepted the post of secretary
of war in Asquith's government and in so doing became the first
serving soldier to sit in the Cabinet since General George Monck held
the post in 1660. To the man in the street all was well now that Britain
had secured the services of its most famous soldier in its greatest hour
of need: in their eyes Kitchener could do no wrong. His career had
seen him move from victory to victory in the remote parts of the
empire and his very presence – his huge frame, his luxuriant moustache, the fixity of his gaze – had become the symbol of British pluck
and resolve.

Kitchener took up his post with characteristic energy. From the
outset he disagreed with the prevailing opinion that the war would
be short-lived and largely naval. He also believed that Britain's

professional army was too small to offer anything but limited support to France – it numbered only 247,432 men – and that huge new armies would have to be raised if the country was to make any impact on the direction of the war. On 8 August he called for the first hundred thousand volunteers aged between eighteen and thirty, the aim being to create an army of seventy divisions, approximately 1.2 million men, by 1917. Its arrival would come at a time when Germany's resources would be overstretched, and, according to Kitchener, Britain would then be in a position to crush the enemy and dictate the peace.

Kitchener's methods were also controversial. Instead of expanding the part-time soldiers of the Territorial Force, which had been raised for home defence in 1908, he would build on the existing regimental structure of the British Regular Army. No new formations would be raised but the existing infantry regiments would expand their numbers of battalions to meet the demand for men. These would be known as 'special service battalions': by the war's end a not untypical regiment such as the Highland Light Infantry had twenty-six special service and Territorial Force battalions instead of the normal two active service battalions and one depot battalion. In that way, argued Kitchener, volunteers could be assimilated quickly into the 'New' or 'Kitchener' armies and no new machinery would have to be assembled to deal with them.

From the outset of his tenure at the War Office Kitchener decided not to introduce conscription. He knew little about the Territorial Force, having been out of the country for much of his service, and what little he did know he distrusted, believing its members to be amateurs at best and playboys at worst. Had Kitchener read a diary kept by Major J. Craig Barr, 6th Argyll and Sutherland Highlanders, he would have felt vindicated. Barr's battalion of Territorials recruited from Renfrewshire and were on their summer camp at Machrihanish where there was golf and riding for the officers and everything seemed cosily familiar: 'The camp was similar in most ways to the training camps which some of us had attended for almost twenty years of service. The same canvas city gleaming white in the last rays of the setting sun, the same military routine, the same cheery mess tents and the same holiday spirit and jolly comradeship of old friends!'[27]

As it turned out, 6th Argylls, like every other Territorial battalion, gave sterling service, but that was in the future. At the time Kitchener wanted little to do with them. Showing the same sense of certainty that had guided him throughout his career he plumped for the voluntary principle and quietened doubters with the question 'If you are only ready to go when you are fetched, where is the merit in that? Are you only going to do your duty when the law says you must?' Such was Kitchener's personal standing and the strength of his political connections that he had the full support of the government, even though no one in the Cabinet really knew how the armies would be raised or if a million men would actually volunteer. As for the Territorials, who went on to play an illustrious role in the war, Kitchener was obdurate; Haldane complained that he was 'unable to prevail on him [Kitchener] to adopt, or even to make much use of the Territorial organisation'.[28]

Backed by a huge publicity machine which included the press and the influential all-party Parliamentary Recruiting Committee the national appeal for recruits was loud and insistent and the campaigners quickly showed that they meant business. Before long, Kitchener's instantly recognisable features with the famous luxuriant moustache were assisting in the campaign as Alfred Leete's famous recruiting poster began to be seen everywhere all over the country. Very few young men caught swithering outside an army recruiting office found it easy to ignore Kitchener's pointed exhortation 'Your Country Needs You!' By 12 September the first 100,000 men had been recruited; aged between 19 and 30 they signed on for three years or the duration of hostilities and formed the First New Army or K1 consisting of six divisions, 9th to 14th. By the end of the following month there were sufficient men to form twelve new divisions, which formed the Second New Army (15th to 20th Division) and the Third New Army (21st to 26th Division). In character and manpower two of those New Army divisions were entirely Scottish formations: 9th (Scottish) and 15th (Scottish). On one day in October 35,000 men enlisted, as many as had been recruited during the whole of 1913. In Scotland, as in other parts of the country, the call to arms was shrill and insistent. 'I feel certain that Scotsmen have only to know that the country urgently needs their services to offer them with the same splendid patriotism as they have always shown in the past,' Kitchener told Sir Alexander Baird of Urie, Lord Lieutenant of Kincardineshire, in a letter that was given considerable prominence in the Scottish press. 'Tell them from me, please, that their services were never more needed than they are today and that I rely confidently on a splendid response to the national appeal.'[29]

His words did not fall on deaf ears. Within a day of the declaration of war the army's recruiting office in Edinburgh's Cockburn Street was doing brisk business under the judicious eye of Captain William Robertson, a Gordon Highlander who had won the Victoria Cross in the Boer War, and by the end of August the *Glasgow Herald* reported that 20,000 men had been processed through the recruiting office in the Gallowgate. From other parts of Scotland came news of equally high figures of enlistment during August: 1,500 from Coatbridge, 900 from Clydebank, 940 from Dumbarton and 750 from Alloa. Recruits in Inverness rushed to join a special service battalion of the Queen's Own Cameron Highlanders that was being formed by D. W. Cameron of Lochiel; it would fight as the 5th Camerons, and Lochiel offered his personal guarantee that 'at the end of the war the battalion would be brought back to Inverness where it will be disbanded with all possible dispatch'.

A number of factors prompted those volunteers from all over Scotland to take the King's Shilling. Workers doing repetitive or menial jobs saw a chance to escape the drudgery of their existence. The Scots' traditional respect for militarism also encouraged many a young man who thought he would look a god in a kilt and a Glengarry bonnet. In those days, too, words such as duty, honour and patriotism were not idle concepts but the cornerstone of many young lives: within a year the Rev. Duncan Cameron, minister of Kilsyth, claimed that after painstaking research, he had found that 90 per cent of the country's ministers had seen their offspring ('sons of the manse') volunteer for duty in the armed forces.[30] Unskilled workers or the unemployed looked forward to the prospect of work and a steady wage but, as the *Scotsman* reported on 8 August, the recruits in Cockburn Street (Edinburgh) came from all walks of life: 'Men of all types and classes passed along, some in professions and trades – well groomed and spruce – and others with whom the world had dealt more hardly, but all curious to take their paces in the ranks and shoulder a rifle.' Peer pressure was brought to bear on the undecided and there was a general feeling that the whole thing was a bit of a lark and that it would be a shame to miss the great adventure. Few seem to have given any thought to the dangers that lay ahead or even realised that warfare would bring casualties. That was the impulse that took John Cooper to war when he enlisted in The Black Watch in Dundee:

> The folk at home said never a word to dissuade me, and for that I was grateful. I knew they would not rejoice to see me going, but as the going was in any case inevitable it was better to say nothing about it. Many people went into no end of a flurry about their young lads joining up. It was really all very senseless I thought. The right way to look at it was the way the boys themselves looked at it, and they went joyfully, most of them, even although they may occasionally have had misgivings about the probable end of the adventure. Not that young lads ever thought morbidly of death in battle – we all had a pathetic faith that we should come through somehow.

Others, like Carson Stewart, simply let curiosity get the better of them. In September he went down to the Institute in Cambuslang to watch the crowds of young men queuing to join up and was so enthused by the sight that he joined up himself and was 'duly sworn in and became a Soldier of the king, in the Queen's Own Cameron Highlanders'. The newly enlisted Private Stewart had joined the regiment's 7th (Service) Battalion, which would serve with the 15th Scottish Division in the Second New Army. From Cambuslang he went north to the regiment's depot in Inverness where, a Camerons' officer remembered, conditions were not always of the best: 'Soon the barracks were crowded out, and for a few nights men had to sleep where they could. Even the distillery at Inverness (already with an insect population of its own) was brought into use.'[31]

In the first flush of enthusiasm the War Office's problem was not how to raise sufficient recruits so much as what to do with them once they had enlisted. So great was the pressure on the existing army structure that recruits frequently went without uniforms, weapons with which to train and even accommodation. Vast tented encampments soon mushroomed in civic parks, farmers' fields and in country estates as enthusiastic recruits drilled with broomsticks while still wearing their best suits. To meet the shortages, production of khaki uniforms and boots had to be increased, supplies were purchased from the United States and the Post Office helped out with blue uniforms surplus to requirements. Stewart and his fellow Cameron volunteers did not feel that they were proper soldiers until the first kilts were issued later in the year.

One of the most popular manifestations of the volunteering craze in that unreal late summer and autumn of 1914 was the formation of 'pals battalions', so called because they kept together volunteers from the same cities or towns, or from working, sporting or social clubs. All told, 215 'pals' or locally raised battalions had been formed in the UK by the summer of 1916, and although the title was never fully recognised in Scotland the concept of men serving together did catch on, especially in the big cities. Shortly after the declaration of war the Glasgow Boys' Brigade, inspired by their treasurer, David Laidlaw, had volunteered to form a special service battalion for the Highland Light Infantry. Finding that the regiment was not enthusiastic, Laidlaw, formerly of the Lanarkshire Engineer Volunteers, approached the Cameron Highlanders, but he did not achieve recognition until 1 September when the Glasgow Corporation gave the go-ahead for the formation of a Highland Light Infantry battalion drawn from the city's public transport system. Wearing their green uniforms and marching behind a pipe band, the motormen and conductors of the tramways department paraded through the city, where they presented themselves for enlistment on 7 September. Under the direction of James Dalrymple, Glasgow's transport manager, the Coplawhill tramways depot became a giant recruiting hall and it took just sixteen hours to enlist the members of what would become the 15th (Tramways) Battalion, Highland Light Infantry.

Encouraged by that success, official approval was given to the Boys' Brigade to form a 16th (Boys Brigade) Battalion, a move which caused a great deal of public excitement in the city. 'Never will it be said that men who were connected with the Boys' Brigade throughout the length and breadth of the United Kingdom and Ireland funked in the hour of Britain's need', noted a patriotic journalist in the *Glasgow Post*. A few days later, a third 'pals' battalion, numbered 17th, was formed at the instigation of the Glasgow Chamber of Commerce, with recruits being enrolled in the Lesser Hall of the Merchants House.[32] Not to be outdone, the Glasgow Stock Exchange formed a special company for the Cameron Highlanders. Edinburgh also followed suit, the first calls for a regiment of city volunteers appeared in the *Scotsman* on 12 August but it was not until 12 September that Lord Provost Robert Kirk Inches announced that a 'City of Edinburgh Battalion' would be formed. By then the local regiment, The Royal Scots, had formed three service battalions for the New Armies (11th, 12th, 13th), but Inches was keen to see a designated Edinburgh regiment that would be the equal of the three Glasgow battalions. Then as now, rivalry between the two cities was intense and no excuse was needed to bring it into play. The result was the formation of two battalions, which served with The Royal Scots as 15th (1st City of Edinburgh, Service) and 16th (2nd City of Edinburgh, Service). As they both owed their existence to local commanding officers, they were also known by the men who served in them as Cranston's Battalion and McCrae's Battalion.

Both men were prominent members of the local business community. Sir Robert Cranston had served as treasurer and provost on the city council and had interests in local drapery stores and temperance hotels, and, like many of his class, he enjoyed a long association with the old Volunteer movement. Sir George McCrae was equally well regarded, but he was a self-made man who had set up in the drapery business on his own account, having managed to bury the secret that he had been born an illegitimate child, a fact that could have hindered his advancement. Hard work had made him a wealthy man and he was elected to parliament as a Liberal MP in 1899. Like Cranston, he had also served as a Volunteer.

Both battalions were raised in the latter months of 1914 and both went on to serve on the Western Front, but McCrae's battalion was unique in that it contained a large number of footballers, most of whom played for one of the local football clubs, the romantically named Heart of Midlothian. Shortly after the battalion was raised one of the new recruits penned a suitable verse for McCrae to read out when he appeared in uniform at a special performance of the annual Christmas pantomime in the King's Theatre: 'Do not ask where Hearts are playing and then look at me askance. If it's football that you're wanting, you must come with us to France.' By then McCrae had recruited over a thousand officers and men, and his battalion assembled in George Street on 15 December with each volunteer being told to bring with him 'one pair good Boots, Topcoat, two pairs Socks, and shaving outfit'.[33] The occasion prompted a good deal of local excitement as they marched off to their temporary billets in the examination halls of George Heriot's School and in the nearby Castle Brewery.

Despite initial doubts, the volunteer principle worked: by the end of 1915, the British total was 2,466,719 men, more than would be achieved after the introduction of conscription in May 1916 and just under half the wartime total of 5.7 million men who served in the army during the war years. Of their number, 320,589, or 13 per cent, of those who volunteered in 1914–15 were Scots. By the end of the war, the number of Scots in the armed forces rose to 688,416, consisting of 71,707 in the Royal Navy, 584,098 in the army (Regular, New and Territorial) and 32,611 in the Royal Flying Corps and Royal Air Force.[34]

At that point in the war the reality of the fighting on the Western Front had not yet sunk in and the enthusiasm for volunteering was still high. But the intervening months had also seen changes which made the people of Scotland realise that they were now on a war footing. The authorities wanted to get across the message that 'the war has falsified every prophecy [of panic]' and that it was a case of 'business as usual', but in those first anxious weeks it was difficult to believe the official line as there were too many instances of unusual occurrences. In the weeks that followed the declaration of war three special liners were chartered to take 2,800 US visitors back to their homes; they sailed from the Clyde on 15 August and their departure marked the first serious downturn in the Scottish tourist trade. The shooting season was a washout, not because the Glorious Twelfth was wet – a recurring problem – but because there was no mood to pursue sport during a time of national emergency. Ironically the weather held fair and most of the big Highland sporting estates reported plentiful numbers of grouse. The holiday trade was also constrained by a rash of spy mania especially after the passing of the first of the Defence of the Realm Acts on 8 August when the government took over control of vital resources and communications. The public was advised to be on the lookout for spies, with the result that strangers in country areas were often thought to be German intelligence agents and there were a number of newsworthy incidents.

On 18 August John Campbell of Dalwhinnie came across a strange motor car, with one female and three male passengers, parked on the main Perth to Inverness road. He reported the matter to the police at Newtonmore because he noticed that 'one of the men and the woman were about 80 yards off the road on the south side and near the bank of the River Truim. The man had a theodolite mounted on a tripod, and was apparently taking a survey of the district on the south side of the River as the needle of the theodolite was pointing southwards'. Clearly the matter had to be investigated, but when challenged the party said that they were government surveyors. Even so, Campbell did not believe them, as they failed to produce official papers apart from a telegram, and despite his misgivings – 'they spoke good English and I did not think they looked like foreigners' – Campbell passed on the information to the authorities.[35] Other cases were often more risible. In Edinburgh the *Evening Dispatch* reported that an elderly man had been arrested for discharging a shotgun at a pigeon in the mistaken belief that the bird was being used by an enemy spy. There were also reports of defeatism and these were duly passed on to the authorities. On 30 August the War Office received a letter addressed to Kitchener from Sidney Herbert of Stonehaven stating that a message had been read from the pulpit of Fettereso parish church in Kincardineshire claiming that 'the British Expeditionary Force had been practically cut to pieces'. As the message had come from the Lord Lieutenant Sir Alexander Baird of Urie, who said that he had received the news from the battle-front it carried weight but, as Herbert argued, the announcement caused no little local panic. Herbert continued:

I learn here that there is no foundation, as yet, for such a statement, and I venture to suggest that had it been true it would have been unwise to have proclaimed it so baldly, but being untrue it is a most cruel action.

May I appeal to you to prevent the Laird from running riot. When I left Stonehaven knees were shaking and hearts quailed.

Given the person involved, the letter called for discretion and it received only a brief acknowledgement from the War Office: Baird of Urie played a role in local recruiting efforts and had been one of the first lords lieutenant to respond to Kitchener's call for volunteers.[36]

The other example of abnormality which no one could miss was the first appearance in the press of wartime casualty lists. As most people thought that the war would be won by the superiority of the Royal Navy it was not surprising that the first casualties were sailors. In fact the war was only twelve hours old when the first hostilities took place in the North Sea, in the area between Harwich and Antwerp. In the early morning of 5 August the light cruiser HMS *Amphion*, commanded by Captain H. C. Fox and accompanied by two destroyers, *Lance* and *Landrail*, came across the German minelayer *Königin Luise*, formerly a Hamburg–America excursion liner, which had been sowing her mines in the approaches to the estuary of the River Thames. In a short and decisive action the German ship was sunk and 56 of her crew of 130 were taken on board the British cruiser. It was their last piece of luck. At six-thirty in the morning on 6 August *Amphion* hit a mine which had most certainly been laid by the German warship and settled in the water. As the sailors began to abandon ship two huge explosions ripped through the crippled cruiser and, her back broken, she quickly went to the bottom – Fox later remembered that 'the foremost half of the ship seemed to rise out of the water'. Despite the best efforts of the escorting destroyers 132 British sailors and 27 German prisoners were killed in the explosion: they were the first casualties of the war and *Amphion* was the first naval vessel to fall victim to a magnetic mine. Amongst those killed were John Maxwell of Edinburgh, a signal boy and the son of the church officer of St Giles'; Stoker William Douglas of Aberdeen, son of the green-keeper of the local links golf course; and William Carson Mair of Freuchie in Fife whose parents had the melancholy experience a few days later of opening his last, hopeful letter home.

Another milestone was reached a month later, on 3 September. The light cruiser HMS *Pathfinder* was leading a patrol of the 8th Flotilla in the mouth of the Firth of Forth when it became the first British warship to be sunk by a German submarine, *U-21*, commanded by Lieutenant Otto Hersing. Although the submarine was sighted there was no time to take evasive action. *Pathfinder* was torn apart by a huge explosion in the forward magazine and sank within four minutes, drowning all but nine of her crew of 259. The briefly blazing wreck could be seen from the Fife coast and the East Lothian shores and Hersing's successful attack led to an immediate outbreak of nerves,

known as 'periscopitis', as the Royal Navy came to terms with this
new undersea threat. Worse followed three weeks later with an even
more audacious attack. On 22 September the small kerosene-powered
submarine, *U-9*, commanded by Otto Weddigen, torpedoed three
elderly British armoured cruisers, *Aboukir*, *Hogue* and *Cressy*, which
were operating a patrol in the 'Broad Fourteens' off the Dutch coast.
First to be hit was *Aboukir*, and as her sister ships attempted to pick up
survivors they too fell victim to *U-9*'s torpedoes. The casualty list was
high – 1,459 officers and men – and once again the pride of the Royal
Navy had been severely dented. But all three ships should never have
been at sea. Not only were they ancient rust-buckets, having been
held in reserve on the Medway, but they were crewed by reservists,
most of whom had not been at sea for years. In an attempt to make
them battle-worthy all the cruisers had regular navy captains and
senior officers, but tragically each ship had been assigned nine young
midshipmen from the Royal Naval College, Dartmouth. Amongst
the thirteen midshipmen killed in the action was the fifteen-year-old
nephew of Lord Erskine, the heir to the Mar and Kellie earldom, who
was serving with the army in France. A letter from Erskine's mother
written two days after the sinking summed up the sense of loss and
waste: 'Of course, one is proud of him but it is desperately young to be
called upon to give one's life for one's country . . . It is wicked to have
sent those children into that frightful strain. They were doing patrol
work all the time in the North Sea and had sent their destroyers into
port on account of the bad weather and should never have been
cruising about without them. Those slow old boats were absolutely
defenceless.'[37]

As the war progressed letters like that would become commonplace
as grieving families attempted to come to terms with the losses. It was
not the end of the bloodletting at sea. Three weeks later Weddigen
struck again, hitting the elderly cruiser HMS *Hawke* as it was slowly
patrolling in the North Sea off Aberdeen. A destroyer sent to search
for the cruiser found a lifeboat holding twenty-nine sailors, but over
five hundred men had been drowned earlier when the cruiser capsized
and quickly sank after being hit by *U-9's* torpedoes. *U-9* survived the
war, the only submarine of her class to do so, but Weddigen was less
fortunate. Decorated with the Pour le Mérite, Germany's highest
gallantry award, he was killed on 18 March 1915 off the north-east

coast of Scotland when his submarine, *U-29*, was rammed and sunk by HMS *Dreadnought*. In the meantime, for the Royal Navy at least, the war was becoming painful reality: ships were being sunk by modern sophisticated weapons such as mines and submarines, and hundreds of lives were being lost.

2 The Flower of Scotland

At the beginning of the First World War, as at any other time in history, Scotland was no stranger to the business of warfare. The country's story is bloody with battles: some fought against the nearest neighbour, England; many more fought amongst the Scots themselves, family against family, clan against clan, Lowlander against Highlander, Catholic against Protestant. Scotland's history of warfare is long and varied and it includes long periods of fighting abroad: from the sixteenth century onwards Scots mercenaries fought in the service of the kings of France, Spain, Russia and Sweden. Scots made good fighters and in common with many other minorities on Europe's fringes – the Croat cavalry in Wallenstein's army, for example – they exported their skills, becoming soldiers of fortune who gave good value for money. At least 25,000 were in the service of Gustavus Adolphus of Sweden, half as many fought for King Louis XIII of France, often confronting their fellow countrymen on the field of battle, neither giving quarter nor expecting to receive it. One, Sir John Hepburn, scion of an old East Lothian Catholic family, fought in the Swedish and the French armies and rose to become a marshal of France, having raised the formation which became The Royal Scots, the 1st of Foot and the senior line infantry regiment in the British Army's order of battle.

A further reason for the Scots' interest in soldiering was provided by recent history and the creation of dubious military traditions. In the middle of the previous century Scotland had been gripped by the Volunteer craze, that Victorian fancy for part-time amateur soldiering which involved some gentle shooting practice and drills and, best of all, dressing up in turkey-cock uniforms. In Scotland the recruitment figures for the Volunteer units were twice the British average, a figure which was undoubtedly assisted by the creation of units with

Highland affiliations, most of them in the Central Belt. Their panoply of kilts, tartan trews, ostrich feathers and ornate sporrans were an irresistible attraction and everywhere men rushed to wear them. Most of these outlandish uniforms owed nothing to tradition but were invented by local colonels and they came to represent one of the flowerings of a self-conscious nationalism or what the military historian John Keegan has described as 'a force for resistance against the creeping anglicisation of Scottish urban life'.[1] Nostalgia for a half-forgotten romantic past was a factor, as was the existing iconography of the Scottish soldier, which found its apotheosis in Roger Fenton's Crimean War photographs of the sternly bearded Highland soldiers of Queen Victoria's army. However, there was more to soldiering than putting on fancy dress. Being a part-time soldier meant following an honourable calling: it was companionable, offered self-respect and produced steadiness of character, all important moral virtues in Presbyterian Scotland.

The vogue for soldiering can also be traced back to the defeat of the Jacobite army at Culloden in 1746 and to the subsequent subjugation of the Highlands and the despoliation of its Gaelic culture. In time it came to be considered a romantic episode in Scotland's history – Bonnie Prince Charlie, the Young Pretender, at the head of his kilted Jacobite army – and it became a sentimental myth in poetry and song, one which most Scots were happy to swallow. The facts, though, were rather different and far from glorious. The army commanded by Prince Charles Edward Stewart was not a professional force in the sense that his opponent and near relative the Duke of Cumberland would have understood it. True, many of the officers had seen service in Europe, and, equally true, it was based on regimental lines which gave it a sense of orderliness to distinguish it from being a rabble of revolutionaries, but it relied on tactics which were fast becoming an anachronism in the middle of the eighteenth century. Cavalry was lacking, modern weapons were in short supply, the commissary arrangements were not of the best and all too often the soldiers had to rely on their own resourcefulness to make up for the deficiencies of the command structure.

Against them on the government side were soldiers who had seen service in the recent European campaigns. They were well trained, well fed and strong in artillery and cavalry, and many of them were

Scots fighting in regiments which survived into the twentieth century:
The Royal Scots of St Clair's Regiment, The Royal Scots Fusiliers of
Campbell's Regiment and The King's Own Scottish Borderers
of Sempill's Regiment. Add on the Argyll Militia and the Earl of
Loudon's Independent Companies of the Highland Watch and it is
impossible to view the defeat at Culloden as a battle between the
English and the Scots. Rather, as Cumberland saw it and as he
addressed his men before the battle, it was an action fought by the
government's internal security forces to put down a rebellion by a
group of disaffected rebels. His policy was clear. Cumberland was
determined 'to bruise those bad seeds spread about this country so as
they might never shoot again' and in so doing to prevent the
Highlands from offering their traditional threat to the body politic.
It was a chance, he said, to demonstrate to the clans that they were not
above the law and that it was in the power of the government's
security forces to march into lands previously considered inaccessible.
After the defeat the clans were forced to disarm, their centres of power
destroyed: around 7,000 houses were razed and steps were taken to
garrison the areas concerned. Finally, measures were taken for 'disarming and undressing those savages' through the Disarming Act of
August 1746. Not only were traditional weapons and the plaid made
illegal but Highlanders were forced to swear an oath of allegiance
which left the clansman in no doubt that his day was over.

The destruction of Highland Scottish military power and the
Clearances of the traditional clan lands have been described as the
beginning of the end of a way of life which was barely understood by
outsiders, not least Lowland Scots, but it has to be said that, at the
time, the process was largely welcomed. In the aftermath of the union
of the parliaments and the economic benefits of 'heavenly Hanover-
ianism' it was thought no bad thing to have this lawless area with its
savage population and their heathen way of life (for so it seemed)
brought under control. What to do with them was another matter.
Either they could accept modernity and the union or they could be
moved elsewhere to make new lives, courtesy of landowners who
regarded themselves not as destroyers but as liberal reformers. As for
the soldierly instincts of their tenants, these could be offered to the
British Army at a time when it was being used as an imperial
gendarmerie to expand the country's growing colonial holdings.

During the Seven Years War the elder Pitt, acting on a suggestion made by King George II, opened the door for the creation of the Highland regiments. It was a simple concept. Highlanders were regarded as good soldiers: their powers of endurance and their fighting qualities had become evident during the earlier Jacobite rebellions. Here was a ready supply of soldiers who would do their duty, were known for their abilities as fighters, displayed hardihood in the field and gave unbending loyalty to their commanders. One other factor intruded: the traditional clan structure produced a sense of coherence and loyalty which would translate into good military practice. As the days of the clan system were numbered after Culloden and would soon disappear – other than as a sentimental entity based on chief-doms, tartan and yearning for a lost past – the Highland regiments became handy substitutes for the old clan way of life.

Through the barbaric allure of their uniforms Scottish soldiers became an instantly recognised and widely feared element of the British Army, and their service in Africa, India and North America helped to consolidate Britain's growing mercantile empire. The long tradition of soldiering was also a powerful factor in establishing the Scottish people's relationship with the army. While it is true that there had been a falling-off in the numbers and the quality of recruits in the second half of the nineteenth century, leading to higher numbers of English and Irish soldiers joining the Scottish regiments, the army was not in itself considered a dishonourable calling. The career of Hector Macdonald is a case in point. The son of a crofter in the Black Isle, he left a steady job as a shop assistant to join the 92nd (Gordon) Highlanders and was granted a commission while serving in Afghanistan in 1871. He was eventually knighted in the rank of major-general and was a much-lauded national figure who was praised as a good example of Scottish pluck and determination, the epitome of the upright Highland soldier. Men like him provided young Scots with an example of what could be achieved and Macdonald helped to create the ideal of the kilted soldier as one of nature's gentlemen, a lion in the field but a lamb in the house. (Macdonald's career ended in disgrace when he committed suicide in 1903 rather than face charges of sexual misconduct; but so great was his reputation in Scotland that many chose to believe that he had been framed by jealous senior officers.) War Office figures showed that 26.9 per cent of the men aged 15 to 49 volunteering for the army in 1911 were Scots, compared to 24.2 per cent in England, and in her study of the composition of the Highland regiments between 1870 and 1920 Diana Henderson insists that, despite seasonal man-power problems, 'soldiering was widely looked upon as a respectable profession in Scotland'. Military matters were widely reported and discussed in the Scottish press – the *Scotsman* published regular 'Military and Naval Notes' – and regiments returning from overseas were always given a warm welcome as they marched from the quayside back to their barracks.[3]

There was, of course, another side to the question of recruitment. Young men also joined the army because they had no option. In the poorest families an unemployed boy was an extra mouth to feed and in every Scottish regiment there were large numbers of young men who had escaped grinding poverty by becoming soldiers. A return by the Army Medical Department in 1903 showed that of 84,402 recruits examined on enlistment the majority, 52,022, came from the lower stratum of the working classes. This was especially true in Lowland regiments where recruits often came from backgrounds where families lived below the poverty line and overcrowding and lack of decent sanitation were commonplace. Conditions in Glasgow and many parts of Lanarkshire were particularly bad. Although the prevailing squalor and degradation of the previous century had been addressed by a combination of philanthropy and the introduction of radical im-provements in public health, the physical conditions for most workers in Glasgow were not good, with the population density in 1911 being twice that of Edinburgh and Dundee.[4] In 1917 a Royal Commission on Housing revealed a situation which was bedevilled by 'gross overcrowding and huddling of the sexes together in the congested villages and towns, occupation of one-room houses by large families, groups of lightless and unventilated houses in the old burghs, clotted classes of slums in the great cities'. Faced by those conditions, and the low pay which caused them, the army was often seen as an escape route. Peter Corstorphine, a poorly paid fourteen-year-old apprentice plumber in Edinburgh, tried to join the army in 1907 but was considered to be 'too small and too young'. Three years later he got his wish. It helped that his brother was already serving in The Black Watch:

What made me want tae join the army at that time wis merely the fact that there were no jobs goin' around, especially for the likes o' me. And workin' as an apprentice joiner ah was gettin' about 3/6d a week.

Ma mother used tae give me a sixpence pocket money. And life became very hard, especially when you got to the length of fifteen and sixteen. You were still only gettin' 4/6d a week and you were gettin' very little pocket money. Ye couldnae even go tae the theatre. And the young lads at that time were a' beginnin' tae wear bowler hats and what have you. I was goin' about like Coconut Tam [a well-known, diminutive Edinburgh street vendor].

Now the army wis seven shillins a week and ye're all found, plus the fact that ye got your uniform and boots and everything. Ye were well fed and a good bed. What more did a fellow want?[5]

Like his brother, Corstorphine also joined The Black Watch, serving in Ireland and Edinburgh before going to India with the 2nd Battalion. Although he found the training hard and the conditions in the barracks in Edinburgh Castle 'terrible' he made the grade and like other men in his position soon appreciated the order, cleanliness, regular meals and close companionship which were central to army life. For Corstorphine, as for every other recruit to a regiment's rank and file, the initial period of service was seven years, after which they could be discharged to the Reserves for a five-year period or elect to spend that time with the Colours, provided that they were found to be efficient and of good conduct. At the end of the twelve-year period they could opt for a discharge or sign on for another nine years to complete twenty-one years of service. The best soldiers were promoted and in time became senior non-commissioned officers or warrant officers, the backbone of any self-respecting infantry battalion.

The commissioned officers were a different breed. The purchase of commissions had ended in 1871 but Britain's military officer class was still one which Wellington or Marlborough would have recognised, as most of its members, including the Scots, came from the aristocracy, the landed gentry, the clergy and the professions and had been educated at Britain's great private schools. All were expected to have private incomes, as the annual pay of a second lieutenant, the entry rank, was just over £95 a year and that was insufficient to cover his uniform costs and mess bills which amounted to roughly £10 a month. In 1914 the War Office recommended that the minimum needed to survive was £160 a year but even that amount meant that a young officer would have to lead an abstemious existence. Some regiments were extremely expensive. Officers in cavalry or foot guards regiments had to purchase a variety of uniforms to meet all the variations in service and mess dress; they were expected to live well in the mess and to keep at least two hunters and three polo ponies. It was not considered unusual for a smart cavalry regiment to insist on a young officer being in possession of a private income of up to £1,000 a year, an enormous sum in 1914. For the Scottish regiments this made the Royal Scots Greys and the Scots Guards the most expensive, but smarter Highland regiments such as The Black Watch or The Argyll and Sutherland Highlanders required a private income close to £400 a year. Lowland regiments were a little less costly at an average of £250 a year and the implied differences in social scale were not only understood but accepted by the men involved. So too were the differences in rank within a battalion. Officers were meant to be a breed apart but they were also supposed to put their men's best interests before theirs and prided themselves on setting high personal standards of behaviour. Soldiers like Peter Corstorphine knew only too well that the creation of mutual trust precluded any intimacy: 'Relations between the other ranks and officers before the war were, oh, very much apart, you were very much apart. They were a different class altogether. They could be comradely enough, ye know, but ta, ta a lot. Each rank was segregated.'[6]

Although it is dangerous to generalise, the Scottish infantry regiments of the regular army in 1914 were very much the nation in uniform. In each battalion there would be representatives of the different social classes, from well-connected and wealthy aristocrats or landed gentry in the officers' mess to the rank and file who had known only the subjugation of extreme poverty. In between were small numbers of the professional classes – clerks and shopkeepers and trained artisans and farm labourers – but the bulk of Britain's regular army was drawn from what one historian has called 'the lower end of the working class'.[7] There would be a fair share of men who drank too much or gambled away their modest pay; equally there would be temperance men and others who used their spare time to improve their education. There would be officers who did not fit in with the battalion's way of life and behaved irresponsibly, while there would be those who took a Jesuitical interest in their calling and put a high premium on personal honour and courage. There were battalion commanders who would fail the test of combat and men who forgot to die like heroes in the hellish fear of battle. But there would also be those, the majority, who were bound up in the common cause: to serve the regiment which had become their physical and spiritual home. They might have spent a great deal of time grumbling, they probably thought they were better trained and more professional than they really were, but warts and all they represented the first flowering of Scotland's contribution to the war effort in the late summer of 1914.

The most visible elements of Scotland's 'army' consisted of its ten infantry regiments, each of which consisted of two Regular line battalions, one at home and one stationed abroad on service in the empire. This two-battalion system had been evolved in 1881 by Edward Cardwell, the innovative Secretary for War, allowing the home-based battalion to provide both a training facility for drafts and reliefs when they were required. Regiments numbered 1 to 25 in the army's order of battle already had two battalions and they were left alone, but the remainder were rearranged into new paired relationships, some of which were unhappy and took time to settle down. Thus it was that in August 1914 the 2nd Battalion Royal Scots was based in Plymouth where it formed part of 8th Brigade in the 3rd Division, while the 1st Battalion had been based in Allahabad in India since 1911 where it formed part of the British garrison in a country which one military historian has described as 'the greatest formative influence on the life, language and legend of the British army . . . India, with its heat, stinks and noise, its enveloping dust, became the British army's second home − perhaps its first.'[8] That arrangement worked with no rancour between the battalions but matters were less settled in The Cameronian Regiment. Its 1st Battalion had been the 26th Foot, which had been founded in 1689 by the Earl of Angus, while the 2nd Battalion began life in 1794 as the 90th (Perthshire) Light Infantry, a regiment raised for service in the wars against France by Lord Lynedoch. Each considered themselves to be a cut above the other: the 1st had a long and distinguished history which stretched back into the seventeenth century, while the 2nd Scottish Rifles (as they always styled themselves) were proud of their light infantry heritage, which was considered socially superior, leaving a regimental historian to remark that 'there was a good deal of animosity between the battalions, which was not really killed until the 1930s'.[9] All line infantry regiments also had a third Reserve battalion, which was based at the regimental depot and was largely an administrative formation to provide reinforcements for the two Regular battalions.

These infantry regiments, plus two battalions of Scots Guards and one cavalry regiment, The Royal Scots Greys, were the symbol of the country's military prowess and, with their kilts or trews, they were held in high regard by the Scottish public. Yet in August 1914 only three battalions were resident in Scotland: the 1st Cameron Highlanders were stationed in Edinburgh Castle, the 1st Cameronians were in Glasgow and the 2nd Argyll and Sutherland Highlanders were at Fort George outside Inverness. Eight Regular battalions were based in England or Ireland, helping to form the six infantry divisions which would make up the British Expeditionary Force (BEF) created before the war to provide an army to fight in Europe in the event of a major conflict breaking out on the Continent. These were: 1st Scots Guards, based at Aldershot, 1st Brigade, 1st Division; 2nd Royal Scots, based at Plymouth, 8th Brigade, 3rd Division; 1st Royal Scots Fusiliers, based at Gosport, 9th Brigade, 3rd Division; 2nd King's Own Scottish Borderers, based in Dublin, 13th Brigade, 5th Division; 2nd Highland Light Infantry, based at Aldershot, 5th Brigade, 2nd Division; 1st Black Watch, based at Aldershot, 1st Brigade, 1st Division; 2nd Seaforth Highlanders, based at Shorncliffe, 10th Brigade, 4th Division; and 1st Gordon Highlanders, based at Plymouth, 8th Brigade, 3rd Division. Another ten battalions were based abroad, seven in the garrison in India – 1st Royal Scots (Allahabad), 1st King's Own Scottish Borderers (Lucknow), 1st Highland Light Infantry (Ambala), 2nd Black Watch (Bareilly), 2nd Camerons (Poona), 1st Seaforths (Agra), 1st Argylls (Dinapore) – one in Malta (2nd Scottish Rifles), one in Cairo (2nd Gordons) and one in Gibraltar (2nd Royal Scots Fusiliers). The 2nd Battalion Scots Guards were at the Tower of London as part of London District while The Royal Scots Greys were in York as part of 5th Cavalry Brigade, which had also been committed to the BEF.

The home-based battalions would be the first to fight in France and Flanders: most crossed over the Channel with the BEF in August, including the three Scottish-based battalions, which were deployed as lines of communication troops. However, the overseas battalions followed close behind. The Seaforths arrived in England on 21 September, The Black Watch on 12 October, The Royal Scots and the Camerons on 16 November, The Argylls on 19 November and The King's Own Scottish Borderers on 28 December. All crossed over to France and all were in action with the BEF by the beginning of 1915.[10]

The fighting strength of the BEF was 247,432 officers and men, about one third of whom were based in India, and the official historian of the war has called it 'incomparably the best trained, best organised and best equipped British Army which ever went forth to war'. (Ominously, he added the caveat 'except in the matter of numbers'.[11]) Of those, it is difficult to estimate the total number of Scottish Regular soldiers as not every Scottish battalion was manned entirely by Scots and many Scots served in other formations in the army. However, as twenty-two Scottish-named infantry battalions were committed to the BEF in August 1914 the figure must be at least 20,000, with more serving in the artillery, engineers and support arms. This closely mirrors the demographics of the British Isles in that accepted population figures for 1914 showed that Scotland made up 10.6 per cent of the British and Irish population.

At the time, an infantry battalion consisted of around a thousand soldiers under the command of a lieutenant-colonel, usually an experienced officer in his forties. His executive consisted of a second-in-command, an adjutant in the rank of captain who was responsible for the smooth running of the battalion and a quartermaster who dealt with stores and supplies. Also part of the team was the regimental-sergeant-major, the battalion's senior non-commissioned officer who ran the battalion headquarters and the orderly room. The fighting strength of the battalion lay in its four rifle companies of six officers and 221 infantrymen under the command of a major or a senior captain; each company had four platoons, each one having four sections and the men were equipped with the recently introduced

Short Magazine Lee Enfield rifle and an 18-inch bayonet. The battalion itself formed part of an infantry brigade with three other battalions under the command of a brigadier-general. Beyond that, and well beyond the imagination of most soldiers, were the Division, the Corps and the Army.

For most soldiers, especially the pre-war Regulars who made up the BEF, the first loyalty was to the regiment and the battalion in which they served. This was their home and one whose honour and history they would go to great lengths to protect. As John Baynes put it in his account of the 2nd Scottish Rifles at the Battle of Neuve Chapelle in March 1915 'all the ranks in the battalion were caught up, whatever their origins, in the powerful grasp of the Regiment. By the time they had lived for two or three years in the atmosphere of the Regimental tradition, had made the strongest friendships of their lives within the Regiment, and had been constantly reminded of their duty to it, the Regiment could claim them as its own . . . I do not suppose Regimental spirit will ever mean so much again as it did to those Regular soldiers of 1914.'[12] It helped that the regiments had their own recruiting areas with the depot being central to the local community and a focus for recruitment. The majority of the men in The Cameronians' two battalions came from Glasgow and industrial Lanarkshire, with a handful having their original homes in other parts of Scotland and England, the latter mainly in London and Newcastle. For them the regiment had become home, perhaps the only home they would ever know. As one Cameronian, Company Sergeant-Major Robert Leggat, remembered the period before 1914, 'in those days the regular army carried its own life with it, wherever it went, and you lived pretty much the same, whether you were in India or any other place. You lived between the barrack-room and the wet canteen, without any social life at all.'[13]

That understanding lies at the heart of the regimental tradition in the British Army and the Scots were no strangers to upholding its mystique, part family and part fighting formation. Indeed, given the tribal nature of much of Scottish society and the allure of the Scottish regiments' uniforms with their tartans and feathered bonnets, Scottish soldiers had a good conceit of themselves and were not slow to parade the fact that they thought themselves a superior breed. Regimental attachments ran deep. The Royal Scots were proud of the fact that they were the oldest line infantry regiment in the British Army, the 'First of Foot', and rejoiced in their nickname of 'Pontius Pilate's Bodyguard'. The Black Watch was the senior Highland regiment, wore the distinctive black and green government tartan kilt with a red hackle in the soldiers' bonnets and in common with the other Highlanders took a great deal of interest in their traditions and heritage. Scotland's only cavalry regiment, The Royal Scots Greys, rode exclusively on the type of big grey horses which had charged at Waterloo and Balaklava, and The Scots Guards traced their history back to King Charles I's civil wars. Of course, English, Irish and Welsh regiments were equally proud of their histories and traditions, and the rifle regiments' dark green uniforms were thought particularly smart, but the kilts of the 'tartan curtain' were difficult to ignore even by those who resented the attention given to the Highland regiments. In 1916 Private Ernest Parker, 15th Hussars, watched a Scottish formation marching up towards the line:

> One thing I shall never forget is the sight of thousands of rhythmically swinging kilts as a Division of Highlanders swept towards us. Skirling at the head of the column strode the pipers, filling the air with their wild martial music. Behind glinted a forest of rifle barrels and the flash of brawny knees rising and straightening in rhythm. Were these the freemen of yesterday, peaceful citizens who a few months ago strolled to work? These men seemed to us a crack military unit ready to carry out its mission.[14]

Not everyone was so impressed. The adjutant of the 2nd Royal Welch Fusiliers, in which the poet Robert Graves served, accused the Scots 'both the trousered kind and the bare-arsed kind' of being loud-mouthed braggarts who left trenches in a filthy condition and were indifferent to basic hygiene, while a private soldier in the South Staffordshire Regiment was moved to complain, 'It's no use an English regiment trying to get on when there's a regiment with the kilts. The kilts put all the other regiments in the dark.' Insults were common and it took little to start a fistfight when rivals clashed. A shout of 'two pints of broken squares' in the pub or wet canteen would cause Highland soldiers to clench fists and unbuckle belts as they defended their honour against the allusion that The Black Watch had allowed the square, then the infantry's basic defensive formation, to be broken at the Battle of Tamai in 1884 during the campaign against Osman Digna in the Sudan. The cry of 'who shot the cheese?' would rouse the Gordons to fury – an 'allegation that they had once opened fire on a ration cheese, mistaking its pallor in the dusk for the pale face of an enemy' – and The Royal Scots would take on anyone daring to hail them as the 'first and worst'. Even outsiders would respond to any insult, real or imagined. English and Irish soldiers serving in Scottish regiments quickly became per-fervid Scots and would take a savage delight in refusing to obey orders other than from their own officers; they would often be found at the forefront in inter-regimental scraps.[15]

This was the old Regular Army, which had come into being after the Boer War and which was destined to undertake the first fighting of the war as the BEF in France and Flanders in 1914. It was professional, well equipped and well led. Its commander-in-chief, Field Marshal Sir John French, was a cavalryman who had performed well, and the two corps commanders, Douglas Haig and Horace Smith-Dorrien, also enjoyed good reputations. In addition to those Regular regiments there were two other armies which would fight alongside them: the volunteers of the Territorial Force, which had been raised in 1908 to provide the country with a second line of home defence manned by part-time soldiers, and the New Army, which was created as a result of Kitchener's call for manpower in the immediate aftermath of the declaration of war. As we have seen, Kitchener entertained misgivings about the worth of the Territorial Force – he dismissed the force as a 'town-clerk's army' consisting of skylarkers who would disrupt army discipline – but his criticisms were belied by the fighting spirit and courage of the fourteen first-line divisions of the Territorial Force which were raised during the war, four of which, 51st Highland, 52nd Lowland, 64th Highland and 65th Lowland, were Scottish. All ten Scottish infantry regiments had Territorial battalions based in their recruiting areas where local county Territorial associations, presided over by the lord lieutenant, were responsible for running their property and supplying their equipment.

However, most of their weapons were obsolescent: Territorial soldiers were not trained on the Short Lee Enfield, were forced to use earlier models of the rifle and possessed little or no artillery. This led senior Regular commanders to argue that the force was of little practical use and could only be used to fulfil its original role of home defence. Even then their abilities were open to question: Territorial soldiers only trained twice a week and attended a fortnight's camp once a year, attendance was not compulsory, recruiting was lax (at the start of the war the force was 47,317 men short of its establishment) and there was a widespread feeling in military circles that Territorial soldiers looked on their service as a pleasing diversion and preferred organising dinners and dances to studying tactics. The yeomanry were considered to be even worse, based, as many of their regiments were, on local hunts. Just as the cavalry demanded officers with good private incomes so too did yeomanry regiments, with the exception that even troopers had to be able to afford their mounts and purchase their expensive uniforms. Scotland had seven yeomanry regiments, in order of precedence: the Ayrshire Yeomanry (Earl of Carrick's Own), the Lanarkshire Yeomanry, Lothians and Border Horse, Queen's Own Royal Glasgow Yeomanry, Fife and Forfar Yeomanry, the Lovat Scouts and the Scottish Horse.

Although yeomanry regiments thought themselves second to none so too did many Territorial Force battalions. When John Reith was commissioned in the 1/5th Cameronians (Scottish Rifles) in 1911 he observed that the 'social class of the man in the ranks was higher than that of any other regiment in Glasgow'. Whole companies were formed from staff of Glasgow's leading business firms and one was raised from the University of Glasgow, with the result that many of the rank and file were educated members of the middle class who thought themselves equal to, if not better than, any Regular formation. By way of contrast the same regiment's 1/6th Battalion drew its men from the industrial towns of Lanarkshire, and the 1/7th Battalion had one company of total abstainers while the 1/8th Battalion drew one of its companies from Glasgow's breweries. The same was true on the other side of the country where the 1/5th Royal Scots recruited heavily from George Heriot's School while the 1/9th Royal Scots had close links with George Watson's College; as a result both battalions had many professionals in the ranks whereas the 1/7th Royal Scots was composed of men who worked in the Leith docks or the East Lothian coalfield.[16] Inevitably the Territorial soldiers had a variety of reasons for serving. One was a chance to wear uniform without facing the normal dangers of a soldier's life. The opportunity to earn extra pay was also a factor as was the possibility of going on the summer camp, which many of the poorer soldiers regarded as a holiday. That was one of the considerations which persuaded Bill Hanlan, a coal miner at Newbattle, to try his luck with the 1/8th Royal Scots which recruited in Midlothian and Peebles-shire: 'When we got tae camp we got a shillin' a day and our food and we got a uniform and we got sleepin' in tents, because it was summer weather. It wis always in July, when the pit holidays wis on, that we went. We went for two weeks. And if ye had to stay over and above the two weeks ye got your pay that ye had at your work. Ye always got paid full up, ye never lost anything.'[17]

In July 1914 the 1/8th Royal Scots were at Stobs Camp near Hawick where they heard their first rumours of war and Hanlan was one of the majority of his battalion who volunteered for additional service overseas, a practice that allowed Territorial battalions to cross over to France. Once introduced on 13 August the idea caught on and group pressure made it difficult for serving Territorials to refuse to serve overseas if the majority of the battalion volunteered. This was the case with the 10th King's Liverpool Regiment, or Liverpool Scottish, which produced a 'miserable response' when volunteers were requested but, as Colour-Quartermaster Robert Scott Macfie noted in a letter home, by 1 September more and more men were coming forward with the result that it was very difficult for individuals to stand aside and refuse:

> I have one member who did not intend to volunteer for foreign service, but when appealed to agreed to go. He was an only son, and his parents heard from somebody else that he had volunteered and sent a long telegram forbidding him to go abroad. He came to me almost crying and withdrew his name. Then he wrote to his parents and said he felt like a coward and that he hoped they would not write to him for a long time. Last night we had another telegram from his mother. 'It is we who are cowards, you must go' – so he came to me again almost crying and said that it was the best news he had ever heard in his life. This is the sort of fellows we have in E Company and I'm very proud of him.[18]

Macfie was aged 46 and had rejoined his unit on mobilisation; the chairman of a sugar-refining firm he refused a commission and like many other Territorials was happy to remain in the ranks.

The Liverpool Scottish crossed over to France at the end of October by which time the Territorial Force had already been blooded. The first to see action was the London Scottish which had come into being in 1908 as the 14th (County of London) Battalion, the London Regiment (London Scottish), and was manned by Scots living in the London area and along with the 13th (Kensington) and 28th (Artist's Rifles) was one of the London Regiment's smarter battalions, as much a social and sporting club as a military formation. They went into action on the Messines ridge on 30 October, attacking the heavily defended German position at Wytschaete during the First Battle of Ypres. The attack was made by 750 soldiers, with their pipers playing encouragement, but raw enthusiasm was no armour against the German machine-gunners: 394 London Scots were killed in the action. Just as bad, the battalion's War Diary recorded that 'the rifles Mark I were proved to be very bad and nearly 50% were useless for rapid firing owing to faulty magazines'. Amongst the survivors was Ronald Colman, who would later emerge as a film star in Hollywood.[19] By the end of 1914 the London Scottish had been joined by seven other Scottish Territorial formations: 1/8th Royal Scots, 1/5th Cameronians, 1/9th Highland Light Infantry (Glasgow Highlanders), 1/5th Black Watch, 1/4th Seaforth Highlanders, 1/6th Gordon Highlanders and the Liverpool Scottish. Amongst their number was Private James Marchbank from Dalkeith who was serving with the 1/8th Royal Scots, and at the age of fourteen years and four months he was the youngest soldier recorded to be on active service in November 1914. The bulk of the Scottish Territorial Force deployment came in the spring of 1915 when the 51st (Highland) Division moved over to France and the 52nd (Lowland) Division took part in the operations in Gallipoli.

The creation of the New Armies and the gradual use of Territorial Force formations meant that the country's line infantry regiments expanded massively during the course of the war and became huge organisations handling thousands of men. To take one example, The Royal Scots raised thirty-five battalions at various stages of the war and all played a role, from seeing active service to raising and training soldiers at home in Scotland, England or Ireland:

1st Battalion (Regular Army): Western Front, Salonika, Russia
2nd Battalion (Regular Army): Western Front

3rd (Reserve) Battalion: Scotland, England, Ireland

1/4th (Queen's Edinburgh Rifles) Battalion (Territorial Force): Gallipoli, Egypt, Palestine

2/4th (Queen's Edinburgh Rifles) Battalion (Territorial Force): Scotland, Essex, Ireland

3/4th (Queen's Edinburgh Rifles) Battalion (Territorial Force): Scotland

4th (Reserve) Battalion (Territorial Force: Scotland, Catterick

1/5th (Queen's Edinburgh Rifles) Battalion (Territorial Force): Gallipoli, Egypt, France

2/5th (Queen's Edinburgh Rifles) Battalion (Territorial Force): Scotland

3/5th (Queen's Edinburgh Rifles) Battalion (Territorial Force): Scotland

1/6th Battalion (Territorial Force): coastal defence Scotland, North Africa, France

2/6th Battalion (Territorial Force): Scotland

3/6th Battalion (Territorial Force): Scotland

5/6th Battalion (Territorial Force): Western Front (formed in 1916 from 1/5th and 1/6th Battalions)

1/7th Battalion (Territorial Force): Gallipoli, Egypt, Palestine

2/7th Battalion (Territorial Force): coastal defence Scotland, England (Essex), Ireland

3/7th Battalion (Territorial Force): Scotland

1/8th Battalion (Territorial Force): Western Front

2/8th Battalion (Territorial Force): Scotland, England (Essex)

3/8th Battalion (Territorial Force): Scotland

1/9th (Highlanders) Battalion (Territorial Force): Western Front

2/9th (Highlanders) Battalion (Territorial Force): Scotland, England (Essex)

3/9th (Highlanders) Battalion (Territorial Force): Scotland, England (Catterick)

1/10th (Cyclist) Battalion (Territorial Force): Scotland, Ireland

2/10th (Cyclist) Battalion (Territorial Force: coastal defence Scotland, Ireland, England (Aldershot), Russia

11th Battalion (New Army): Western Front

12th Battalion (New Army): Western Front

13th Battalion (New Army): Western Front

14th (Reserve) Battalion (New Army): Scotland

15th (Cranston's, 1st City of Edinburgh) Battalion (New Army): Western Front

16th (McCrae's, 2nd City of Edinburgh) Battalion (New Army): Western Front

17th (Rosebery's Bantams) Battalion (New Army): Western Front

18th (Reserve) Battalion (New Army): England

19th (Labour) Battalion (Mixed): Scotland, France

1st Garrison Battalion (Mixed): Greece (Mudros), Egypt, Cyprus

2nd Garrison Battalion (Mixed): Scotland[20]

The Royal Scots' make-up and its experiences during the war were not untypical and from the regiment's order of battle a pattern emerges. Both the Regular battalions saw action, as did the first battalion of each Territorial Force formation and all but the 14th Battalion of the New Army formations. Two battalions (1st and 2/10th) served in Russia in 1919 during the operations against Bolshevik forces and the regiment fought on every battle-front except Mesopotamia and East and West Africa.

By the nature of the army's prearranged strategy for going to war in Europe the first Scottish units to go into action were the ten Regular battalions of line infantry and foot guards regiments which crossed over to France with the first four (1st, 2nd, 3rd and 5th) divisions of the BEF. Before leaving they had to be brought up to strength and all regiments had been in a state of heightened activity since 29 July when the War Office issued its orders for a 'Precautionary Period' prior to full mobilisation. As we have seen, for the 1st Cameronians this meant an abrupt departure from their summer camp near Blair Atholl and a return to Maryhill Barracks in Glasgow where they began receiving their reservists to bring them up to a full war establishment of 1,022 infantry soldiers. These were part of the 145,347 soldiers who had completed their service in the Regular Army but were still obliged to serve in the event of war and as one officer remarked they required 'tuning up' in the short period available. Only two reservists failed to make an appearance. Full mobilisation was completed on 8 August and five days later the battalion left Maryhill station in four special trains which took them to Southampton and then across the Channel to Le Havre.[21] For the Scottish regiments based in England the position was more complicated as the reservists had to be summoned from all over the country to go to their regimental depots before being sent south by train. At the end of July the 2nd Royal Scots were taking part in a field firing exercise when they were ordered to return to Plymouth in preparation for mobilisation. At the same time some 500 reservists were being processed by the regiment for service with the 2nd Battalion. As one of their number remembered, the system worked with cool efficiency: on the morning of 5 August, having said his farewells to his wife and family, he left his home in Mussel-burgh by train. He was not at all surprised to find other Royal Scots joining him before they arrived at the regimental depot at Glencorse, near Penicuik:

> I reported myself at the guardroom, and the sergeant, after taking all particulars, gave me a form and directed me to the hospital to go before the doctor. I wasn't long in his hands, and being fit and sound, I was told to go over to the Orderly Room to pass before the Commanding Officer. At the same time I was to hand in my old discharge papers. That done the next move was towards the Keep. There I got my kit and equipment, all bundled into a blanket, and with these thrown over my shoulder and my rifle in hand, I marched to the drill shed, which was our temporary quarters, changed my clothes, and lo and behold, there I was, a soldier once again. The whole proceedings only took about an hour all told, as everything was ready. It was just a case of in one door a civilian and out the other a soldier.[22]

The anonymous diarist and his fellow reservists were then sent by train to Plymouth that same night. Earlier in the day he had told his wife that he might be home again in three weeks and if he had to stay at Glencorse she and the children would be able to visit him. In common with many others he thought that the fighting would be over by Christmas.

The BEF began moving across the Channel on Monday 10 August, sailing in cramped steamers to Boulogne, Rouen and Le Havre and receiving warm and often tumultuous welcomes from the local populations. Within eight days the War Office was able to report that the first 80,000 soldiers of the BEF had landed in France with their equipment and were preparing to deploy in their agreed sector around Maubeuge and Le Cateau just south of the Belgian border, prior to taking up their position on the left flank of the French Fifth Army. Travelling by train in forty wagons whole battalions were moved into the area with a speed and efficiency which said much for the pre-war planning even if it meant that the men travelled in extreme discomfort through the summer heat in packed railway wagons. On 14 August 2nd Royal Scots arrived in Boulogne where the pipers responded to the welcome by playing 'La Marseillaise'; on the following day it entrained for Landrecies where the men went into billets at Taisnieres. A routine of daily route marches and musketry practice was introduced to get the reservists into shape; this was much needed as most of them had not had any practice with the new Short Magazine Lee Enfield rifle.[23] At that stage of the operation the Scottish regiments were deployed as follows:

I Corps (Haig)
   1st Division, 1st Brigade
     1st Scots Guards
     1st Black Watch
   Positioned at Grand Reng, Rouveroy and Givry

   2nd Division, 5th Brigade
     2nd Highland Light Infantry
   Positioned at Paturages

II Corps (Smith-Dorrien)
   3rd Division, 8th Brigade
     2nd Royal Scots
     1st Gordon Highlanders
   Positioned at Nouvelles

   9th Brigade
     1st Royal Scots Fusiliers
   Positioned at Frameries

   5th Division, 13th Brigade
     2nd King's Own Scottish Borderers
   Positioned at Wasmes[24]

In addition, two battalions were acting as lines of communication troops – 1st Cameronians and 2nd Argylls – but on 22 August these formed a new 19th Brigade with 1st Middlesex and 2nd Royal Welch Fusiliers. (1st Cameron Highlanders were deployed as lines of communication troops but joined 1st Brigade in September to replace 2nd Royal Munster Fusiliers.) All were in action by 23 August, the day after the first encounter between the British and German armies had taken place when C Squadron, 4th Dragoon Guards, under the command of Major Tom Bridges, had attacked a patrol of German cavalrymen of the 4th Cuirassiers and routed them near the village of Le Cateau. The first shot of the war was fired by Trooper Ted Thomas who was reported to have said that 'it seemed to me to be more like rifle practice on Salisbury Plain'.

The role of the BEF had been agreed before the war but by the time it deployed in support of the French Fifth Army on the northern end of the French line the situation was changing day by day. The German attack into France and Belgium was based on the pre-war Schlieffen Plan, aimed at knocking out France quickly and decisively. When the attack began the French underestimated its strength and a counter-attack was quickly repulsed. To make matters worse, on 22 August General Lanzerac's Fifth Army was defeated on the Sambre with the loss of over 4,000 casualties. The setback forced him to withdraw, leaving the BEF isolated in its defensive positions on the Mons–Conde Canal with I Corps deployed to the east and II Corps stretched out along a twenty-mile front to the west. Bearing down on them from the north were six divisions of General Alexander von Kluck's First Army. French agreed to hold the position for twenty-four hours and his men began digging-in for the expected onslaught, using the features of the mining area with its spoil heaps and buildings to enhance their defences.

The expected German assault began on the morning of 23 August and for the attacking enemy infantrymen it was a sobering experience. Trained to fire fifteen rifle rounds a minute the British regiments poured their fire into the advancing German lines with predictable results; the rate was so rapid and concentrated that the Germans believed they were facing machine-gun fire. The 75th Regiment lost 381 men in their attack on the 2nd Royal Scots' positions on the Mons–Harmignies road while the defenders' casualties were slight:

one officer and one soldier wounded and four others reported missing.* By the end of the day the attack had faltered as exhausted and frightened Germans attempted to regroup, but, despite halting the assault, the BEF was obliged to retire and in the coming days its regiments were to receive increasingly high casualties. (The exact numbers are impossible to compute as War Diaries were written up later and information about casualties was understandably, given the circumstances, incomplete.) At one point in the retreat D Company 2nd Royal Scots was reduced to one officer and seventeen soldiers and the battalion lost its commanding officer Lieutenant-Colonel McMicking.[25]

The Great Retreat, as it was known, towards the River Marne would allow the German Army to push on to the outskirts of Paris, and the BEF suffered further casualties on 26 August when II Corps turned to face the advancing Germans at Le Cateau some 30 miles from Mons. It was the British Army's biggest set-piece battle since Waterloo and their 55,000 soldiers faced German opposition which numbered 140,000. Smith-Dorrien's three divisions, supported by the Cavalry Division, were able to hold the line by dint of their superior firepower but by evening they were outnumbered and only a German failure to press home their advantage allowed II Corps to resume their retreat. Even so, the casualties were heavy – 7,812 killed – and gave a stark indication of worse things to come. Exhausted by the battle and the summer heat the BEF continued to pull back amidst rumours that the war was lost and that the French government had evacuated Paris for Bordeaux. It was a time of confusion when the fog of war seemed very real indeed as the battle-weary infantrymen continued to sleepwalk, as Captain R. V. Dolbey, the medical officer of 2nd King's Own Scottish Borderers, put it, through the French countryside: 'In a dream we marched, unconscious of the towns we passed, the village we slept in; fatigued almost beyond endurance; dropping for sleep at the five-minute halt that was the reward for four miles covered. All companies, dozing as they marched, fell forward drunkenly on each other at the

---

* On the previous day the regiment had lost its first casualty. Lieutenant G. M. Thompson, on secondment to the Gold Coast Regiment, was killed in action leading a company of Senegalese *tirailleurs* against German forces on the Chra river north of Nuatja in the German protectorate of Togoland. He was also the British Army's first officer casualty.

halts; sleeping men lay, as they halted, in the roads and were kicked uncomplainingly into wakefulness again.'[26]

For the men of The Kings Own Scottish Borderers, ahead lay the next battle on 13 September when they reached the River Aisne where the long retreat ended and the Allies were able to counter-attack. During the battle the Scottish regiments won their first Victoria Crosses (VC) of the war. They were awarded to Private Ross Tollerton, 1st Camerons, for his courage under fire when he carried a wounded officer to safety, despite being wounded himself, and to Private George Wilson, 2nd Highland Light Infantry, who captured a German machine-gun position at Verneuil by charging it with sufficient resolution to give the impression that he was in command of a superior force. However, they were not the first Scots to win the medal, which is only awarded for 'most conspicuous bravery, or some daring or pre-eminent act of valour or self-sacrifice or extreme devotion to duty in the presence of the enemy'. The first Scottish VC had been won on 23 August when Lance-Corporal Charles Alfred Jarvis, 57th Field Company, Royal Engineers, successfully demolished a bridge over the Mons–Conde Canal despite being under heavy enemy fire while he packed twenty-two slabs of gun cotton on to the girders to bring them down. A native of Angus (although born in Fraserburgh he was brought up in Carnoustie), Jarvis had enlisted in the Royal Engineers in 1899 and was one of the thousands of reservists who were called up from civilian life in 1914. Two months later he was badly wounded and invalided home. Captain James Jack, now a staff officer in the newly raised independent 19th Brigade, won a different kind of award at Le Cateau where he was awarded the French Légion d'honneur for his gallantry under fire while helping to extricate two companies of the 2nd Argyll and Sutherland Highlanders.

Not every incident resulted in heroism and honours. In the confusion of the retreat some battalions became isolated and were unaware of the orders coming down from brigade or divisional headquarters. That was the predicament facing 1st Gordon High-landers on the night of 25 August as 8th Brigade covered the 3rd Division's retreat from Le Cateau. With the exception of A Company the battalion found themselves isolated at Caudry together with elements of 2nd Royal Scots and 1st Royal Irish as the rest of the brigade, unknown to them, withdrew. The Gordons' commanding officer, Lieutenant-Colonel F. H. Neish, was disinclined to follow suit without receiving orders but his second-in-command urged him to see sense and order a withdrawal. The subordinate's warning carried weight: Major & Brevet Colonel William Eagleson Gordon was not only superior in army rank but had been awarded the VC during the Boer War at Krugersdorp where his gallantry under fire had saved the British guns. A furious row broke out between the two men and Gordon exercised his right to take over command as the senior officer in charge of a mixed force of Gordons, Royal Scots and Royal Irish. The force started pulling out in the early hours of the morning but it was too late. On the outskirts of the village of Bertry the Germans were waiting and the mixed force was surrounded. In the confusion of night most of the men were either killed or taken prisoner and 500 survivors were forced to surrender. As a result the battalion almost ceased to exist and had to be reinforced but that did not stop other soldiers giving the Gordons a new name: 'The Kaiser's Bodyguard'. It was a poor jest. The men involved were in an impossible position and the most reasonable comment was left to the *Official History*, which dryly remarked that 'the fortune of war was hard upon the 1/Gordons', adding the solace that their 'gallant resistance' had saved others during the retreat.[27] Unfortunately, because there was confusion over the actual surrender – Gordon wanted to continue fighting, as did other officers, but Neish gave the order to avoid unnecessary casualties – it was not the end of the matter. The battle was re-fought after the war in both an army board of investigation and a libel case instigated by Colonel Gordon (see Chapter 11).

The Aisne marked a new phase of the operations and signalled the end of a war of manoeuvre as both sides struggled to fill the gap between the Aisne and the Channel coast before it was exploited by the other. This was known as the 'Race for the Sea' and it ended in stalemate with the only potential gap in the battle-lines being the wastes of the Flanders plain, an unprepossessing region peppered with names which would soon become drearily familiar to the soldiers who fought over it: Ypres, Passchendale, Messines, Langemarck, Vimy, Arras. The style of the fighting was also changing as the armies faced one another in the fields of Flanders. Trenches were dug, barbed-wire obstacles were thrown up and field fortifications constructed; the

German plan to encircle Paris had finally stalled in the mud of Flanders and the first great set-piece battles were about to be fought.

The town of Ypres was the fulcrum of the German attempt to break through and the first battle was fought there between 20 October and 22 November. For the British it was the first large-scale killing battle of the war. Athough the BEF stemmed the German attack it paid a heavy price: 8,631 officers and men had been killed, 37,264 were wounded and 40,342 were missing. Amongst the casualties was Captain Ortho Brooke, 2nd Gordons, who was awarded the VC for leading a counter-charge which saved many lives. Corporal George Matheson, 1st Camerons, now with 1st Brigade, spoke for many of those who took part in the action when he said that while his regiment had made a name for itself in the course of the fighting, what they had experienced was 'pure murder, not war'.[28] During the fighting the 2nd Royal Scots Fusiliers held their position south of the Menin Road and paid the price for their courage, the regimental historian noting tersely that their losses 'need not be discussed for the battalion had simply disappeared'. Three months later they received their thanks in a message from their brigade commander that could have been replicated in many other regiments which had fought at Mons, Le Cateau, the Marne, the Aisne and Ypres:

> The Germans came pouring through, and it soon became obvious that our position was untenable, and we were asked to take up a position further back. I tried to telephone [Lieutenant-] Colonel [A. G.] Baird Smith, but the wires had been cut by shrapnel. I sent two orderlies with a message to withdraw, but the message was never received. Both orderlies must have been killed or wounded.
>
> Colonel Baird Smith, gallant soldier that he was, decided – and rightly – to hold his ground and the Royal Scots Fusiliers fought and fought until the Germans absolutely swarmed into the trenches.
>
> I think it was absolutely splendid. Mind you, it was not a case of 'Hands up' or any nonsense of that sort; it was a fight to the finish. What more do you want? Why, even a German general came to Colonel Baird Smith afterwards and congratulated him and said he did not understand how his men had held out so long.[29]

By then other overseas Regular Army battalions had arrived in France and had taken their places with the BEF in the front line. Soon they would be joined by the soldiers of the Territorial Force and the New Armies. Soon, too, their lines would form part of the pattern of trenches which ran from the Channel coast to the frontier with Switzerland as all hope of attacking vulnerable flanks disappeared. When 1914 drew to an end the Western Front, as it would be known, was quiet as the three armies took stock of the situation, regrouped and restocked their depleted supplies of men, stores and ammunition. At home in Scotland, as in the rest of Britain, families were coming to terms with the fact that many of the men who marched away so blithely in the late summer would not be coming home in the near future.

One last rite remained. In common with many other frontline troops, Scottish regiments took part in the 'Christmas Truce', a brief period over Christmas when hostilities ceased in many sectors of the Western Front as soldiers from both sides put down their arms and fraternised with the enemy in no-man's-land, the area between their trenches. Souvenirs, cap badges and luxuries such as cigars and whisky were exchanged as men celebrated their Saviour's birth after trying their best to kill each other. The War Diary of the 1st Scots Guards recorded that one of their men had met a German on patrol who 'was given a glass of whisky and some cigars, and a message was sent back saying that if we didn't fire at them they would not fire at us'.[30] Impromptu games of football were played, one of which took place in the Frelinghien–Houpline sector and involved a battalion of Seaforth Highlanders playing against the 113th Royal Saxon Regiment. The Germans won 3–2 but everyone involved, including the German Lieutenant Johannes Niemann who recorded the incident, agreed it was an opportunity to savour an unexpected few hours of peace:

The Scots marked their goal mouth with their strange caps and we did the same with ours. It was far from easy to play on the frozen ground, but we continued, keeping rigorously to the rules, despite the fact that it lasted an hour and that we had no referee. A great many of the passes went wide, but all the amateur footballers, although they must have been very tired, played with huge enthusiasm. Us Germans really roared when a gust of wind revealed that the Scots wore no drawers under their kilts – and hooted and whistled every time they caught an impudent glimpse of one posterior belonging to one of 'yesterday's enemies'.[31]

It could not last. Although the truce lasted for up to a week in some sectors and was welcomed by the troops – Private Bill Hanlan, 1/8th Royal Scots met two German soldiers who had worked in a footwear shop in Edinburgh – the British high command was determined that it should be the only instance of that kind of behaviour. From his headquarters at St Omer French issued strict orders to prevent a recurrence of fraternisation and warned that local commanders would be punished if there was any slackening of offensive spirit. As the year ended the BEF, Britain's small professional army, counted the cost of five months of fighting and estimated that its losses amounted to 89,969 casualties, killed, wounded or missing. This was almost half its original number of professional Regular soldiers and time-expired volunteers; of the 84 battalions which had taken part in the fighting to date only nine had more than 300 fit men on their strength.[32] Now it would be the turn of Kitchener's New Armies.

3   First Blood: Neuve Chapelle, Aubers Ridge and Loos 1915

The raising of the New Armies is one of the great British stories of improvisation in the face of adversity, allied to a reliance on the innate patriotism of thousands of young men. It was also a huge risk. Never before in the history of warfare had a country decided to create new armies while engaged in combat, and when the German high command heard of the decision they figured that the divisions would never be a professional force and would only be used as cannon fodder in mass attacks. Even Kitchener, the creator of the New Armies, was worried about the experiment and later in the war admitted to members of parliament that he had embarked on unknown territory: 'Armies, it had always been argued, could be expanded within limits, but could not be created in time of war. I felt, myself, that, though there might be some justice in this view, I had to take the risk and embark on what may be regarded as a gigantic experiment.'[1] Not only did the army have to find sufficient volunteers, those men had to be trained, equipped, housed, fed and hardened for the shock of battle. At the same time, the forces already in contact with the enemy on the Western Front had to be serviced and reinforced, all of which placed an immense strain on the country's economic and industrial infrastructure.

It also stretched the army's capacity to the limit, and to meet the need for instructors hundreds of retired soldiers were called up to instil the basic elements of drill and discipline in the rapidly expanding new regiments. They were referred to as 'dug-outs'. When the 15th (Scottish) Division first mustered, there were no more than five Regular Army officers in each of its brigades and most of the senior training staff were retired Regular, Militia or Territorial officers. One battalion, 7th Royal Scots Fusiliers, was under the command of a recently promoted quartermaster-sergeant.

Needless to say, given the difficulties of raising divisions from scratch, serving commanders were critical of the idea, not least because it was believed that the effort would keep back reinforcements and supplies for the regiments already engaged in the fighting. The foremost critic was French's deputy chief of staff, Brigadier-General Henry Wilson, a committed Francophile and the officer responsible for developing military co-operation with France. In his diary he said that Kitchener was either mad or stupid and that the creation of the New Armies would bring nothing but disaster:

> K's 'shadow armies' for shadow campaigns, at unknown and distant dates, prevent a lot of good officers, NCOs and men from coming out [to France]. It is a scandalous thing. Under no circumstances can these mobs now being raised, without officers and NCOs, without guns, rifles or uniforms, without rifle-ranges or training grounds, without supply or transport services, without *moral* [sic] or tradition, knowledge or experience, under no circumstances could these mobs take the field for 2 years. Then what is the use of them? What we want, and *what we must have* is for our little force out here to be kept to full strength with the best of everything. Nothing else is any good.[2] [italics original]

A close ally of Sir John French, Wilson was no friend of Kitchener but his disdainful attitude would have surprised many of the men who made up those first formations of the New Armies. This was a true citizens' army, with the men coming from every walk of life and representing every social class. Because the New Army battalions carried the names of famous regiments and men were allowed to make a choice when they volunteered, esprit de corps was quickly formed, and because the divisions trained as independent formations their component parts quickly learned to operate as a single entity. For all that equipment and uniforms were slow in arriving and the physical conditions were frequently uncomfortable – the good autumn weather was followed by cold and rain – the volunteers proved to be remarkably resilient. Having enlisted in the army at Maryhill Barracks on 10 September, John Jackson, a native of Cumberland but working at the time with the Caledonian Railway Company in Glasgow, plumped for the Queen's Own Cameron Highlanders and was promptly dispatched by train for Inverness where his draft was given 'a miserable breakfast of bread and cheese and some half-cold tea'. It was to be a short stay: with 100 others Jackson was sent south to Aldershot to join Lochiel's 5th Battalion, which was in training before embarking for France. Following a journey which lasted twenty-one hours there was further chaos when only a handful of the draft were selected for service in the 5th Battalion. The remainder were sent to Maida Barracks and told that they would form the basis of a new 6th Battalion; meanwhile they would just have to make do with the Spartan conditions:

> This was the beginning of the roughest period of my experience as a soldier at home. We were each given a boiled potato (skin included) and a piece of meat for our dinner. We did not have plates, knives or forks, nor yet tables to sit at. No, our tables were the floor-boards. Perhaps allowances should be made at this time, for the unpreparedness of the authorities, with regard to the abnormal numbers of recruits, but with all things considered it was sickening to men who had previously known decent home-life. We became more like animals than humans, and only by scrambling and fighting like dogs were we able to get food to eat.[3]

A few days later the skeleton 6th Battalion made its way to Rushmoor Camp on the outskirts of Aldershot where they were joined by a number of other Scottish New Army battalions and told that they would form the 15th (Scottish) Division, the first of the divisions in the Second New Army. In September 1914 its infantry component was made up of three brigades, each brigade numbering four battalions. In common with all infantry divisions the component battalions changed at regular intervals throughout the war, but initially they were as follows:

44th Brigade
   9th Black Watch
   8th Seaforth Highlanders
   9th Gordon Highlanders
   10th Gordon Highlanders

45th Brigade
  13th Royal Scots
  7th Royal Scots Fusiliers
  6th Queen's Own Cameron Highlanders
  11th Argyll and Sutherland Highlanders

46th Brigade
  7th King's Own Scottish Borderers
  8th King's Own Scottish Borderers
  10th Cameronians
  12th Highland Light Infantry

With the end of the year fast approaching the weather worsened, making life in camp wet and uncomfortable, but it was not until the middle of November that the Scots were moved into new hutted accommodation at Bramshott Camp. They were also issued with their first uniforms, most of which were ancient scarlet jackets with white facings from a bygone age. According to one officer in the 15th Division this made them look more like participants in a comic opera than soldiers of the king and steps were quickly taken to give the men a more soldierly appearance: 'A few of us made the best of a bad job by purchasing glengarries and badges to show that we belonged to a Highland regiment and not to a Red Alsatian Band.'[4] Kilts and khaki tunics were only issued when they moved to Basingstoke early in 1915. Jackson's memoirs make it clear that, while conditions were harsh, the men put up with them and retained their keenness largely because they were given sound training and reasonable amounts of food. In addition to learning the basics of drill and musketry they were taught battlefield tactics and the importance of building sound trenches was impressed on them. Route-marching was a regular part of the training and there were few complaints because the men realised that they were being 'hardened up' for battle. Bonding also played a part: another soldier in the battalion, quoted by Jackson, remembered eating and drinking with men who had become close friends and then sleeping 'under the open air of heaven'. Other pleasures came from the novelty of living and training in the southern counties; few of the men had ever been in England and they were impressed both by the rolling hills and hidden villages and by the kindness of the local population. Even when regiments were billeted on towns such as Basingstoke there was plenty of goodwill and the Scots reciprocated with pipe and drum displays. As Jackson noted, 'no doubt a Highland regiment was an unusual sight in this inland town'. Slowly but surely, the division was being licked into shape to play its part on the Western Front:

> Our training, if hard, was very interesting, and allowed us much freedom of movement; moreover it kept us very healthy, and from the open-air life we were in a hard and splendid condition. We were fast becoming finished soldiers, and knew our time in this country would be short, but everyone was anxious to be out among the real fighting. Perhaps we did not fully understand what it meant, but we were full of enthusiasm and confidence in our ability as a regiment to make a good name once we had a chance.[5]

At no point in his narrative does Jackson complain. On the contrary, his account is enlivened by the sheer pleasure he took in his surroundings, from features such as the great natural depression of the Devil's Punch Bowl to Lord Curzon's elegant estate at Hackwood Park, which had been given over to the army for field sports. For Scots used to a harsher landscape, or whose only experience had been the confines of the city, the softer southern countryside with its pubs and village greens came as a welcome and exotic change. Even watching games of cricket proved a novelty as the spring gave way to early summer.

The enthusiasm displayed by the New Army battalions during training was welcomed by Kitchener, who made a point of inspecting each new division before it left for active service. As Jackson conceded, the men might have been unaware of what lay ahead but at least they had received a solid grounding. The rest would have to be learned on the battlefield. For the Territorial Force formations which had volunteered for service abroad the transition was not so well ordered. Several Scottish battalions had already crossed over to France before the end of 1914 and it took time for the two Scottish Territorial divisions, 51st (Highland) and 52nd (Lowland) to come to a state of battle readiness. The 51st Division had its training area in

Bedford, where thousands of Scottish soldiers were billeted on the local population, an experience that was a novelty for both sides. Like those of the New Army, most of the Scottish soldiers had never been in England and most of the people of Bedford had never met Scots. For both it was to be a steep learning curve. At the outset there was bound to be some confusion but, as Private Alexander Rule of U Company, 1/4th Gordon Highlanders recalled, the Scots were happy enough to play up to the image. No sooner had they arrived than they got out their bagpipes and danced reels outside the station, to the astonishment of the local population:

> We revelled in our barbarian role and solemnly assured our hosts that the kilt was our normal civilian garb; we even had the effrontery to tell them that our wild hoochs represented the semi-articulate call of primitive ancestors, and were still used to communicating from one rocky Hielan' crag to another. 'But don't you wear longer kilts in winter?' The question came from a woman spectator and she was promptly enlightened on the point. Our landladies were equally ingenuous; they gravely showed us how to flush a lavatory and how to turn a gas jet out – obviously fearing that we might blow it out. But we somehow managed to keep a straight face all through.[6]

Rule and the other members of his company were all students or graduates and they recorded their impressions of life in Bedford for the Aberdeen University magazine *Alma Mater*. From its pages it is possible to understand what life was like in a Territorial battalion on the eve of war. Just as had happened with the New Army volunteers, the Territorial soldiers were prepared to put up with the discomforts of training as most of them had some military experience. Like them, too, they had to use antiquated weapons and most of their technical stores were in short supply. Being part-time soldiers they had up-to-date uniforms and the Highland battalions wore the kilt, but there were differences that marked out the Territorial soldiers from their New Army brethren. Although they had learned the basics of drill and discipline in the carefree years before the war it took time for them to knuckle down to the more serious aspects of soldiering. As Kitchener and other critics had feared, attitudes were inclined to be unsoldierly and field discipline was often lax. The following conversation was not an untypical occurrence in the battalion's orderly room:

'Well, Private M'Turk, here you are again. You are charged with being drunk and absent without leave. Were you drunk?'
  'No sir.'
  'But the Sergeant says you were drunk.'
  'Ach! He disnae ken, sir, what drunk is.'

Elsewhere, the novelist John Buchan remembered hearing about another battalion which brought an exercise to a standstill when the men fell out and started picking wild blackberries.[7]

There was also a tendency to maintain civilian standards of behaviour and this was particularly true in battalions with large numbers of educated men or dedicated professional companies. J. D. Pratt, the colour-sergeant of U Company 1/4th Gordons, was a lecturer in chemistry with two first-class honours degrees and he found it difficult to call Captain Lachlan Mackinnon, his company commander and social equal, anything but 'Lachie'. The men under their command were also unusual in that they were well educated and while they were willing to obey orders they also bridled at anything which seemed unfair or illogical. One of their number, a remarkable man called John Keith Forbes, was studying for the ministry and always carried with him a copy of the *Book of Job*, which he read in the Hebrew original. He also found the time to translate it into German. At one stage in their training the men complained about the lack of promotion or opportunity to see action and half the company demanded the right to be transferred as casualty replacements to other Scottish battalions already serving in France. Mackinnon attempted to reason with his men by appealing to the need to maintain group solidarity, but as one of their number, James Anderson, wrote in a letter to his father, these were men who were used to debating issues:

It was too late to take the men into his confidence now, this they plainly told him and this they told him plainly – he could say nothing. They were too exasperated with his tyranny and not a man withdrew. He then asked the reasons, and we told him that he treated us like dogs and not rational beings. He was called anything

but a gentleman, but he made no reply. The Colour–Sergeant
[Pratt] was then detailed to see what influence he had, and if the
Captain got his character, the Col. Sgt. got it worse.[8]

Eventually the incident was resolved by the intervention of the
commanding officer, Lieutenant–Colonel Tommy Ogilvie, who told
the men of U Company that as they would soon be crossing over to
France there was no need to break up the battalion. The student
soldiers felt that they had won a moral victory but it could have turned
out very differently: in some regiments insubordination of that kind
would have been penalised with a field punishment and the men
could have found themselves being tied to a wagon wheel for their
pains.

The Highland Division did not complete its deployment to France
until the end of April but by then some of its component battalions were
already serving as reinforcements in the front line. The 1/4th Gordons
crossed over on 19 February in a converted cattle boat, the *Archimedes*,
and landed at Le Havre, which the men of the North-East thought
was 'like any seaport'. From there they were taken by train to Bailleul,
about ten miles from Ypres, where they became part of 8th Brigade,
3rd Division. The Jocks were not impressed. The train travelled at less
than 15 miles an hour – 'worse than the Buchan train' noted John
Knowles in his diary – and they were surprised when 'every time we
came to a wayside estaminet the engine driver descended for a glass of vin
blanc and a chat'.[9] In the spring of 1915 the 51st (Highland) Division
consisted of the following three brigades:

152nd Brigade (1st Highland)
    1/5th Battalion Seaforth Highlanders
    1/6th Battalion Seaforth Highlanders
    1/6th Battalion Argyll and Sutherland Highlanders
    1/8th Argyll and Sutherland Highlanders

153rd Brigade (2nd Highland)
    1/6th Battalion Black Watch
    1/7th Battalion Black Watch
    1/5th Battalion Gordon Highlanders
    1/7th Battalion Gordon Highlanders

154th Brigade (3rd Highland)
    1/4th Battalion King's Own Royal Regiment
    1/8th Battalion King's (Liverpool)
    2/5th Battalion, Lancashire Fusiliers
    1/4th Battalion, Loyal North Lancashire

The latter brigade was formed initially of Lancashire Territorial Force battalions of the 55th (West Lancashire) Division and these were replaced in January 1916 by four Scottish battalions: 1/4th Battalion Black Watch, 1/5th Battalion Black Watch, 1/4th Battalion Seaforth Highlanders and 1/4th Battalion Gordon Highlanders with its student soldiers. Later, it was recognised that it had been a mistake to send the division's battalions across to France in a piecemeal fashion and that as a result the Highlanders lacked the cohesion of a New Army division. According to Haig, the 51st arrived in France 'practically untrained and very green in all field duties'; it would take some time for the men to become battle-hardened but by the war's end the division was considered to be one of the best in the British army.

The 9th (Scottish) Division under the command of Major-General H. J. S. Landon followed shortly after the Territorials and one of the officers serving in the 10th Argyll and Sutherland Highlanders celebrated the move in a poem which summed up his men's feelings as they set off for France and war:

> And now today has come along,
> With rifle, haversack and pack,
> We're off a Hundred Thousand strong,
> And – some of us will not come back.
> But all we ask, if that befall,
> Is this. Within our hearts be writ,
> This single-lined memorial:
> He did his duty and his bit.[10]

The poet's name was John Hay Beith and he wrote for *Blackwood's Magazine* under the pseudonym of 'Junior Sub' in order to preserve his identity as a serving officer. A popular light novelist who had been educated at Fettes College in Edinburgh, Beith was also better known as 'Ian Hay' and had been a Territorial Force officer before the war. At the beginning of the war he was in uniform serving with one of the New Army battalions and by November the first of a series of his sketches appeared in *Blackwood's* with an account of the tribulations of learning close-order drill. Throughout the autumn and winter 'Junior Subs'' musings took the reader through the training of the fictional battalion referred to as the 'Bruce and Wallace Highlanders' until it was ready to cross over to France to go into action. Brilliantly conceived, and narrated in the first person and present tense, it was akin to a homely correspondence and the sketches became an immediate bestseller when they were published in December 1915 under the title *The First Hundred Thousand*.

Hay's book is an intensely Scottish account, seen from the perspective of a man who, though born in England, was deeply proud of his heritage; he tells his readers early on 'we are Scotsmen, with all the Scotsman's curious reserve and contempt for social airs and graces'.[11] Beyond that, the novel also provided a keen insight into the military mind, so much so that many brigade and divisional commanders recommended it as reading matter for their newly joined officers. For readers at home it was an accurate portrayal of the enthusiasm and optimism of those early days before the New Armies went into action at Loos. The reviewer in the *Spectator* praised Hay's ability to capture the mood of the New Armies while the *Saturday Review* claimed that finally the British soldier had found a voice, making their experience appear 'irrepressibly brave, comical, devoted, prosaic, glorious or dull'.[12]

In his introduction to the war history of Hay's battalion H. G. Sotheby reminded his readers that the first draft had already been written in *The First Hundred Thousand*, and a glimpse at the diaries and letters of contemporaries confirms the authenticity of Hay's descriptive powers. Jack Russell from Cambuslang volunteered on 2 September 1914 and chose the Gordon Highlanders, serving in the regiment's 10th Battalion. His diary contains a portrayal which any reader of *The First Hundred Thousand* would recognise and a range of characters who could have come out of the Bruce and Wallace Highlanders: 'We are a funny lot – not that I use the word in the literal sense. The only time we are really funny is on pay nights, when there are a few buckets running. Then we hear humour in all its phases, pure and sullied, bright and heavy. I think I would say we are a curious lot, for reasons which will be obvious to you later on.'[13]

Just as Hay had a standard drunk whose heart was in the right place in the shape of his fictional Private Robb, the 10th Gordons contained a real–life counterpart in Private Johnston from Partick whom Russell describes as 'the brave, brave man on pay nights, but on other nights, unless he comes across a sailor [softy], the veriest recruit could cow him'. Russell's company also has an Irishman to match Hay's Private McOstrich – 'Irish' Murphy 'who keeps us all awake with singing a song about Sir Edward Carson and his cat'. The tough Regular Army Sergeant Jamieson could have appeared as a fictional character in *The First Hundred Thousand* – 'he took us in hand away back in September, a raw lot of civilians, and now he is very proud of us' – as could the enthusiastic subaltern Lieutenant Robinson or 'Cock Robin' who was 'not a bad sort'.[14] From the point of view of accuracy, as revealed by Russell's diaries, Hay was spot-on in describing the members of a New Army infantry battalion and capturing the idea that they represented the nation in arms. Later, *The First Hundred Thousand* would be dismissed as propaganda in that it put the experience of the New Armies in the best possible light, but in 1915 it was widely praised for its insights into a world which was alien to most of the civilian readers.

It would take the great killing battles of 1915 and the first heavy losses inflicted on the New Armies to change any idea that it was a romantic adventure. At that stage in the war the 9th (Scottish) Division contained the following infantry battalions:

26th Brigade
    8th Black Watch
    7th Seaforth Highlanders
    8th Gordon Highlanders
    5th Queen's Own Cameron Highlanders

27th Brigade
    11th Royal Scots
    12th Royal Scots
    6th Royal Scots Fusiliers
    10th Argyll and Sutherland Highlanders

28th Brigade
  6th King's Own Scottish Borderers
  9th Cameronians
  10th Highland Light Infantry
  11th Highland Light Infantry

The strategic situation at the start of the second year of the war was dominated by the stalemate on the Western Front where, as the war historian of The Royal Scots points out, the soldiers were having to come to terms with the reality of trench warfare:

> The trenches were only taking shape, and once a man was dumped in them, there he had to remain until he was relieved. With practically no communication trenches in existence, the men were like prisoners, for normally there could be no daylight journeying between the support and front trenches, and a man had little more to do than sit in mud and water gazing at the sloppy breastworks in front of him. With movement so greatly restricted it is not surprising that men sometimes fell into moods of profound despondency; they had no water except for drinking, they were limited to a diet of bully beef and bread or biscuits, and their chief companions were their own thoughts. Only at night, under showers of bullets and shells, was exercise with any freedom possible. On the conclusion of a spell of trench duty a man resembled a scarecrow, every furrow of his face filled with mud and a stubbly beard on his chin.[15]

Later in the year, conditions would improve and the trench system on both sides of the line became relatively sophisticated and reasonably habitable. They might have been basic, occasionally insanitary and frequently verminous but they offered safety to their inhabitants with a complicated system of underground shelters, and support and communication trenches protected by breastworks and barbed-wire. Between them and the German line lay no-man's-land, a space of open ground which could be as wide as 300 yards or as narrow as 25 yards. From the air it looked orderly and secure but the creation of the trench system also dominated the tactics used by both sides and would scarcely change until the return to more open warfare in the last months of the war.

In 1915 the dilemma facing British and French planners was how to break the German trench line by attacking key points which would force the enemy to fall back on their lines of communication and in so doing return some fluidity to the fighting. Lines of advance had to be chosen and in January the Allies agreed to mount offensives against both sides of the German salient which ran from Flanders to Verdun. These would be made at Aubers Ridge and Vimy Ridge to the north and in Champagne to the south, the intention being to squeeze the Germans and perhaps even converge to complete the encirclement of the salient. In this spring offensive the British and the French would attack in Flanders and Artois, the French alone in the Champagne. For the British this would involve them in battles at Neuve Chapelle, Aubers Ridge and Festubert and later in the year at Loos. All failed to achieve the Allies' objectives and all produced large numbers of casualties. As a result the reality of trench warfare on the Western Front was brought home to the people of Scotland, especially at Loos in September where two of the six British assault divisions were the 9th and 15th (Scottish) Divisions of the New Army.

The first battle, Neuve Chapelle, was initiated by French to win back a German salient captured in October 1914. This position gave the Germans the freedom to fire on British positions from both flanks and the danger had to be eliminated, but French also hoped to exploit any success by threatening the German lines of communication between La Bassée and Lille. The British field marshal was also anxious to demonstrate to his doubting French allies that his forces had retained their offensive capability and had a significant role to play in the war. By then the British military presence in France and Flanders had expanded and the attack would be made by formations of the British First Army under Haig's direction: IV Corps (7th Division, 8th Division and the Lahore Division and Meerut Division of the Indian Corps). Neuve Chapelle provided other 'firsts'. It would be the first battle of the trench system, it would be the first to involve Indian troops – the Garwhal and Bareilly brigades of 7th (Meerut) Division attacked on the right – and it would be the first to use new artillery tactics with the British guns firing in support of the infantry. The plan was to attack on a narrow front of only 2,000 yards using four infantry brigades in the initial assault phase. Amongst those taking part were 2nd Scottish Rifles, which had been deployed to attack on the right flank of 23rd Brigade with 2nd Middlesex on the left.

When the attack began at 7.30 a.m. on 10 March it achieved complete surprise. The huge British bombardment also encouraged the waiting infantrymen to believe that no one could have survived the shelling and when they began their attack half an hour later hopes were high that an early breakthrough could be achieved. Subsequent war histories and contemporary documents referred to the British and Indian infantry sweeping through the German lines unopposed and creating a huge breach, opening up the prospect of a quick local victory by advancing a mile into German-held territory. Unfortunately that was not the case in the 23rd Brigade attack. Both the Middlesex and the Scottish Rifles' lead companies came under heavy and sustained German machine-gun fire when they reached the intact German barbed-wire. Following the example of Captain E. B. 'Uncle' Ferrers, commanding B Company, most of the officers in 2nd Scottish Rifles carried their swords into battle, but that chivalric style was no armour against the rattling machine-gun fire and the Scottish riflemen were 'forced to fall back and lie in the fire-swept open'. The monocled Ferrers was wounded sword in hand and within an hour the battalion had lost most of its officers and sergeants, killed or wounded. From hospital he wrote to a fellow officer giving a vivid picture of what it was like to face the brunt of the German machine-gun fire:

I got over the parapet just to the right of where your hedges ended. When I got there the cupboard was bare and someone shot me, as I thought in the right ankle, as I started for the next trench. This was really rather a relief as no one else was up and I was feeling exceedingly lonely. I couldn't walk so I leant up against the parapet and waved my sword and generally marked the distant point. I could see some of the lads all hung up in wire and I fancy some were firing half and quarter right but before I could appreciate the situation I took it again in the right thigh. As it came out very low down right in the middle of the stomach I accepted that as final and being fallen on my back partly on sand-bags and partly in a puddle I concluded to stay as long as I was and take stock of my worldly affairs. I doubted that I'd live very long but as I'd had all I ever wished for I didn't worry much over that.[16]

As the battalion regrouped, a fresh artillery bombardment on the German positions finally silenced the enemy fire but by mid-morning 23rd Brigade was unable to continue the attack and the 2nd Scottish Rifles took up a defensive position to the north of Neuve Chapelle. There was further fighting the following day and on 12 March there was a renewed attack to try to break out of Neuve Chapelle but by then the battle was already slipping out of the hands of the British commanders. Communications between the front lines and rear areas broke down quickly and decisively. There was no radio or telephone link and messages had to be sent by runners, with the result that the assault formations were unable to make contact with headquarters. For the battalion commanders this proved to be fatal, as orders were painfully slow to get to the front lines or did not arrive at all, which led to a complete breakdown in command and control. Initially taken by surprise, the Germans responded with a will, rushing reinforcements into the line, and were soon in a position to counter-attack. However, these assaults failed to make any headway, due to the fact that the British forces had also been able to regroup their defensive lines and when the battle was finally called off that same evening the losses on both sides were high: the British lost 11,652 casualties, killed, wounded or taken prisoner, and the Germans an estimated 8,500. When the 2nd Scottish Rifles were relieved on the night of 14/15 March they consisted of 143 men under the command of a young officer, 2nd Lieutenant W. F. Somervail, and Regimental-Sergeant-Major Chalmers. The battalion had lost 13 officers, 112 other ranks had been killed and 344 were either lost or wounded. Amongst them was its commanding officer Lieutenant-Colonel W. M. Bliss, whose arrival a year earlier had caused consternation because he was 'a 1st battalion man'.[17] Two other Scottish battalions also lost their commanding officers at Neuve Chapelle: Lieutenant-Colonel Henry Uniacke, 2nd Gordons, and Lieutenant-Colonel Colin McLean, 1/6th Gordons.

Although neither side had gained any particular advantage both learned important lessons from the experience. For the British, Neuve Chapelle presaged the later battles of 1915 and gave those who survived a first experience of the kind of warfare which would dominate the fighting on the Western Front for the rest of the war. It would take time, though, for them to learn that the advantage gained by the attacking force had to be consolidated and reinforced before the defenders regrouped and counter-attacked. For the Germans, the ease with which their front line was broken showed the need for heavily defended second defensive lines. As John Baynes summarised the condition of the 2nd Scottish Rifles in the aftermath of Neuve Chapelle, they would never again be the same battalion: 'It lived on in name, and certainly in spirit, but those men who had gone over the top on 10 March were always in a minority in the years after the battle. Sadness at this fact is only lightened by remembering that, in spite of everything, nothing had been able to break the morale of such men. They were probably as near unconquerable as any soldiers in the history of the world.'[18]

With a new commanding officer and adjutant and reinforced by men from the regiment's 3rd and 4th battalions the 2nd Scottish Rifles were in action again two months later in the assault against Aubers Ridge. Once more, the failure to cut the wire caused high British casualties as the infantry made their way over the unpromising terrain towards the German positions, and 458 officers and 11,161 other ranks were killed during three days of fighting. Other Scottish formations involved in the fighting at Neuve Chapelle, Aubers Ridge and the subsequent battle at Festubert were 2nd Scots Guards, 2nd Royal Scots Fusiliers, 1st Highland Light Infantry, 1/9th Highland Light Infantry (Glasgow Highlanders), 1st Black Watch, 2nd Black Watch, 1/4th Black Watch, 1st Seaforth Highlanders, 1/4th Seaforth Highlanders, 1st Cameron Highlanders, 1/4th Cameron Highlanders, 2nd Gordon Highlanders, 1/5th Gordon Highlanders, 1/6th Gordon Highlanders and 1/7th Gordon Highlanders. All lost substantial numbers of men in the fighting, which was frequently confusing and which brought no tangible results.

In some places death or survival depended on luck. As the 1/4th Black Watch waited to go into the attack at Aubers Ridge the men noted the casualties caused by the intense German machine-gun fire against the first wave and fearing the worst shook hands with one another before going over the top. At the last minute the assault was cancelled and the men, all Territorial Force soldiers from Dundee, were spared, if only for the moment. Amongst them was a group of journalists, artists and writers who became known as 'Fighter Writers', which included Linton Andrews, news editor of the *Dundee Advertiser*, and Joseph Lee, editor of the *People's Journal*. Both wrote accounts of their service, Andrews in his autobiography and Lee in his verse, and both had gone to war in February with the cheers of the people of Dundee ringing in their ears: 'It was a well–set–up gritty battalion upon which the citizens of Dundee last night showered thunderous cheers as they marched from Dudhope Castle to the West Station.'[19] Within three months, the City of Dundee battalion had been blooded in action and Lee had seen his first casualties:

> I mind o' a field, a foughten field,
> Where the bluid ran ruth and red
> Now I am dead.
> I mind o' a field, a stricken field,
> And a waeful wound that bled –
> Now I am dead.[20]

Lee was to have more to lament after the next great battle of 1915 which involved for the first time the first of the New Army divisions: Loos, where the Scottish losses were so appalling that scarcely any part of the country was unaffected as the casualty figures rose inexorably. So high were they in Dundee that each year on 25 September, the first day of the Battle of Loos, the light still shines from the city's granite war memorial on the Law to remember the city's war dead, among them the local men who fell while attacking the heavily defended German positions in the vicinity of the town of Loos. The majority were killed while serving in the six battalions of the Black Watch which took part in the battle; one, 9th Black Watch, was an assault battalion and lost 680 casualties, including 20 officers, in the first hours of the fighting.

Loos has been called many things by the soldiers who fought in it and also by historians who have picked over its bones but most are agreed that the best description is that it was both an unnecessary and an unwanted battle. In strategic terms it was meaningless. Although the attacking British divisions gained a salient two miles deep, and in the early stages of the battle some Scottish battalions had the heady sensation of advancing steadily across no-man's-land ('the scene resembled nothing so much as a cross-country race with a full field'),[21] the end result did little to help the French offensive in Artois and

Champagne, the main reason why Kitchener insisted that the battle should take place. At the same time, the Germans had learned the lessons of the Allied attacks earlier in the year and had created second defensive lines on the reverse slopes to compensate for their lack of reserves, and by occupying the higher ground they enjoyed an open field of fire. Both were used to good effect when the Allied offensive opened on 25 September and the high casualty figures tell their own story.

From the outset, the planning for the battle was a story of improvisation and optimism that the weight of the French attack would lead to an early breakthrough, thereby taking some of the strain off the attacking divisions. Under the direction of Marshal Foch the British First Army (Haig) would attack from its lines in the north along a wide front which stretched from a position known as the Hohen-zollern Redoubt to the town of Loos, while the French Tenth Army (d'Urbal) would strike at the German defensive positions on the Vimy Ridge. Further south, in Champagne, the French Second and Fourth Armies (Pétain and de Langle) would strike a convergent blow aimed at destroying German lines of communication at Sedan and Douai. Joffre hoped that the massive assault would lead to a collapse in the German centre and drive the enemy back to the Ardennes, but he was already at loggerheads with his allies.

Even before the battle began Haig was forced to extend his line and was concerned that the First Army's objectives included the obstacle of the huge industrial complex within the coalmining triangle of Loos–Lens–Lievin. As he noted in June after visiting the surrounding countryside and riding the ridge north of Ablain, the country was 'covered with coal pits and houses . . . this all renders the problem of an attack in this area very difficult.'[22] He was also worried about the lack of available artillery and ammunition to neutralise the German positions in advance of the main infantry assault and he questioned 'the suitability of New Army Divisions for this duty on their first landing.'[23] There was also a muddle over the command and use of the reserve divisions which would be ordered forward to exploit any breakthrough: these would remain under the strategic command of French at GHQ but Haig reckoned that the congested nature of the ground precluded any rapid deployment.

The matter was settled by Kitchener, who visited Joffre in the middle of August and promised that British support would be forthcoming, not just to help the French but also to take some pressure off Russia, which was facing sustained German attack along a 300-mile front stretching from Riga in the north to the River Dnieper in the south. Following his meeting with Joffre, Kitchener informed Haig that co-operation with the French was essential and that he had decided that Britain 'must act with all our energy and do our utmost to help the French, even though by doing so we suffered very heavy casualties indeed'.[24] As to the planning, this would be left to Haig, who insisted that in the absence of a reliable artillery bombardment gas should be used in the initial stages of the battle. In an ideal world Haig would have preferred to make the attack using over a thousand artillery pieces and thirty-six divisions but only six were at his disposal for the initial attack, supported by two cavalry corps (III and Indian). Unfortunately, Haig failed to solve the problem of using the reserves (1st, 2nd, 3rd Cavalry Divisions, Guards Division, 21st Division and 24th Division), even when it was raised with Kitchener, with the result that he went into the battle knowing that his reserve divisions were deployed too far in the rear and would be unable to make any immediate impact on the battle. Even a loyal staff officer such as John Charteris was gloomy about the prospects facing the men: 'Whatever the issue of the battle, the casualty list will be huge. That is the sad part of it. And if any of us have made an error in our work, it will mean more lives.'[25]

Despite those misgivings, Haig was not unhopeful about his army's prospects and went to bed on the night before the battle noting in his diary that his men were on the eve of 'the world's greatest battle'. He counted on surprise and placed great hope on the use of chlorine gas, which would be released from cylinders but depended on a favourable wind blowing it towards the German lines. The plan was to unleash the gas at first light, after a crescendoing artillery bombardment, and then to attack with six divisions in line along a broad front. From the north of the line the order of battle for the assault formations was: 2nd Division, 9th (Scottish) Division, 7th Division, 1st Division, 15th (Scottish) Division, and 47th (London) Division. Of these, two were New Army (9th and 15th), one was Territorial Force (47th) and three were nominally Regular Army (1st, 2nd and 7th). The overwhelming representation came from Scottish battalions. In fact, as several historians have noted, Loos deserves to be called a Scottish battlefield: some 30,000 Scots would take part in the attack, and not since Culloden in 1746 had so many Scots been involved in such a serious military undertaking.[26] Of the seventy-two infantry battalions which took part in the first phase of the battle, half of them bore Scottish titles. In addition to the twenty-four battalions which made up the two Scottish New Army divisions a dozen other Scottish formations were serving in the three Regular Army divisions: 1st Black Watch, 1st Camerons and the London Scottish with the 1st Division; 2nd Highland Light Infantry, 1/9th Highland Light Infantry, 1st Cameronians, 1/5th Cameronians and 2nd Argyll and Sutherland Highlanders with the 2nd Division; and 2nd Royal Scots Fusiliers, 1/4th Camerons, 2nd Gordon Highlanders and 1/6th Gordon High-landers with the 7th Division. Two battalions of the Scots Guards served in the Guards Division, which formed part of the reserve.

In view of their fate – Loos was not a success and according to Haig's biographer it became 'a symbol of the shattered Allied hopes of 1915'[27] – it is tempting to write off the battle as a futile waste of the lives of men who were ill-prepared to face the shock of modern warfare. Certainly, in the aftermath of the war that was how Loos came to be viewed, but at the time the soldiers in the two Scottish New Army divisions had a good conceit of themselves and their ability to take on the enemy. As the 6th Camerons waited in the front-line trenches on the eve of battle John Jackson exulted in the idea that the 15th Scottish Division was finally to be tried in battle after the long months of training and preparation. Having been issued with their rations and 250 rounds of ammunition apiece the men set about preparing to put their training into practice: 'Instead of going to rest for a few hours in the usual manner, we gathered in groups talking over our chances in the morning. Then the absolute coolness of everyone was shown by the fact that we commenced singing. All the old favourites were sung one by one, bringing back memories of training days, and old scenes of sunny, southern England. Then friends wished each other "Good Luck", friends who knew that the next day would find many of them in the casualty list.'[28]

Jackson was also intensely proud of the fact that Loos was being described as a 'Camerons' day out' as five battalions of the regiment would be going into the attack. Although the 2nd Scottish Rifles would not be taking part in the first phase of the battle, being held in reserve for a subsidiary move to the south undertaken by 8th Division, they too were in good heart. By then Captain James Jack was serving with them as commander of B Company, having spent time in England on sick leave, and he was not disappointed by what he found on his return: 'All ranks here, some 700, of the 90th Light Infantry, the old "Perthshire Grey Breeks" . . . are in fine fettle. What else could they be with such a Commanding Officer? [Lieutenant-Colonel G. T. Carter-Campbell] I do not believe that a better battalion landed in France.'[29] Also taking part in another subsidiary attack to the north, at Hooge, undertaken by 3rd Division, were the student soldiers of 1/4th Gordons, who had provided an intellectual diversion by starting an informal debating club known as 'The Jocks' Society'. As one of its members, Robert Stewart, wrote later in *Alma Mater*, it held its final meeting in the evening of 22 September over a simple meal of potatoes and meat sauce:

> Those of us who were privileged to attend will recall the scene – Sergeant Crichton in the presidential chair maintained order with zest in debates. The speeches of such as Privates Mason and Surtees were received with keen relish, and appreciated as literary delicacies by their hearers, while Peterkin's caustic humour, usually directed against some members of the Society, and Sunny's [McLellan's] subtlety added greatly to the enjoyment of the evening.
>
> Supper over, we gathered round the heart of the open fireplace and the past occupied our thoughts. Marischal College, with all its joys and associations, was discussed, and many a wish expressed that soon, notebook in hand, we would again cross the quadrangle. No mention of the morrow was made.[30]

It was not all sombreness. As the 10th Gordons made their way to the front line they passed other kilted regiments of the 9th (Scottish) Division in the darkness and Jack Russell remembered the glee each encounter provoked amongst his fellow soldiers.

> One would shout to a kent face, 'Whaur do ye come frae?'
> 'Fife.'
> 'Fife! Gies your haun'. Whit part o' Fife?'
> 'Kirkcaldy.'
> 'Kirkcaldy! Gies yer ither haun'. Gies baith hauns!'[31]

These were not sheep going to the slaughter but men who were confident in their abilities and training and who took comfort in the fact that they were going into battle in the company of friends. They would need all that high morale and more to support them in the hours that lay ahead.

As the roar of the artillery grew to a crescendo the first gas was discharged shortly after five o'clock in the morning of 25 September in advance of the first attacks. In some sectors it drifted listlessly towards the German lines on the soft south-westerly wind but to the north it blew back on the lines of the 2nd Division, whose role was to provide flanking cover for the 9th Division's attack on the formidable obstacle of the Hohenzollern Redoubt and Fosse 8 where the German observation posts were sited, causing it to halt its attack along both banks of the La Bassée Canal. As the Scots pushed their way through the smoke and gas with four battalions in line, each split into three waves, the lead units of 26th Brigade suffered heavy casualties: the 1/6th King's Own Scottish Borderers on the right lost twelve officers killed and seven wounded in the opening minutes, and the 10th Highland Light Infantry on the left had its battalion headquarters signalling staff wiped out by a shell blast. But some units achieved their objectives: shortly after eight o'clock 8th Gordons had reached the German second line trenches and the German trenches on the faces of the redoubt had been taken by 7th Seaforths and 5th Camerons with 8th Black Watch in support. Further to the south the attack of the 15th (Scottish) Division was more successful and by eight o'clock Loos was in British hands although the next objective, Hill 70, was fiercely contested by the German defenders. For a watching staff officer the attack on Loos had been carried out in an exemplary fashion by men who only nine months earlier had been civilians unversed in warfare:

Once in No Man's Land they took up their dressing and walked – yes coolly walked – across towards the enemy trenches. There was no running or shouting; here and there a man finding himself out of line would double for a pace or two, look to his right and left, take up his dressing and continue to advance at a steady walk. The effect of those seemingly unconcerned Highlanders advancing upon them must have had a considerable effect on the Germans. I saw one man whose kilt had got caught in our wire as he passed through a gap; he did not attempt to tear it off, but, carefully disentangling it, doubled up to his correct position in the line and went on.[32]

By midday there was optimism in the British ranks. The German line had been broken and there were reports of panic in Lens where the headquarters of the German Sixth Army was making preparations to pull out. In some places there had been little opposition, a result of the gas and sustained bombardment, but already the Germans were rushing their reserves into the line and fighting hard to protect key points such as Hill 70 and the Hohenzollern Redoubt. Everything now depended on the deployment of the reserve divisions and the renewal of accurate artillery fire to support the units which were still engaged with the Germans. At Hill 70 the Scottish battalions were pinned down on the forward slopes by German machine-gun fire and were forced to dig in. At nightfall the 6th Camerons made a determined but suicidal bid to drive the Germans off the hill:

> The situation was serious, and anxiously we looked back for reinforcements but no help could we see. A third time we charged on that awful hillside, but the enemy with his reserves at hand, were too many for us and again we fell back. Truly we were holding to the motto of the regiment 'A Cameron never can yield'. We numbered at this stage less than 100 all told, and for all we knew might be all that was left of 6th Camerons. As the evening drew on we made a fourth and final attempt to win and hold the ridge. This time we meant to do or die. Led by our brave old colonel, bareheaded and with no other weapon than his walking stick, we made for the top of Hill 70 through murderous rifle and machine-gun fire, while shells crashed all around us. Our action was a sort of last desperate chance, but in the face of such heavy odds it could only end in failure. The white-haired old man who led us was shot dead, and shortly afterwards Capt. Milne, cool and unruffled to the last, paid a similar penalty.[33]

John Jackson's commanding officer, the 'white-haired old man', was Lieutenant-Colonel Angus Douglas-Hamilton and Captain Milne was the battalion's adjutant. For his bravery and leadership under fire Douglas-Hamilton was awarded the Victoria Cross (VC) posthumously, one of five to be awarded to Scots after the battle. Before rescuing two wounded men on Hill 70 Private Robert Dunsire, 13th Royal Scots, was warned that his mission was suicidal, and the following day, 27 September, Corporal James Dalgleish Pollock, 5th Camerons showed equally cool courage in holding up a German attack from the Hohenzollern Redoubt. By a coincidence, Pollock's cousin, Corporal James Lennox Dawson, 187th Field Company Royal Engineers, was also given the highest award for gallantry after firing bullets into three leaking gas cylinders and saving many men from being gassed during a British attack. All the VCs were bravely won but the deed which captured the public imagination was the behaviour of Piper Daniel Laidlaw, 7th King's Own Scottish Borderers, on the morning of 25 September. A reservist who had served in the Durham Light Infantry, Laidlaw sensed that his company had been badly shaken by the effects of the gas and started playing the regiment's march, 'Blue Bonnets Over the Border', to lead the men into the attack. With 2nd Lieutenant Martin Young he led the men forward, only to be hit in the left leg; undaunted he continued playing and as the men approached the German lines changed the tune to 'The Standard on the Braes o' Mar', which he later described as 'a grand old tune for charging on'. Despite his wounds, Laidlaw was able to get back to the battalion lines and was later awarded the VC by King George V. He was not the only piper in action that day: the 6th King's Own Scottish Borderers were piped into action by 60-year-old Pipe-Major Robert Mackenzie, who was later fatally wounded.

The gains made on the first day of the battle were the high water mark for the British divisions at Loos. Now was the time to deploy the reserves but it was at this point that Haig's plan began to unravel. Before midday French put the three reserve divisions – Guards, 21st and 24th (the latter two both inexperienced New Army divisions) – under Haig's command but it took time for them to make their way to the front and by the time they assembled between Loos and the Hulluch–Vermelles road on the morning of 26 September they were tired and hungry. Overcrowding in the rear of the British line had added to their difficulties, the roads were heavily congested and in some sectors units were forced to bypass British obstacles, compounding the confusion. At the same time the Germans had been busy reinforcing their own positions and by the time the two reserve New

Army divisions began their attack they were met with sustained machine-gun and artillery fire. Later, German regimental historians recorded the amazement of their gunners as they saw the serried lines of British infantrymen marching relentlessly towards them, offering targets which could not be missed: 'Never had machine-guns had such straightforward work to do, nor done it so effectively . . . The effect was devastating. The enemy could be seen literally falling in their hundreds'.[34] Although the attack battalions continued their advance with great gallantry and determination, the men were doomed and by nightfall those who had not been killed were either in retreat or were pinned down under the inexorable German fire. So great was the slaughter that the German gunners showed compassion and eventually held their fire as the survivors began the long retreat. Total disaster was avoided when the Guards Division stabilised the situation and the Germans, too, were in no position to counter-attack decisively, but by nightfall on 27 September any hope of a successful 'Big Push' had evaporated.

At the end of the month the French attack in Champagne was brought to a standstill and coupled with the failure at Vimy the Allied autumn offensive had achieved little in return for huge losses. Bowing to the demands of the French, Haig kept the battle going in the British sector until 16 October, by which time the British casualties at Loos and the subsidiary attacks amounted to 2,466 officers and 59,247 other ranks, killed, wounded or missing. Assessing the actual number of deaths is difficult. Regimental War Diaries tabulated the casualties after the battle but the number listed as 'killed' invariably increased in the aftermath as men died of their wounds and those listed as 'missing' were found to be dead. For example, the War Diary of the 10th Cameronians listed 239 missing, but of those 192 were later found to be dead and the adjutant admitted the impossibility of verifying the actual numbers.[35] Even so, the casualty figures at Loos were high, and for the Scots they were even higher; as Ian Hay put it, 'There is not a name on the list of those who died for Scotland which is not familiar to us . . . big England's sorrow is national; little Scotland's is personal.'[36] Jackson recorded that of the 950 men of the 6th Camerons who had gone into action, 700 had become casualties; at the roll-call the survivors simply called out 'over the hill' when the name of a missing man was read out.

Some idea of the losses can be seen from the official figures. The commander of 9th (Scottish) Division, Major-General Sir George Thesiger, was killed near the Fosse 8 dump and the following battalions lost their commanding officers: 11th Royal Scots, 1/4th Black Watch, 9th Black Watch, 6th Camerons, 7th Seaforths, 2nd Gordons and 1/6th Gordons. Of the 12 British battalions which lost more than 500 casualties, 8 were Scottish: 7th Camerons (687), 9th Black Watch (680), 6th King's Own Scottish Borderers (650), 10th Highland Light Infantry (648), 7th King's Own Scottish Borderers (631), 12th Highland Light Infantry (553), 8th Black Watch (511) and 8th Seaforths (502). It has been estimated that of the 20,598 names on the memorial to the missing at Loos one in three is Scots.[37] The memorial is situated at Dud Corner on the Loos–Vermelles road, where the old British front line ran and from which the 15th (Scottish) Division attacked. It was unveiled on 4 August 1930, fittingly by a Gordon Highlander, General Sir Nevil Maccready.

Amongst them the names of the missing were 104 men of D (or U) Company, 1/4th Gordons who became casualties while attacking the German positions at Hooge on the Ypres Salient as part of a diversionary attack to the north of the Loos battlefield. As a result the company of student soldiers ceased to exist in its earlier form and was changed inexorably by the arrival of new drafts and the transfer of many of the survivors to serve in other battalions. The battalion suffered 334 casualties 'as far as is known', recorded the adjutant, and he was right to be circumspect. After the battle a Gordons' officer saw six men under the command of a junior non-commissioned officer and asked why they were not marching as a platoon. 'Platoon?' came the reply. 'This is D Company.'[38] Also killed during the battle was the poet Charles Hamilton Sorley, who fell victim to a sniper's bullet while assuming command of his company during an attack on German trenches south of the Hohenzollern Redoubt on 12 October. Hastily buried the next day, an undated pencil–written sonnet was found in his kitbag. With its direct approach and controlled syntax it proved to be his finest creation and led John Masefield to claim that Sorley showed the greatest potential of all the poets killed in the war. The lines are certainly a fitting memorial to those killed in action, many witnessed by Sorley while serving with the Suffolks at Loos:

When you see millions of the mouthless dead
Across your dreams in pale battalions go,
Say not soft things as other men have said,
That you'll remember. For you need not so.
Give them not praise. For, deaf, how should they know
It is not curses heaped on each gashed head?
Nor tears. Their blind eyes see not your tears flow.
Nor honour. It is easy to be dead.
Say only this, 'They are dead.' Then add thereto,
'Yet many a better one has died before.'
Then, scanning all the overcrowded mass, should you
Perceive one face that you loved heretofore,
It is a spook. None wears the face you knew.
Great death has made all his for evermore.[39]

Hardly a community in Scotland was left unaffected by the action at Loos and the late September and early October newspapers were thick with the casualty lists and heroic descriptions of the fighting. Press reporting of the war was constrained by the Defence of the Realm Act which created a system of strict censorship of stories from the battle-front. It was not until May 1915 that the *Glasgow Herald* shared reporting facilities on the Western Front with the *Daily Chronicle*, but even then the war correspondents were kept well clear of the actual fighting and had to submit their stories to military censors before they were filed, a routine which meant that all dispatches were sanitised before publication. Officially the system was supposed to prevent confidential information reaching the enemy but the reality was that only good news was published and disasters were camouflaged or ignored.[40] However, that did not stop news from the front being published, albeit with the names of places and military formations omitted: during the initial part of the war local papers continued to publish soldiers' letters from the front and these provided romanticised and frequently fanciful descriptions of the fighting from soldiers. Loos was no exception. Readers of the *Inverness Courier*, for example, might have been spared the exact details of what actually happened, but from a published letter from Lieutenant-Colonel D. Y. Cameron of Lochiel, written while he was on leave at his estate at Achnacarry, they were left in no doubt that the men of their local regiment, the

Camerons, had just experienced an heroic though no doubt bloody and terrifying battle:

> Instances of personal bravery in my battalion are too numerous to recount, but two might be cited as examples. A lance-corporal, finding the [telephone] connection the Brigadier and myself cut, climbed to the top of a slag heap to get into visual communication. Here he went on waving his flags amidst a perfect tornado of shell fire, until finally a shell burst right over him, and all that was found afterwards was a piece of his kilt and his notebook.
>
> Another corporal did yeoman service as a bomb-thrower. The German bombers were coming along a trench, and owing to the presence of snipers it was courting disaster for our men to get out of the trenches. The corporal in question, however, volunteered to go, and taking up a bag of bombs, he got on to the parapet of the enemy trench and continued to throw bombs down on the Germans. While so occupied he was exposed to fire from all directions, but he succeeded in driving back the other bombers until he was himself wounded.[41]

That refusal to be downhearted was typical of the soldiers' response to the fighting at Loos and, as John Keegan has pointed out, the feelings of bloody-mindedness ran deeply amongst the Scots in the two New Army divisions, who 'seem to have shrugged off casualties and taken the setback only as a stimulus to renewed aggression'. His comment is backed up by much of the contemporary evidence. In the wake of the battle an officer in the 4th Camerons wrote to the *Inverness Courier* telling the people of Inverness-shire that the battle had provided his men with an important rite of passage and that they should be proud of what they had achieved: 'The men were in splendid spirits and feel that they have passed from what might be called the drudgery of war to the romance of war, where, instead of the monotonous trench life so long endured, they can now view war in a broader state and see something of that dash and glory which have appealed to the soldier nature from time immemorial.'[42] Lest that be taken as officer-class bluster, similar feelings coursed through the ranks, even in battalions such as the 6th Camerons, which had taken heavy casualties. Having been reinforced with a new draft the survivors were ready to begin all over again, Jackson noting that 'in spite of the horrors we had passed through in the great battle, we began to pick up again our jaunty devil–may–care ways'.[43]

As Charteris and other staff officers had feared, the casualties had been high but it had not been all loss and gloom. Commanders had learned the value of the creeping artillery barrage and sustained machine-gun fire and there had been moments when it seemed as if a breakthrough could have been made, especially in the opening phases when 15th (Scottish) Division and 47th (London) Division swept through the German lines at Loos, an attack which the *Official History* characterised as 'an ample demonstration that the plans of the commander of the First Army were not altogether founded on vain hopes'.[44] Two contemporary anecdotes sum up the fighting spirit that survived intact in the Scottish regiments after Loos. As the battalions regrouped, Major-General H. F. Thullier, the senior officer commanding the Royal Engineers in 1st Division came across a sergeant and eight soldiers from the 7th King's Own Scottish Borderers who were intent on retrieving the bodies of two dead officers from Hill 70, by then once again in German hands. Told by Thullier that their mission was suicidal and would achieve nothing, the men were doubtful and it took a direct order to prevent them going back to the line. Even then, the sergeant needed the reassurance that he was acting under orders: 'Well, sir, if you order me to go back I must go, but I can't face the colonel and say I haven't carried out his orders unless I show him in writing the order you've given me. I must also ask you, sir, if you will excuse me, to give me a note with your name, rank and regiment on it.' Thullier duly obliged. Later in the war he would take over command of the 15th Scottish Division.[45]

The second story might be apocryphal, but only just, because it typifies the Scots' relish for the reductive idiom in any incident involving a confrontation with authority. As a weary and battered Gordon Highlander passed through Vermelles in pouring rain, his head bandaged and his kilt in tatters, he passed a smart military policeman with highly polished boots and the distinctive red cap. '*Some* fight, Jock!' said the MP from the shelter of the old church. 'Aye,' came the rejoinder, after a long hard look at the polished apparition that stood before him. 'And *some* don't!'

4 End of Innocence: The Somme 1916, Arras 1917

After the Battle of Loos Scotland would never again provide half the number of infantrymen for a massed attack on the Western Front, but there were to be two other battles in which Scots played a leading role and suffered a disproportionate number of casualties. The first of these was the Somme in 1916, in which three wholly Scottish divisions took part as well as Scottish battalions serving in other divisions. (During the course of the battle between July and November a total of fifty-one Scottish infantry battalions took part in the fighting on the Somme sector, but they were never in the front line at the same time.) The second was Arras, in 1917, which saw the deployment of forty-four Scottish battalions on the first day plus seven Scottish-named Canadian battalions, making it the largest concentration of Scots ever to have fought together. The novelist John Buchan estimated that the Scots' presence at Arras was seven times greater than the army that fought under Robert the Bruce at Bannockburn in 1314, and it was larger than the total number which had fought at Loos.[1]

The Battle of the Somme, 1916

In the aftermath of Loos there was one more casualty: Sir John French was sacked as a result of his handling of the battle. The main faults were brutally summarised by Haig, who complained that his superior had failed to deploy the reserve divisions when a breakthrough seemed possible in the early hours of the battle and that it had been 'courting disaster' to use two inexperienced New Army divisions 'with staffs and commanders inexperienced in war'. Haig, who enjoyed impeccable social and political connections in London, wrote to Kitchener four days after the battle making a powerful case for the importance of his own part in the battle while subtly foisting any blame on to French:

> You will doubtless recollect how earnestly I pressed you to ensure an adequate reserve being close in the rear of my attacking Divisions and under my orders. My attack was a complete success. The enemy had no troops in the second line which some of my plucky fellows reached and entered without opposition. The two reserve divisions, under the Commander in Chief's orders, were directed to join me as soon as the success of the 1st Army was known at GHQ. They came on as quickly as they could, poor fellows, but only crossed our trench lines at 6 pm. We had captured Loos twelve hours previously and the reserves should have been at hand then. We were in a position to make this turning point of the war and I feel annoyed at the lost opportunity.[2]

Haig was in reality using the facts to his own advantage. Even if the reserve divisions had been available and in position at the time that he required them, their march to the front had left them tired and disorganised and they could not have taken any significant part in the fighting before the early afternoon of 25 September. By then it was too late as reinforcements had strengthened the Germans' second line of defence. If the British reserves had advanced at that moment they would have done so without heavy artillery support, across open ground and against barbed-wire which had not been broken. What would have happened to them became only too evident on the following day, when Haig ordered an attack and the two reserve divisions walked into a maelstrom of German machine-gun and artillery fire and thousands of men died. None the less Haig managed to get across the message that French had not only failed at Loos but was now incapable of directing the British Army's operations in France. He said as much to King George V during a royal visit to the front on 24 October, and in the weeks that followed French's position became untenable. On 8 December French resigned as commander-in-chief and was replaced by Haig. At the same time, French's chief of staff, Sir William Robertson, became Chief of the Imperial General Staff – the senior officer responsible for directing operations on all fronts – and command of the new Fourth Army was

given to Sir Henry Rawlinson, who shared Haig's reservations about
the misuse of the reserves at Loos. These three generals would be the
guiding figures behind the major British campaign of 1916, a large
offensive along the River Somme to the north of the French lines.

No other commander of the First World War has been the subject
of so much praise or vilification as Douglas Haig. Born in Edinburgh
in 1861, the son of a Scottish whisky distiller with long-established
connections in the Borders, Haig was educated at Clifton School,
Brasenose College Oxford and Sandhurst before being commissioned
in a fashionable cavalry regiment, the 7th Hussars, where he proved to
be an energetic and inquiring officer, keen to make his mark. He had
his first experience of warfare when he accompanied Kitchener's re-
conquest of the Sudan in 1897–98 and he came to prominence as a
first-class staff officer during the Boer War. Backed by powerful
patrons such as Kitchener, Haldane and Lord Esher, a prominent
Liberal grandee, his career prospered with postings in India as
inspector-general of cavalry and he was also helped by an advanta-
geous marriage to a maid of honour to Queen Alexandra. Considered
to be one of the coming men in the army, and in the words of one of
his biographers an 'educated soldier', Haig thoroughly deserved his
promotion to lieutenant-general and command of the I corps at
Aldershot on the eve of the outbreak of war. Reserved and inarti-
culate, he was much misunderstood even by those close to him; he
could appear cold and remote, yet that constraint often masked
sentimental feelings which he felt unable to express. Stories are legion
about his long silences and his inability to communicate, but against
that he was a deep-thinking soldier who understood what was
expected of him and who possessed an unshakable determination
to put his thinking into practice. John Masefield came close to
delineating the man when he wrote after a visit to general headquarters in the autumn of 1916, 'I don't think anyone could have been
nicer, & I don't think any race but the Scotch could have produced
just such a one.'[3]

It was a fair comment. While Haig was a member of the Anglo-
Scottish upper class and had only a passing relationship with the land
of his birth, he was deeply influenced by his Scottish background and
heritage. More than anything else, he was a child of the Church of
Scotland and his Presbyterian upbringing instilled in him a powerful

sense of Christian duty allied to a highly developed work ethic and a mystical belief in the relevance of self-sacrifice. As his padre, the Rev. George Duncan, summed up Haig's religious nature: it was driven by a resolute spiritual reliance in an Almighty providence and by 'a calm recognition of the challenges and needs of everyday life'.[4] Haig's military philosophy and approach to the strategic situation on the Western Front were equally clear-cut. Looking at the trench system which separated the rival armies, he argued that far from being permanent or an insuperable obstacle, it was the key to victory. Once the Allies had built up large enough armies backed by overwhelming firepower, they could attack and destroy the German positions with complete confidence. Successful infantry and artillery assaults would then allow cavalry to exploit the breakthrough by sweeping into open country to turn the German system of defence and ultimately defeat the enemy by removing its ability to resist. It was against that background that Haig contemplated the planning for the major offensive battle of 1916.

The tactics produced by Haig were deceptively simple. He aimed to attack the German lines using the maximum force at his disposal, to break the defences and then to move forward to take possession of the area to the rear. To do this the British would attack with Rawlinson's Fourth Army, numbering nineteen divisions, who would, in the words of the tactical notes produced for the battle 'push forward at a steady pace in successive lines, each line adding fresh impetus to the preceding line'.[5] Following an enormous week-long bombardment involving the firing of a million shells along a 25-mile front the Germans would be in no condition to resist and the British infantry would simply brush the opposition aside as they took possession of the German lines. A creeping barrage would keep the surviving Germans cowering in their trenches. Some brigade commanders were extremely confident of the strength and power of the artillery barrage; one of their number, Brigadier-General H. D. Tuson of 23rd Brigade. even issued a special order telling his men that their attack on Pozieres would be a cakewalk: 'This is only the first step in what is hoped will prove to be a decisive and signal victory. Many divisions will pour through the gap opened for them by this Brigade.'[6] Behind the front lines, from Albert to Amiens the British created a huge rear area with new roads, ammunition dumps and encampments in preparation for the push which would win the war.

For all the careful planning which went into the battle, Haig's optimism had little connection with the reality of the situation. The Somme had been a quiet sector for most of the war and the Germans had used the long periods of relative inaction to good effect by creating a formidable defensive alignment in the firm chalk downlands. Some of the trenches were 30 feet deep and had been constructed to withstand the heaviest bombardments. The lie of the land also favoured the Germans. A first line incorporated several fortified villages such as Thiepval and Fricourt and a second defensive line had been constructed behind the ridges of the higher ground, stretching from Pozieres to Combles. Protected by barbed-wire these would provide stern defences, yet Rawlinson likened it to the familiar surroundings of Salisbury Plain and reassured the king's private secretary, Clive Wigram, that the Somme was 'capital country in which to undertake an offensive when we get a sufficiency of artillery for the observation is excellent and we ought to be able to avoid the heavy losses which infantry have suffered on previous occasions'.[7] Alas for those fond hopes the Somme was to be remembered not for the expected breakthrough but as the killing ground of the British Army: no other battlefield of the First World War created more casualties per square yard, and the opening day of the battle, 1 July 1916, was to produce the bloodiest day for the infantry regiments which took part in the initial attack. From the 11 divisions which began the assault, 57,470 men became casualties: 21,392 killed or missing, 35,493 wounded and 585 taken prisoner. It would take another 140 days before the fighting in the sector finally came to an end.

The Somme also became the graveyard of Kitchener's New Armies and in no other formations were the losses more grievously felt than in the 'pals' battalions, the units whose soldiers all came from the same locality or profession. Ten New Army divisions took part in the battle and for the more recently arrived soldiers this would be their first and for many their only experience of combat. Three Scottish divisions were involved at the Somme – 9th and 15th (Scottish) Divisions and the 51st (Highland) Division – but there were, of course, Scottish battalions serving in other divisions. For example, The Royal Scots had three battalions serving in the 34th and 35th Divisions – 15th (Cranston's Battalion), 16th (McCrae's Battalion) and 17th (Rosebery's Bantams) – and all had been raised on the 'pals' principle. As happened in the rest of the country, whole areas were affected when the casualty lists began to appear. Both Cranston's and McCrae's battalions of The Royal Scots were no exception: they took part in the initial assault with 34th Division which attacked the heavily fortified German position at La Boiselle and suffered accordingly. The 15th lost 18 officers and 610 soldiers, killed, wounded or missing, while the casualties in the 16th were 12 officers and 573 soldiers. As the historian of the latter battalion points out, the casualties were the eleventh highest suffered by the attacking battalions and were similar to those suffered by the better known 'Accrington Pals' (11th East Lancashire Regiment), whose losses have come to typify the bloodshed on the opening day of the Somme.[8]

If the battle had gone according to plan, Rawlinson's Fourth Army divisions would have advanced on a broad front from Serre in the north to Maricourt in the south while a subsidiary attack was mounted by the Third Army against the German salient at Gommecourt. Once the breakthrough had been made, reserves would move quickly to push through the gap to take the high ground beyond Guinchy. Ahead would lie the promised land of Bapaume, Arras and Cambrai as the British forces, infantry backed by cavalry, made the long-expected breakthrough. To help them on their way the British gunners laid down the biggest and most sustained barrage of the war, so heavy that its echoes could be heard on the English side of the Channel. Five days of heavy bombardment built up to a final crescendo in the last hour when 224,221 shells were fired and ten huge mines were detonated ahead of the British advance.

At 7.30 a.m. on 1 July whistles blew along the front lines as the first wave of British infantrymen went into the attack. As the noise of the explosions died away men clambered up the scaling ladders and began their advance in the suddenly eerie silence of a summer's morning; afterwards an officer in 34th Division remembered hearing the sound of pipes being tuned as the pipers of the Tyneside Scottish battalions prepared to play their men over the top. Bucked up by the sound and fury of the earlier bombardment most of the men in the first wave were confident that nothing could have survived such a maelstrom, and while naturally nervous and anxious they believed that they were about to participate in one of the glorious moments of the war. Sergeant Francis Halcrow Scott of the 16th Royal Scots proudly told his parents that 'man to man we could beat them every time' and later, David Laidlaw, commanding 16th Highland Light Infantry, remembered that his men were 'singing and whistling as if they were going to a football match instead of one of the most serious encounters in the world's history'. Waiting to go over the top with the 2nd Scottish Rifles, James Jack noted that his men were 'in grand form, quite carefree, itching to cross the parapet to meet the Hun, and sure of victory'. Before they clambered over the parapets they said their last farewells and wished each other luck as they shook hands, while in Jack Russell's battalion his fellow Jocks engaged in the kind of banter which they hoped would keep bad luck at bay:

> 'Ye'll be shair tae write hame an' let the wife ken if I kick the bucket?'
> 'I'll dae that wi' pleasure,' was the well-meant response. 'Whaur dae ye want to be burrit?' asked Tod of Sanny.
> 'Oh, Westburn'll dae for me. I'm no' that particular.'
> 'I'm wantin' cremated,' says Job.
> 'Hoots awa, man!' someone shouts. 'You cremated! Ye widna mak' a licht for a cigaur.'[9]

As we have seen, senior commanders encouraged a feeling of optimism to lift morale, but it did not take long for the attacking soldiers to find that they were engaging well-defended positions and that the wire had not always been cut by the artillery fire. Accuracy was poor, far too many shells failed to explode and shrapnel proved useless in destroying the heavier barbed-wire defences. During the 29th Division's attack on Beaumont Hamel the 1st King's Own Scottish Borderers found themselves in open ground and pinned down by accurate German machine-gun fire. In the fire-storm they sustained 550 casualties and had to withdraw as best they could. To the north of them the 2nd Seaforths suffered similar casualties during the 4th Division's attack, while the 2nd Gordons became trapped in a sunken lane in front of Mametz and lost 450 casualties to heavy artillery fire. In the opening hours of the attack on the Leipzig Salient carried out by 32nd Division, the 16th Highland Light Infantry lost 20 officers and 534 men, most of them members of the Boys' Brigade from the Glasgow area, and in the days that followed the casualty lists in the *Glasgow Herald* were thick with local names. Amongst the casualties was David Laidlaw, who was badly wounded by shrapnel. Soldiers later compared the bullet shower to a heavy hail–storm or to an unstoppable water cannon as their comrades fell and the ranks were inexorably thinned. A sergeant in the London Scottish spoke for many who took part in the first day's attack when he recorded 'They were simply knocking hell out of us all day.'[10]

Inevitably, as happens in any battle, it was not all failure and disaster. During the attack of the 30th Division, on the right of the British line, a brigade containing the 2nd Royal Scots Fusiliers succeeded in taking its objective at Montauban by mid-morning. Soon elements of the division were pushing through the area towards Guillemont and Longueval, prompting thoughts of an early breakthrough on the sector between Fricourt and Maricourt. Further north, at Thiepval, the 36th Ulster Division succeeded in breaking through to the Germans' third line; many of the soldiers in the division were of Scots descent and had joined the Ulster Volunteers, which had been raised before the war to protect the province from home rule. But despite those isolated successes, the first day of the Somme told a sorry story of frightful casualties and bodies broken for no tactical advantage. 'The extended lines started in excellent order, but gradually melted away,' recorded the *Official History*. 'There was no wavering or attempting to come back, the men fell in their ranks, mostly before the first hundred yards of No Man's Land had been crossed.'[11] In the onslaught the wonder is that so many soldiers pressed home their attacks and did not waver in the face of such terrible bloodletting. Noticing the strain on the faces of his men, before going over the top Jack took out his handkerchief and made a great show of dusting his well-polished boots complete with spurs.

Two days later what was left of the assault battalions were relieved and withdrew into the rear areas. Amongst them were the two Royal Scots battalions in 34th Division which had taken their objectives south of La Boisselle, despite taking heavy casualties. The reaction of the survivors in 16th Royal Scots provides another example of the doggedness and courage of the soldiers of the New Army. It had been a dreadful few days but life went on:

The most wonderful thing of all was that no man seemed to realise that he was doing anything heroic or out of common. Hungry and thirsty the men had been but there was no grousing. Amid all the scenes of horror and tragedy their sense of humour never failed them. Once two Germans (caught in no-man's-land) came tearing across to our trench, being shot at by their own people in front of us. They dropped into our trench. When one of them, over six feet in height, overcome with thankfulness at finding himself in safety, with blood streaming down a wounded nose, took a dapper officer of ours round the neck, and with a bloody nose attempted to kiss him, the men nearby roared with laughter at the consternation depicted on the British officer's face.[12]

Despite the huge losses, which were not immediately apparent at general headquarters, Haig decided that the 'correct course' was to press ahead with attacks on an enemy which, he believed, had been 'severely shaken'. In making that estimate he was relying on guess-work but he was not far wrong in backing his hunch. Although the Germans had beaten off the attack on their right, they had to rush reinforcements to the front and as a result were forced to cancel all further attacks against Verdun in the French sector. The next stage of the battle began on 14 July with the intention of straightening the line before mounting a fresh offensive planned for September. The attacks were centred on the German defensive positions between Guinchy and Martinpuich at Delville Wood, High Wood and Bazentin-le-Petit Wood, names that would always be remembered by the men in the attacking divisions. Amongst them was the 51st (Highland) Division which went into the attack on High Wood with 5th Division on its right and 19th Division on its left flank. For one officer in the division the ground over which they fought was a scene of devastation that had no equal: 'A giant of steel seemed to have ridden over the proud German defences. Villages were wiped completely out of existence; woods were laid waste. Saddest sight of all, there was not a blade of grass visible. A tumbled heap of rubble marked the spot where the church of Fricourt once stood. Its very gables were powdered to dust. A few gable ends still stood in Mametz. These were gradually being demolished by enemy fire. Trenches were everywhere blown out of recognition.'[13]

The damage done to the attacking divisions was equally ruinous. Despite the courage shown by the infantrymen in pressing home the assault on High Wood, wave after wave was beaten off. One attack by the 1/4th Seaforths on 25 July came to nothing when 'an intense machine-gun fire was opened on the British trenches at the moment when the attackers were mounting the parapet. The troops suffered such losses from this fire that the attack never materialised.' The 51st (Highland) Division suffered 3,500 casualties following two attacks on the heavily defended German position, a situation which their historian recorded as being 'disappointing and dispiriting to all'.[14] There was better fortune on the right, where the 9th (Scottish) Division took part in the attack on the village of Longueval and Delville Wood. The 9th Cameronians and 11th Royal Scots took their objectives but the 12th Royal Scots unhappily lost their commanding officer and a large number of casualties as the battalion moved up towards the start line. Ferocious German counter-attacks meant that ground won had to be defended, often against superior odds, and for many of the Scottish battalions this phase of the battle was marked by close-quarter fighting and the inevitable casualties. A sergeant in the 1/9th Royal Scots, the 'Dandy Ninth', called the fighting 'absolute slaughter' after his men had run into a barrage of machine-gun fire without any hope of shelter or protection. British casualties amounted to 9,000 for the day's fighting but, crucially, ground had been taken on the Longueval Ridge and in some places British troops had advanced almost three miles into enemy territory. However, it was won at a cost.

As the summer wore on, the attrition rate began to affect morale and the will to fight, and some of the earlier optimism began to evaporate. Contemporary evidence still points to a widely held belief that it was only a matter of time before the Germans were worn down, and that the next year would bring the long expected 'knock-out blow', but the beginnings of disenchantment were also evident. Perhaps because he was an older and more experienced man who felt that he could speak his mind, Scott Macfie of the Liverpool Scottish was moved to reveal to his father that the fighting on the Somme was not only costly but increasingly pointless:

Our performance was no exception to the rule: of my company 177 went up – 20 were killed, 42 wounded, and about 8 missing (i.e. in all probability dead). The want of preparation, the vague orders, the ignorance of the objective and geography, the absurd haste, and in

general the horrid bungling were scandalous. After two years of war
it seems that our higher commanders are still without common
sense. In any well regulated organisation a divisional commander
would be shot for incompetence – here another regiment is ordered
to attempt the same task in the same muddling way.[15]

Although the battle on the Somme ran on into November, the
attacking battalions were not constantly in the front line and soldiers
were given a respite from combat. Units were relieved regularly and
were able to recuperate in rear areas where soldiers could bathe and
have their uniforms washed and repaired. The 9th (Scottish) Division
proved to be particularly adept at looking after the soldiers' comforts,
providing two mobile canteens, nicknamed 'Wee Macgregor' and
'Rob Roy', as well as a mobile cinema. Men who had been wounded
were evacuated; the lucky ones had a 'Blighty one', which sent them
back to Britain for treatment. Wounded men were given leave and,
while this was welcomed, it could also be a dislocating experience.
John Jackson was sent back to hospital at Monifieth near Dundee to
have his wounded leg treated and on his return found he was going to
be posted to the 1st Camerons. This did not appeal to him as he feared
he would not be amongst friends, having spent his previous service in
the regiment's 6th Battalion. As it turned out he was given a 'kindly
welcome' from a battalion which still contained a number of Regular
soldiers, the 'Old Contemptibles' who had crossed over to France in
August 1914. By that stage in the war the distinctions between the
Regular, Territorial and New Army battalions were already being
diluted by the need to find reinforcements for battlefield casualties.
Jack Russell had also been injured during the 10th Gordons' attack at
Loos the previous year but he returned to the front and died of
wounds on the Somme in August when 8/10th Gordons, by then a
composite battalion, attacked east of Guinchy.

Given the Scottish involvement in the Battle of the Somme, it was
fitting that the last moves involved a large number of Scottish
formations including the 51st (Highland) Division, which was finally
able to put behind it the setbacks encountered at High Wood. Not
that the task facing the assaulting forces was any easier: following a
dreadfully late summer the weather deteriorated again in the autumn,
making the ground conditions so bad that, according to one Highland

officer, 'The country had become water-logged owing to excessive downpours of rain. Continual mists and the absence of wind prevented the rain from being absorbed in the atmosphere. The ground thus remained sodden, the roads were reduced to a pulp, and tracks and paths became lost in oozing mud of the consistency of porridge.'[16] Against that background Haig decided to make one last push against Beaucourt and Beaumont Hamel, a first-day objective which had come to be regarded by both sides as being impregnable. The attack was due to begin on 24 October but after many postponements finally commenced on 13 November with the explosion of a mine in front of the German lines and the customary artillery barrage.

Under the command of Major-General George 'Uncle' Harper the 51st (Highland) Division attacked with two brigades and one in reserve, using 'leap-frog' tactics as they advanced towards the German lines of defence. On the right 1/6th Black Watch and 1/7th Gordons quickly reached the German front line and took it without difficulty, and although 1/8th Argylls and 1/5th Seaforths were checked on the left they were able to fight their way through to the second line. Harper's tactics worked in that the division achieved its objectives with only 2,200 casualties, killed, wounded or missing (to put this into perspective, the 29th Division lost 5,115 casualties attacking the same position on 1 July). To the soldiers this was a source of great satisfaction, as the failure to take High Wood had drawn to them the unattractive nickname of 'Harper's Duds', a play on their HD divisional badge. All that changed after the assault on Beaumont Hamel. As Harper watched the walking wounded making their way back to the line two days later he overheard one of his Jocks remarking 'Onyway, they winna ca' us Hairper's Duds noo.'[17] From that point onwards the 51st (Highland) Division was held in high regard by the Germans as one of the crack infantry formations in the British Army.

One last act remained to be played. Although Beaumont Hamel had fallen, the British had failed to take two German defensive systems called Munich Trench and Frankfurt Trench. An attempt to put that right was launched on 18 November when 32nd Division attacked the objectives 'in whirling sleet which afterwards turned to rain, the infantry groping their way forward as best they could through half-frozen mud that was soon to dissolve into chalky slime'.[18] Amongst those attacking were 16th and 17th Highland Light Infantry, the Boys'

Brigade and Chambers of Commerce pals' battalions, which had already been over the same ground on the first day of the battle when the former battalion had almost been wiped out. The division fared little better than it had done five months earlier: the attack fizzled out with 1,387 casualties killed or wounded, most of them from the 16th Highland Light Infantry. Of the 21 officers and 650 other ranks who went into action, 13 officers and 390 other ranks did not make it to the final roll-call three days later when ranks had to be closed up before the battalion was inspected by General Sir Hubert Gough, commander of the Fifth Army. But even when the last attack of the Somme was finally called off it was not the end of the suffering for the Boys' Brigade 'pals' from Glasgow.

During the attack three platoons of D Company had fought their way into the Frankfurt Trench, where they were marooned with a small party from the 11th Border Regiment while the rest of the force withdrew. About a hundred men remained and, finding themselves cut off with no hope of escape, they set about barricading a section of the trench to repel the expected German counter-attack. As the battalion's historian pointed out, it was one of the most bizarre and unexpected situations for any soldier and one which almost defied explanation:

> If the average experienced soldier were to be asked to imagine three platoons of men to be marooned in the second line of the enemy's trenches without food or water, who would yet resist capture or total destruction for eight days in spite of savage assaults upon their position, he would gravely doubt the sanity of the proposition. But this was the actual feat of arms performed. Its only military value could have been the moral effect of such resistance upon the enemy; but the accidental fact that the deed served no purpose in the scheme of battle does not rob it of any of its glamour or greatness. It stands as a tremendous tribute to the character of the Scottish soldier.[19]

It soon became painfully clear that the men of the 16th Highland Light Infantry were in no position to offer protracted resistance – of their number only half were uninjured and they only had four Lewis guns with limited ammunition – but they possessed a stubborn will and fierce pride. They were also well led by their senior non–commissioned officer, Company Sergeant–Major George Lee, who had been a roads foreman with Glasgow Corporation in civilian life, and against the odds they managed to hold out until 25 November, a week after the original attack. Frantic attempts to save them were made by men of the 16th Lancashire Fusiliers, and aircraft of the Royal Flying Corps flew overhead to offer encouragement but the men from Glasgow were on their own. To their credit the Germans sent a party under a white flag with a captured Inniskilling Fusilier to try to encourage the remaining men to surrender, but the offer was spurned even though food had run out and the Scots had been without water for several days. Eventually the Germans lost all patience and mounted a huge attack on the position only to find that the opposition had been reduced to fifteen able-bodied men and around thirty wounded who were 'isolated, [and] exhausted with little ammunition left'. The rest, including Lee, were dead.[20] Understandably, the Germans were not amused and ordered the exhausted Scots to remove the dead and wounded from the trench. With tensions running high the survivors fully expected to be executed, especially when a sudden British barrage killed a German soldier, but they were treated with grim respect by the senior officer present. 'Is this what has held up the brigade for more than a week?' he asked as the unkempt Scots were brought before him. Of the fifteen who survived, two died in captivity and one man was shot 'for the unwarlike offence of accepting a piece of bread from a French inhabitant'.[21]

The last stand of the 16th Highland Light Infantry marked the end of the Battle of the Somme. Winter had now taken a grip on the land and, following the earlier bad weather, offensive operations were no longer possible. Arguments still rage about the winners and losers of a battle that came to symbolise the worst of the fighting and slaughter on the Western Front. The Allies lost 600,000 casualties, two-thirds of them British, while the German losses cannot have been much less. (These are difficult to compute as they did not include wounded who were expected to survive.) In the cold statistical analysis of modern warfare the Allies did better out of the battle than the Germans and most modern military historians are agreed that it was 'a win on points'.[22] Although the expected breakthrough never occurred and the ground gained was a modest return for the expenditure of so many lives and so much materiel, pressure had been taken off the French and valuable lessons had been learned. After the war, senior German commanders complained that the Somme was 'the muddy grave of the German field army' while their opposite numbers in the British Army argued that their inexperienced divisions came of age during the battle, even though most of the lessons were bloodily learned. That was the generally accepted view within the 9th (Scottish) Division, which had performed well throughout the five months of fighting:

> With the opening of the Battle of the Somme there was a noticeable change in the attitude of the men. They now realised the full seriousness and gravity of the business that they had undertaken, and they no longer entered into battle with the exuberant optimism that had filled the men at Loos with the belief that they could sweep away the defences of Germany at one blow. Their confidence was unshaken and their belief in ultimate victory assured, but if the Somme became for the enemy a Gehenna, it was also a supreme trial and test for the soldiers of the British Empire.[23]

In common with all the assault formations, the casualties of the 9th (Scottish) Division were high – 314 officers, 7,203 other ranks, killed wounded or missing – but, as their historian insists, their morale remained high. Even so, the Somme is a dreadful punctuation mark in British military history; few communities were left unaffected by the huge casualty list and the battle has become a byword for senseless slaughter. As viewed by Lieutenant Ewart Alan Mackintosh, 1/5th Seaforths, in his poem 'High Wood', the easy enthusiasm of the summer of 1914 had given way to deeper and darker feelings:

> The wild war pipes were calling,
> Our hearts were blithe and free
> When we went up the valley
> To the death we could not see.
> Clear lay the wood before us
> In the clear summer weather,
> But broken, broken, broken
> Are the sons of the heather.[24]

Amongst the many casualties was Lieutenant-Colonel John Collier Stormonth-Darling, who was killed by a sniper on 1 November while leading 1/9th Highland Light Infantry in the assault at Le Transloy. He had spent his last leave with his family at Lednathie in Glen Prosen where he had caused some mild astonishment by giving vent to his feelings and talking about the beauties of the glen.[25] One of the first of fifty-one Victoria Crosses (VCs) awarded after the battle was won on the first day by Sergeant James Turnbull, 17th Highland Light Infantry: after rallying his men at Authuile he took the German position but was killed while repelling a counter-attack. Long after the operational phase of the battle had ended Captain John Lauder, 1/8th Argylls, was killed near Courcellete on 28 December. He was the son of the prominent entertainer Harry Lauder, who was told the news a few days later while appearing in the revue *Three Cheers* at the Shaftesbury Theatre in London. Ironically, one of the show's best-known songs was 'The Laddies who Fought and Won'. Following his death there were persistent rumours that Lauder was an unpopular officer and had been shot in the back by his own men, although this is not borne out by letters his father received from other officers in the battalion.[26] Whatever their rank, though, and however they died, the soldiers' sacrifice is commemorated by the 51st (Highland) Division memorial, a magnificent cairn topped by a kilted Highland soldier which stands on the Beaumont Hamel battlefield close to the old German lines. Its inscription would have raised a wry smile from those who died there. Translated from Gaelic (*Là a' bhlàir's math na càirdean*) it reads simply, 'Friends are good on the day of battle'.

The Battle of Arras 1917

Rightly fearing the renewal of a bigger Allied offensive on the Somme in the new year, the German high command decided to shorten the line between Arras and the Aisne by constructing new and heavily fortified defences which would be their new 'final' position behind the Somme battlefield. Known to the Germans as the Siegfried Stellung and to the Allies as the Hindenburg Line, this formidable construction shortened the front by some 30 miles and created an obstacle which would not be taken until the end of the war. The withdrawal began on 16 March and as the Germans retired they laid waste to the countryside, leaving a devastated landscape in which the cautiously pursuing Allies had to build new trench systems. To test the reality of the withdrawal and to ascertain the potency of the new German positions, raids were ordered on the enemy trenches and inevitably these caused high casualties. They were also dreaded by the men who took part in them: in one such raid on 21 March the 11th Royal Scots sustained seventy-five casualties. Raids took place at night and usually involved up to three sections, consisting of eight men each who had to cross no-man's-land armed with grenades. According to one soldier, 'the object of the raid was to kill Germans, damage his trenches and obtain his identification'.[27]

By then Joffre had been replaced as commander-in-chief of the French army by General Robert Nivelle, an artillery officer and a veteran of the fighting at Verdun, who proposed a new attack on the shoulders of the Somme salient, with the French attacking in the south at Chemin des Dames while the British and Canadians would mount a supporting offensive at Arras and Vimy Ridge. Prior to the British attack there would be a huge and violent bombardment with 2,879 guns firing 2,687,000 shells over a five-day period. Writing about its effects a company commander in 15th (Scottish) Division thought it heavier and more lethal than the barrage that had preceded the Somme in the previous summer: 'Guns seemed to be firing from behind every house, and, to cap all, German shells fell continually in the city, the noise of their explosions being accentuated by the rebounding echo of the narrow streets. Language on all sides was hot and flowery, and generally the place might have been mistaken for Hades instead of Arras.'[28]

The overall direction of the British and Canadian forces was under the command of General Sir Edmund Allenby, a thrusting cavalryman of uncertain temper who was known as 'The Bull'. While four Canadian divisions attacked the Vimy Ridge (amongst them were Scottish-named regiments: 13th Royal Highlanders of Canada, 15th/48th Highlanders of Canada, 16th Canadian Scottish, 17th Seaforth Highlanders of Canada, 43rd Cameron Highlanders of Canada, 72nd Seaforth Highlanders of Canada and 85th Nova Scotia Highlanders), ten divisions made their assault on a broad front, twelve miles wide, straddling the valley of the River Scarpe to the east of Arras. Also serving in 9th (Scottish) Division were four battalions of

South African infantry, who formed a South African brigade. (The division's 28th Brigade was broken up on 6 May 1916 and was reformed on 11 September 1918.) The Scottish formations which took part in the first and subsequent phases of the battle were:

9th (Scottish) Division
    26th Brigade
      8th Black Watch
      7th Seaforth Highlanders
      5th Queen's Own Cameron Highlanders
      10th Argyll and Sutherland Highlanders
    27th Brigade
      11th Royal Scots
      12th Royal Scots
      6th King's Own Scottish Borderers
      9th Cameronians

15th (Scottish) Division
    44th Brigade
      9th Black Watch
      8th Seaforth Highlanders
      8/10th Gordon Highlanders
      7th Queen's Own Cameron Highlanders
    45th Brigade
      13th Royal Scots
      6/7th Royal Scots Fusiliers
      6th Queen's Own Cameron Highlanders
      11th Argyll and Sutherland Highlanders
    46th Brigade
      7/8th King's Own Scottish Borderers
      10th Cameronians
      10/11th Highland Light Infantry
      12th Highland Light Infantry

51st (Highland) Division
    152nd Brigade
      1/5th Seaforth Highlanders
      1/6th Seaforth Highlanders

1/6th Gordon Highlanders
1/8th Argyll and Sutherland Highlanders
153rd Brigade
1/6th Black Watch
1/7th Black Watch
1/5th Gordon Highlanders
1/7th Gordon Highlanders
154th Brigade
1/9th Royal Scots
1/4th Seaforth Highlanders
1/4th Gordon Highlanders
1/7th Argyll and Sutherland Highlanders

2nd Division
2nd Highland Light Infantry
1st Cameronians

3rd Division
2nd Royal Scots
1st Royal Scots Fusiliers
1st Gordon Highlanders

4th Division
2nd Seaforth Highlanders

5th Division
2nd King's Own Scottish Borderers
6th Argylls

29th Division
1st King's Own Scottish Borderers

30th Division
2nd Royal Scots Fusiliers

34th Division
15th Royal Scots
16th Royal Scots

The battle began in the early morning of 9 April in a biting wind which sent snow flurries scudding across the countryside, but despite the wintry weather the portents were good. For the first time, the assault battalions found that the artillery had done its job by destroying the wire, and new types of gas shells had fallen in the rear areas, killing German transport horses and making the movement of guns impossible. Within a few hours the German line had been penetrated to a depth of two miles and in one of the most astonishing feats of the war the Canadian divisions swept on to take the previously impregnable German positions on the gaunt features of Vimy Ridge. The first day of the assault was a triumph for the British and the Canadians, who suffered reasonably small casualties and succeeded in taking their first objectives and then regrouping to attack the second and third lines of defence. According to the War Diary of the 12th Royal Scots the advance was 'effected just like a drill parade, correct dressing and distances between "waves" being maintained throughout' and, over-all, the 9th (Scottish) Division likened their advance to 'a Salisbury Plan ceremonial manoeuvre'.[29]

The first phase of the battle encouraged hopes that this might be the long-awaited breakthrough and some units were surprised both by the ease of their attack and the lack of German resistance. For example, all five Seaforth battalions achieved their first-day objectives and the 1st Gordons, attacking towards Monchy-le-Preux with 3rd Division, were at the German front or 'Black Line' within twenty minutes of leaving their trenches. At Rolincourt 1/8th Argylls succeeded in capturing second (Blue) and third (Brown) lines, the 7/8th King's Own Scottish Borderers found themselves half a mile beyond their objective, near Monchy, and in other sectors Scottish battalions enjoyed equal levels of success, some moving forward so quickly that they found themselves coming under friendly fire from their own guns. It was at this point that things began to fall apart.

Despite the initial successes, the British advance had been irregular and some units were held up by German defensive positions which had escaped the barrage and were still able to inflict heavy casualties on the attacking forces. A huge explosion triggered by German sabotage of one of their own dumps held up the attack of 1/5th Seaforths, and 1/4th Gordons lost so many men in the opening hour – 24 officers and 570 other ranks – that they ceased operating as a coherent unit. In the assault on the Blue Line near Bois de la Maison, 15th Royal Scots were reduced to four officers with around a hundred men, and according to the regimental historian 'once again raw courage was called for before the enemy could be silenced, and officers and men immediately rose to the challenge'. Attacking with them were the men of McCrae's Battalion (16th Royal Scots) who lost two officers during an attack on a particularly tenacious German machine-gun position.[30] Their day ended, as it did for all the attacking battalions, with ground gained and the possibility of taking more. Allenby was anxious to continue the momentum and ordered forward units 'to press the enemy, leaving any strongpoints to be dealt with by parties in the rear', but already the steam was running out of the assault. As night fell the weather deteriorated, leaving the infantrymen in forward positions exposed, hungry and bitterly cold as they had been forbidden to wear or carry their greatcoats during the attack. Battalion war diaries speak of men lying huddled together for warmth, their condition being made worse by failure to get supplies through to them due to congestion on the roads behind Arras.

Despite those problems Allenby ordered the attack to be resumed the following day with an assault on the final German line, the Green Line, at Monchy. He was optimistic of success but already the opposing German commander in the Arras-Vimy sector, General von Falkenhausen, had roused himself and had started moving his reserves from their pre-battle positions fifteen miles behind his lines. At headquarters Haig ordered Allenby to keep up the momentum, believing that a rupture was imminent, writing in his diary 'As to the battle of Arras, I know quite well that I am being used as a tool in the hands of a Divine Power.' Spurred on by his commander-in-chief, Allenby urged his men to press on with the next phase of the battle and to 'understand that the Third Army is now pursuing a defeated enemy and that risks must be freely taken'.[31] Monchy fell on 12 April but time was fast running out for the ever more exhausted assault battalions. Increased German resistance and reinforcement meant higher casualties for the attackers. The 11th Royal Scots lost 150 casualties and the 12th Royal Scots 250 in the course of an attempt to take the unlovely village of Roeux with its chemical works north of the Scarpe between Fampoux and Plouvain. On 15 April, almost a week after the first attack, Haig succumbed to reason and to the pleas

of three divisional commanders and called a halt to the first phase of
the battle to allow reinforcements to be brought up.

At the same time, the French launched their attack on the German
lines on the Aisne between Reims and Soissons with a huge creeping
bombardment preceding the infantry attack. Nivelle had high hopes
that the twenty attacking infantry divisions would achieve a breakthrough, but he was to be disappointed. Not only was the barrage
mismanaged; as a result of lapses in French security the Germans had
reinforced the area and their machine-gunners were able to mow
down the advancing French forces. Within five days it was clear that
the offensive had failed, with the French army losing 134,000
casualties for the gain of a minuscule amount of territory. Worse,
the high attrition rate led to mutinies in many frontline formations as
battle-weary soldiers refused to continue fighting. Officers spoke of 'a
sort of moral nihilism' as men went on strike and refused orders or
simply sat down with their arms folded. In the aftermath Nivelle was
sacked and replaced by General Henri Philippe Pétain, whose good
sense and firmness finally restored order, although the unrest in some
units continued into the early part of 1918.[32] Under pressure from the
French, Haig ordered Allenby to resume the offensive on 23 April but
by then the Germans had reinforced their defensive positions and
were able to counter-attack. The result was that the roles were
reversed and the British came under a heavy artillery bombardment.

The ferocity of the offensive was an unnerving experience and later
a Highland Division officer remembered hearing a sergeant encouraging his frightened men with the far from optimistic words: 'Great
God A-michty, ye canna a' be killed.'[33] Despite the fear and the
turmoil, in the midst of the fighting there were moments of black
humour. Commanding 1/6[th]Gordons at Arras was the Hon. William
Fraser, a Regular officer with high standards, who asked a battalion
runner from the front line where he had come from, only to receive
the answer, 'Aberdeen'. With the battle raging, the conversation
became yet more surreal:

'No, no, where do you come from now?'
'Yonder,' replied the runner.
'Well,' said the colonel, 'what's happening yonder?'
'Well, a Boche officer comes up to us and says surrender.'

'Well?'

'We told him, to hell with surrender.'

'Where's the officer now?'

'Yonder.'

'What's he doing yonder?'

'Doing?' said the runner. 'Doing? He's deid.'[34]

It was to be one of the few things to smile about at Arras. This time there were to be no easy gains and the British attack soon faltered as the assault battalions came up against stronger German opposition, leaving the historian of the 9th (Scottish) Division to lament, 'Little can be said in defence of this battle, which the Division fought with great reluctance. The preparations and arrangements were hurried to a deplorable degree.'[35] For men who had been in continuous action in the first phase of the battle, this second assault along the Scarpe proved to be a battle too far, and five days later Allenby was forced to scale down the offensive. Some of the fiercest fighting was at Roeux, which had been captured briefly by the 51st (Highland) Division only to be retaken by the Germans. On 28 April, a fresh assault on the village was made by 34th Division and in common with other operations at this stage of the battle it was hurried and improvised. The preceding artillery barrage failed to unsettle the German defenders, who were in the process of rushing reinforcements into the village for an attack of their own. In the confusion forward elements of 16th Royal Scots found themselves cut off, having reached their objective ahead of the other attacking battalions, and as a result sustained heavy losses. Amongst the battalion's 300 casualties was Captain Gavin Pagan, the minister of St George's Church in Edinburgh, who was in command of the cut-off men. The *Official History* referred to Roeux simply as 'a melancholy episode' while the 15th (Scottish) Division called it 'a black day for the British Army', but a Scottish private offered a soldier's perspective of the fighting when he commented later, 'To be in the Comical [chemical] works made a body windy whether it was shellin' or not.'[36]

Arras is not one of the better-known battles of the First World War but it deserves to be remembered for a number of reasons. The initial attacks demonstrated that the British had learned from the Somme by concentrating their artillery to pin down the enemy in his deep trenches and make life easier for the attacking infantry. The barrage was also more accurate and proved to be more effective against wire. On the first day, the advance took the attackers as far as three miles into German territory, with the 4th Division leap-frogging over the 9th (Scottish) Division to make one of the biggest single advances made by infantrymen fighting on the Western Front. For the Canadians, supported by 51st (Highland) Division, the first day was even more spectacular: after taking the Vimy Ridge they enjoyed the heady sensation of looking down on to the Douai plain and watching the Germans in full retreat. Casualties on the first day were a third of those suffered in the comparable period on the Somme and large numbers of German prisoners had been taken. From the point of objectives being reached and casualties kept down, the first day of fighting at Arras deserves to be called a 'triumph'. Thereafter matters did not run so smoothly and the impetus was lost. Bad weather was one reason – the snow and rain did not make life easy for the men on the ground and delayed the transport – but it proved impossible to sustain the attack with exhausted troops. Any opportunity for an early breakthrough was lost when the Germans pushed reinforcements into the line, and their arrival quickly nullified Allenby's earlier tactical advantage.

By the time that the fighting ended at the beginning of May, any hope of defeating the Germans at Arras had disappeared and the losses had multiplied. The British suffered around 159,000 casualties, a daily rate of 4,076 (higher than the Somme's 2,943), and the stuffing had been knocked out of many of the formations which had been involved in a month of hard fighting against a heavily reinforced enemy. Given that so many Scottish battalions were involved in the fighting, roughly a third, a high proportion of the casualties were Scots; one brigade in the 51st (Highland) Division lost 900 casualties in the final and bloodiest phase of the battle, the majority being killed or wounded by shrapnel. Amongst the Scots killed at Arras was Alastair Buchan, the brother of John Buchan, who fell on the first day during the attack of the 6th Royal Scots Fusiliers. One of the letters of sympathy to his family was written by Winston Churchill, who had commanded the battalion for five months in 1916 in the period following his resignation from Asquith's administration. There are two battlefield monuments to the Scots who fell at Arras: the Seaforth Highlanders' Memorial at Fampoux, which also commemorates the award of the Victoria Cross to Lieutenant Donald Mackintosh, and the 9th Scottish Division Memorial at Point du Jour. It was the last time in the war that so many Scottish formations would be on the same battlefield at the same time.

Later in the year, at the Third Battle of Ypres, also known as Passchendaele, all three Scottish divisions were again involved in the fighting to deepen the British-held Ypres Salient. The battle lasted four months and accounted for 250,000 casualties, 70,000 of them killed or drowned in the lagoons of mud which covered the battle-field. Having returned to the battle line after a period of home leave, John Jackson was never to forget the shell holes which littered the battlefield: 'These holes were often ten to twelve feet deep and full up at this time with dirty, slimy water. At the bottom of them in many cases could be seen the bodies of dead men and mules, together with parts of wagons, the whole creating a stench that was rotten and sickening.'[37] The year ended with the Battle of Cambrai when tanks were first used in large numbers to smash through the German lines. This time the expected breakthrough occurred, with tanks penetrating the German lines to a depth of five miles within the first ten hours, but the action was not exploited and 1917 ended in frustration for the Allies on the Western Front. Cambrai also saw the death of the poet Ewart Alan Mackintosh, who was killed in action on 21 November with 1/4th Seaforths when the 51st (Highland) Division advanced over Flesquieres Ridge with the pipes and drums of 1/4th Gordons leading the assault. The final lines of his last-ever poem, 'War, The Liberator', were a fitting epitaph, not just for him but for all of the Scots who had served as Regulars and Volunteers between 1915 and 1917 and knew what it was like to face the shock of battle:

> Now in all the time to come, memory will cover us,
> Trenches that we did not lose, charges that we made,
> Since a voice, when first we heard shells go shrilling over us,
> Said within us, 'This is Death – and I am not afraid!'

Mackintosh had no need to be taking part in the battle. Having been badly wounded on the Somme at High Wood he was employed in Cambridge training officer cadets and could have stayed there. No one would have blamed him, but the easy option was not for him.

Despite the hardships and terrors of life in the front line, which he deplored, he had come to believe that the experience was a privilege and a rite of passage which had been denied others. He was not alone in his optimism. In a letter written to his father on 5 October Lieutenant James Burnett Lawson, 2nd Scottish Rifles, argued that the best was still to come and that the fighting spirit in his battalion was as high as it had ever been: 'No wonder there are wars. No wonder Haig's men have to smash their way up the Passchendaele heights. He is taking the inevitable road to victory. That's why there must be no faltering. Give way to nerves now, and all our suffering will have been in vain. Let us rather steel our hearts for the second half of the great fight which begins next Spring and ends with complete victory in October 1918.'[38]

Lawson was only one month out in his calculations but he did not live to see the 'complete victory' which he forecast with such enthusiasm. A medical student from Glasgow, he had enlisted in The Cameronians in 1915 and was killed in action leading a counter-attack at Meharicourt during the Germans' spring offensive. For his parents the tragedy was compounded when they learned that their son had sent in his application to be allowed to return to his medical studies under a scheme introduced by the government early in 1918.

5 Battles Far Away: Gallipoli, Mesopotamia, Salonika and Palestine

The Western Front was the fulcrum of Britain's war against Germany. It consumed the greatest part of the country's war effort and in four and a half years of fighting the western European battlefields claimed a higher proportion of lives: roughly 750,000 British and Commonwealth soldiers died in the fighting. It has been estimated that for every nine British soldiers who served in France and Flanders five became casualties (killed, wounded or missing), or, as the historian Richard Holmes puts it, '4 million [British] men went to France and nearly three-quarters of a million stayed there for ever'.[1] So fixed in modern memory has the experience become that the Western Front has come to represent all that was wrong and unlovely about the fighting of the First World War. Its trenches and its battlefields gave it historical substance, the mud of Flanders represented the awfulness of its conditions in winter and everywhere firmly etched place-names recalled the great battles of attrition where thousands of soldiers were killed in what has come to be represented as senseless death-dealing attacks. As an arena of combat the Western Front certainly does not lack critics. In the immediate aftermath of the war David Lloyd George, prime minister from 1916, excoriated the 'policy of flinging masses of our troops against concrete machine-gun emplacements, with the result that hundreds of thousands of them were put out of action' and another politician involved in the direction of the war, Winston Churchill, later admitted that while he said nothing at the time he viewed 'with the utmost pain the terrible slaughter of our troops and the delusions that were rife' during the Battle of the Somme.[2] From there it was but a small jump to the literature of disillusionment in the late 1920s which spoke of horror and waste; the

expansion of that argument forty years later insisted that the fighting
on the Western Front was an appalling aberration in which brave
British soldiers were sent to their deaths by criminally incompetent
generals. Non-historical manifestations such as the television series
Blackadder Goes Forth (1989) or Joan Littlewood's play, later filmed, *Oh
What a Lovely War!* (1963) helped to solidify the idea that the Western
Front was the First World War, pure and simple, and that it was a
colossal piece of bungling. The concept is even cemented by the
much-visited battlefield sites and the achingly beautiful but mournful
military cemeteries with their serried rows of white gravestones, so
lovingly tended by the Commonwealth War Graves Commission. In
his poem 'Ghosts of War' Ewart Alan Mackintosh caught a glimpse of
the Western Front in the future, long after he and his fellow Seaforths
were dead and buried:

> This is our Earth baptizèd
> With the red wine of War.
> Horror and courage hand in hand
> Shall brood upon the stricken land
> In silence evermore.[3]

And yet, for all its well-worn familiarity, born also of its relative
closeness to the British isles, the Western Front was not the only front
on which British soldiers fought and died. The First World War took
place on a global scale and Scottish soldiers fought on its other main
battle-fronts: Gallipoli, Mesopotamia, Salonika and Palestine. Two
battalions – 2nd King's Own Scottish Borderers and 2nd Gordon
Highlanders – have the distinction of being part of the British and
French forces sent to assist the Italians in the autumn of 1917 following
their heavy defeat by Austro-German forces at Caporetto and the
subsequent collapse of the home government. During the winter they
took part in offensive operations against the Austro-Hungarian army.
The King's Own Scottish Borderers returned to the Western Front in
April 1918 and were replaced by 10th Black Watch, but the Gordons
saw out their war in northern Italy, taking part in the successful repulse
of Field Marshal Boroevic's attack along the River Piave north of
Treviso. Food shortages and industrial unrest fed a belief that revolution was in the air in Italy but the formation of a coalition government

and the sacking of the inept General Luigi Cadorna helped to steady the situation. Also, shorn of much their German support, the Austro-Hungarian armies failed to make any headway. The final battle was fought at Vittorio Veneto where British troops served in the Tenth Army under the command of the Earl of Cavan; an armistice brought the fighting to an end on 3 November 1918.

Gallipoli 1915

Allied forces had been sent to Italy to stabilise the front at a time when this vital ally was in danger of collapsing as a result of defeats and mass desertions in its army. The other major operations against Ottoman forces in Gallipoli, Mesopotamia and Palestine were all part of a wider initiative to break the impasse of the Western Front by opening new fronts elsewhere. (The deployment in Salonika was part of an initiative to support Serbia by creating a bridgehead in northern Greece.) Kitchener summed up the strategic situation in a revealing letter written to French on 2 January 1915, arguing that the stalemate on the Western Front had brought Allied offensive operations to a standstill: 'I suppose we must now recognise that the French Army cannot make a sufficient break through the German lines of defence to cause a complete change of the situation and bring about the retreat of the German forces from northern Belgium – if that is so, then the German lines in France may be looked upon as a fortress that cannot be carried by assault and also cannot be invested, with the result that the lines can only be held by an investing force while operations proceed elsewhere.'[4] Something more dexterous was needed and so began the debate between the 'westerners' and the 'easterners'.

The former argued that Germany could only be defeated convincingly in Europe, while the 'easterners' believed that the impasse on the Western Front could be broken by using the navy to gain military advantages elsewhere. The latter school, of which Churchill was a leading exponent, believed that the war could be won more effectively and more cheaply by employing the ships of the Royal Navy to attack the Dardanelles as part of a wider campaign against Turkey, which had entered the war on Germany's side at the end of October 1914. While this declaration was not unexpected it put Britain under additional pressure: she had land forces in Egypt,

ostensibly an Ottoman possession but in reality a British protectorate;
vital oil interests in Mesopotamia had to be guarded; and it was
essential to prevent Russia becoming embroiled in a potentially
disastrous confrontation with Turkish forces in the Caucasus and
to keep open her supply route into the Mediterranean through the
Black Sea.

Inspired by a Greek plan to attack the Gallipoli peninsula, which
guarded the Dardanelles, Churchill had begun gathering political
support for an attack which would allow the Allies to enter the
Black Sea and threaten Constantinople. Various grandiose plans were
put forward at the end of 1914, some of the more ambitious of which
involved the participation of troops from Serbia, Greece and Bulgaria
(the latter two being still neutral), but eventually it was agreed to
mount a purely naval attack through the Dardanelles, involving older
but heavily gunned battleships, to attack and destroy the Turkish
forts on the peninsula. At a sombre meeting of the War Council on
13 January Churchill mooted the plan 'lucidly but quietly and without
exaggerated optimism' and clinched the issue by offering the services
of the navy's latest dreadnought, the mighty *Queen Elizabeth*, which
would calibrate and test her 15-inch guns against the enemy targets.[5]
At that stage there was no up-to-date intelligence about the strength
of the Turkish defences; all that was known was that British warships
had successfully bombarded the entrance to the Dardanelles at Sedd el
Bahr and Kum Kale in November 1914, causing panic amongst the
Turkish defenders. The planners in London were not to know that the
attack had encouraged the Turks to increase their minefields and to
strengthen the Gallipoli defences with modern mobile howitzers.

The naval plan was put into operation on 19 February under the
command of Vice-Admiral Sackville Carden, commanding the British
naval forces in the Eastern Mediterranean. A cautious man, he
proposed to destroy the outer defences first, using his ships' long-
range heavy weapons against targets at the entrance to the straits where
the Dardanelles meets the Aegean. Once these had been breached he
would move in closer to destroy the remaining gun positions, and the
reduction of the defences would allow the minefields to be swept
safely. At that point it would be safe to land ground forces to complete
the capture of the peninsula and to neutralise the Turkish garrison.
The creation of these forces was not achieved without difficulty and

some reluctance on the part of the War Office, which was under pressure to deploy more soldiers in France, but at the beginning of March it was agreed to earmark the British 29th Division to support landings by light infantry battalions of the Royal Naval Division. Kitchener then ordered the deployment of Australian and New Zealand troops training in Egypt, while the French agreed to deploy the Corps Expéditionnaire d'Orient, a mixed force of French and North African troops. Although the slow build-up did not immediately signify the creation of an attacking force, the British and the French were slowly drifting into a major campaign. The naval attack did not go according to plan: Carden's ships failed to make much impression on the Turkish defence as the trajectories were too shallow and the high explosives failed to damage the heavily defended Turkish forts, and it proved impossible to sweep minefields due to the accuracy of the Turkish field guns and the strength of the local currents. By the middle of March the British naval campaign was in deadlock and Kitchener was forced to agree to the creation of contingency plans for an offensive by ground forces.

Command of the Mediterranean Expeditionary Force was given to General Sir Ian Standish Monteith Hamilton, a Gordon Highlander and a veteran of the Boer War and many other Victorian campaigns, who was perhaps the most experienced soldier in the British Army. He had twice been recommended for a VC. In the first Boer War at Majuba Hill in 1881 his bravery should have earned him one, but it was rejected as he was considered too young; in the second Boer War he distinguished himself at Elandslaagte in 1899 but the recommendation for a VC was again turned down, this time because, being a brigadier, he was thought to be too senior. But this engaging and educated general travelled east with several drawbacks in his baggage: at 62 he was relatively old and heading towards retirement, and his orders from Kitchener were muddled and inexact. Later, in his diary-memoirs, Hamilton created an unforgettable image of the moment when he was summoned to the War Office to talk to Kitchener, with whom he had served in South Africa: 'Opening the door I bade him good morning and walked up to his desk where he went on writing like a graven image. After a moment he looked up and said in a matter-of-fact tone, "We are sending a military force to support the fleet now at the Dardanelles and you have command."' By then that command had grown to 70,000 soldiers, a sizable force which Kitchener said was more than enough to take on the Turks. However, such was the haste with which Hamilton's departure was planned that his headquarters staff had only twenty-four hours to make their arrangements. One of their number, Captain Aspinall, quickly realised that they were being deployed without any precise idea of what was being asked of them: 'I shall never forget the dismay and foreboding with which I learnt that apart from Lord Kitchener's very brief instructions, a pre-war Admiralty report on the Dardanelles defences and an out-of-date map, Sir Ian had been given practically no information whatever.'[6]

Aspinall would later become the campaign's official historian and he had every right to be so alarmed. Hamilton's orders were vague and couched in the most general terms. He was to do nothing until his force had been assembled, he was to undertake no ground operations until the fleet had finished its work and he was to avoid any action which might suck his men into a lengthy campaign. Kitchener was emphatic about this final point, telling his protégé that 'once we begin marching about continents, situations calling for heavy reinforcements would probably be created'.[7] Hamilton was left with the decided impression that he was to command a force which would not take on offensive operations but would in essence be responsible for mopping up operations in the wake of the naval attack. It was also made clear to him that the operations were not to be dragged out and that the forces under his command, especially the 29th Division, were only on loan as they were needed for service on the Western Front.

However it soon became brutally apparent to Hamilton that the battleships were not the solution to the neutralisation of the Turkish defences. On 17 March he and his staff arrived at the Greek island of Tenedos and the next day the British and French warships, now under the command of Vice-Admiral Sir John de Robeck, made a fresh attack in three lines against the fortifications at Kilid Bahr and Chanak which guarded the narrows and the entrance into the Sea of Marmara. The idea was to open fire at long range and then to reduce the range for a final onslaught, but this depended on the successful sweeping of known minefields in Eren Keui Bay where the fleet would begin the assault. To begin with, the battleships seemed invincible and those watching them guessed that the Turks would be unable to withstand

such an onslaught from the heavy guns. Early in the day the fire from
the forts began to slacken, encouraging hopes of a quick victory, but
shortly after two o'clock disaster struck when the French battleship
Bouvet hit a mine and exploded. Only a handful of her crew of 700
survived. At the same time howitzer fire forced the Allied mine-
sweepers to scatter. It was obvious that Eren Kui Bay was littered
with mines – unknown to the Allies a Turkish minelayer had carried
out the operation ten days earlier – and the hidden weapons
began inflicting more losses. Minutes after the sinking of the *Bouvet*
HMS *Inflexible* hit a mine followed in short order by HMS *Irresistible* and
HMS *Ocean*, both of which sank after their crews had been saved. Not
surprisingly de Robeck called off the attack. Not only had he lost
three battleships with another three disabled, including the French
ships *Suffren* and *Gaulois*, but the Turkish forts had not been destroyed.

A storm the following day prevented further naval operations, but
while the British commanders on board HMS *Queen Elizabeth* were
taking stock of the situation they found themselves reaching the fateful
decision to use land forces to attack the Turkish forts. Hamilton was
the main protagonist, sending a message back to Kitchener claiming
that success depended on 'a deliberate and progressive military
operation carried out at full strength so as to open a passage for
the Navy'. In London Kitchener agreed, telling Hamilton that 'these
operations must be undertaken after careful consideration of the local
defences, and they must be carried through'.[8] Having lost so many
ships, and worried about the dangers posed by the minefields, de
Robeck was in no position to complain and agreed to the proposal
that the new operations should begin on 14 April at the every earliest,
to allow Hamilton to assemble his ground forces in Alexandria. It
would be a combined operation but it would be an operation like no
other mounted in the war: it was decided on the spot without
reference to London or Paris, there was no overall commander, there
was little in the way of logistical planning and there was to be no
attempt at surprise. Worse, both Hamilton and de Robeck laboured
under misunderstandings. The general thought that the navy would
continue shelling the forts, while the admiral decided not to risk his
battleships until the invasion began. Once the big naval guns had fallen
silent the Turkish garrison guessed that there would soon be a fresh
assault and that next time it would come from ground troops.

They were right. Little attempt was made to disguise the Allied preparations as Hamilton drew together his landing forces, which consisted of the following formations: 29th Division (Major-General Aylmer Hunter-Weston); Royal Naval Division (Major-General Archibald Paris); Australian and New Zealand (ANZAC) Corps (Lieutenant-General Sir William Birdwood) and French Corps (General Albert D'Amade). The Turks too had been busy. Command of their forces (Fifth Army) was given to an experienced German soldier, General Otto Liman von Sanders, who had been sent to Constantinople in 1913 as the Inspector-General of the Turkish army. Under his direction the Turkish Fifth Army in Gallipoli was redeployed in its position by concentrating their resources into three defensive areas on the peninsula itself with other defensive positions on the European side and the Asiatic side between Besika Bay and Kum Kale. Beaches were wired and mined and new defensive positions with deep trenches were hurriedly constructed: no easy matter given the hard unyielding ground, and Liman von Sanders later admitted that his forces benefited hugely from the 'four good weeks of respite' allowed by the Allies. When the British came, he argued, they would be stopped and thrown back into the sea.

Against these modern defences Hamilton and his fellow commanders hoped that their superior firepower and military abilities would win the day. Schooled in the belief that a modern European army would be no match for inferior 'native' opposition they took comfort from an earlier incident involving Turkish forces the previous December at Alexandretta in Syria, where a British raiding party landed to cut the railway line. Not only did the sailors meet no opposition, the Turkish defenders agreed to carry out the demolition themselves and insisted that the lieutenant in charge should be treated as a Turkish officer for the day. The official account recorded the raid as a 'comedy' and added to the belief that the average Turkish soldier was a slothful and incompetent coward, or as one staff officer put it, he had 'never shown himself as good a fighter as the white man'. Basically, Hamilton hoped that the mere presence of the battleships and the sight of disciplined troops would quickly destroy the Turks' will to resist. In his mind the main assault would be over within two days and he optimistically forecast that his forces would 'take a good run at the Peninsula and jump plump on – both feet together . . . And stake everything on the one hazard'.[9] That meant landing the 29th Division at five small landing beaches at Cape Helles (codenamed S, V, W, X and Y) while the ANZAC forces landed further north at Ari Burnu and the French Corps attacked the Asiatic side at Kum Kale. The attack was planned to begin on 25 April, six weeks after de Robeck's naval bombardment had spluttered to a halt.

The main offensive was aimed at the Cape Helles beaches and was directed by Major-General Aylmer Hunter-Weston, a Royal Engineer who had been born at Hunterston in Ayrshire in 1864. Known as 'Hunter-Bunter', he was a hard and aggressive commander who frequently stated that he cared nothing about casualties; with his gruff red-faced ferocity he might have been a figure of fun had he not been in such an important position. His division ('The Incomparable') was considered to be one of the best-trained in the army and contained two Scottish infantry battalions, 1st King's Own Scottish Borderers and 1/5th Royal Scots, a Territorial Force battalion, together with IV (Highland) Mountain Brigade, Royal Field Artillery; but before they could give an account of themselves in the fighting they first had to be taken ashore. That proved to be no easy task. In addition to a specially adapted Clyde-built collier, the *River Clyde*, which was run ashore at V beach carrying 2,000 men, the main force was landed in ships' cutters pulled by a variety of tug boats. The intention was to secure the beaches and then to advance on the ridge between Krithia and Achi Baba which would be the key to taking control of the peninsula. As was the case throughout the campaign, things did not turn out that way.

In the initial stages the Turks seemed confused by the breadth and strength of the Allied attack but they soon regrouped and at V and W beaches the British forces took heavy casualties when they found themselves pinned down by heavy and accurate machine-gun fire. On the other hand, at X and Y beaches the landings were unopposed, but there were serious communication failures between those two landing forces which meant that they were unable to exploit the situation even though they faced minimal Turkish opposition. Attacking Y beach was a combined force of 2,000 comprising 1st King's Own Scottish Borderers, the Plymouth Battalion Royal Marines and a company drawn from 2nd South Wales Borderers, but their progress was stymied by a muddle over who should take command. The Kings

Own Scottish Borderers' commanding officer, Lieutenant-Colonel Archibald Koe, thought that he held command but no one had told him that the Marines' colonel was senior to him. The result was a fatal indecision which allowed the Turks to regroup and by nightfall the British forces were under heavy and sustained counter-attack. Captain Robert Whigham, an officer in the King's Own Scottish Borderers, could see them approaching in the light of the full moon and later described what he had observed:

> One could see line upon line of Turks advancing against our position. They fought with extraordinary bravery and as each line was swept away by our fire another one advanced against us and the survivors collected in some dead ground to our front and came on again. The attack worked up and down our whole front as if they were looking for some weak spot to break through our line. I saw one man, during one of these advances, continue to run towards us after his companions had stopped. He ran at full speed towards us, dodging about all over the place. He got up to within about fifty yards of the trench and than I saw him drop. Four times during the night they got right up to my trench before they were shot and one Turk engaged one of my men over the parapet with his bayonet and was then shot.[10]

Forced to dig in quickly, the Scots used their packs to reinforce their defences and later admitted that the 'trenches' never deserved the name. By the next day the King's Own Scottish Borderers' position was becoming untenable and both sides had taken large numbers of casualties; the British alone had lost 700 killed or wounded. With Hunter-Weston unable or unwilling to comprehend the importance of the position and the need for immediate reinforcement a decision was taken to retire to the beaches for re-embarkation, a move which was covered by 1st King's Own Scottish Borderers. Koe was killed during the fighting and his body was never recovered. The failure to act decisively at Y beach was compounded by Hamilton's unwillingness to intervene in Hunter-Weston's direction of the battle and, according to the Official Historian, such blunders typified the operation with its confusion over command, the lack of initiative after landing and the absence of any support from the staff:

Cleverly conceived, happily opened, hesitatingly concluded, miserably ended – such is the story of the landing at Y beach. In deciding to throw a force ashore at that point Sir Ian Hamilton would seem to have hit upon the key of the whole situation. Favoured by an unopposed landing, and by the absence of any Turks in the neighbourhood for many hours, it is as certain as anything can be in war that a bold advance from Y beach on the morning of 25th April must have freed the southern beaches that morning, and ensured a decisive victory for the 29th Division. But apart from its original conception no other part of the operation was free from calamitous mistakes, and Fortune seldom smiles on a force that neglects its own opportunities.[11]

Within the King's Own Scottish Borderers the feeling was that they had been left to their own devices and the high command had failed to respond to urgent signals. The battalion and the South Wales Borderers were in action again in the fighting for Krithia, but even at that early stage stalemate had come to the battlefield. The Allies were confined to their beachhead while the Turks held on to the higher ground and could not be dislodged, largely due to their doggedness and the Allies' lack of field artillery. At the same time, the Turks failed to drive their enemy back into the sea and the fighting degenerated into as bitter a struggle as anything seen on the Western Front. By the end of the month, less than a week after they had landed, the British had lost some 400 officers and 8,500 other ranks, around a third of the attacking force.

At the beginning of May the first reinforcements arrived in the shape of the 29th Indian Infantry Brigade and the 42nd (East Lancashire) Division but it was clear that Hamilton needed a much bigger force to dislodge the Turkish defenders; on 10 May Kitchener sanctioned the dispatch of the 52nd (Lowland) Division which had been training in the Stirling area. It was made up of the following formations:

155th Brigade
    1/4th Royal Scots Fusiliers
    1/5th Royal Scots Fusiliers
    1/4th King's Own Scottish Borderers
    1/5th King's Own Scottish Borderers

156th Brigade
  1/4th Royal Scots
  1/7th Royal Scots
  1/7th Cameronians (Scottish Rifles)
  1/8th Cameronians (Scottish Rifles)

157th Brigade
  1/5th Highland Light Infantry
  1/6th Highland Light Infantry
  1/7th Highland Light Infantry
  1/5th Argyll and Sutherland Highlanders

The division began deploying immediately, with the battalions being sent south by train to Liverpool and Devonport for passage to Gallipoli through Mudros or Alexandria. It was a well-oiled operation but tragedy hit one battalion even before it had reached the seat of war. Half of the Leith-based 1/7th Royal Scots were travelling south on Train 18 when it slammed into a local service at Quintinshill Junction near Gretna at 6.45 a.m. on 22 May as a result of a disastrous misunderstanding by the local signalmen. The carriages were strewn across the main line. Within minutes the disaster was compounded when a London to Glasgow overnight express travelling north at high speed crashed into the wreckage, causing even greater damage. Then, to the horror of the rescuers, 'a few wisps of smoke were seen to start in different parts of the mass, and soon the wreckage was blazing furiously – and there were no available means of coping with the fire'. Three officers and 207 other ranks were killed; five officers and 219 other ranks injured, and the battalion travelled out to Gallipoli at half strength.[12] When the funerals were held in Leith's Rosebank cemetery, Edinburgh's port area was in mourning with blinds drawn, shops closed and huge crowds lining the route of the mass funeral procession. Both the signalmen involved in the accident, James Tinsley and George Meakin, were tried at the High Court in Edinburgh and found guilty of negligence; Meakin was imprisoned for eighteen months while Tinsley received three years but suffered a nervous breakdown while in prison. It was the biggest disaster in Britain's railway history and a terrible blow for a city which would soon be mourning even greater numbers of dead from Gallipoli and from the autumn battles in Flanders.

During the 156th Brigade's first major offensive, at Helles on 28 June, the assault battalions were 1/4th and 1/7th Royal Scots and 1/8th Cameronians and they all suffered terribly from the intensive Turkish machine-gun fire and from the failure of the British artillery to suppress it. The Edinburgh battalions lost heavily: the 1/4th Royal Scots lost 16 officers and 204 soldiers, killed or missing, while the 1/7th Royal Scots was reduced to six officers and 169 soldiers, roughly the size of a company.[13] As the casualty lists started appearing in the Edinburgh newspapers it was impossible to disguise the fact that whole areas of the city had been affected and that, as the *Evening Dispatch* reflected, death had been unsparing of class or background:

> In its ranks are many former pupils of such schools as George Watson's College, not a few of whom joined after the outbreak of the war. There is something at once inspiring and pathetic in the fate of these young fellows. They had grown up together almost from infancy, sitting on the same bench at school, romping in the playground together, running shoulder to shoulder on the football field, and then after the parting that comes at the end of school life, finding themselves side by side once more on the field of battle, playing the biggest game that men have ever played.[14]

The sentiment comes close to delineating the ethos of the volunteer army, its tight solidarity and its optimism in the face of hardship and violent death. As Ian S. Wood explains in his study of the Royal Scots' Territorial battalions, the losses were made more poignant because they mirrored not just Edinburgh's social structure but also the close-knit composition of the Territorial battalions across the country, in which many professional men served as private soldiers either because there were not enough commissions or because they wanted to stay with their friends. Listed in the daily and ever-growing catalogue of death was Captain George McCrae, 1/4th Royal Scots, the elder son of the founder of the 16th Royal Scots. All across the Central Belt of the Scottish Lowlands families were left to mourn the loss of young lives as the casualties began to mount in the battalions of their local regiments. After the unsuccessful attack on Achi Baba Nullah on

12 July Alexander Burnett, 1/4th Royal Scots Fusiliers, looked back at the battlefield and regretted the loss of men who had joined up with him in Kilmarnock at the beginning of the war: 'We were all boys together at school, we'd started jobs as apprentices, we'd formed friendships. And there they were a line of them all killed at one time, none of them over seventeen.'[15]

In an attempt to humanise the process the local newspapers printed brief details about each casualty and, wherever possible, a photograph of the young man in uniform. What the writers could not do was to describe the dreadful conditions being faced by the men. Not only was the fighting conducted at close quarters, with some trenches so close as to be almost in touching distance, the physical hardships were worse than anything faced on the Western Front. Despite the best efforts at maintaining basic sanitation, disease was rampant, especially dysentery and enteric fever, which was spread by the absence of proper latrines and washing facilities and by the ever-present swarms of black buzzing flies. One medical officer said it was impossible to eat in their presence as they quickly swarmed on to any spoonful between plate and mouth. Like everyone else on the peninsula the Scots had to live with this plague although, as George Waugh, 1/4th King's Own Scottish Borderers, remembered, some even managed to turn the flies into a joke: 'There was raisins and currants he [the cook] shoved in the rice. But this day when they were dishing it out there was no currants in it. One of the men beside me said, "Nae currants, Davie?" The cook replied, "Nae currants today. Oh, half a minute." He lifted the Dixie lid and all the flies went in!'[16] In the heat of high summer the swarms were especially bad and even the advent of colder autumn weather brought little respite as the sun gave way to long days of freezing rain.

Despite the arrival of reinforcements – in all Hamilton was given five new divisions – the deadlock could not be broken and the men on the peninsula were becoming increasingly weakened. An ambitious amphibious landing at Suvla Bay failed in August because the Turks were able to rush reinforcements into the area to prevent the creation of a bridgehead. The novelist Compton Mackenzie was acting as an official war correspondent at Hamilton's headquarters and as he watched the operation unfold he felt as if he had 'stood by the death of an old order' and that the British had finally lost their 'amateur status'.[17] The news of the failure was met with dismay in London and compounded the idea that 1915 had been a year of military disasters, with no change in the position on the Western Front and stalemate in Gallipoli. Disease and searing heat added to the difficulties facing the men on the peninsula and in August alone over 40,000 soldiers had to be evacuated, the majority suffering from dysentery. The strategic situation worsened the following month, when Bulgaria began moves to enter the war on the opposite side and an alarmed Serbia made urgent requests for British and French reinforcements. In October the inevitable happened: Hamilton was sacked, rightly so, as his leadership had become increasingly feeble and sterile, and he was replaced by General Sir Charles Monro, a veteran of the fighting on the Western Front who was also a disciple of the westerners. Having taken stock of the situation he recommended evacuation, although this was not accepted until the beginning of November, when Kitchener himself visited the battle-front and found himself agreeing that the difficulties were insuperable. A heavy and unexpected winter storm also helped to decide the issue: over 280 British soldiers died of exposure including a number from the Worcestershire Regiment who were found frozen to death on the fire steps of their trenches. In a brilliant operation, which was all the more inspired after the fiascos which preceded it, the British finally withdrew their forces at the end of 1915, remarkably without losing any casualties. The great adventure to win the war by other means was finally over but the survivors, such as Captain C. S. Black, 1/6th Highland Light Infantry, had mixed emotions when they said farewell to one of the harshest battlefields of the war:

Cape Helles had no happy memories for us; no one wanted to see the place again. But what of the men we were to leave behind us there? The good comrades, who had come so gaily with us to the wars, who had fought so gallantly by our side, and who now would lie for ever among the barren rocks where they had died. Never a kindly Scot would there be to tend their graves; their memory was left to the mercy of foes and strangers, though thank heaven, gallant foes. No man was sorry to leave Gallipoli; but few were really glad.[18]

One statistic will stand for many: when the 1/4th Royal Scots were evacuated they had been reduced to two officers and 148 men.[19] As happened on other fronts, the exact British death toll was difficult to compute but most estimates agree that 36,000 deaths from combat and disease is not an unreasonable tally. (The official British statistics show 117,549 casualties: 28,200 killed, 78,095 wounded, 11,254 missing. Total Allied casualties are put at 265,000.) The failure of the Gallipoli campaign has provided history with one of its great conundrums, the conditional 'if only' being applied to most aspects of it. If only the tactics, the leadership, the reinforcements and the munitions had been better, if only the execution had matched the conception, then a sordid defeat could have been a glittering triumph. The original reasons for the deployment had much to recommend them but an absence of clear thinking and the half-hearted conduct of the campaign must account for its failure and for the waste of so many lives and so much equipment. The Official History summarised the campaign in words that speak only of disillusionment and despair: 'Few memories are sadder than the memory of lost opportunities, and few failures more poignant than those which, viewed in retrospect, were surely avoidable and ought to have been avoided. The story of the Dardanelles is a memory such as these.'[20]

The failure of the campaign left a lasting bitterness amongst those who had taken part, not least in Australia and New Zealand, where 25 April is still commemorated as ANZAC Day. Unlike the Western Front, where optimism survived for a surprisingly long time, there were no good words to be said about Gallipoli and soldiers who served on both fronts admitted that the conditions on the peninsula were worse than anything they encountered in France and Flanders. Some, like John Brown who served in the Lovat Scouts* as part of the Highland Mounted Brigade, 2nd Mounted Division, came to believe that they had been forgotten and condemned to die of starvation or disease, and very few of the men who fought at Cape Helles or Suvla would have disagreed with the words of Brown's commanding officer,

---

* Two regiments of Lovat Scouts were raised in 1903 and both served as dismounted troops in Gallipoli. In September 1916 the two formations were amalgamated and served as 10th (Lovat Scouts) Queen's Own Cameron Highlanders with the 27th Division in Macedonia. In June 1918 they were transferred to France as lines of communication troops.

Lord Lovat: 'It will be up to date and probably to all eternity as sordid and miserable a chapter of amateur enterprise as ever was written in our history.'[21] However, it was not the end of the war for the survivors. The original three divisions – 29th, ANZAC and Royal Naval – were sent to France in time to take part in the Battle of the Somme and were followed by the 11th (Northern) and 42nd (East Lancashire) divisions after a brief period of rest in Egypt. The 13th (Western) Division was dispatched to Salonika to assist the Serb war effort and the rest of the Mediterranean Field Force, including the 52nd (Lowland) Division remained in Egypt to guard the Suez Canal and for the operations against Ottoman forces in Palestine and Syria.

Salonika 1915–18

The withdrawal from Gallipoli allowed the British and the French to build up forces in the Balkans, both to support Serbia and to prevent Bulgarian forces from influencing events in the region – on 5 October 1915 its army had been mobilised and it entered the war on the side of the Central Powers. The Allied response was to send two divisions to the port of Salonika (present-day Thessaloniki) under the command of the French general Maurice Sarrail, a radical socialist and rival of the commander-in-chief, Joffre. At the time, German and Austro-Hungarian forces under the command of Field Marshal August von Mackensen★ had invaded Serbia and had entered Belgrade while Bulgarian forces had pushed into Macedonia, a move which stymied any Allied attempt to relieve pressure on the Serbs. As a result Sarrail's divisions were pushed back into Salonika, which rapidly became a huge military base: by the end of the year three French and five British divisions, together with a huge amount of stores and ammunition, were encamped in a perimeter which was 200 miles square and defended by acres of barbed-wire. For entirely political reasons the British supported the deployment, which the Germans ridiculed as

---

★ During his lifetime this outstanding East Prussian cavalry officer was thought to be of Scottish descent, a claim he always denied. There were also rumours in the post-war period that his identity had been adopted by Major-General Sir Hector Macdonald, following his faked suicide in a Paris hotel in 1903. The full story is told in Trevor Royle, *Death before Dishonour: The True Story of Fighting Mac* (Edinburgh, 1982).

'the greatest internment camp in the world' and which prevented vital reinforcements and equipment from being deployed on the Western Front. The new French prime minister, Aristide Briand, had made Salonika a plank in his war strategy and the British did not want to provoke a crisis by insisting on withdrawal. There was also a need to maintain pressure on Bulgaria as a means of helping the Russians, who had suffered a heavy defeat at Gorlice-Tarnow in September.

Together with IV (Highland) Mountain Brigade Royal Field Artillery and 1/1ˢᵗ Lothian and Border Horse, who served as Corps or General Headquarters troops, 11 Scottish infantry battalions served on the Salonika front between 1915 and 1918: 1ˢᵗ Royal Scots, 8ᵗʰ Royal Scots Fusiliers, 11ᵗʰ Cameronians, 10ᵗʰ Black Watch, 13ᵗʰ (Scottish Horse) Black Watch, 1ˢᵗ Garrison Battalion Seaforths, 2ⁿᵈ Camerons, 10ᵗʰ (Lovat Scouts) Camerons, 1ˢᵗ Argylls, 12ᵗʰ Argylls, 2ⁿᵈ London Scottish. However, they did not see action until the summer of 1916 when British XVI Corps moved up the valley of the River Struma towards the border with Bulgaria. The move was made to encourage Romania to join the war on the Allied side and most of the fighting was undertaken by the French divisions, which had to face determined Bulgarian counter-attacks. Most of the British effort was confined to the Struma valley, where the participants found that the style of fighting seemed to come from a different age. On 30 September three Scottish regiments – 1ˢᵗ Royal Scots, 2ⁿᵈ Camerons and 1ˢᵗ Argylls – moved across the Struma to attack Bulgarian positions in the fortified villages of Karajakoi Bala and Karajakoi Zir, with pipers leading them into battle. For Lieutenant R. W. F. Johnstone of the 1ˢᵗ Royal Scots, who left a vivid description of the fighting, it was not the only archaic touch of the day:

> Behind us we could see on the heights spectators watching the battle. On our level we could see the artillery galloping into action, the guns being swung into position and the teams galloping back to a position of safety while the guns opened fire and the noise of the shells above our heads was at times quite deafening. There was also a cable wagon in front of the gun line galloping across the front with mounted linesmen paying out the cable as they rode. It was in all a scene of the old South African type battlefield which no one who was there would ever forget.[22]

Both objectives were captured with the loss of 1,248 casualties and it was the biggest operation undertaken by British forces in Salonika in 1916. However, it was quickly becoming apparent that the main British losses were not battlefield casualties but men who fell victim to malaria: for every casualty from enemy action, ten found themselves in hospital as a result of illness, and some units were unable to function.[23] Dysentery and various enteric diseases also caused havoc and put a great strain on the medical services, but malaria was a constant problem mainly because it was endemic in the area and proved difficult to eradicate. Re-infection was also a problem, for although malaria did not kill men in great numbers – fatalities were confined to one per cent of hospital admissions – it did remove soldiers from operational service, and in the worst cases incapacitated men had to be evacuated.

Christopher Murray Grieve, a quartermaster-sergeant in the Royal Army Medical Corps, was one of the many who suffered from bouts of malaria. Born in Langholm in 1892 he had enlisted in the Territorial Force while working as a student teacher in Edinburgh and had joined up in July 1915. Within a year he was serving with the 42nd General Hospital, which was located on the outskirts of Thessalonica and which contained so many Scottish medical personnel that Grieve wrote to his mentor George Ogilvie suggesting 'that it should be called not Thessalonica but Thistleonica'.[24] Another unmistakable Scottish medical presence was provided by volunteer units of the Scottish Women's Hospitals which had been founded by an Edinburgh graduate, Dr Elsie Maud Inglis, and which had already seen service in Serbia (see Chapter Eight). However, no sooner had Grieve arrived in Salonika than he was infected with the first of three bouts of malaria and was eventually invalided home in the summer of 1918. The experience in Salonika touched Grieve in other ways. After the war he adopted the name of Hugh MacDiarmid and became one of the great poets of the twentieth century, embracing at various stages of his life both communism and nationalism. As a result of his wartime experiences he also became a convinced Anglophobe. Shortly before his death in 1978 Grieve/MacDiarmid admitted that while serving in the army he and his fellow Scots only got on well with Irish and Welsh soldiers 'but we always had a difference from the English, we didn't get on with the English at all and I became more and more anti-English as the time went on'.[25]

The main action in Salonika took place in May 1917 with an operation by the French and Serb forces to break through the Bulgarian defensive lines. The British objectives, undertaken by XII Corps, were the heavily defended positions to the west of Lake Doiran, but the Allied offensive failed and had to be abandoned on 23 May with the loss of 5,024 British casualties. As happened on the Western Front the Allied artillery failed to cut the wire and the attacking infantry soon found themselves pinned down by accurate Bulgarian artillery and machine-gun fire. In their attack the 10th Black Watch broke through the line on the Petit Couronne position but then found themselves under fierce counter-attack: 'Had it not been for their bombs and the increased machine-gun fire from the flanks, this attack might have got through the wire, but it was impossible to hold on as it was getting lighter every minute, and they had to withdraw.'[26] The mountainous terrain also helped the defenders and the commander-in-chief of British Salonika Forces, Lieutenant-General G. F. Milne, was forced to concede that 'our men are not a match for the Bulgar in hill fighting, though superior on the flat'.[27] Other problems came from manpower shortages, lack of reliable equipment, especially heavy artillery, and the absence of coherent plans. For the rest of the year the front remained surprisingly quiet while XVI Corps' activities in the Struma valley were confined to operations which the latest historians of the campaign describe as 'a series of limited actions, none on a scale large enough to be defined as battles in the Official History'.[28]

During the winter Greece finally entered the war on the Allied side, following the abdication of the pro-German King Constantine, and at last the Allies were rewarded for their long-standing military presence in Salonika. At the same time Sarrail was sacked and replaced first by General M. L. A. Guillaumat and then by General Franchet D'Esperey who brought the campaign to a conclusion in the summer of 1918. Weakened by German troop withdrawals, the Bulgarian army failed to halt the last assault of the war, which began on 15 September and ended a fortnight later when the Bulgarian front was split. On 29 September French forces entered Skopje and the following day Bulgaria requested an armistice. D'Esperey was keen to continue his advance up through the Balkans to threaten Germany's southern flank and his troops were already crossing the Danube when the war came to an end on 11 November. At the same time Milne moved his British forces up to the Turkish frontier, but his hopes of attacking Turkey ended when the Turks signed an armistice on 31 October. Elements of British forces remained in the area into 1919, serving as peace-keepers, and for most of them it was a dispiriting end to a campaign which had tied up huge numbers of men and materiel for no obvious strategic gains. Although the British Salonika Force listed a modest 18,000 casualties from combat, this was overshadowed by the 481,000 who had succumbed to illness, mainly malaria.

Mesopotamia 1915–18

When it became clear that Turkey was going to enter the war on the side of the Central Powers in the late summer of 1914 the British government authorised the dispatch of an Indian expeditionary force (Force D), consisting of three infantry brigades, to the Ottoman province of Mesopotamia (present-day Iraq) to safeguard the oilfields and refineries of the Anglo-Persian Oil Company at Ahwaz. The force landed near the mouth of the Shatt-al-Arab waterway and by the end of November it had secured the city of Basra and the surrounding area, having defeated Turkish forces in a number of small but fiercely contested engagements. All the objectives had been achieved: access to the Persian Gulf had been secured and local Turkish resistance had been neutralised. Even when the Turks counter-attacked at the beginning of 1915 they were repulsed with heavy losses and this success encouraged thoughts of pressing the attack up the River Tigris to take Baghdad. For the Allies this was a tempting prospect, for although there was no strategic need to make an immediate move, the capture of such an important city would do wonders for western prestige following the setbacks at Gallipoli. From a military point of view it also made sense as the nearest Turkish reserves were believed to be at Aleppo in present-day Syria or fighting the Russians in the Caucasus. None were thought to be within 400 miles of Baghdad. Command of the Mesopotamian forces was given to Lieutenant-General Sir John Nixon and he was later reinforced with two Indian divisions from France: 3rd (Lahore) and 7th Meerut. Serving with them were three Scottish battalions – 1st Highland Light Infantry (3rd Division), and 2nd Black Watch and 1st Seaforths (both 7th Division) – which moved to Basra in December 1915.

All three would take part in the operation which has come to symbolise the failings of the campaign in Mesopotamia: the relief of the forces besieged in the town of Kut-al-Amarah. This came about as a direct result of the move to take Baghdad, which had begun in May with a move up the Tigris by a mixed British-Indian force* commanded by Major-General Charles Townshend, an experienced if somewhat arrogant Indian Army officer. From the outset the odds were stacked against him as the advance would overstretch his lines of communication and he was operating during the intense heat of summer, but Townshend made good progress with his 14,000-strong ground force backed by a number of gunboats. The town of Al-Amarah fell on 3 June, allowing him to move up the eastern bank of the Tigris towards Kut-al-Amarah, which was captured on 28 September, and to Nixon's delight the 'Tigris regatta' seemed to be fulfilling all its objectives as the Turks retreated towards Baghdad. However, even at that stage Townshend's forces were running into problems. He was almost 400 miles north of his base at Basra and, although he did not know this, the Turks would soon be reinforcing their Mesopotamian garrison with forces from the Gallipoli front. Townshend was cautious about continuing the operation but Nixon was enthusiastic and the first signs were encouraging. Continuing his approach on the west bank of the river, Townshend defeated a Turkish force at Aziziye and by 12 November he was within 30 miles of Baghdad. Ahead lay a heavily fortified Turkish position at Ctesiphon which was manned by 30,000 soldiers backed up by German advisers. Townshend's force was half that number but on 22 November his forces attacked and seized the Turks' first lines. That was the only success: the Turks rushed reserves into the area and after three days of fighting Townshend's force had lost 4,511 casualties, killed or wounded. Forced to retreat, the rump of the force reached Kut-al-Amarah on 3 December and began preparing for a lengthy siege.

Military logic suggested that Townshend should have continued his retreat, but he shared Nixon's confidence that the relief force would arrive before the position became untenable. Perhaps he was too sure

---

* The force consisted of four British infantry battalions, twelve Indian Army infantry battalions, one Gurkha battalion, two squadrons of Indian cavalry and various supporting units.

of his abilities. In 1895 Townshend had come to prominence as the 'Hero of Chitral', having weathered a 46-day siege surrounded by hostile tribal forces in the north-west Indian town of Chitral while serving as a captain in the 2nd Central Indian Horse. It was only natural that he believed that it was possible to repeat the experience in Mesopotamia. Kut (as it is commonly called) was situated in a loop in the Tigris and although that feature added to the position's defensive properties it also made it easy to besiege. Having failed to break into Kut, two Turkish divisions began the investment and within a week of Townshend's arrival they had completed their blockade. According to the German commander of the Turkish Sixth Army, General Colmar von der Goltz, the British had been 'bottled with the cork in'; they could neither escape nor take in fresh supplies. Inevitably conditions began to deteriorate inside Kut, which was little more than a collection of mud huts and compounds, and life for Townshend's force soon became intolerable. Sanitation was a problem and because some positions were below the water level it proved difficult to build trenches to protect the men from constant Turkish attack. Supplies began running out and by the beginning of March the average daily ration was 10 ounces of barley flour and 4 ounces of barley grain. Horse and mule meat were also available, although usually refused by the Indian soldiers.[29]

With the arrival from France of the two Indian Army divisions the first attempts were made to relieve Townshend's force, but from the outset it was clear that this would not be the easy operation forecast by Nixon. The winter rains made the going difficult, the supply lines were no better than they had been for the first operation and the Turks had been able to reinforce in strength and had occupied strong defensive positions. Haste also played a part. The forces were dispatched north as soon as they arrived in Basra, often without their horses, supply wagons and ambulances, and the commander of the operation, Lieutenant-General Sir Fenton Aylmer, had no clear idea about how he should proceed. The result was one disaster after another. The first attack took place on 7 January against heavily defended Turkish positions at Shaikh Saad where the British and Indian infantry battalions attacked without artillery or cavalry support.

A second attack, at Umm al Hanna a fortnight later, fared little better. Although the men of 2nd Black Watch reached the Turkish

lines they became isolated from the main attacking force: 'As the
bombardment lifted, The Black Watch advanced at a slow double,
and were at once greeted by a storm of bullets. Despite the heavy
mud, despite the losses, perfect order was kept, and after a momentary
halt at the irrigation channel every man rose up simultaneously and
swept forward into the Turkish trench. There for a few moments the
Turks met them hand-to-hand.'[30] So fierce was the fighting that
when the men of The Black Watch withdrew they had been reduced
to ninety-nine men under the command of a subaltern, 2nd Lieutenant
Stewart Smith. The 1st Seaforths had suffered equally high casualties
and as a result the survivors from the two formations were grouped
together as a composite Highland battalion which was involved in the
next stage of the operations at Sannaiyat. This took the relieving force
12 miles short of Kut, but despite the gallantry shown by the British
and Indian soldiers the attempt to relieve Kut ended in failure when
Townshend was forced to surrender the city on 27 April. The siege,
the longest in British military history, had lasted 147 days and had cost
over 2,500 casualties, dead and wounded. For those who survived,
though, the future was bleak. Put into Turkish captivity and marched
north under deplorable conditions only 837 of the 2,592 British
soldiers survived the war, while of the 10,486 Indian and Gurkha
soldiers 7,423 survived. The relief force, now under the command of
Lieutenant-General Sir George Gorringe, had also lost heavily, having
sustained 23,500 casualties in four months of fruitless fighting along
the River Tigris.

Coming on top of the debacle at Gallipoli the surrender at Kut was
a serious blow to British morale in the Middle East. Not only had
neither campaign done anything to shorten the war or discomfort the
enemy, they had also been expensive in terms of personnel and
equipment. The defeats had also damaged British prestige and it was
clear that much-needed stability had to be brought to the British
and Indian forces in Mesopotamia. Command was given to Major-
General Sir Frederick Stanley Maude, a veteran of the Western Front
who spent the rest of 1916 consolidating his forces and renewing their
arms and equipment. Both 2nd Black Watch and 1st Seaforths were
brought up to strength with drafts from home and, along with
1st Highland Light Infantry, they took part in the renewed offensive
which began on 12 December 1916. Two months later Kut was

recaptured and Maude pushed on to Baghdad, continuing his campaign in the furnace-like heat of summer, with the temperature reaching almost 50 degrees Celsius in the shade. As one Black Watch officer remembered 'this was not for a day or two days but week after week' and after nine o'clock in the morning 'a death-like stillness would creep over everything, both sides suffering too much to be able to add any more suffering to each other'. Small wonder that another Black Watch officer, Brigadier-General A. G. Wauchope, was 'lost in wonder' when they eventually reached the outskirts of Baghdad and saw 'its mosques and minarets'. It had been a long and bruising campaign: 'For although I am lying in a grove of date-palms, it is fifteen months since I have seen a tree of any kind; it is fifteen months since I have seen a house or lain under a roof; and this girl coming towards me with hesitating steps, clothed in rags and patches, this little date-seller with her pale face and dark eyes, her empty basket resting on her small well-shaped head – this is the first woman I have seen or spoken to for a year.'[31]

Baghdad eventually fell on 11 March 1917. Maude's success was helped by the fact that the Turks had been forced to withdraw forces to serve on a new front which had opened in Palestine, but he deserves full credit for restoring the badly battered British and Indian divisions and for taking the war back to the Turks. Over 9,000 prisoners were taken and the fall of the city was the first solid Allied triumph of the war; The Black Watch still count the 'Baghdad Bell' as one of their proudest battle trophies. Unfortunately Maude died of cholera in November, but by then he had created plans for his forces to advance up the Tigris towards Mosul, with its vital oilfields, and further up the Euphrates towards Ramadi, while another force proceeded up the Diyala towards Kirkuk.

Palestine 1917–18

The next great prize was the defeat of the Turkish forces in Palestine and the operation was entrusted to an Egyptian expeditionary force of 88,000 soldiers under the command of Allenby, who had been sacked after his failure at Arras in April 1917. Before taking up his new command he had been warned by Lloyd George that he had to take Jerusalem by Christmas as a gift to the British nation and that he

should demand what he needed to make sure the enterprise succeeded. In fact there was already a pressing need to attack the Turkish
forces, who were being reinforced in Aleppo in present-day Syria for
an offensive which would be known as 'Yildirim', or lightning strike,
aimed at retaking Baghdad. If Allenby could engage the Turks
through Palestine it would force them to divide their forces, passing
the initiative back to the British. There were other imperatives. With
no sign of a breakthrough on the Western Front Lloyd George hoped
that the defeat of Turkey would be a major blow to the Germans and
perhaps hasten the end of the war without further costly offensives in
France and Flanders. From a strategic standpoint, the British and the
French had already drawn up secret plans to carve up areas of influence
in the Middle East following the expected collapse of the Ottoman
Empire.

From the outset Allenby recognised that he needed overwhelming
superiority over the Turks if he were to avoid the setbacks that
doomed the forces at Gallipoli and Kut, but getting those reinforcements in the second half of 1917 was another matter. The priority
continued to be the Western Front and with the Battle of Passchendaele eating up resources it took time and much subtle diplomacy to
build up his forces. Eventually these consisted of a desert mounted
corps consisting of ANZAC and British cavalry and yeomanry regiments, and two infantry corps, one of which, XXI Corps, contained
the 52nd (Lowland) Division. This latter division now included, in
addition to the battalions previously listed, the Lowland Mounted
Brigade (1/1st Ayrshire Yeomanry). Their objective was to break into
Palestine through Gaza and Beersheba and destroy the defending
Turkish Eighth Army under the command of Freiherr Friedrich Kress
von Kressenstein. Allenby had also requested and received modern
warplanes, and the use of DH4 bombers to carry out air strikes was
central to his plans, which were based on hitting the enemy hard and
then deploying mobile forces, including cavalry, to take them by
surprise.

Allenby's battle-plan was innovatory, yet simple, and was based
largely on his reading of the terrain over which the fighting would
take place. On 27 October, following a huge bombardment from
artillery and from British and French warships lying off the coast, Gaza
was attacked while XXI Corps prepared for the break-in battle which

would follow. This confirmed to the Turks and their German advisers that Allenby was using the tactics of the Western Front and that assault would come from the waiting ground troops.[32] However, at the same time and in great secrecy Allenby shifted the emphasis of his attack towards Beersheba which was quickly surrounded by a brilliant flanking attack to the east. At the end of a battle which lasted all day on 31 October, the issue was decided with a full-scale cavalry charge into the town carried out by the 4th Australian Light Horse.

The fall of Beersheba allowed Allenby's forces to put greater pressure on the Turkish positions at Gaza and its defences were successfully stormed on 7 November, leaving the defenders no option but to retreat north up the coastal littoral towards Askalon and Jaffa. During this mobile phase of the battle the Turks fought with great determination but they were demoralised by the weight of the attack and by the use of British warplanes to strafe their fleeing columns. Although there were concerns in London that Allenby might repeat Townshend's mistakes during the Kut operations by overstretching his lines of communication, the strength and aggression of the British attack brought them to the western approaches to Jerusalem by the end of November. In some awe, a medical officer in 52nd (Lowland) Division recorded that his fellow Scots were not only fighting over the biblical lands of the Old and New Testaments but they were also following in the footsteps of the crusaders: 'We felt that every rock was hallowed by sacred memories. Every peak as it looked down on us in its stern unchanging dignity, had watched the hundred holy battles that swayed to and fro along the valleys round Jerusalem. And we felt that they stood over us in judgement.'[33] To great acclaim the holy city fell on 8 December after a determined attack by the 53rd and 60th divisions forced the remaining defenders to evacuate their positions. Three days later, in a carefully stage-managed operation, Allenby and his staff entered the city to take possession of it and secure the holy places. To avoid hurting Islamic feelings the Mosque of Omar was put under the protection of Indian Muslim troops and the guards lining the streets came from the four home countries, and Australia and New Zealand and France and Italy. It was not the end of the war in Palestine, but it was the beginning of the end.

Allenby's next objectives were to move into Judea and to regroup to prevent Turkish counter-attacks before moving on to his next

objectives, Beirut, Damascus and Aleppo. However, to accomplish
that he would need additional troops to reinforce his own men and to
protect the lines of communication as he pushed north; at the very
least, he told the War Office, he would need an additional sixteen
divisions, including one of cavalry. In the short term his forces
invested Jaffa, which fell after the 52nd (Lowland) Division seized
the banks of the River Auja in an operation which demanded surprise
and resulted in 'the most furious hand-to-hand encounters of the
campaign'. Finding their way blocked by Turks who fought to the last
round the men of 1/5th King's Own Scottish Borderers 'drove them
towards the river, and as the Turks would not surrender, into it'.[34]

This proved to be the last action undertaken by the majority of the
Scottish regiments in Palestine. Before the question of reinforcing
Allenby could be addressed by the War Office the Allies were faced by
a crisis on the Western Front in March 1918 when a German offensive
pushed back the British line some 40 miles between Arras and La Fere,
the old Somme battlefield (see Chapter Ten). During the fighting the
British lost 163,000 casualties and the need for rapid reinforcement
had come at the very moment when Allenby wanted to continue the
push towards Aleppo and he was forced to order two infantry
divisions, nine yeomanry regiments and one divisional artillery unit
to move to France. One of the divisions was 52nd (Lowland), which
embarked for Marseilles at Alexandria aboard seven troopships escorted by six Japanese destroyers. Later they were replaced by the two
Indian divisions from Mesopotamia, which allowed the 1st Highland
Light Infantry, 2nd Black Watch and 1st Seaforths to see out the war in
Palestine. All three took part in the final operations, which did not
begin until September to allow for reinforcements from India, and the
decisive battle took place at Megiddo on 19–21 September. After a
fierce artillery assault infantry and cavalry pushed through the Turkish
lines, harrying the enemy as they tried to escape and pushing north
into the Plain of Esdraelon. The way to Damascus was now open and
with Turkish authority collapsing the end of the campaign was in
sight. On 31 October an armistice was signed. It was one of the
cheapest and most successful campaigns of the war: in the space of five
weeks Allenby's forces had advanced 300 miles, captured 75,000
Turkish soldiers and 360 guns for the loss of 6,000 casualties. And as
Allenby's biographer makes clear, it was a resounding success for a

general who thought his career had been blighted by his failure at Arras eighteen months earlier: 'in the course of operations three Turkish armies had been destroyed and three provinces, Palestine, the Lebanon and Syria, liberated'.[35]

All told, some 50,000 Scots served in the four operations which were devised by the 'easterners' to produce an alternative way of defeating Germany. The expected breakthrough never happened but Allenby's operations defeated the Turks and helped to settle, for good or ill, the post-war shape of the Middle East: the former Ottoman provinces were divided up between Britain and France and a Jewish homeland was settled in Palestine. By far the bloodiest and most wasteful campaign had been Gallipoli, which was a story of avoidable failure and wasted opportunities, and the memory of the fighting on that barren peninsula lingered longest in the minds of the soldiers who fought there. In an open letter to the *Scotsman*, Dr William Ewing, a chaplain with the 52nd (Lowland) Division, said simply that 'the sights I have seen will never be erased from memory' and that the spectacle of so many wounded and mutilated men provided 'some conception of what this strife costs'.[36] With conditions worse than anything witnessed on the Western Front and a more concentrated rate of attrition Gallipoli was a long nightmare, and although some soldiers had positive memories, even those were deeply shadowed by the brutality of the campaign. William Begbie, 1/7th Royal Scots, looked back with pride and some amusement when he thought of his sixteen-year-old self attacking the Turkish lines (in common with many other soldiers Begbie was under-age and had lied about his age when he enlisted in 1/7th Royal Scots in August 1914 – he was in fact only fifteen). However, he also recorded that the fighting was brutal and deadly, with the enemy producing 'such a terrific fire that our Company fell in bundles'.[37]

Not everyone was sorry to have served in such exotic climes. For the British Regulars who served in the Indian Army divisions in Mesopotamia, the valley of the Tigris and the Euphrates carried memories of service in India, albeit in a much hotter climate and against a more determined enemy. They were also doing what the British Army had been doing for generations and, like most old soldiers, simply got on with the task in hand. Even so, it has to be said that during the campaign to relieve Kut the 2nd Black Watch and 1st Seaforths suffered casualties at a rate which equalled the worst fighting on the Western Front.

Provided that malaria was avoided Salonika was a safer front, with fewer set-piece battles and without the stress caused by non-stop bombardment. It also offered moments of reverie when the war seemed to be a distant drum and it was possible to experience a different kind of pleasure. Even allowing for poetic licence, the future Hugh MacDiarmid was able to 'shake off the dust of Macedon' in a rest camp and tell his former pupils that he had 'little to do but eat, sleep and bathe and remember old friends' in a landscape where 'the bathing is splendid, along a long sweep of beach (reached by a break-neck of goats' track down steep cliffs) in waters clear to a great depth and with a fine, smooth, sandy bottom'.[38] Added to that was the sheer animal pleasure of being abroad in an age when travel was generally the preserve of the wealthy and even travel within Scotland could be costly. Many soldiers' diaries record the pleasure of travelling through the Mediterranean on great liners pressed into service as troop carriers, almost as if, bar the fighting, it were all a delightful cruise.[39]

However, all told, the fighting against the Ottoman forces had been a long and unforgiving experience. The historian of the 52nd (Lowland Division) recorded that in three years of service in the Mediterranean theatre the Scots had 'fought in all kinds of country, and in all weathers and temperatures, ranging from the hard frost and blizzards of the moorlands of Gallipoli, and the bitterly cold hail storms of the Judaean Highlands, to the midday heat of summer in the desert'.[40]

6 The Land, the Sea and the Clash of the Battle Fleets

Soldiers coming home on leave were a regular sight in Scotland's towns and cities throughout the war. Other manifestations of the conflict were the returning wounded who were landed from their hospital ships at Leith and Dundee before being dispersed to hospitals all over Scotland. To treat wounded or recuperating servicemen hospitals in Scotland allocated agreed numbers of beds, which were administered by the army's military hospital system, and the political activist Harry McShane never forgot the wail of ambulances as they drove their charges through nighttime Glasgow from Central Station to Bellahouston Hospital, reminding people of the harsher realities of war.[1] For most families, though, it was the men in uniform who provided the best reminder that there was a war being fought. Leave was granted to men serving on the Western Front – soldiers serving in the Mediterranean theatre received local leave in Cairo or Alexandria, a very different experience – and it was not uncommon to see service personnel in uniform, sometimes still bearing the signs of wear and tear of life in the front line. Fourteen days away from the front line was a coveted privilege but for many Scots it was a bittersweet experience, as travelling time was included in the pass. At best a journey home could take 24 hours, at worst it could be three times longer. For everyone the long trail home began at a railhead catching a train to Boulogne or Le Havre, followed by a Channel crossing, a leave train to Waterloo or Victoria and then a dash across London to King's Cross or Euston for the journey north. Even when set against today's timetables it is easy to see that home leave for a soldier from the Highlands or Western Isles involved a huge amount of travelling. There were canteens along the route, run by the Young Women's Christian Association (YWCA) and other organizations, but for the homecoming Jock the journey could be a lengthy and tiring business.

For Private Alex Brownie, 1/4th Gordons, the journey in winter proved to be even more arduous. Having arrived at Huntly from Aberdeen he found himself in the middle of a violent snowstorm and had to walk the last 10 miles to the family croft at Forgue. Getting as far as Carlisle also proved to be a marathon for John Jackson who received his first home leave in October 1917 and spent 'a very busy, very tiring, week visiting friends in the district'.[2]

The irrepressible Jackson enjoyed his time at home but others thought it a dislocating experience. On leave in London, John Reith, a Territorial Army officer serving with 1/5th Cameronians and later to be the first director-general of the BBC, found a place he did not recognise, a brash metropolis far removed from the harsh realities of front-line life in Flanders. The city 'irritated him beyond expression' and the sheer tawdriness of civilian life prompted him to ask, 'was this what one was fighting for: loafers, profiteers, the whole vulgar throng on the streets?' Reith's prickly temperament had already led to quarrels with the commanding officer and adjutant of 1/5th Cameronians over matters of discipline and dress, and by September 1917 he had transferred to the Royal Engineers (1/2nd Highland Field Company RE), a posting which was more suited to his earlier training. But he was not alone in feeling awkward while on leave. A soldier in the amalgamated 4/5th Black Watch found himself back home in Dundee towards the end of the war and could not bring himself to say anything to his family about the conditions on the Western Front, even though the state of his uniform did not leave much open to doubt. Like others of his generation he found it easier to keep his feelings to himself and preferred not to worry his parents lest they started to fret about his safety.[3] Perhaps the best articulation of that emotion came from Harry Lauder. After the death in action of his son, Lauder threw himself into war work by entertaining troops in the field with a series of concerts on the Western Front. By meeting and talking to his audiences he reached a deeper understanding of what the frontline soldiers were experiencing. One such visit in 1917 prompted him to imagine a soldier – 'Donald, or Jock might be his name, or Andy' – as he came back home on his first leave to his home town:

And at last he comes to his own old home. He will stop and look around a bit. Maybe he has seen that old house a thousand times out there, tried to remember every line and corner of it. And maybe, as he looks down the quiet village street, he is thinking of how different France is. And, deep down in his heart, Jock is glad that everything is as it was, and that nothing has been changed. He could not tell you why; he could not put his feeling into words. But it's there, deep down, and the truer and the keener because it is so deep.[4]

Lauder's reputation has been sullied by criticism of his vaudeville songs and his comic portrayal of music-hall Scottish characters but he had a keen insight into the character of the soldiers he met in France. He certainly deserved the knighthood he received in 1919 for his services to the war effort.

Other soldiers had different experiences of homecoming. As soon as they reached home they wanted to get out of uniform and put on civilian clothes, but even that simple desire had its dangers. It was not uncommon for soldiers on leave to be given a white feather – the sign of cowardice – by young girls who thought that the man in question was shirking his military duties. Leave also helped to sharpen the differences between life at home and life in the front line and made men aware of what they were missing. Bill Hanlan, an orphan, came back to Edinburgh after serving with 1/8th Royal Scots at the Battle of the Somme and decided not to return to the front at the end of his fortnight's leave. This was desertion, for which the penalty could be death, but he managed to avoid arrest for five months before he joined up again under a different name, this time as a gunner in the Royal Artillery. Ironically, he witnessed a military execution when his machine-gun team provided cover for the grim event 'because when anybody was bein' shot there might ha' been other sojers no' pleased at that, no' wantin' it and goin' tae cause a bit o' trouble'.[5]

Of the 346 British and Commonwealth soldiers executed during the war – mainly for desertion, cowardice or murder – 39 were Scots, reflecting the proportional representation of Scots in the forces. All of them were convicted under the terms of the military law of the day and the murderers amongst them could have expected execution under civil law, but it is also clear that a number were condemned to death while suffering from 'shellshock', the catch-all description for a wide range of nervous and mental disorders brought on by the stresses of combat. Amongst that number of unfortunates was Private John Docherty, 9th Black Watch, a veteran of Loos, who was executed in February 1916 after deserting for a second time, despite the fact that two doctors found that he was 'suffering from a marked degree of neurasthenia'.[6] His fate was sealed because he had already been sentenced to death for an earlier desertion, and although it had been commuted to five years' penal servitude by then, he had deserted again. The fact that there had already been five other desertions in the battalion also counted against him and he was shot with eleven other soldiers on 15 February 1916. It seemed to have escaped the notice of the authorities that the site of the execution could not have been more appropriate: within the abattoir at Mazingarbe. Along with the others his execution was hushed up during the war and only recently have the official court-martial papers been made available for public consultation. It is still a highly sensitive subject. In 1998 the government refused a request to grant a blanket pardon to those executed; the call was backed by the Scottish parliament and the lobbying for a pardon continues through a number of bodies including an organisation aptly named 'Shot at Dawn'. To modern sensibilities it was a barbarous practice. Only one in ten death sentences was actually carried out, but at the time the threat of execution was taken seriously and was clearly a deterrent. Bill Hanlan could have remained on the run, working in his brother's fruit-mongering business, but, as he remembered later in life, 'if ah wis caught ah was feared for what the result wid be. Ah got the wind up.'[7]

What saved him was his change of name when he rejoined the army. By that stage in the war conscription had made it more or less impossible for any able-bodied male to avoid detection and measures such as the Defence of the Realm Act had been put in place to tighten up internal security. Passed on 8 August 1914 and with half a dozen subsequent extensions DORA (as it became known) provided the government with a wide range of powers, from press censorship to the imprisonment of war protesters, and it allowed civilians to be tried by courts martial under section 5 of the Army Act.[8] As we shall see, DORA was also used to imprison a large number of people, many of them Scottish members of the Independent Labour Party (ILP) who objected to the war on moral or ethical grounds (see Chapter Nine).

However, it was the move towards conscription that brought the male population of the country under closer control. Long resisted, compulsory service became inevitable as the number of volunteers began to fall off in 1915. Under the terms of the National Registration Act of July 1915 all persons, male and female, aged between 15 and 65 registered for possible service while men from the register aged 18 to 41 would sign up or 'attest' but would only be called up as and when they were needed, depending on such factors as the importance of their jobs or whether or not they were married. The object of the exercise was to enlist bachelors engaged in unskilled work, but because the attestation was left in the hands of local tribunals, who were not always the best judges of a man's suitability or were open to influence, the scheme frequently fell foul of corrupt practices. In 1916 the army's director of recruiting complained that tribunals were more lenient in Scotland but this was refuted by the Scottish Office which used census figures to show that Scotland had less surplus labour than any other part of the country.[9] Charles Murray, Aberdeenshire poet, captured the spirit of the process in his poem 'Dockens Afore his Peers (Exemption Tribunal)' in which a garrulous farmer, John Watt o' Dockenhill, puts the case for his son and plays a trump card by reminding the members of the tribunal of the debts they owe him:

> Hoot, Mains, hae mind, I'm doon for you some sma' thing wi' the bank;
> Aul' Larickleys, I saw you throu', an' this is a' my thank;
> An' Gutteryloan, that time ye broke, to Dockenhill ye cam' –
> 'Total exemption.' Thank ye, sirs. Fat say ye till a dram?[10]

The registration scheme helped to maintain the Liberals' belief in the voluntary principle – most Scottish Liberal MPs were opposed to conscription – but its operation proved to be cumbersome and unworkable and the Military Service Acts of January and May 1916 brought in conscription for the first time in the country's history. The first Act introduced conscription of all single men and childless widowers aged 18 to 41 and the second extended the age range to 50. (A further act in 1918 put the age up again to 56 but it was never enacted.) Under the terms of the legislation men could apply for exemption on grounds of ill health, or if they were employed on war work of national importance, or if they were the sole breadwinner with dependents. There were also clauses dealing with objection to service on the grounds of conscience but, far from providing a liberal alternative, the treatment of conscientious objectors became one of the scandals of the war and involved large numbers of Scots who were opposed to taking part in the fighting. The acts also changed the complexion of the army. Of the 5,704,416 soldiers who served between 1914 and 1918 over half, 3,257,697, were conscripts, the majority infantry, and as a result the regional identity of many regiments was gradually eroded. By the end of the war, men who joined one regiment would find themselves wearing a different cap badge and the Scottish regiments were not exempt from the changes. For example, the poet Donald MacDonald of North Uist (Domhnall Ruadh Choruna) joined up in the Camerons but served in the West Riding Field Regiment, Royal Artillery, where he insisted on wearing his Cameron cap badge.

If the familiar figure of the kilted Scottish soldier home on leave was a constant reminder of events in France it was not the only sign that the country was engaged in a long and increasingly arduous war. By far the most visible presence of the war effort was provided by the warships of the Royal Navy, which had major bases at Rosyth in the Firth of Forth, at Invergordon in the Cromarty Firth and at Scapa Flow in Orkney. The other naval bases in Scotland were Dundee (3rd Sloop Flotilla and Northern Destroyer Patrol), Granton (4th Sloop Flotilla, 16th Minesweeping Flotilla and Southern Destroyer Patrol), Oban (13th and 14th Minesweeping Flotillas) and Kirkwall (21st Minesweeping Flotilla). However, the most dramatic manifestation of British naval power was to be found at the Rosyth base, which was home to the navy's Battle Cruiser Fleet (Battle Cruiser Force from November 1916), an impressive fleet of ten battle-cruisers and attached cruisers and destroyers under the command of the flamboyant Vice-Admiral Sir David Beatty in his flagship HMS *Lion*. Moored to the west of the Forth Railway Bridge, these sleek warships trumpeted Britain's naval superiority. Here was the shield against German's bombastic pre-war pretensions to create a bigger and more powerful naval force, and here was one of the swords which would one day 'meet and overwhelm the [German] High Seas Fleet in some second and even greater Trafalgar'.[11] The German Navy felt the same way:

the expected confrontation with the Royal Navy was known to them as 'Der Tag', 'The Day'.

The senior officer in Scotland was Vice-Admiral Sir Robert Swinburne Lowry, who had been appointed Senior Officer to the Coast of Scotland on 1 July 1913 but was promoted to Admiral Commanding on the Coast of Scotland shortly after the outbreak of war. Later, this was amended to Commander-in-Chief, Rosyth, and despite minor amendments this was the title used by Lowry's successor, Admiral Sir Frederick Tower Hamilton, when he took over command on 1 July 1916.[12] However, despite the grand titles both Lowry and Hamilton presided over a confused situation, albeit not of their making. Although the Royal Navy's fleet was the most powerful naval force in the world, all three of its Scottish bases were scantily defended. None had defences against submarine attack; Rosyth and Invergordon had some shore artillery but the guns were only capable of engaging light surface ships. The problem was not just lack of money but also a turf war conducted within the Admiralty about which base should house the Grand Fleet.

Central to this squabble was the First Sea Lord, Admiral of the Fleet Sir John 'Jacky' Fisher, who used his six years in office before the war to stymie any attempt to develop Rosyth as the navy's main North Sea base, both for the defence of the British coastline and to prosecute any war against Germany. Designated by the government as such on 5 March 1904, Rosyth, on the north shore of the Forth estuary, had much to recommend it. It was only 375 miles from the German coast, it possessed sufficient accommodation for a modern battle fleet and it had access to the main London to Aberdeen railway line, an important consideration for supply and re-supply and the movement of ships' crews. Rosyth's only drawback was the presence of the huge railway bridge which had come into service in 1890: if it was attacked and destroyed the wreckage could trap the warships in their mooring places. (Given the strength of the bridge and the relative weakness of contemporary aerial bombs, this was an unlikely eventuality.) Fisher thought that Cromarty was a better bet, despite its remoteness, and would have preferred using the Humber in England but for its shallow waters and the difficulty in defending it against mine and submarine attack. As a result he prevented any sizable sums of money being spent on Rosyth because of its 'beastly bridge', with the result that the port's two dry docks were not due for completion before 1916 and when war broke out the base was poorly defended.[13]

During the same period Scapa Flow became the main base for the summer manoeuvres of the Grand Fleet, which on 4 August 1914 came under the command of Admiral Sir John Jellicoe, a gunnery specialist and Second Sea Lord, whose flagship was the dreadnought HMS *Iron Duke*. With its huge expanse of water, 10 miles long and 8 miles wide, Scapa Flow was a natural remote anchorage and it provided quick access to the waters to be patrolled between Scotland and Norway as part of Britain's naval policy of 'distant blockade'. This involved cutting off the approaches to the Atlantic and staging aggressive patrols to wear down Germany's strength while trying to tempt the Imperial Navy into the North Sea for what would be the decisive naval battle of the war. The Orkney base possessed three main entrances, each of which had strong currents and awkward tides, one reason why it had been thought unnecessary to spend money on defending them. From a strategic point of view Scapa was an ideal base but, as we have seen, for the crews of the Grand Fleet and the sailors who manned the base the posting was not popular. There were also problems with supply. Everything had to be brought in by sea and the journey south meant crossing the uncertain waters of the Pentland Firth and then a long winding rail trip from Thurso to Inverness and then on to England through Perth or Edinburgh. The weather too could be unkind. While the summer was often a delight, with its long days and blue skies, the winter was the exact opposite, with short dark days, constant storms and, for the men, constant gloom.

From 1909 onwards Orcadians became used to the sight of up to a hundred grey-hulled warships using their waters as a secure anchorage during the long summer days. It was no different at the end of July 1914, when the Grand Fleet slipped into its moorings under cover of a seasonal fog following its summer manoeuvres. In 1914 the Grand Fleet consisted of four battle squadrons, a battle-cruiser squadron, two cruiser squadrons and a light cruiser squadron plus accompanying destroyer flotillas, and by 1 August ninety-six ships were in position in the Flow together with an armada of coalers, auxiliary vessels and drifters pressed into service as temporary minesweepers. The only defence against submarines was provided by destroyers patrolling the main entrances at Hoxa, Switha and Hoy, and Jellicoe was uneasily aware that despite the base's distance from Germany his fleet was still prey to submarines.

His disquiet was confirmed on 9 August when the cruiser HMS *Birmingham* rammed and sank a German submarine, *U-15*, off Fair Isle to the north of Orkney. The previous day the same boat had tried to attack the dreadnought HMS *Monarch* while it was engaged on gunnery practice, and while the sinking pleased Jellicoe it was an unpleasant reminder of the reach of the German submarine fleet. Three weeks later there was a further scare when lookouts reported a submarine inside the Flow while a dozen dreadnoughts were engaged in the time-consuming and potentially dangerous business of re-coaling. The incident, later known as the First Battle of Scapa Flow, caused a good deal of panic before the ships managed to slip into the safety of the Pentland Firth. No trace of any attack was ever found but the incident convinced Jellicoe that the safest place for his dread-noughts was on the high seas. He was further persuaded in the middle of October when one of Beatty's battle-cruiser squadrons reported seeing a submarine as they approached the anchorage at Invergordon. An accompanying destroyer opened fire but the only casualty was a baby, slightly injured when a shell fell on a house in the village of Jemimaville on the shores of the Cromarty Firth. But after the 'Battle of Jemimaville', as the action became known, Jellicoe had had enough. Following the torpedoing of the *Pathfinder* and three elderly cruisers in September (see Chapter One) he took the Grand Fleet to sea and they took refuge on the west coast of Scotland, at Loch Awe and Loch Na Keal in the island of Mull, and at Lough Swilly in Northern Ireland; they did not return to Scapa until the middle of November.

The scares prompted the government to act and steps were taken to defend Scapa Flow against attack. More anti-submarine nets were hung, minefields were sown, 48 trawlers were converted to gunboats and block ships were sunk to narrow the entrance channels, which were protected further by defensive booms which could be raised and lowered. The defences at Rosyth and Cromarty were also strengthened. However, an unusually stormy winter meant that none of the work was completed until the beginning of 1915. During that period there was a further incident which raised questions about using Scapa Flow as a main base. On 16 December, under the command of Franz von Hipper, a squadron of German cruisers and battle-cruisers protected by destroyers shelled Whitby, Scarborough and Hartlepool in a daring hit-and-run raid aimed at luring the Grand Fleet into the North Sea for a pitched battle with the Imperial Fleet. This did not happen, as neither side made contact – having reached the Dogger Bank the Imperial Fleet withdrew due to poor visibility – but the raid on the east coast towns humiliated the Royal Navy. The damage was slight but the outrage was great and in the aftermath it was decided to deploy the navy's faster battle-cruiser squadrons at Rosyth, where they became the Battle Cruiser Fleet (BCF) at the beginning of 1915, charged with the responsibility of acting as the Grand Fleet's advance scouts. At the same time the bulk of the fleet, now renamed the Battle Fleet (BF), remained at Scapa Flow under Jellicoe's command.

Beatty's three battle-cruiser squadrons left a lasting impression on Fife and nearby Edinburgh, not least because the fast and powerful warships were distinctive and attractive to the eye. Developed in the period between 1904 and 1910, they were very much Fisher's creation and were supposed to combine the speed and reach of the armoured cruiser and the strength and firepower of the new dreadnought battleships. With a maximum speed of 25 knots they were fast, but that speed and agility had been bought at the expense of armoured protection. Even so, they were still thought to be capable of taking on and destroying larger battleships by virtue of the longer range of their large-calibre guns. As the navy's spearhead, they were engaged in the first heavy fighting of the war and had proved their worth, sinking German battleships and grabbing the headlines. On 28 August 1914 a mixed force of battle-cruisers, cruisers and destroyers fought a running battle with German warships in the Heligoland Bight, north-west of the German coast, which resulted in the sinking of three German light cruisers with the loss of 1,200 lives. This was followed by the Battle of the Falklands in December when Vice-Admiral Frederick Doveton Sturdee's battle-cruiser squadron sailed to the South Atlantic and used their speed and superior firepower to destroy the German warships *Scharnhorst*, *Gneisenau*, *Leipzig* and *Nürnberg*. Sturdee's victory was particularly gratifying as the German squadron had already sunk two British warships at the earlier Battle of Coronel. At a time when British naval superiority was taken for granted, the lean powerful lines of Beatty's battle-cruisers in the Firth of Forth became a reassuring sight and helped to convince the public that all was well at a time when there seemed to be nothing but bad news coming out of France and Flanders.

The presence of Beatty added to the high romance. At the age of 29 he had been one of the navy's youngest captains and in 1910 he became the youngest rear-admiral since Nelson. Married to an American heiress he was a wealthy man and he enjoyed rarefied social connections which saw him become Churchill's naval secretary and thus an important influence on policy. With his raffish looks, his cap worn at a slant and his elegantly cut six-buttoned wide-lapelled reefer jacket he was a distinctive figure whose name was never far away from newspaper headlines. He encouraged his men to be equally flam-boyant and his squadron commanders and ships' captains were his equals in seeking the limelight. Being a member of the BCF was not just a duty: Beatty wanted it to be an obligation which demanded responsibilities, and a cult of brotherhood quickly sprang up amongst the ships' crews. For example, the ships of the 1st Battle Cruiser Squadron – HMSs *Lion*, *Tiger*, *Princess Royal* and *Queen Mary* – were nicknamed the 'Splendid Cats' and much was forgiven of their captains provided that they displayed Nelsonian dash and élan. However, there was a negative side to the pomp. The gunnery skills of the ships left much to be desired, signals communication was poor and discipline could be lax. Compared to the hours spent training in the unpromising surroundings of Scapa Flow, where there were few home comforts, the BCF crews seemed to enjoy one long round of action at sea followed by adulation at home. This perception was increased when the BCF engaged a German squadron at the Battle of the Dogger Bank on 24 January 1915 when their battle-cruisers and the Harwich destroyer force sank the German battleship *Blücher* and badly damaged the *Derfflinger* and the *Seydlitz*. The victory was met with acclaim when the ships returned to their bases, but inside the navy the reaction was more sanguine.[14] Far from being the rout claimed by the press the action had revealed that the gunnery had been so bad that the severely damaged *Derfflinger* and *Seydlitz* had been allowed to escape. Equally disconcerting, *Lion* had been hit sixteen times and had revealed to the Germans her vulnerability to the flash of bursting shells. Even Jellicoe was displeased, angrily dismissing the action as 'a terrible failure'.[15]

However, at a time when the British badly needed victories and an antidote to the stalemate on the Western Front, Beatty's battle-cruisers were fêted, especially in their home base in Scotland, where they were quickly adopted by the people of Edinburgh and Fife. Unlike the crews of the BF in Orkney, the BCF's sailors could leave their ships and experience the pleasures of life ashore. For the ratings this was restricted to organised football matches and to a 'wet' canteen at Rosyth which had been established by the Edinburgh brewers William McEwan Ltd for the sale of beer at three pence a pint, but for the officers it was rather different. Edinburgh was a short distance away by train or ferry and uniformed officers made regular pilgrimages to the capital where sporting and social clubs made them honorary members for the duration of the war. (The prestigious New Club on Princes Street limited the privilege to ranks above commander.)[16] Those with social connections were invited on local shoots or played tennis and golf or simply enjoyed a time out of life when they were free to 'lunch in Edinburgh, go to the cinema or walk down Princes Street looking at the shop windows'.[17] For those of an amorous disposition there was even the chance of assignations. Beatty used a room in the smart North British Hotel (today the Balmoral) to carry on an affair with a fellow officer's wife, and when one of his squadron commanders, Rear-Admiral William Pakenham, was asked at a civic reception if he was married, he replied, 'No, madam, no. I keep a loose woman in Edinburgh.'[18] There was method behind this seemingly lackadaisical approach. To make sure that officers returned to their ships in the event of a sudden emergency there was a sophisticated recall system whereby Edinburgh cinemas would flash a message on their screens, and the hall porters of various hotels and clubs were kept in discreet telephone contact with the flagship, *Lion*.

It was difficult to keep such goings-on secret and the many freedoms enjoyed by the BCF were fiercely resented by the men of the BF at Scapa who thought that they were doing a real job of work while 'the show-offs had all the glamour'. For their part, the BCF believed that they were the real fighters in the front line whereas the BF skulked in its northern fastness without hearing a shot fired in anger.[19] Rivalry in any force is usually a good thing but at times there were real tensions between Beatty's boys and the main BF, leading to allegations that the BCF was only interested in personal glory. Those feelings were exacerbated in May 1915 when Jellicoe detached the

5th Battle Squadron to reinforce Beatty at Rosyth, thus giving him command of five modern dreadnoughts, including HMSs *Barham*, *Warspite* and *Queen Elizabeth*. This was done to allow one of the BCF's formations – Hood's 3rd Battle Cruiser Squadron – to leave for some much-needed gunnery practice at Scapa, but the change gave Beatty command of a much more powerful force in the event of any German breakout into the North Sea. This was to come sooner than any of the British commanders expected.

At the end of February Admiral Hugo von Pohl, the commander in chief of the German fleet, died of cancer of the liver and was replaced by Reinhard Scheer, an aggressive and forceful commander who believed in taking the naval war to the British. Whereas von Pohl had carried out the wishes of the high command not to risk the fleet in a set-piece battle with Jellicoe's Grand Fleet and had put to sea only five times since the outbreak of hostilities, Scheer was anxious to provoke the Royal Navy into action by attacking the British mainland. He was also committed to using every weapon at his disposal – not just surface ships but also submarines and airships – in combined air-sea operations. His ideas were well received and there followed a succession of offensive operations against British targets aimed at prompting Jellicoe into responding. At the end of March Lowestoft was bombarded and a few days later, on the night of 2/3 April, two airships bombed Edinburgh. One of them, *L14*, made landfall at St Abbs Head and attempted to attack Rosyth and the Forth Railway Bridge but only succeeded in bombing the centre of Edinburgh, hitting the Castle Rock and George Watson's College and damaging property in the Marchmont and Grassmarket areas. A second airship, *L22*, arrived over Newcastle and attacked Edinburgh from the south. Amongst the houses destroyed was a family home at 39 Lauriston Place, which received a direct hit, giving the McLaren family an unwelcome experience of what modern warfare had become: 'The 100lb Zeppelin bomb exploded on hitting the roof, causing extreme damage throughout the house, particularly to the roof, top landing and staircase, also blowing out all the windows. The nose cap travelled down through the middle landing, then the sitting room and finally was stopped by the stone floor in the kitchen pantry.'[20] During the raid thirty-three bombs were dropped by the two airships and ten lives were lost – seven adults and three children – but due to wartime reporting restrictions the locations of the raid were not mentioned in any of the Scottish newspapers. A second raid took place a month later but on this occasion the results were farcical: *L14* overshot the Forth estuary and found itself flying over Arbroath at the mouth of the Tay estuary where its bombs were dropped harmlessly on farming land. It made its escape over Fife Ness. Things went no better for its sister ship: *L20* arrived over Montrose at 9.53 p.m. on the night of 2/3 May but continued flying westwards until it reached Loch Ness at midnight. Although it managed to leave Scottish airspace over Peterhead at 2.40 a.m. the following morning and limp back to Norway, it was forced to crash-land after running out of fuel.[21]

Frustrated by the failure of the raids – during the Lowestoft attack the only opposition had come from the Harwich destroyer force – Scheer decided to use Hipper's squadron to bombard Sunderland, which was close enough to Rosyth to allow Beatty to put the BCF to sea. A screen of submarines was waiting for him, with the main German surface fleet lying further out in the North Sea in the Dogger Bank area but still close enough to engage the British battle-cruisers. Scheer reckoned that it would take up to eight hours for Jellicoe to put to sea from Scapa and in that time the damage would have been done. On 17 May four mine-laying submarines were dispatched to lay their deadly weapons off the Forth estuary (*U72*), the Cromarty Firth (*U74*), and Orkney (*U75* and *UC3*). At the same time, seven attack submarines were deployed off the Firth of Forth while three others patrolled further to the north to intercept any warships leaving Scapa Flow. The trap had been set but a combination of bad weather and delays in making the German fleet battle-worthy meant that Scheer had to abandon the plan to attack Sunderland as by 1 June the U-boats were running out of fuel. Unwilling to lose the threat posed by the U-boat screen and their sown mines, Scheer decided to make a feint toward the Norwegian coast with Hipper's battle-cruisers while moving his main fleet into the North Sea. The result would be the same: Beatty would take his battle-cruisers towards the minefields and submarines and any ships which survived would be picked off by the waiting German warships.

It was a sound plan but unknown to Scheer its main details were known to the Royal Navy. From the outset of the war the Admiralty cryptanalysts, led by Dundee-born Sir Alfred Ewing, had cracked

German radio codes and the Naval Intelligence Department in Room 40 was able to intercept and read German directional signals used to control their ships and submarines in the North Sea. From intercepts of radio traffic picked up by a network of listening stations which stretched from the Wash to the Shetland Islands, Room 40 was able to build up a fairly precise picture of German ship and U-boat movements, the type of craft used, their characteristics and sometimes even their commander.

The records of Room 40's intelligence about German movements in May 1916 show that the Admiralty had a good idea of Scheer's intentions and was able to pass this on to Jellicoe in Orkney.[22] There were also other sources of evidence: on 27 May *U-74* was sunk by four armed trawlers to the east of Peterhead and there were numerous other U-boat sightings. However, the main evidence for Scheer's plans came from the decrypts. One signal in particular, received on 30 May, roused interest: the code '31. G.G. 2490' suggested to Ewing's cryptanalysts that a German attack had been planned for the following day. It was in Jellicoe's hands by that afternoon and at 5.28 p.m. he was ordered to raise steam and to take his fleet to sea to engage the enemy.

At Rosyth the BCF started its preparations with men hurrying back on to the ships from football matches and other shore activities, and by 10.08 p.m. the first of Beatty's battle-cruisers had slipped their anchor buoys and were heading down the estuary through the outer defences towards the open sea. By midnight they were off May Island and heading towards the position where they would rendezvous with Jellicoe's BF off the coast of Jutland. Alongside them escorting destroyers played sheepdog as the 96 ships of the BCF headed out towards the dark of the North Sea. Rumours abounded of a raid by airships but the night was moonless and, later, sailors would remember seeing only the crackle of summer lightning against the far horizon. As one young officer recalled the moment, 'Night, and the mystery of darkness, enfolded them. The battle-cruisers were unleashed.'[23] Half an hour earlier the boom defences had been lifted at Hoxa and the first of 70 of Jellicoe's warships, including 16 dreadnoughts, moved through the growing darkness towards the open sea. At the same time, 23 ships of the 2nd Battle Squadron, eight of them dreadnoughts, had also raised steam at Invergordon and were heading out into the

North Sea. The British Grand Fleet was sailing towards a position known as Horns Reef where they would meet to take on the German naval might. It was only 10.30 p.m. and Scheer's fleet was still at anchor in their base at Wilhelmshaven waiting for the following day.

Unfortunately, by then Jellicoe was of the opinion that the Germans were not at sea and that they were engaged in a wild goose chase. This was due to confusion in Room 40 when Captain Thomas Jackson, Director of Operations, misunderstood information given to him about the whereabouts of Scheer's flagship, *Friedrich der Grosse*, which used the call sign 'DK' when in harbour. Jackson was suspicious of the cryptanalysts and thought them amateurs with no knowledge of naval affairs. When he asked the location of 'DK', the call-sign for Scheer's flagship, he was told that it was in Wilhelmshaven. Unfortunately this response was forwarded undigested to Jellicoe: 'no definite news of the enemy'. A further inquiry would have revealed the information that Scheer switched his call-sign when at sea but Jackson chose not to ask for explanation or comment, and as a result the British fleet lost some of the priceless advantage gained by Room 40's intercepts.[24] The result was that neither side fully understood the other's intentions when the first elements of the two fleets clashed in the afternoon of 31 May. The first shots were fired by the British light cruiser *Galatea* which sighted Hipper's force and began engaging its destroyer screen. At the time Beatty was concentrating on the rendezvous with Jellicoe's fleet but he reacted quickly to the signal from *Galatea* and abruptly turned his squadron south-east to try to get behind Hipper's ships. In the confusion signal flags were not properly seen and 5 miles away the big battleships of the 5th Battle Squadron were left behind as their commander, Hugh Evan-Thomas, continued as ordered to move to the north. The mistake was rectified but it meant that Beatty was going into action without the 15-inch guns of his four battleships. At 16,500 yards his battle-cruisers opened fire, well within their range, and Hipper's ships responded. For one of the British officers in the BCF, the engagement was:

. . . magnificent, inspiring, awful. The din of battle was stunning, stupendous, deafening as hundreds of the heaviest guns in the world gave voice. Great masses of water rose in the air like water spouts, mast high, as the shells of the Germans fell short or went over. Now and then a shell found its mark but it left one absolutely cold as to its effects. To each man at a time like this, his task. A dozen may be knocked out at one's side. It makes no difference. It is war.[25]

The anonymous officer was writing under the constraints of censorship – his account was published later – but behind the bravado things were quickly going wrong for Beatty's battle-cruisers. The German fire was more accurate and although both sides were scoring hits the British ships were being badly punished. Beatty's flagship, *Lion*, was almost knocked out when a shell from *Lützow* hit her amidships, but worse was to follow when HMS *Indefatigable* blew up following some heavy German punishment. *Queen Mary* was the next to go, blown up after being engaged by two German battleships, and by late afternoon it was clear that Beatty was in danger of losing the battle before the main battle fleets appeared on the scene. Beatty's idea was still to get behind Hipper's force and to cut it off before it turned for home; equally, Hipper hoped to lure Beatty into the trap posed by Scheer's fleet which, unknown to the British, was now at sea and rapidly coming into focus 14,000 yards away on the eastern horizon.

The unexpected appearance of the German ships changed the character of the battle. Hipper hoped that Beatty would continue his attack so that he could finish off the British battle-cruisers, but Beatty now had the chance to lure Sheer's fleet north where Jellicoe was waiting, and he took it. Known as the 'Run to the North' this phase was a running battle between the retreating British warships and their pursuers. Again both sides suffered damage and again another British battle-cruiser, HMS *Invincible*, was blown to pieces, suffering the same fate as her sister ships when a shell ignited powder in the main magazines, with disastrous results. Contemporary descriptions make it clear that in all three cases the ships exploded and sank within minutes, giving their crews no chance of escape. However, the formidable presence of Jellicoe's Battle Fleet put pressure on Scheer, who was enough of a realist to understand that his fleet was out-gunned and liable to be destroyed. Shortly before 7 p.m. he ordered his ships to execute a 180-degree manoeuvre and under cover of the smoke and encroaching mist took them westwards. Inexplicably, Scheer then repeated the movement and returned to take on Jellicoe's fleet, but the moment had gone and his ships faced such tremendous fire that the counter-attack lasted only ten minutes. This so-called 'death ride' resulted in huge damage being done to Scheer's fleet with *Derfflinger*, *Lützow* and *Seydlitz* all being severely damaged. In the same phase Jellicoe's losses were limited to a hit on HMS *Colossus* and the death of five sailors. As darkness fell the big guns of the dreadnoughts finally fell silent.

Running battles between destroyers and cruisers continued throughout the night but the following day Scheer was able to withdraw his fleet under Jellicoe's nose and by early afternoon on 1 June most of his ships had returned to Wilhelmshaven. The battle, known to the British as Jutland and to the Germans as Skagerrak, was over and for the admirals the balance sheet was far from clear. Hipper had lured out the British battleships but had failed to inflict a decisive defeat. Beatty had come off worse in the duel of the battle-cruisers but had succeeded in bringing Scheer north. Scheer lost the element of surprise and was forced to retreat when it became clear that his fleet was outnumbered; and Jellicoe's fear of torpedo attack led him to turn away and lose contact at two decisive points during the second phase of the battle. In terms of casualties the Germans were clear winners and Hipper deserves credit for the handling of his battle-cruisers in the fighting against Beatty's superior force. The Germans had lost only one battleship (the pre-dreadnought *Pommern*), one battle-cruiser (*Lützow*), four light cruisers and five destroyers (3,099 casualties), whereas Jellicoe's losses were three battle-cruisers, three armoured cruisers and eight destroyers (6,784 casualties). But in strategic terms it was a victory for the Royal Navy. Not only was their fleet still numerically superior – all the losses were covered by ships under repair in dry dock – but never again would the German High Seas Fleet attempt to meet the British Grand Fleet to contest the mastery of the North Sea.

Scheer made three further sorties before the end of 1916 but none of them resulted in any significant action and his High Seas Fleet was destined to spend the rest of the war in port. From that perspective, for all the British losses, the inaccurate fire and the faulty design which led to three modern battle-cruisers blowing up, Jutland was a triumph of sorts. Most of the Royal Navy's ships, including the stragglers, returned to their home ports or limped into Aberdeen or Newcastle to off-load the dead and wounded. Many of the ships showed signs of battle with holed hulls and blackened shell-torn superstructures, but by the evening of 2 June Jellicoe reported that his fleet was once more battle ready.

Arguments about who won Jutland and which admiral deserved the most credit or censure continued for years and are still the subject of debate amongst naval historians,[26] but in the immediate aftermath of the battle there was a fresh tragedy when it was announced that Kitchener had been drowned en route to a meeting in Russia. By the middle of 1916 the secretary for war's star was waning. He bore much of the responsibility for the fiasco in Gallipoli, a crisis over the provision of shells for the Western Front in 1915 almost brought him down and responsibility for overall strategy had passed from him to the General Staff under Sir William Robertson. He had also lost the confidence of his fellow politicians, narrowly surviving a vote against him in the House of Commons on 31 May, and it was with some relief that Asquith gave him permission to head a delegation to visit Russia at the beginning of June. It was agreed that he and his staff would travel from Scapa Flow to Petrograd (as St Petersburg had become) on 5 June on board the fast armoured cruiser HMS *Hampshire* (6,655 tons, Captain H. J. Savill) which had served at Jutland as part of the 2nd Cruiser Squadron. Kitchener travelled by rail to Thurso and crossed over to Scapa on the morning of 5 June to join the *Hampshire* and its two escorting destroyers, HMS *Unity* and HMS *Victor*, after lunching with Jellicoe. All day a gale had been blowing from the north-east and the deteriorating meteorological conditions forced a change of plan. Instead of sailing eastabouts and into the main mercantile route north the convoy would enter the Pentland Firth westabouts and then north along the west coast of Hoy, which would offer the ships a lee from the islands. It was also thought that this route provided the least chance of attack by submarines or mines.

On both points it was the wrong decision. Shortly after the *Hampshire* slipped into the Pentland Firth at 4.45 p.m. the winds began backing to the north-west, bringing in a violent storm from the Atlantic. Although the *Hampshire* had the strength to cope with the conditions the escorting destroyers, small K-class ships displacing 928 tons, were forced to turn back in the heavy seas. Now alone in a force-nine gale *Hampshire* turned north, and it was in the seas, roughly 1.5

miles from shore between the Brough of Birsay and Marwick Head on mainland Orkney that she met her fate while shaping a course of N.30'E. Around 7.45 p.m. a huge explosion ripped through the cruiser, 'shaking her from stem to stern' as one survivor remembered. As she pushed her way through the storm *Hampshire* had dropped onto a mine moored some 30 feet below the water, which tore a huge hole between the bows and the bridge. The cruiser settled quickly by the bows and although frantic attempts were made to launch the ship's boats these were smashed to matchwood; only a number of Carley life-rafts were launched and reached the shore where twelve fortunate survivors were pulled from the sea by local people. In those conditions escape was difficult and fifteen minutes later *Hampshire* went down by the bows, her stern rising high in the water before seeming to somersault forward as she plunged out of sight below the waves.[27] Amongst the 655 drowned were Kitchener and his staff.

Jellicoe called the loss 'a national disaster of the first magnitude'. When the news was announced the following day busy London streets came to a standstill and crowds gathered outside the War Office where blinds were drawn and the Union flag flew at half-mast.[28] The shock of Kitchener's death was so profound that years afterwards many people remembered in exact detail what they were doing when it was announced. To them it seemed that the centre had been torn from their lives, that a rock-like presence had crumbled, leaving them alone in a world which was suddenly unsafe and unsure. Inevitably perhaps, given the shock caused by the announcement, conspiracy theories were soon in evidence suggesting that Kitchener had been betrayed and that the details of his journey had been leaked to the Germans, allowing them to position a submarine to sink the *Hampshire*. There were also rumours that he was not dead at all but would return like King Arthur to save his country, and on Orkney there were stories, still told to this day, about armed soldiers preventing the rescue of survivors, the navy's refusal to launch the Stromness lifeboat and the unexplained presence of German spies.[29] The truth was probably more prosaic: *Hampshire* fell victim a mine laid by the German submarine *U-75*, commanded by Lieutenant-Commander Kurt Beitzen as part of Scheer's plan to lure Jellicoe's fleet into a trap prior to Jutland. The naval headquarters at Longhope knew that a submarine was operating off Orkney – two intercepts showed her to be in the vicinity and on 5 June she was reported to be '10' NE of Cape Wrath steering W' – but in the confusion after Jutland these warnings were either ignored or misplaced.[30]

After the war Kitchener's death prompted a number of bizarre theories about spies or sabotage and for many years the 'Kitchener Mystery' played on the minds of assorted cranks and publicity seekers. A lack of openness by the authorities only encouraged the rumblings. Following the sinking of the *Hampshire* a court of inquiry was held on board HMS *Blake* but its findings were never made public. Ten years later a White Paper was produced but it was less than candid about the sightings of the *U-75* and concluded that the accident was due to happenstance rather than any human error and that 'the loss of the ship was not due to treachery'.[31] Today, Kitchener's death is marked in Orkney by a solitary tower which stands on Marwick Head looking out to the spot where *Hampshire* foundered. The seas, 300 feet below, crash on to the huge rugged rocks which guard those formidable cliffs, and even on a calm day it is possible to imagine the plight of the crew as they attempted to leave the ship for the inhospitable shore. The monument was raised by the people of Orkney and is reached by a path leading from the road where the first civilians and military patrols arrived on the scene of the disaster all those years ago. For going to the assistance of *Hampshire*'s crew the farming folk of Sandwick and Birsay received scant reward. A week after the incident Vice-Admiral Brock wrote to Jellicoe suggesting that some acknowledgement should be made to recognise the part played by the Orcadians in the rescue. Such appreciation, he counselled, should not be money as the crofters were 'not of a class to which money could be sent; I am of the opinion that a letter of thanks would be much more highly prized, although the people concerned are mostly poor'.[32] As for Beitzen, he too fell victim to mines when his boat *U-102* entered a British minefield in September 1918; ironically, by then *U-75* had met a similar fate, going down with all hands off Terschelling in the Netherlands in December 1917.[33]

Mines were a continual menace off the Scottish coast throughout the hostilities. From the very outset of the war Germany laid an estimated 25,000 mines in the North Sea, concentrating on the main shipping lanes and the approaches to the Allied ports. A large number of minelayers were used in the exercise – older destroyers, converted merchant ships and specially adapted UC-class submarines – and one of the first German ships to be sunk was the minelayer *Königin Luise* (see Chapter One). The British response was tardy, partly because the mine was considered a cowardly weapon but mainly because no thought had been given to mine-laying, with only ten elderly gun-boats having been converted to mine-laying operations. A defensive minefield sown in the Channel caused all manner of problems when mines started drifting away or exploding without contact. Respon-sibility for mine warfare lay in the hands of the Royal Navy's Torpedo Branch at HMS *Vernon* at Portsmouth but, compared to the German effort at the outset of the conflict, it was very much a Cinderella service. It soon became clear in 1914 that German mines would cause the most trouble when they scored the first high-profile casualty of the war.

In October 1914 the converted North German Lloyd liner *Berlin* sailed from the North Sea and then down the west coast of Scotland to lay mines in the approaches to the Firth of Clyde and its vital shipping lanes to North America. If the captain had succeeded in sowing his mines in the North Channel he could have inflicted severe damage to Britain's shipping trade, but he decided to place 200 mines off the north-west coast of Ireland, close to Tory Island and the approaches to Lough Swilly. It was still a good choice. Not only did the area contain the main sea lanes for ships crossing the Atlantic from Liverpool but, unknown to the *Berlin*'s captain, Lough Swilly had been designated as an anchorage for Jellicoe's fleet in the anxious early days of the war when the submarine threat kept Britain's battleships at sea. A mer-chant ship, the *Manchester Commerce*, was the first to fall into the trap, on 26 October, when it was holed and sunk, but that success was nothing compared to the next victim. Two days later eight modern dreadnoughts crossed the area to engage in gunnery practice and one of them, HMS *Audacious*, hit a mine and began settling in the water. Desperate measures were put in place to keep her afloat and to try to beach her on the Irish coast 25 miles away, but every attempt to bring her in tow failed. A passing White Star liner, *Olympic*, sister ship of the ill-fated *Titanic*, made a last-ditch effort, but it was a hopeless struggle and the towing line eventually broke in the heavy seas. Later that night *Audacious* capsized and blew up, thus achieving notoriety as the first and only British dreadnought battleship to fall victim to the enemy during the hostilities. (Another dreadnought battleship, HMS *Vanguard*, exploded in Scapa Flow in 1917 as a result of unstable ammunition. Only two crew members survived.) So appalled was the Admiralty that the news of the loss of *Audacious* was not released until after the war and she remained a phantom name on the navy's list of operational ships.

Before the war the Admiralty had acknowledged the danger of mines when Admiral Lord Charles Beresford, commanding the Channel Fleet, had proposed the use of fishing trawlers as mine-sweepers on the grounds that their deployment would free other naval vessels for active service and that 'Fishermen, by virtue of their calling, are adept in the handling and towing of wires and trawls, more so than are naval ratings.'[34] The result was the formation of the Royal Naval Reserve (Trawler Section), a fleet of 100 steam trawlers which could be mobilised and taken out of commercial service during any period of heightened tension. These would be manned by 1,000 officers and ratings who would act as reservists and would be called up in the event of war. In recognition of their special role the naval trawler captains were given the rank of 'Skipper RNR' and on 3 February 1911 the first fishing captain to be commissioned was Peter Yorston of Aberdeen. By 1912 the Royal Naval Reserve (Trawler Section) consisted of 142 trawlers manned by 1,279 personnel, and following the outbreak of war the service consisted of 7,888 officers and men. Most of them came from east-coast fishing communities, the majority from Scotland, and their main areas of responsibility were the Pentland Firth, the Cromarty Firth, the Firth of Forth, the Tyne, the Humber, Harwich, Sheerness, Dover, Portsmouth, Portland and Plymouth, where they worked alongside the navy's growing minesweeping fleet which was largely under the command of merchant seamen serving in the Royal Navy Reserve or the Royal Naval Volunteer Reserve.

All told, the Royal Navy commandeered around 3,000 steam trawlers and drifters during the war, and while the majority served as minesweepers or mine-hunters they were also used as boom defence vessels, convoy escorts and mobile airship moorings. In Aberdeen a third of the fleet was commandeered, a drastic move which forced the Aberdeen Fish Trade Association to complain on 15 September 1914 that it was 'a greater proportion to the total fleet of trawlers at that port than in the case of other ports'. A fortnight later the Admiralty was forced to admit that 'the grievance was well founded'.[35] The steam drifters were particularly useful as all-purpose vessels, so much so that in 1916 the navy commissioned its own class of 'Admiralty Drifter' based on the design of a pre-war steam drifter *Ocean Reward* built by Hall Russell of Aberdeen. The same company also provided one of the three designs for 'Admiralty Trawlers'. The design was based on its Strath class, the model boat concerned being the *Strathlochy*. Altogether 540 Admiralty Trawlers and 335 Admiralty Drifters were ordered at a total cost of £11,958,000 (the equivalent in purchasing power of around £400 million in 2005) with the hope being expressed that some of the costs could be recouped by selling the boats on to the fishing industry after the war.[36] For the crews of the minesweeping boats it was a difficult and dangerous occupation, for not only were the mines often unstable – exploding them by rifle fire was one method use to disarm them – but all fishing boats were liable to attack by enemy submarines.

During the war 675 fishing boats were sunk by enemy action while fishing or flying the colours of the Royal Naval Reserve, the majority in 1917 when the Germans introduced the policy of unrestricted warfare in an attempt to cripple Britain by sinking ships bringing in much-needed supplies. Of that number 89 were boats manned by Scottish crews. Amongst them was the Arbroath-registered boat *Maggie Smith* which hit a mine and was blown up while sailing into the Bell Rock fishing grounds in February 1918. All the crew were killed. A Peterhead crew was somewhat luckier when they were intercepted by a German U-boat skipper with a sense of fair play. Ordered to abandon his fishing boat before it was sunk by gunfire the Peterhead skipper replied that he carried no lifeboat and could not therefore escape certain death. His fear turned to astonishment when the German captain spared him with the admonishment that the Scottish fishermen were contravening international maritime regulations by going to sea without a lifeboat.[37] It was not just in Scottish waters that the Scottish fishermen found themselves in the front line. Scottish-based trawlers and drifters were in action during the naval operations in Gallipoli and they also served in the English Channel keeping the approaches free for the warships of the Dover Patrol. The first VC to be awarded to a skipper RNR was won by Joseph Watt of

Banff while commanding HM Drifter *Gowanlea* (FR105) in mine-sweeping operations in the Straits of Otranto in the Adriatic on 15 May 1917. Called on to surrender by an Austrian cruiser he opened fire with his boat's 6-pounder gun and continued fighting despite coming under heavier fire from the enemy warship. Although his crew sustained casualties Watt survived the action and he returned to fishing after the war.

The last major naval incident in Scottish waters took place at the beginning of 1918 when Beatty, having succeeded Jellicoe as commander-in-chief, took the Grand Fleet into the North Sea on 31 January. With them was a new K-class of fast steam-powered fleet submarines which had hinged funnels to allow them to revert to diesel power when submerged. They weighed 2,565 tons and were 338 feet long but were only 27 feet in the beam, disadvantages which meant that they had poor sailing and undersea characteristics. One of these new K-class monsters had already been lost on its first test dive in the Gareloch, but the unhappily numbered *K13* was raised and renumbered *K22*. Its luck had not changed; part of the submarine flotilla that made its way out of Rosyth, once again disaster was not long in coming *K22*'s way. While the fleet was manoeuvring off May Island *K14*'s rudder jammed and she was rammed by the newly raised *K22*, which was in turn rammed by the battle-cruiser HMS *Inflexible*. Worse followed when the light cruiser HMS *Fearless* rammed and sank another K-class boat, *K17*, while *K4* met a similar fate at the hands of *K6* and *K7*. Over a hundred submariners were drowned in the Firth of the Forth as a result of the accidents: many of the men in the water were cut down by destroyers screening the battleships of the 5th Battle Squadron. Two K-class submarines were lost and three submarines and a light cruiser were badly damaged. In common with the earlier incidents at Scapa Flow and Jemimaville the fate of the K-class submarines was given the ironic nickname within the Royal Navy of the 'Battle of May Island'.[38]

As the war progressed the Royal Navy's use of mines became more sophisticated. E-class submarines were converted as minelayers to establish minefields off the German and Dutch coasts as well as sectors of the English Channel. Destroyers patrolling the areas would attempt to drive German submarines into the minefields and this tactic was particularly successful at night, when the boats tended to be on the

ABOVE. A Black Watch soldier lends encouragement to potential recruits outside a recruiting office. Note the sheepskin jacket which was adopted by front-line troops during the bitter winter of 1915. (© *Trustees of the National Museums of Scotland*)

RIGHT. National sentiment, as well as patriotism, found their way into recruiting posters. The poet Robert Burns followed his own advice and enlisted in the Royal Dumfries Volunteers in 1795 at a time when Britain was threatened with invasion by Revolutionary France. (© *Trustees of the National Museums of Scotland*)

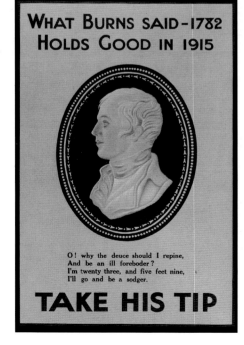

WHAT BURNS SAID - 1782
HOLDS GOOD IN 1915

O! why the deuce should I repine,
And be an ill foreboder?
I'm twenty three, and five feet nine,
I'll go and be a sodger.

TAKE HIS TIP

TOP. A contemporary postcard showing the aftermath of the railway disaster at Quintinshill Junction near Gretna on 22 May 1915. Two hundred and ten soldiers of 7th Royal Scots were killed when their train crashed into a local service. The tragedy was compounded when the overnight London to Glasgow express slammed into the wreckage.
(© *Trustees of the National Museums of Scotland*)

ABOVE. Medical staff of the Scottish Women's Hospital in Serbia. The Serbian government accepted Dr Elsie Inglis's offer to provide a field hospital in October 1914.
(© *University of Glasgow*)

OPPOSITE TOP. The Scottish Women's Hospital at Royaumont was housed in a Cistercian Abbey which was founded by King Louis IX in 1229. The Blanche de Castille Ward, shown here, was on the first floor. (*By courtesy of Mrs Anne Murdoch*)

OPPOSITE BELOW. The cloisters and terrace of the Scottish Women's Hopsital at Royaumont were used as outside wards during the summer months. Winter was less enticing: the building was described as being "picturesque, impressive and most abominably chilly".
(*By courtesy of Mrs Marion Proctor*)

Female auxiliaries handle an airship at East Fortune airfield in East Lothian. By 1917 the base was home to the Royal Air Force's Torpedo Training School. (© *Trustees of the National Museums of Scotland*)

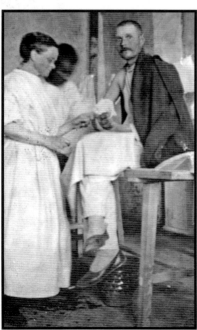

OPPOSITE TOP. Breaking the bale in a clothing factory in Greenock. By 1918 around 31,000 women were employed in essential war work in Scotland, often doing work which had been previously reserved for men. (© *Dumfries and Galloway Libraries, Information and Archives*)

OPPOSITE LEFT. Dr Elsie Inglis, founder of the Scottish Women's Hospitals, treating a wounded Serb soldier. Having raised the money to start the project she moved to Serbia in May 1915 and served later in southern Russia. (© *Mitchell Library, Glasgow City Libraries and Archive*)

OPPOSITE RIGHT. Ewart Alan Mackintosh, dressed for the winter cold, was one of the finest poets of the First World War. He was killed while serving with 1/4th Seaforth Highlanders at the Battle of Cambrai in November 1917. (© *Rosemary Beazley from* Can't Shoot a Man with a Cold, *Argyll Publishing, 2004*)

ABOVE. Standing beside his mother in a posed photograph, the poet Hugh MacDiarmid (Christopher Murray Grieve) served with the Royal Army Medical Corps on the *Salonika*. After the war he instigated the Scottish Renaissance movement and became in time the country's greatest poet of the 20th century. (© *Gordon Wright*)

The architect of victory: Field Marshal Earl Haig of Bemersyde towards the end of the war. His name still rouses more passion – for and against – than any other commander of the conflict. (© *National Portrait Gallery*)

HOME FLEET AT SCAPA FLOW, ORKNEY. T.K.

TOP. The Russian armoured cruiser Rurik lies alongside the British battleship Agamemnon in William Beardmore's fitting-out dock at Dalmuir in 1908. During the war years there was a rapid expansion of warship building at all the Clydeside yards. (© *University of Glasgow*)

ABOVE. At the outbreak of war the Royal Navy's Grand Fleet moved to Scapa Flow in Orkney and it remained a strategically important naval base throughout the war. (© *Orkney Library*)

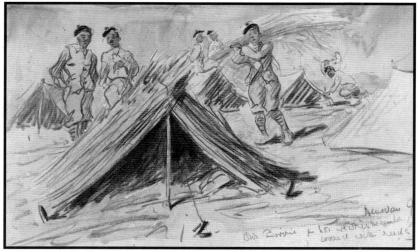

TOP. Vice-Admiral Sir David Beatty's flagship HMS *Lion* receives a hit on Q turret during the Battle of Jutland fought at the end of May 1916. Considered a "draw", it was the only major naval battle of the war. (© *Imperial War Museum*)

ABOVE. Ridiculed by the Germans as 'the greatest internment camp in the world', the Franco-British front in Salonika was created in 1915 to engage German and Bulgarian forces. Sketch by Lance-Corporal Joseph Adam, 13th (Scottish Horse) Battalion, Black Watch. (© *Trustees of the National Museums of Scotland*)

TOP. An army cookhouse belonging to the 52nd (Lowland) Division in Gallipoli in 1915. It was taken by Corporal Henry Flint of the Royal Army Medical Corps. (© *Trustees of the National Museums of Scotland*)

MIDDLE. The conditions in Gallipoli were as bad as any endured on the Western Front, largely due to the difficulty of digging trench systems. Photograph taken by Corporal Henry Flint, Royal Army Medical Corps. (© *Trustees of the National Museums of Scotland*)

ABOVE. The pipes and drums of the 7th Highland Light Infantry in Palestine. The men served with 52nd (Lowland) Division which also fought in Gallipoli and on the Western Front. The photograph was taken by Sapper T. Milne, Royal Engineers. (© *Trustees of the National Museums of Scotland*)

TOP. Egyptian officers pose with a Jock from the 52nd (Lowland) Division during the operations in Palestine. Photograph from Sapper Milne's album. (© *Trustees of the National Museums of Scotland*)

ABOVE. A group of nine officers serving with 1st Seaforth Highlanders in Mesopotamia. All had the distinction of being promoted from the ranks and two became battalion commanders. (© *Imperial War Museum*)

TOP. The pipes and drums of 8th Black Watch play following the capture of Longueval in 14 July 1916. During the operations, which formed part of the Battle of the Somme, the battalion sustained 495 casualties. (© *Imperial War Museum*)

ABOVE. As part of the armistice terms the German High Seas Fleet was ordered to be interred in Scapa Flow. Under Royal Navy escort SMS *Seydlitz* steams toward the rendezvous point off the Isle of May in the Firth of Forth. (© *Trustees of the National Museums of Scotland*)

Men of the 14th (County of London) Battalion, The London Regiment (London Scottish) march up to the front on 27 June 1916 in preparation for the Battle of the Somme. (© *Imperial War Museum*)

TOP. The first widespread opposition to government policy arrived with the rent strikes in Glasgow in 1915. Attempted evictions were opposed by the formation of tenement committees made up of women who forced the government to rush through a Rent Restriction Act which not only met the strikers' demands but, equally to the point, ensured continued production of essential wartime supplies. (© *Glasgow Museums: The People's Palace*)

ABOVE. John Maclean with his supporters in Glasgow during the strike action of 1919. After the war he was increasingly isolated and his Scottish Workers Republican party failed to make any political impact. (© *Glasgow Museums: The People's Palace*) surface. By far the most ambitious minefield was constructed in 1917 during Germany's period of unrestricted marine warfare. This Northern Barrage was huge, bridging the gap between Shetland and the Norwegian coast, and was put in place both to reinforce the concept of distant blockade and to prevent German submarines from entering the Atlantic. It stretched for 250 miles and of the 70,177 mines used in the defensive system, the US Navy's First Mine Squadron planted 56,571, working from bases at Invergordon and Inverness. (The barrage was a mixed success: by the end of the war only seven German submarines were reported to have been sunk.)

At the same time, the Highlands west and north of the Great Glen became a restricted area, closed to anyone without the relevant permit, in order to safeguard the naval bases and coastal defence installations. In addition to the bases at Invergordon and Scapa the west-coast harbour of Kyle of Lochalsh had to be guarded in the latter stages of the war when it became the main base for the US Navy's operations in the North Sea. Naval patrol boats kept watch on the Caledonian Canal and to all intents and purposes the Highlands became an annex of the navy. Travel became complicated and arduous, not least because the Highland railway line between Perth and the north was given over almost entirely to military traffic. The difficulty of getting about and receiving supplies was not just an irritation: it brought great inconvenience to local communities in remote townships in the West Highlands and along the western seaboard. In 1916, when a crofter in Coaigh in Ross-shire, a small settlement between Loch Broom and Enard Bay, told commissioners from the Board of Agriculture in Scotland that the war was a time 'when the mantle of darkness had descended on the land' he meant exactly what he said: failure to land oil supplies meant that they had had no artificial light in the previous winter.[40] There is an excellent description of the problems of wartime travelling in the restricted area in John Buchan's novel *Mr Standfast*. The hero, Richard Hannay, finds himself in the West Highlands without the necessary 'passport' while hunting a network of German spies who are using well-meaning pacifists as cover.

One other element came into being during the war: flight. Scotland was integrated into the country's national air defence system which was in the hands of the Royal Naval Air Service (RNAS) until the end of 1915 when the responsibility was handed over to the Royal Flying Corps (RFC). The principal RFC base was at Turnhouse outside Edinburgh, which was home to 77 Squadron, part of Number 46 Home Defence Wing. The other main RFC bases were at Ayr Racecourse (No. 1 School of Aerial Fighting), Charterhall (landing strip near Greenlaw, Borders), Crail (27 Training Depot Station), Drem (2 Training Depot Station), Edzell (26 Training Depot Station), Loch Doon (School of Aerial Gunnery), Montrose (6 Squadron and 32 Training Depot Station), Renfrew (Beardmore Flying School and 6 Aircraft Acceptance Park), Stirling (43 Squadron), Turnberry (School of Aerial Gunnery) and Winfield (landing strip near Berwick-on-Tweed). Scotland's strategic position by the North Sea meant that aircraft and airships flew coastal patrols and operations in support of the Grand Fleet. Towards the end of the war aircraft were also used in anti-submarine operations and the two main RNAS bases were at Dundee Stannergate and East Fortune, which was situated close to the mouth of the Firth of Forth. Both operated different types of aircraft. Dundee was home to the Short 184 and Felixstowe F2A flying boats of 249 and 257 squadrons, while East Fortune was used as an airship base including the rigid 'R'-class, which came into service in 1917, necessitating the construction of larger hangars. Following the formation of the Royal Air Force in April 1917 East Fortune became the RAF's Torpedo Training School but the war ended before there was an opportunity to attack the German High Seas Fleet in this way. Other RNAS stations were at Donibristle (salvage park and repair depot), Inchinnan (Beardmore airship station), Leuchars (airfield), Longside (airship patrol station) and Machrihanish (airship patrol station).[41]

Unlike other parts of the United Kingdom, the Scottish mainland did not suffer any major German assault during the war. The only recorded attack from the sea came on 15 May 1918, when the remote island of St Kilda was shelled by a German U-boat. Over 70 rounds were fired, damaging the church and two houses, one of them occupied by the island's nurse. No lives were lost because the German captain gave a general warning before opening fire: his target was an Admiralty radio station which formed part of the country's coastal defences. The news reached Edinburgh after the minister, the Rev. Alexander McKinnon, wrote to the offices of the United Free Church of Scotland reporting the attack and demanding some protection: 'I think it is most essential to have a large gun on the island for many a time there is a shot on a submarine here if there was a gun on the island. There is neither gun nor patrol.' The matter was passed to the Admiralty and an official replied on 31 May that there could not be regular patrols 'owing to other Naval requirements' but the matter did not end there. St Kilda was owned by Macleod of Macleod, who had handed over St Kilda and its adjacent islands for naval use and he argued that the Admiralty should pay for the damage. The matter was then referred to the Air Raids Compensation Committee, which dealt with payments to civilian buildings damaged by enemy action, but they rejected an application for compensation owing to the military nature of the target of the German attack. A year later questions were asked in parliament about the government's tardiness in dealing with the matter and it was not until the summer of 1919 that the Admiralty agreed to pay £530 and sent four workmen from Edinburgh to make good the damage.[42]

Despite the fact that there was, fortunately, only one naval and one airship raid of any significance on Scotland, the encroachment of modern means of waging war was to change the face of the Scottish landmass in the years after the conflict. The navy's main submarine training and testing facility was established on the west coast at Faslane and during the Cold War years it would house Britain's main nuclear deterrent in the shape of strategic submarines carrying Polaris, Poseidon and Trident missiles. In the inter-war years the big ships of the Royal Navy were a regular sight at Invergordon and Rosyth and from the 1920s onwards Leuchars was developed as a major RAF base, as were other bases on the east and north-east coasts, such as Kinloss and Lossiemouth. In that sense at least the experience of the First World War encouraged military planners to regard Scotland as a major facility for developing the country's forward maritime defence strategy, both in the Second World War against Germany between 1939 and 1945, and then during the long years of Cold War confrontation with the Soviet Union and its Warsaw Pact allies.

7 The Workshop of War

The war had an immediate impact on the Clydeside shipyards where 90 per cent of Scotland's shipbuilding capacity was concentrated and where the bulk of Britain's biggest commercial and naval warships were built. It was clearly a national asset which had to be defended to safeguard ships under construction as well as the future ships, mainly destroyers, which would be required for the war effort. Three firms were immediately designated as naval dockyards under Admiralty control: William Beardmore at Dalmuir, John Brown at Clydebank and Fairfield at Govan, all of which had long experience in constructing warships and armaments for the Royal Navy. Other yards followed suit in 1915 as a result of the passing of the Munitions of War Act, which brought essential industries under government control. This was a sensible move as it secured production and in Clydeside's case put the shipbuilding industry on a war footing. Glasgow was beyond the reach of air raid and the approaches to the Clyde could be protected by the navy from submarine and mine attack, an important consideration as the estuary was used for ships' trials. The move also safeguarded jobs and held out the promise of more to come as most people in 1914 believed that Britain's war effort would be concentrated at sea. Many of the ships which fought at Jutland were Clyde-built: the battleship HMS *Barham*, the flagship of Evan-Thomas, commander of the Grand Fleet's 5th Battle Squadron, and the battle-cruiser HMS *Tiger* were products of John Brown's yards at Clydebank; two of Fisher's *Invincible*-class battle-cruisers, HMSs *Inflexible* and *Indomitable*, were constructed at Fairfield's and launched in 1908 and, in addition to warships, Beardmore made huge 15-inch calibre naval guns at their Parkhead Forge munitions works. All told, the pre-war naval race with Germany had meant good business: by 1913 the volume of shipbuilding on the Clyde had grown to 757,000 tons and the total number of workers dependent on the industry was estimated to be 100,000 or 14 per cent of the male working population. By way of comparison the UK total was 2,264,000 tons for the same period.[1] At the outbreak of war Clydeside was buoyant and ready for further expansion, its rapid growth in the middle of the previous century having been assured by the development of steam propulsion and the increasing use of iron and then mild steel in place of wood.

Like many other facets of Scotland's past it is easy to dramatise the shipbuilding industry and to make heroes of the men who were involved in what the novelist George Blake called 'the high, tragic pageant of the Clyde'. In its heyday, shipbuilding was central to the prosperity of Glasgow and the west of Scotland and gave sustenance to the heavy industries and other trades that supported it. Clydeside yards were also innovators. In 1879 William Denny of Dumbarton launched the *Rotamahana*, the world's first ocean-going steamer constructed from mild steel, and he followed this up the following year with the first steel passenger liner, the *Buenos Ayrean*, for the Allan Line, which ran regular transatlantic passenger services from Glasgow. In the same period John Elder and Company developed the triple-expansion engine, and the first turbine engine was introduced by Denny in 1901. Together with the other great firms – Robert Napier and the Thomson brothers – the Clyde shipbuilders were market leaders, and the banks of the Clyde near Glasgow sprouted the yards, wharves, sheds, cranes and railway lines that defined the industrial landscape.

On that score – the perception of a giant enterprise at work – there was something brave and admirable about the industry. It bred hard men who had a good conceit of themselves and their worth and for the skilled time-served workers it provided a good living and transferable expertise. All were highly specialised in the trades that they followed, whether they were engineers, electricians, boilermakers, riveters, carpenters, painters or plumbers, and those skills were jealously guarded, with entry into the work being subject to varying degrees of apprenticeship. Wages had been kept low in the nineteenth century – one reason for the area's ability to keep manufacturing costs down and productivity high – but by the time of the 1906 census on industrial wages Clydeside shipbuilders were as well paid as any others in Britain.[2] Being a skilled shipyard worker was a passport to a decent wage and reasonable (if sometimes seasonal) job security, although it has to be said that by 1914 in real terms wages had been eroded by increases in the cost of living. It was a craft-based industry and men took great pride in the ships that they built and in ensuring high quality.

Naturally there was a downside. Not all the workforce were natural aristocrats and the work itself involved long hours and heavy labour with the possibility of accidents ever present. Excessive drinking could also be a problem although this was eased as a result of wartime restrictions, and great outrage was expressed when Lloyd George complained that productivity was being lost as a result of over-indulgence. In the first weeks of the war the secretary of the Scottish Christian Social Union wrote to the secretary of state for Scotland, Thomas McKinnon Wood, complaining about 'deplorable scenes of drunkenness in our city at present. Some say this open drunkenness has increased since the war. It is asserted, on what seems to be good authority, that the money given to soldiers' and sailors' wives is in many cases, or in a considerable number of cases, spent in intoxicating liquor. It is also asserted that territorials in uniform are frequently seen under the influence.' However, when the matter was investigated the chief constable of Glasgow responded on 7 October that according to the crime statistics drunkenness had diminished in the city since the war had begun and that there had been a decrease in the number of arrests. While admitting that there had been scenes of drunken excess in the first weeks he said that this had happened as a result of people 'treating' soldiers when they were called up or were preparing to leave Glasgow.[3]

Britain's defence policy of giving preference to the navy meant that there was almost no let-up in the production of warships. This constant production was also encouraged in part by the completion in 1906 of the ultra-modern HMS *Dreadnought*, a powerful new battleship which made all its rivals obsolete overnight. Its construction gave Britain a huge lead in the naval arms race but it was followed in 1907 by an unexpected contraction in shipbuilding caused by defence cutbacks and a dearth in worldwide merchant shipping orders. Clyde-side was not exempt from the phenomenon and yards were forced to lay off labour and tighten their belts, leaving the *Glasgow Herald* to lament at the end of 1907 that the lack of orders was 'a condition of affairs quite unprecedented in recent years'.[4] At Dalmuir, having been launched with a flourish, the battleship *Agamemnon* languished in its fitting-out berth and did not begin sea trials until the following year, while the other yards were forced to subsist on the construction of smaller vessels such as destroyers and a reduced diet of merchant ships.[5] The situation did not improve until the production of the 1909–10 Naval Estimates which introduced a new period of expansion following a lengthy campaign which was supported by the popular press. (The Admiralty wanted six new super-dreadnoughts but the cry was 'we want eight and we won't wait'.) The people of Britain took great pride in the iron walls of their battleships, seeing naval superiority over rival powers as a means of maintaining Britain's place and prestige in the world; sea power was the apotheosis of the country's superiority and its maintenance attracted a good deal of interest. With the construction of modern battleships and battle-cruisers in the period between 1908 and 1914 the people of Britain were not disappointed either in the scale or fighting capacity of the ships in question. Heavily armoured, with huge guns capable of firing shells weighing up to 2,000 pounds, as well as being fast, elegant and powerful, the Royal Navy's latest warships were the most potent in the world, and as many of them were Clyde-built (a self-conscious synonym for reliability) the people of Scotland had good reason to take pride in them. (That being said, the launch of the *Barham* in August 1915 was somewhat marred when the guests found themselves stuck in one of the new electric elevators after a visit to the engine room.)[6] As a result of the wartime boom Clydeside experienced a period of bonanza, with the three leading yards winning orders worth over £16 million. It was a fillip for Clydeside, although Hugh Peebles has demonstrated in his history of the warship-building industry that, for a variety of reasons, the orders did not make the expected huge profits, a result mainly of poor management practices, inefficient budgeting and shortages of skilled labour.[7]

Any fears of a new recession were dispelled when war broke out and Britain's shipyards, including those on the Clyde, experienced a boom. At the start of the war 13 battleships were under construction and nine battle-cruisers were on the stocks, and during the course of the war Britain's shipyards built a further 842 warships and 571 auxiliary vessels. Skilled workers could not volunteer for the armed forces and were exempted from conscription after its introduction in 1916; in steel consumption the Admiralty was given precedence over other industries and until 1917 warship production took priority over merchant tonnage. Clydeside itself at the outbreak of war was a busy place with three battleships (*Barham*, *Valiant* and *Ramillies*), three *Arethusa*-class light cruisers and six destroyers under construction and the promise of more to come. Due to the exigencies of war – the need for more surface warships, especially destroyers, and the growing loss of merchant ships – the Clydeside yards entered a profitable period with a total of 481 warships aggregating almost 760,000 tons being constructed between 1914 and 1918. The other yards which profited from wartime expansion were Scott's of Greenock, Denny of Dumbarton and Yarrow's of Scotstoun and, all told, the six Clydeside shipyards accounted for the following Admiralty orders for warships during the war years:

Clydebank (John Brown)
  2 battle-cruisers
  1 aircraft carrier
  3 light cruisers
  37 destroyers
  3 submarines
  1 depot ship

Govan (Fairfield)
  2 battle-cruisers
  5 light cruisers
  29 destroyers
  13 submarines

Dalmuir (Beardmore)
  1 aircraft carrier
  2 light cruisers
  19 destroyers
  13 submarines

Greenock (Scott)
  3 light cruisers
  19 destroyers
  8 submarines
  1 12-inch-gun monitor

Dumbarton (Denny)
  1 aircraft carrier
  3 flotilla leaders
  27 destroyers
  8 submarines

Scotstoun (Yarrow)
  29 destroyers
  1 submarine
  16 river gunboats
  1 depot ship[8]

These are impressive figures, made more so because they do not include the substantial merchant tonnage which was also part of the Clyde's war effort. It also suggests that the war brought prosperity to the area and to a major extent this was true. At Clydebank all-day Saturday working and Sunday nightshifts were introduced to speed up work on the battle-cruiser *Tiger* and the battleship *Barham* and by the end of the war wages in the industry had increased by 10 per cent, keeping earnings above wartime inflation.[9] At one stage the weekly wage bill at Dalmuir rose to £47,000 from a weekly average of £14,700 in 1914. There was an influx of new workers who brought fresh spending power into the area, adding to the sense of prosperity, but there was a downside to this emphasis on productivity. *Barham* and *Tiger* were completed by the summer of 1915 but once they had been commissioned Brown's had to lay off over 2,000 workers at Clydebank. This was normal practice in the trade, there being little or no job security, but the fluctuations made it difficult for the yards to meet the ever-increasing demands from the Admiralty to increase production, especially of the much-needed battle-cruisers. At the beginning of 1915, when John Brown responded to Admiralty pleas to speed up work on the construction of the battle-cruiser HMS *Repulse* (originally planned as a battleship), the yard struggled to find the additional heavy-iron workers needed to complete the job within the requested 15 months.

The Admiralty's infatuation with battle-cruisers reached its apogee in the construction of perhaps the most famous warship to be built on the Clyde during the war: HMS *Hood*, which has the distinction of being the largest warship ever built for the Royal Navy. Laid down at John Brown's yard at Clydebank in September 1916, *Hood* was to be one of four enhanced battle-cruisers which would meet the threat posed by the proposed construction of the German *Mackensen* class of fast heavily-armed battle-cruisers capable of taking on and beating Britain's fleet. The *Admiral* class was the Royal Navy's response: they would be 42,000-ton monsters with eight 15-inch guns and they would be capable of running at 32 knots. Lessons learned at Jutland meant that *Hood* and her sisters would have thicker plating on their armoured belts but speed would be maintained by utilising more powerful turbine engines. With her great length (860 feet), her raked bows and elegant lines *Hood* was destined to be one of the navy's most beautiful ships, but she owed her existence solely to the efficiency of the Clydebank workforce. By the end of 1916 it became clear that the *Mackensen* class had been cancelled and the Admiralty decided to follow suit by suspending work on its *Admirals*. Work on a sister ship, HMS *Rodney*, was brought to a halt at Fairfield's but because *Hood* was so advanced it was decided to push ahead with her construction, albeit it at a reduced rate. At any one time 1,000 men were working on the ship but due to a succession of design changes and a lack of urgency from the Admiralty *Hood* was not launched until 22 August 1918 and did not begin her sea trials until after the war, in the spring of 1920.★ When she left the Clyde it was the end of a period which had seen continuous full-time employment and high wages for all, and viewed in retrospect the mighty *Hood* was the high-water mark of the wartime Clyde-built ship. No expense had been spared to build her and the work on her had been labour-intensive; she was innovative, unique and powerful, with all the basic materials and technology coming from industries in the surrounding area.

During the wartime construction of the Clyde's warships the yards faced increasing competition in the local labour market from the growing munitions industry as well as from other heavy industries such as the North British Locomotive Company at Springburn and

★ Neither her speed nor her strength could save *Hood*. On 24 May 1941, while leading HMS *Prince of Wales* into action against the German warships *Bismarck* and *Prinz Eugen* in the north Atlantic, *Hood* received a succession of direct hits and exploded with the loss of all but three of the 1,418 crew.

Polmadie which had come into being in 1903 as a result of the amalgamation of Glasgow's three leading locomotive companies: Sharp, Stewart and Company; Neilson, Reid and Company and Dubs and Company. By the beginning of 1915 Beardmore's Parkhead Forge had expanded to employ 20,000 workers and the same company would soon extend its activities into aircraft and airship production at Dalmuir and Inchinnan. Shipbuilding was incredibly labour-intensive and the labour pool was finite. At any one time a shipyard such as Brown's at Clydebank required up to 2,500 iron-workers with various different skills, but the intensity of wartime production and its unexpected fluctuations meant that it was difficult to retain the workforce. In calmer times men would switch between yards, taking employment as and when it became available but the war freed up the employment market making it easier for men to be absorbed elsewhere whenever work dried up. Travel was also a problem, especially for the Clydebank yards where many of the workforce (estimated at 16,000) lived in Glasgow or elsewhere and had to travel to work by train, adding extra hours onto the working day. In an attempt to ease the problem, both Brown's and Beardmore extended their peacetime policy of constructing modern tenement buildings near their yards for their key workers. The result was the appearance of a number of tenement buildings along and off the Dumbarton Road which were rented to foremen and under-foremen at market rates. With two or three rooms and with inside water-closets and bathrooms (albeit with only cold water) they offered superior modern accommodation at a time when nearly half the population lived in houses of two rooms and one in eight families lived in a single room. They also provided an immediate solution to the problem of holding on to and rewarding the foremen whom all shipyards quaintly characterised as the 'non-commissioned officers' of their operations: skilled men who acted as the link between the management and the workforce. Beardmore even created a large workers' hostel with small and simple bedrooms in a building called the Benbow Hotel, which also had a dining hall and recreational facilities such as a billiard room. It was destroyed during the Clydebank Blitz of the Second World War but many of the tenement buildings are still standing and the engraving of the battleship *Agamemnon* can still be seen on the stonework of the tenement building at the corner of Dumbarton Road and Agamemnon Road.[10]

The influx of workers into the area put a huge strain on the local housing market and inevitably led to difficulties, not least amongst English workers who also objected to the climate and the indifferent diet. At least 70 per cent of Glasgow's housing stock consisted of one- or two-room flats and the demand for more rented accommodation simply could not be met.[11] Much of the accommodation was sub-standard even before rents became an issue. With many tradesmen fully occupied in industry, lack of maintenance brought about deterioration and many tenement buildings in Glasgow badly needed modernisation or repair to the fabric. Unfortunately, the response from landlords was simply to increase rents and to evict those who were unable to meet their demands. Those who could pay soon found that their hard-earned wages and overtime were being whittled away while those who could not pay, including families with men serving in uniform, faced the probability of eviction by sheriff's officers. With the added problem of the rising price of foodstuffs the situation became so unbearable by the beginning of 1915 that there was an inevitable response from those affected. This came not just from the trade unions and political parties such as the Independent Labour Party (ILP) but also from the specially created Glasgow Women's Housing Association, which was formed on 16 February specifically to protect tenants against rent rises. Its secretary was Helen Crawfurd, a leading suffragette and anti-war campaigner who had already spent four terms in prison. Together with other activists – Mary Barbour, Agnes Dollan and Jessie Stephens – Crawfurd's association took the fight back to the landlords by encouraging the tenants to combine to resist the increases.

On one level they made it physically impossible for the bowler-hatted sheriff's officers to carry out their evictions. No sooner was an eviction attempted than women would rally to the scene and do whatever was necessary to prevent tenants being forcibly evicted from their homes, from cramming into tenement closes to pelting the sheriff's officers with bags of flour. Although the resistance was essentially peaceful in tone – Crawfurd and her associates made it clear that they were acting to prevent profiteering and to support wartime production – the landlords responded with court orders, a move which simply added to the sense of moral indignation as defaulters were forced to appear in court. In May 1915 the first rent strike was held in South Govan close to the Fairfield works, and by the end of the year at least 25,000 tenants had joined the movement, including a number of Labour councillors. Mass meetings were held to support the rent strikers and local women's housing associations were set up to galvanise support for the rent strikes and to back those who faced court orders.

Inevitably, with men at work the bulk of the organisation fell to women, who formed tenement and kitchen committees to protect their localities. In that sense the movement had a political aspect but its emphasis was more anti-profiteering than anti-war. When munitions workers were taken to court in the middle of October for refusing to pay rent increases their defence counsel explained to the court that they were not troublemakers but women engaged in essential tasks helping to win the war: 'They are not working for the proprietors of their homes. They are working for the purpose of turning out munitions.'[12] Outside in the streets women carried placards stating that while their menfolk were fighting in France or working in factories and shipyards, 'We are fighting the Huns at Home'. (An alliterative alternative was 'fighting Prussians in Partick'.) Paradoxically, perhaps, the strikers were supported by their employers, who did not want to see productivity slowed down by external factors outside their control; the management at Fairfield's issued a statement saying that 'they would allow no workman of theirs to occupy any house of any person victimised for refusing to pay a rent increase'.[13]

Matters came to a head towards the end of the year when a mass meeting was held in Glasgow's George Square on 17 November to protest against the prosecution of 18 tenants due to appear in court for refusing to pay rent increases. By then the rent strikes had escalated, with men taking their own wildcat strike action at Fairfield's and Beardmore's in protest against the actions of the landlords and to agitate for pay increases of their own. Rebellion was in the air but the rent strikes came to an end the following month when the government rushed through a Rent Restriction Act, which not only met the strikers' demands but, equally to the point, ensured continued production of essential wartime supplies. Rents were frozen at pre-war levels and increases were only allowed if improvements had been made to the property. It was a victory for what would later be known as 'people power', and as we shall see (Chapter Nine) the rent strikes also played a part in helping to politicise the Scottish labour force during the war years by encouraging workers to see that they had 'power and could bring about social change'.[14] At the heart of the matter, though, the rent strikes were prompted by a sense of outrage that landlords were taking advantage of the situation to make profits at a time when the country was fighting to win a war. David Kirkwood, a shop steward at the Parkhead Forge and a prominent ILP activist, put the crisis in perspective when he wrote to Sir John Lindsay, Glasgow's Town Clerk, stating that the objective was not special pleading but the creation of a fair deal to provide decent housing for essential workers: 'if the nation is to have an adequate supply of munitions of war, the workers must have healthy housing accommodation'.[15] And it was not just in Glasgow that rent strikes took place; there were also demonstrations against rent increases in Aberdeen and Dundee.

The settlement of the rent issue was a step forward in improving domestic conditions but it did not solve the concerns about main-taining a regular workforce for the shipyards. The other problem in workforce retention was centred on the long-standing employment practices whereby men were hired to carry out specific tasks without security of tenure. Time-served men such as platers and riveters worked together in squads or gangs whose leader would negotiate contracts based on the work in hand. Their work was highly skilled – the plates had to be shaped precisely and rivets were driven home in specific pre-determined places – but the squads also depended on unskilled temporary labourers who had to be sub-contracted. A lump sum was paid to the squad who then divided it amongst themselves in previously agreed proportions, the older time-served men getting a higher rate than the unskilled helpers. The system was built on hard bargaining and it was here that the foremen held a key role between the workforce and the management as they balanced the requirement for tight financial control with the need to maintain high craft standards. It could have been a bear-pit, with men swapping from one yard to the next and taking the best money on offer, but in 1897 a ticketing system known as enquiry notes was introduced by which men could only be employed if they had a note from their former employer confirming that they had completed their contract.[16] With work guaranteed during the war shipyard workers were in a stronger position than ever before to cut good deals, and skilled workers were keen to preserve their standing as craftsmen who had gone through a five-year apprenticeship. This, too, would prove to be an issue when employment in the shipyards became subject to state controls and rationalisation in order to increase productivity.[17]

Shipbuilding was not the only industry to experience a wartime boom. In the steel-working industry Scotland produced 1.2 million tons of the country's total 5-million-ton output, and the demand for steel for munitions meant that the Scottish figure had doubled by 1918 with 24,000 men in full employment in the Clyde valley. By that same year 90 per cent of the country's armour plate was being produced in Glasgow. For many firms the war came as a lifeline. The steelworks at Glengarnock in North Ayrshire were fast becoming obsolete in 1914: the blast furnaces had first been installed in 1843 and there had been little fresh investment since. However, with money from the Ministry of Munitions David Colville and Sons of Motherwell were able to refurbish the works and build a new open-hearth melting shop and a rolling mill. Coal underpinned everything and although the stocks of the west of Scotland fields were gradually being diminished, in 1913 they accounted for 25.5 million tons, roughly 10 per cent of the entire British output. In the east of Scotland output remained lower, at 17 million tons, a result of the loss of exports to Germany and the Baltic and a higher than average local recruitment of miners into the army.[18]

The creation of a state industry under the Ministry of Munitions in May 1915 revolutionised weapons production, and by the end of the war the ministry had expended £2,000 million and employed 65,000 civil servants. To ensure continuity and expansion of employment in the heavy industries the United Kingdom was divided into twelve areas, two of which were in Scotland under the control of a director of munitions. This job was given to Sir William Weir (later Lord Weir), a prominent Glasgow industrialist and millionaire who ran the family firm of marine engineers, G. & J. Weir, which supplied ancillary machinery for the engine-rooms of the new generation of warships. Having been appointed managing director at the early age of 25 in 1902 he emerged as confident, if conservative leader who turned the company into a successful international business, but he was also a perfervid anti-trade unionist and a great believer in rationalising practices within the workplace. In one of his first reports to the ministry Weir made his position abundantly clear: 'The responsibility and duty of a workman as a citizen of the empire is absolutely incompatible with his duty as a trade unionist.' Again this produced problems for the future, but under Weir's direction Glasgow prospered as an armaments centre with the expansion of Beardmore's at Parkhead, the use of the Singer Sewing Machine factory at Clydebank and the construction of subsidiaries such as the National Projectile Factory at Cardonald.

At the beginning of the conflict there were only 16 firms who tendered the War Office for contracts to provide guns and shells and small arms and ammunitions. The number had to be increased as the war became more industrialised and heavier weapons such as trench mortars and tanks were introduced. Diversification became part of the remit of the Ministry of Munitions, and under its direction William Beardmore built a number of aircraft types at Dalmuir under licence. These included Sopwith Pup fighters, Wight seaplanes and giant four-engined Handley Page V/1500 bombers. The construction of a huge steel-framed airship hangar at Inchinnan allowed the construction of airships including the R34, which became the first machine to fly the Atlantic in both directions in July 1919. Beardmore also moved into the construction of artillery pieces, notably 6-inch howitzers and 18-pounder field guns, while John Brown built a number of Mark IV tanks in 1917.[19] The North British Locomotive Company also moved into munitions production by constructing two new factories which made high-explosive shells and sea mines. The first building was christened 'Mons' and it produced 146,770 8-inch shells before switching to 6-inch shells for the army's 18-pounder field guns. The second factory, 'Marne', produced an average of 700 mines a month and later in the war both factories were involved in tank construction.

In common with the other heavy industries the North British Railway Company prospered as a result of the war, but it was not all about making profits. At the outset of the conflict the directors gave over part of their administration building in Flemington Street, Glasgow, to the Scottish Branch of the Red Cross for use as a casualty reception centre. Comprising five wards, the hospital had 400 beds, together with an operating theatre and a number of recreation rooms. During the war 8,211 soldiers received treatment at the hospital in Springburn and all the costs for the construction and alterations were met by the railway company.

All this was progress and it brought employment and wealth into Glasgow and the surrounding industrial area, a conurbation that embraced Clydeside, Lanarkshire, Renfrewshire, Dunbartonshire and North Ayrshire. Despite the difficulties raised by the rent strikes and problems with accommodation the war years were good to the west of Scotland. Not only were its traditional heavy industries booming as a result of the need to produce weapons of war but other trades and businesses were also in fine fettle, creating the diversity that gave the city its economic strength. In the summer of 1915 Glasgow's Town Clerk, Sir John Lindsay, could not forbear from boasting that Glasgow fully deserved its title as the Second City of Empire. He could not have envisaged the hard times that lay ahead once the war was over, when recession would take the place of the wartime boom. At the end of the second year of warfare it was enough that Glasgow was flourishing:

No city has rivalled, far less surpassed, the commercial metropolis of Scotland. This has chiefly arisen from the city being – if the expression may be used – cosmopolitan in its commerce and manufactures. Glasgow unites within itself a portion of the cotton spinning and weaving manufactures of Manchester, the printed calicoes of Lancashire, the stuffs of Norwich, the shawls and mousselines of France, the silk-throwing of Macclesfield, the flax-spinning of Ireland, the carpets of Kidderminster, the iron and engineering works of Wolverhampton, Sheffield and Birmingham, the pottery and glass-making of Staffordshire and Newcastle, the coal trade of the Tyne and Wear, and all the handicrafts connected with or dependent on the full development of these. Glasgow also has its distilleries, breweries, chemical works, tan-works, dye-works, bleach fields, and paper manufacturies, besides a vast number of staple and fancy hand-loom fabrics which may be strictly said to belong to that locality. Glasgow also, in its commercial relations, trades with every quarter of the globe; and its merchants deal in the various products of every country. It hence appears that one branch of manufacture or trade may be dull while another may be prosperous; and, accordingly, Glasgow does not feel any of those universal depressions which so frequently occur in places limited to one or two branches of manufacture or commerce.[20]

By the very nature of its industrial and commercial make-up Glasgow
and its hinterland benefited most from the wartime expansion of
heavy industry and the growing production of munitions. However,
that did not stop other parts of Scotland from enjoying a measure of
prosperity. Although Edinburgh could not match its western rival in
the industrial stakes – the city's largest engineering works, Brown
Brothers, employed only 541 men – it did house Britain's biggest
rubber manufacturer, the North British Rubber Company, whose
Castle Mills works was the largest single industrial employer in the
city. Brought under the control of the Ministry of Munitions the
company produced a huge variety of necessities for the war effort,
including tyres for every conceivable kind of vehicle and aircraft,
surgical appliances, anti-gas apparatus, cables, rubber boots, water-
proof coats and sheets.[21] With the huge volume of traffic from
England to the north of Scotland the railways also prospered in
the capital: Edinburgh was the main operational centre for the North
British and Caledonian railways, which between them maintained a
local workforce of 8,000. On the outbreak of war all railway
companies came under state control and the National Union of
Railwaymen brokered a wartime truce with the Railway Executive
Committee to prevent strike action during the conflict. Edinburgh's
other main industry was printing, and although it was hardly an
essential trade there were few wartime restrictions placed on it. For
long-established companies such as Bartholomew's, Constable's and
Nelson's it was very much a case of business as usual: athough many
men in their workforces had volunteered for military service in the
first two years of the war, their places had been taken by women.

Dundee was home to the British jute industry, with 69 firms
importing jute, and it enjoyed a virtual monopoly on jute production.
(India was part of the equation: most of Calcutta's jute-mills were
owned by Scots.) Dundee too enjoyed a boom as the War Office
approached companies such as Cox Brothers and Baxter Brothers in
March 1915 and asked them to increase production of jute sacks to
meet the army's demands for sacks for packing and supply, nosebags
for horses and above all sandbags for use in the trenches on the war
fronts. To ensure productivity an elaborate pyramid system of profit
margins was introduced at every stage of the process, from spinning
the jute to providing the army with the completed sacks. With a huge

guaranteed market the orders added to the firms' profits and the workers' wages in an industry which provided employment at peak periods for 25 per cent of Dundee's male workers and 67 per cent of the female workers.[22] The stalemate on the Western Front and the growing trench system pushed up demand to such an extent that by 1916 the army was calling for the provision of six million sacks a month and imports of jute rose accordingly. That same year Dundee's jute industry recorded a wartime high of 1.8 million tons imported from Bengal. The rewards were not slow in coming and towards the end of 1918 a leading jute manufacturer was moved to admit that war had been good for business, that 'jute fibres turned into strands of gold'.[23] So great was the demand from the War Office for sandbags that other customers lost out – notably the food industry, which required sacks for dry products such as sugar – and pre-war contracts had to be broken, with financial support being provided by the government.

Not that the boom helped labour relations, which were already poor in the industry: in March 1916 the Jute Workers' Union claimed a 15 per cent wage increase and a shorter working week and, when refused, went on strike until the end of April. The jute managers responded with the threat of a lockout and the strikes soon collapsed. Textiles and clothing production was another beneficiary of the war. The armed forces needed wool and cotton products for uniforms and local linen spinning firms also produced canvas material for tenting. Shipbuilding also benefited Dundee, where the Caledon Yard came under government direction, and to a lesser extent Aberdeen, where the local yards were engaged primarily in the construction of Admiralty Drifters.

Although the east-coast ports had been closed to trade – one of the reasons why coal production in Fife and the Lothians was adversely affected – they were kept open for fishing, albeit on a greatly reduced basis. At the beginning of the war 32,678 men were employed in the Scottish fishing industry and their catches represented around 25 per cent of the UK total. All that changed with the outbreak of war: by 1917 the number of fishermen had dropped to 21,870 and the catches of white fish had been reduced from 1.5 million tons in 1914 to a third of that amount three years later. Only herring remained reasonably stable, with the industry producing over a million barrels a year of cured herring throughout the war, mainly as a result of the west-coast ports remaining open. In September 1914 Scotland's east-coast ports were commandeered by the Admiralty, who also took control of all shipping, including the fishing fleet, and the following month neutral fishing craft were banned from using Scottish ports. Skippers were also warned that 'they might find themselves at any time caught up in the midst of a Fleet action of which no notice can be given' and that there would be no entry to ports after nightfall.[24] The North Sea was almost wholly closed to fishing, with the only permitted Scottish grounds being the area between the latitude of Kinnaird Head and a line joining the Hook of Holland to Sumburgh Head. On the west coast fishing was restricted to inshore areas and the Firth of Clyde and the Pentland Firth were completely closed to fishing. As a result catches were much reduced. It was also necessary to lay up fishing boats as the catches declined: all told, the Scottish fleet was reduced by 421 steam drifters, 45 motor drifters and 1,013 sail drifters. The port of Buckie was particularly badly hit, losing 120 steam drifters and 270 sail drifters.[25] Coming on top of the loss of the traditional herring export market to Russia and north Germany this sent fishing into a slump, and the auxiliary boats of the Royal Naval Reserve (Trawler Section) offered a lifeline to the industry at a time when it was being severely restricted by wartime naval operations. Things improved marginally after 1917 when the Germans introduced unrestricted submarine warfare and the fishing industry was put under pressure to produce more catches, but with the casualties and the loss of revenues it was hardly a case of business as usual.

Fish should have been one of the staples of the country's diet but the wartime restrictions drove down catches and pushed up prices so that by 1918, in common with many other food commodities, white fish was rationed. Feeding the population was one of the major headaches for the government, particularly in 1917, when the merchant fleet was vulnerable to submarine attack and ships were being sunk at an appallingly high rate. The Germans hoped to bring Britain to its knees by June and early in the year it looked as if might just succeed. On 27 April Jellicoe was so alarmed that he told Sir Edward Carson, the First Lord of the Admiralty, that the navy had lost command of the sea and that without the intervention of the United States or a complete rethink of the country's war aims 'the Navy will fail in its responsibilities to the country and the country itself will suffer starvation'.[26] Losses continued to be steady in May (345,000 British losses) and June (360,000 British losses) before the introduction of improved anti-submarine warfare techniques started reducing the losses to more acceptable levels.[27] Convoy systems were introduced and specially disguised and heavily armed 'Q' ships enjoyed a season of success, but the real catalyst for improvement was the appointment of the Scottish businessman Sir Edward Geddes as controller of the navy in May. A former manager of the North Eastern Railway Geddes had worked wonders with the transport system supplying the Western Front, and his no-nonsense approach galvanised the navy's attitude to anti-submarine warfare. Even so, it had been a grim haemorrhage: by the time the war ended Britain had lost 7.6 million tons of merchant shipping, or 55 per cent of the 1914 fleet, and 15,313 merchant sailors had been killed. Many of that number came from the Western Isles, where there was a long tradition of service in the Merchant Navy, leading to the perception locally that the losses were higher there than in any other part of the United Kingdom. Of the 8,000 fishermen who joined the RNR (Trawler Section), around 2,000 came from Lewis.[28]

Clearly it had been a close-run thing. Not only had Britain been hard pushed to counter the submarine threat but its own resources had been found wanting, largely as a result of pre-war increases in food importation. At the end of the first year of the war Conservative MP Sir William Raeburn had boasted that nothing had changed and that food was not only plentiful but still relatively inexpensive: 'The war has falsified every prophecy', was his confident assertion.[29] However, by the autumn of 1916 the situation had suddenly become grim, with food not only difficult to find but increasingly expensive. On 16 October 1916 the Board of Trade announced that the average increase in the price of foodstuffs was 65 per cent and that in some cases it was much higher: sugar had risen by 166 per cent, fish and eggs by 100 per cent and flour by 66 per cent. Even staples such as margarine (up 19 per cent), milk (up 39 per cent) and potatoes (up 53 per cent) were becoming increasingly expensive and scarce.[30] In an attempt to become more self-sufficient the government introduced measures to turn over more farmland to arable use, but this was not particularly successful in Scotland, where the available acreage was lower and where the bulk of the land was given over to hill farming. (Out of a total area of 19 million acres only 5 million were under crops or grass while 9 million acres consisted of mountain terrain suitable only for rough grazing.) Farmers were also sceptical of the value of increasing arable land by extending the numbers and size of allotments near the cities, a proposal which was aired in July 1915 by the Scottish Office. Asked if these smallholdings could help the war effort, James G. Robinson, Organising Secretary of the Scottish Farm Servants' Union, told the committee of enquiry that such endeavours were a distraction from the task in hand:

> I am not greatly in favour of smallholdings myself. I have been through the smallholdings and have seen the houses at Ballencrief and other places, and I don't know if a man is to be much better off than he would be working on a big farm. The tools can never be the same: they are working with antiquated implements. I think the farm worker would rather have reasonable working conditions and a fairly decent wage working on a farm as he is now doing than be a smallholder.[31]

The problem was exacerbated by manpower shortages which saw the agricultural labour market in Scotland drop from a pre-war high of 107,000 to 89,000 by the cessation of hostilities in 1918; as had happened in the coal industry, disproportionate numbers of young Scottish farm-workers had volunteered in 1914 and 1915, taking much-needed men away from the land. Scotland's main agricultural contribution to the war effort came from traditional sheep farming in the upland areas where the demand for wool and meat pushed up prices and provided full employment. Around 9,000 men worked as shepherds or hill farmers, but with 7 million sheep to tend it was hard and unyielding work: on average each man had to look after 800 beasts.[32] In 1916 the whole of Scotland's wool clip was purchased by the government under a scheme to provide raw materials for the clothing trade and to meet the demand for uniforms. As a result shepherds' wages doubled from 20 shillings to 40 shillings a week and even Scottish upland hill farmers benefited from the scheme. Normally the hardy blackface sheep yielded coarse wool suitable only for carpets but the exigencies of wartime life meant that even their clip was used for clothing.

Although the increases in Scottish arable land were small compared to what was happening in England, the acreage given over to oats rose by 25 per cent and there was a corresponding increase in yield. Root vegetable cropping, long a staple in Scottish agriculture, also had to increase its yield to make up for the loss of imports, although H. M. Conacher, Deputy Commissioner for the Board of Agriculture for Scotland, could not forbear from commenting on his fellow countrymen's lack of appreciation of what was on offer: 'The Scots are acquainted with and appreciate a fewer number of vegetables than the English, potatoes and cabbage being their chief "stand-by".'

All told, before the introduction of food controls in 1917 Scottish farming prospered during the war with wages doubling: in 1914 the average wage for a ploughman was 21 shillings and 6 pence, but by 1919 it had risen to 49 shillings and 2 pence, and productivity remained high.[33] While there were food shortages, these were caused mainly by the reliance on imports, mainly wheat from the United States, and the loss of imported staples such as potatoes. In 1914 Leith imported 2,856,300 hundredweight (approximately 145,000 tonnes), mainly from Europe, but this had shrunk to 547,100 hundredweight (approximately 28,000 tonnes) in 1918. At the same time, the farming community had to work hard to meet the demands of a new client, the massed armies, which had a seemingly insatiable appetite for horses, hay, foodstuffs, milk and wool. At the end of the war Dr Charles Douglas, President of the Highland and Agricultural Society, was moved to record his and the nation's gratitude to the unsung men and women of Scotland who had worked the land, often in trying conditions:

No class perhaps in all the nation emerges with a cleaner record from the trial of battle than the Scottish farm servant. They gave their full proportion – perhaps more than their proportion – to the fighting services. But it is to their work on the farms that I refer here. It will be generally agreed that, taken as a whole, they did not make unfair demands or seek to derive undue advantage from a situation which offered them great opportunities. It will not be disputed that their willing and reliable work was a most essential factor in the success of Scottish war agriculture, and that, in their case, improved conditions of service were a stimulus and not a check to industry and that they showed themselves worthy of the trust that was reposed in them.[34]

Despite those heroic efforts, though, food shortages had become a
reality by the beginning of 1918, forcing the government to introduce
more stringent measures. Two 'meatless days' were observed each
week, Scotland's being Wednesday and Friday, when it became illegal
to serve meat at any meal in any public place such as a hotel or
restaurant. In Edinburgh, the New Club had already introduced
meatless and potato-less days but was forced to introduce a new
and draconian measure for its membership: cake would not be served
at lunchtime.[35] Food rationing came into being on 25 February 1918,
first in the London area and by 7 April all over the country. For the
first time there was a uniform system of food control to ensure that the
sale of essential commodities such as meat, sugar, tea, jam and cheese
was properly rationed and the prices regularised. Breaches of rationing
were punished under legislation provided by the Defence of the
Realm Act (DORA), and the Ministry of Food published regular lists
of defaulters. There was also a vigorous propaganda war to encourage
people to eat less and save more for the war effort with regular
exhortations to 'eat less meat', 'be careful with your bread', 'waste
nothing', 'save especially in all things which have to be imported', 'use
home products wherever possible' and 'grow your own vegetables'.[36]
Even the Royal Family joined in the effort. On 2 May 1917 King
George V issued a proclamation urging the people 'to reduce the
consumption of bread in their respective families by at least one-fourth
of the quantity used in ordinary times' and 'to abstain from the use of
flour in pastry'. The price of milk was also fixed at 2 shillings and 8
pence a gallon in 1918 with seasonal variations to take into account
the summer months when grass was plentiful and the milk yield was
higher. Following pressure from the Board of Agriculture in Scotland,
which oversaw production, Scottish prices were adjusted to take into
account late seasonal growth.[36]

Money was also part of the equation and the 'waste not' philosophy
was carried through to savings. Through the Scottish Home and
Health Department and other agencies the government issued appeals
to 'lend your savings to the Country to pay for the War and Victory'.
Special £5 scrip certificates with a total holding allowance of £200
were introduced which promised a rate of interest of 5 pence per
month. The drinking of alcohol was also curbed during the war and
this affected Scotland in many ways. In the previous century huge

quantities of whisky were consumed by the adult population, with the average weekly consumption being one bottle of duty-charged whisky per head of population. Whisky was a staple of Scottish life – beer was a mere accompaniment as a 'chaser' – and so closely was it associated with Scotland that when comic postcard manufacturers or magazines such as *Punch* portrayed Scots as red-nosed drunken tipplers everyone knew what they meant. Public houses were plentiful, especially in industrial areas, and their culture was solidly male: excessive drinking was not only encouraged but was thought by the participants to be acceptable. Its by-products were less satisfactory. Heavy drinking might have offered temporary escape from the drudgery of the workplace and bad housing conditions, but it also encouraged violence and caused untold misery by eating into family budgets. As the medical officer of Glasgow's prisons put it in 1912, the slums would always be a breeding ground for crime as long as public houses were used as a substitute home by male drinkers. Between 1900 and 1909 the average annual conviction rate for drunkenness was 103 for every 10,000 head of population.[37]

During the same period various temperance movements, such as the Band of Hope and Good Templars, picked up support in Scotland and legislation introduced in 1853 prevented public houses from opening on Sundays and forced them to close at 11.00 p.m. on weekday evenings. Public ownership of drinking outlets was another proposal to curb heavy drinking by institutionalising its consumption along the lines of a scheme introduced in Gothenburg in Sweden. A similar version was created in the west Fife coalfield where some 20 public houses were brought under local control and operated as 'Gothenburgs' or 'Goths', large austere public houses which were usually 'of a somewhat grim and forbidding aspect'.[38] There was also a 'Gothenburg' in Prestonpans in East Lothian which was operated by the East of Scotland Public House Trust, one of whose directors was the publisher Thomas Nelson. However, these well-intentioned schemes were the exception and not the rule and at the outbreak of war public houses were allowed to be open for up to 13 hours a day, apart from Sundays, and there were no limits on what could be drunk.

All that was changed by legislation in the DORAs which gradually reduced the opening hours of public houses: by the beginning of 1916 the Scottish drinking public had only five and half hours a day at their disposal and evening closing time was set at 9.00 p.m., with no opening at all on Sundays. The other restriction was provided by the Central Control Board (Liquor Traffic), which brought under government authority brewing and public house outlets in areas where munitions camps were being constructed. In Scotland the board's restricted areas were at the naval base at Invergordon and in the national cordite factory and munitions workers' camps at Gretna on the Scottish border with England, where the drinking of alcohol was effectively put under government control. During the construction of the Gretna munitions facilities over 25,000 workers were involved in the project, many of them from Ireland. Their arrival in the area led to scenes of drunken disorder on paydays and so great was the outcry that the government was forced to act by restricting the availability of alcohol. Also known as the 'Carlisle Scheme', after the city where the board nationalised four breweries and over 400 public houses for an outlay of £900,000, the move achieved its aim of restricting the consumption of alcohol during the war. In Gretna and Invergordon there were no breweries to close but drinking was restricted to a total of 30 public houses and four off-licences. The scheme worked but it was not popular. The hostelries were plain and unwelcoming places – that was part of the intention – but they did achieve their aim of reducing drunkenness with the Scottish conviction rate falling by a national average of 70 per cent. There were other restrictions centred on curtailing drinking habits, but they stopped short of introducing total prohibition.

Towards the end of the war a number of local plebiscites in the west of Scotland showed that such a move would not have been unpopular and the Scottish Office was bombarded by letters from various bodies and local authorities demanding that the government should extend the restrictions imposed by Central Control Board. These resolutions became more frequent and vocal as rationing increased, the argument being that alcohol production used up vital supplies of foodstuffs such as barley, but despite the weight of correspondence no action was taken; the file was closed with the note that 'an acknowledgement would appear to suffice'.[39] However, as early as November 1914 Glasgow Corporation had voted to stop providing alcohol at official receptions and other public-spirited bodies followed their example;

there was a ban on 'treating' (buying rounds of drinks) and public houses were prevented from offering credit to their customers. In April 1915 the royal family also took a lead when King George V announced that he and his household would be teetotal for the duration of the war.[40] Others had their mind made up for them: on 31 August 1915 the Scottish Office issued a memorandum to Scotland's chief constables directing them to take steps 'to protect soldiers undergoing treatment in hospitals and convalescent homes from the dangers involved in the consumption of intoxicating liquor'.[41]

Scotland's long love-hate relationship with drink was changed inexorably when wartime restrictions were carried over into the post-war years of peace. In 1921 a new Licensing Act restricted public house opening times to eight hours a day, with closing time fixed at 10.00 p.m. and there was no Sunday opening apart from a curious system whereby 'bona fide travellers' could be served alcohol in hotel bars provided they signed a register giving the details of their journey. It was not until the 1980s that Scotland's licensing laws were liberalised to allow longer opening hours as well as allowing public houses to open on Sundays. Other post-war changes were more subtle but more deeply felt.

During the conflict Scotland fully justified its title of the workshop of the war but the productivity and the profits were mostly mirage as the heavy industries were already facing a steady decline in 1914. As we shall see, the boom years of full order books in Scotland's heavy industries soon became a distant memory as the world economy slipped towards the slump of the 1920s. Dundee's jute boom also collapsed when price controls were removed and across the country in just about every commercial sector workers were laid off as profits fell and business came to a standstill. Although it was not evident at the time, that post-war slump affected two of the great dreams to emerge from industrial Scotland during the war: the emancipation of women in the workplace and the evolution of socialist idealism amongst the country's working classes. In 1922 Labour won 29 seats in Scotland, and as 19 represented seats in Glasgow and the west of Scotland hopes were high that the New Jerusalem was at hand and that there would be a just reward for the wartime efforts of the men and women of Clydeside who believed that, united in common cause, they could achieve great things for themselves and their families. It did not quite turn out that way, but the failure does not detract from the growing empowerment of women and the dawning of a socialist movement committed to political change. Both were to cast a long shadow over twentieth-century Scottish life.

8 Women's Work

One statistic sums up the role played by women in the pre-war Scottish workplace and the great changes that took place during the course of the war. The population census of 1911 showed that 185,442 men were employed in the heavy industries of Clydeside, but apart from the 2,062 women employed in the Singer Sewing Machine Factory at Clydebank there were only 3,758 women in full employment in the heavy sector, most of them in the chemical industry, itself a minor contributor to the region's economy. Five years later, by the middle of 1916, the number of women involved in heavy industries in the same area had climbed to 18,500 and by the end of the war 31,500 women were working in the munitions industry in Scotland.[1] The driving forces behind the dramatic increase in numbers were the need to increase the production of weapons of war and the introduction by the Ministry of Munitions of 'dilution' into the workplace. This was an agreement brokered between management and the trades unions which permitted skilled engineering workers' jobs to be broken down into skilled and unskilled components so that an inexperienced worker could carry out one single task on a machine while working under supervision. Many of the workers brought into the industry in this way were women and the majority found themselves working in the munitions industries in the west and south-west of Scotland.

The need to employ women in jobs previously held by men helped to change previously held preconceptions about what constituted 'women's work'. Women had always worked in domestic work or on the land, usually in low paid and monotonous jobs, or in the role of unpaid wives helping out with seasonal chores. However, by the beginning of the century, following the changes in working practices ushered in by the Industrial Revolution, women were also being employed in factories and trades such as printing, and there was already a long tradition of women working in the textile industry. In Dundee the jute industry could not have operated without women workers: whereas men stuck to flax-weaving on handlooms, for the linen trade women were absorbed into the spinning of jute, which had become the city's staple industry by the beginning of the century. Out of a total female working population of 84,000, some 34,000 worked in the jute industry and as the importance of flax decreased so jute assumed a greater importance, with the result that women workers were soon outnumbering the male workers three to one. As Billy Kay found while interviewing Dundee mill workers, it was a unique role reversal. One woman, Sarah Craig, told him, 'They used to say the men stayed at home and the women went out to work in Dundee. Well, that's true in a way because there was work for women, no' for men, wi' the result the men "boiled the kettle" as the saying is.'[2] The majority of the workforce were married women: in 1914 54.3 per cent of women over the age of 15 were in work and of them 23.4 per cent were married, the highest percentage in Scotland. Dundee also became a magnet for migrant labour from the Highlands and Ireland. However, the work was seasonal, with the result that lay-offs were common, and there was a distinct pecking-order with the weavers at the top and the sack sewers at the bottom.

One reason for the success of the jute industry lay in the low wages paid to the women workers: before the war women in all sectors were paid an average of 45 per cent of what would be paid to a man. Even in the professions such as teaching there was a difference, mainly because women tended to remain in the lower reaches of the elementary schools. Women occupied 70 per cent of the available teaching posts but the lack of promotion possibilities meant that none would earn the same as their male colleagues. However, in general the differential in wages for men and women was based on several factors. First, much of the work undertaken by women demanded fewer skills or was deemed to be little more than drudgery and therefore commanded lower pay. The work could also be seasonal or liable to fluctuations. Another factor was marital status. The 1911 census figures show that a majority of Scottish women were married and had children: the average age for marriage in 1911 was 26 and the average family size for women in that age group was 5.8. Their impact on the labour market was therefore limited and of short duration, it being uncommon and considered scandalous for women to continue working once they had married. Only one in twenty women in employment in Scotland in 1911 was married, a figure lower than the rest of the United Kingdom. Only the Dundee jute workers bucked the trend. For the middle classes or those who aspired to join them, it was quite different. Successful husbands did not approve of their wives working and a leisured wife was a sign of a man's financial standing. Their role was to run the home and tend to the children while domestic servants dealt with menial household tasks.

The census statistics of 1911 also provide a handy snapshot of the main outlets for female labour in Scotland shortly before the outbreak of war: domestic work 135,062 (22.76%); textile work 134,418 (22.65%); clothing trade 73,393 (12.37%); food and drink trade 44,984 (7.58%); agricultural work 32,423 (5.46%); commercial clerks 29,067 (4.09%), teaching 18,778 (3.16%) and nurses and midwives 10,629 (1.79%). Women clearly made a key, if limited, contribution in the Scottish workplace but most of it was at the lower end of the scale of skills. With the school-leaving age set at 14, working-class girls often had to give up any idea of further education and were forced to go into work immediately in order to contribute to the family budget. All too often this meant going into low-paid or menial jobs with little hope of advancement. For example, the Report on the Conditions of Work in Scotland revealed at the end of the nineteenth century that most women's work produced a pitiful return. Taking one example, that of the wife of an ironworker, a woman might earn 1 shilling and 2 pence for sewing buttons onto two dozen pairs of men's trousers, but that took up 12 hours of intense labour. In that time she had to heat the room in which she was working (3 pence) and pay 2 pence for the delivery of the finished article to the workshop, leaving her with a profit of 7 pence. Outside the sweatshops matters were not much better. Although the pre-war printing trade in Scotland employed 4,083 women in comparison to 11,031 men, most of the female workers, 2,904, were box-makers compared to 348 men in the same position. A woman's place was clearly in the home and those who worked were expected to accept a wage which would always be inferior to anything paid to a man.[3]

The war helped to change all that, albeit temporarily, by opening

up the workplace to female workers who stepped into the shoes of
male workers serving in the armed forces or were employed in the
heavy industries under the dilution scheme to meet the demand for
war materials. Between 1914 and 1918 female employment in the UK
rose from 2.18 million to 2.97 million, the majority, 703,000, being
employed in the munitions industry.[4] Paradoxically, the opening
months of the war did not hint at this rapid expansion. On the
contrary there was an immediate downturn in the number of jobs
available to women as the country struggled to come to terms with a
major conflict: in September 1914 the government estimated that
some 40 per cent of the female labour force had been made
unemployed as a result of the uncertainty caused by the outbreak
of war and there were fears that the lay-offs might have a lasting effect
on the economy. In the domestic market servants were paid off as an
economy measure but it was a short-lived effort: within weeks a
contemporary survey noted that good cooks were much in demand
on the labour market. Luxury trades such as dressmaking and millinery
also suffered and the reductions in the Scottish shipping fleet affected
the 50,000 women who were employed seasonally as fish-gutters in
the east-coast fisheries.[5] There were also contractions in the textile
industry, where workers were put on short time, although full
production was soon restored as the need for soldiers' uniforms
and equipment increased with the rapid expansion of the armed
forces in 1915. Welcome though this was – the late summer panic was
soon followed by acute labour shortages in the textile industry – most
of the jobs were traditionally regarded as women's work and did not
represent any appreciable change in traditional work patterns. That
only came as women began to move into positions occupied by men
who had enlisted in the armed forces.

By the summer of 1915 it was not uncommon to see women in
highly visible roles at bank or post office counters, or working as ticket
collectors or tram conductors. The labour shortage situation was so
critical that on 30 October 1915 the general manager of the Commercial Bank of Scotland wrote to the Scottish secretary warning him
that the bank would have to close branches across Scotland if more
men volunteered. The letter ended with the plea 'that no more be
taken from us until we have an opportunity – say during the next few
weeks – of engaging and training more women clerks'. As a result of

this and other requests the Scottish Office appointed a committee to consider what steps should be taken to employ more women in commerce and within six months its local advisory committee in Edinburgh reported a sharp increase in women's employment in the capital, with 120 women working in men's jobs on the tramways, 48 in the rubber industry and 33 on the railways, where they worked not just as carriage cleaners, a traditional role, but also as guards and porters. In April 1915 two clerical staff from Glasgow became the first women in Britain to be employed as tram conductors.[6] In work of the latter kind women were not supposed to carry out any heavy duties but they proved to be adept at picking up the required skills, and contemporary surveys show that women were more tolerant of jobs which were repetitive and frequently boring.[7]

The process of putting women into positions vacated by enlisted men was known as 'substitution' and, following some initial hesitation by the trade unions, it proved to be an effective way of dealing with the manpower shortages caused by the country's huge appetite for soldiers. Women were just as capable of stamping tickets or guarding a train as men were – most of the jobs were considered to be men's trades by time-honoured custom as opposed to the possession of any particular skill – and by 1917 it was estimated that one in three working women were substituting male workers' jobs. However, their efforts did not mean that they received equal pay: a male postman received 35 shillings a week while his wartime female counterpart received 10 shillings less. However, as many parts of commercial and industrial life would have ground to a halt without women substituting men in key jobs, the employment of women was a bonus for the war effort or, as a leader in the *Glasgow Herald*, explained the position early in 1916, 'We sum up everything in this: the women are magnificent, and the nation is more indebted to them than it can at present express.'[8] In the longer term, though, the employment of women in men's roles proved to be a temporary wartime expedient. By 1924 the Ministry of Labour was reporting that 'the reversal of the process of substitution which was so striking a feature of wartime industry is now practically complete', and in most factories there had been a return to the status quo of 'men's work' and 'women's work'.

The biggest single employer of UK women in roles traditionally reserved for men was the munitions industry, which came under the direction of the Ministry of Munitions and was controlled by the provisions of the Munitions of War Act of July 1915. Under the terms of this legislation the government had wide-ranging powers to manage the way in which the industry operated and to impose strict rules for the employment of its workforce. Limits were set on profits as well as on wages and standard workshop practices were shelved for the duration of the war. Strikes were outlawed and a system of leaving certificates prevented a worker from being re-employed within six weeks of leaving his or her current job. The new policy embraced dilution and in the west of Scotland its implementation was put in the hands of the Clyde Dilution Commission, which came into being at the beginning of 1916. It issued directives ('L' circulars) on wages and conditions and under circulars L2 and L3 women replacing men in the munitions industry were supposed to be paid a minimum rate of £1 a week, with skilled women workers being paid the men's rate. However, this was not mandatory and employers were able to bypass the regulation, paying women the lower rate or what they estimated to be the going rate for the job. Beardmore proved to be an enthusiastic employer of women, especially at Parkhead Forge, but he also restricted their earnings to 15 shillings a week. Of course, at that stage of the war there were no votes in ensuring that women received the correct rate of pay and, as the government was more concerned with achieving a steady supply of munitions and armaments, the system of state control did not make for better conditions as far as most women were concerned.

By the end of the war there were 4,285 'controlled' establishments manufacturing munitions and 103 government factories. In Scotland the main munitions facilities employing women were in Glasgow and Clydebank. However, there was also the huge purpose-built cordite-manufacturing complex at Gretna and a number of other smaller facilities in the south-west such as the Galloway Engineering Company's factory at Tongland near Kirkcudbright, a futuristic confection of glass and concrete which used techniques developed in the US automobile-manufacturing industry to produce aircraft engines. Developed in 1917 by Arrol-Johnston, the largest of Scotland's carmakers, and backed by Beardmore, it was envisaged as 'an engineering college for ladies' and many of its workers had received their initial training at the Glasgow Institute of Technology. Each sector produced differences. Most of the workers at the Gretna factory came from other parts of Britain and their influx into the lowlands of the Solway estuary changed the complexion of the area. Five farms were taken over and the complex stretched from Dornock through Gretna to Longtown, with the main residential area being constructed at East Riggs. At the height of production over 9,000 women were employed at Gretna (plus 5,000 men) and the township or camp where they lived was the first 'new town' to be planned and sponsored by the government. It was connected to the works by a light railway which brought the girls to work and took those coming off a shift back to the camp, where conditions were clean but Spartan. The cost of living was deducted from the women's wages. Administered by the Young Women's Christian Association, the accommodation blocks consisted of 85 barrack-like wooden huts containing small single rooms with a bed and a washbasin. There were larger quarters for managers and 500 married workers and their families. Constructed in neo-Georgian style in red brick, these houses were the prototypes for the post-war council housing schemes conceived under the Housing and Town Planning Act of 1919, although ironically the design was used only in England. Food was produced by a factory bakery, the complex had its own power station and water treatment plant, and entertainment was provided by a cinema, a dance-hall and an institute which held weekly socials.[9]

The government was proud of the facility, which was the biggest in the empire, and encouraged visits from writers associated with Charles Masterman's London-based War Propaganda Bureau, also known as 'Wellington House', who used their literary skills and their popularity to write unofficial propaganda putting the British war effort in a good light. An early visitor to Gretna was the novelist Arthur Conan Doyle, who wrote about the complex in *The Times* in November 1916, giving it the fictional name of 'Moor-side' and describing it as 'one of the miracles of present-day Britain and perhaps the most remarkable place in the world'.[10] However, the most interesting portrait was painted by another, younger novelist, Rebecca West, the adopted name of Cecily Isabel Fairfield, who had been brought up in Edinburgh and had emerged as an influential and combative journalist in the women's suffrage cause before the war. Her account of 'The

Cordite Makers' appeared in the *Daily Chronicle*, also in 1916, and it produced a stunning picture of the surrounding area with its low scattered marshes where 'there lay the village which is always full of people, and yet is the home of nothing but death'. Gretna had been chosen as the site because it was safe from German attack and because it enjoyed good communications north and south, but what attracted West was the sense of otherness she discovered in the complex:

> In the glare it showed that like so many institutions of the war it has the disordered and fantastic quality of a dream. It consists of a number of huts, some like the government-built huts for Irish labourers, and some like the open-air shelters in a sanatorium, scattered over five hundred acres; they are connected by raised wooden gangways and interspersed with green mounds and rush ponds. It is of such vital importance to the State that it is ringed with barbed-wire entanglements and patrolled by sentries, and its pro-ducts must have sent tens of thousands of our enemies to their death. And it is inhabited chiefly by pretty young girls clad in Red-Riding-Hood fancy dress of khaki and scarlet.[11]

As was the case in the rest of the munitions industry those 'pretty young' Gretna girls worked long hours to meet the insatiable demand for munitions: a typical shift lasted twelve hours with roughly one and a half hours allowed for meal breaks and Sunday was the only day of rest. (To put that into context, most people worked long hours before the First World War: a girl in domestic service would only get half a day off a week and one full day a month.) Their work was also dangerous and unpleasant as they were dealing with highly volatile materials. The uniforms were for show but inside the factory the girls donned caps and white waterproofs to protect them before they worked the brown cordite paste or mixed gun-cotton with mineral jelly – a mixture which Conan Doyle memorably called 'devil's porridge'. Before entering the factory they had to put on rubber overshoes and were searched for metal objects such as hairpins, which could spark an explosion. Other safety measures included a ban on corsets because the bones in them could cause further damage in the event of an accident. In Rebecca West's eyes the girls at work at the big vats resembled millers or cooks and in her fancy she compared them to the working women in Velazquez's painting *The Weavers*, but the reality was rather different.

Like every other munitions factory Gretna worked round the clock and the atmosphere inside the factory was often noxious with toxic fumes which were not only unpleasant but sapped energy levels. Given the volatile nature of the work death was never far away. During the war 61 British women workers died of poisoning and 71 were killed as a result of explosions. (The worst incident came in 1917 at Silvertown in east London where 69 women were killed and 72 were severely wounded when an accidental fire ignited 50 tons of TNT. It caused more damage than all the enemy air raids on the capital combined and the sound of the explosion could be heard all over east London and Woolwich.) There were several minor incidents at Gretna which caused injuries and one major accident in 1917 which killed one girl, but on the whole it was reckoned to be one of the safer munitions establishments. Not that there was much respite from the daily grind: anyone falling ill had their wages stopped and, as the average weekly wage at Gretna was 30 shillings, there was clearly an incentive not to report sick. Towards the end of a shift the desire to sleep grew greater and a visiting inspector reported to the ministry that he found 'several women lying, during the meal hour, beside their piles of heaped-up work; while others, later, were asleep beside their machines, facts which bear additional witness to the relative failure of these hours'.[12]

To maintain order within the factory and township the Ministry of Munitions called on the services of the Women's Police Service, which had been formed originally as a voluntary organisation funded by their self-appointed commandant Margaret Damer Dawson. Many of its members had belonged to the woman's suffrage movement or were involved in moral crusades of one kind or another and wanted to make a contribution to the war effort, preferably by wearing uniform. By the end of the war there were 150 policewomen of the Women's Police Service operating at Gretna under the supervision of two male officers, and their presence was not always welcomed by the work-force. Their main tasks were to ensure the safety of the workers by searching them before they began work and to patrol the area to prevent any backsliding during the shifts, but morality was also an issue. When the police service had been founded, originally as the

Women Police Volunteers, one of its roles was the protection of women from the lure of drink and sexual relationships and this was also an issue at Gretna.

The question of alcohol had been addressed by the Central Control Board, which had restricted the sale of alcohol in the local area, but Carlisle with its 'undesirable temptations' lay within reach and, on police advice, to prevent any communication with its larger population evening train services between the two places were cancelled.[13] There were strict rules in force to control the possibility of sexual relationships – girls were given medical examinations every fortnight – but as Sunday was the only holiday and travel was difficult, liaisons outside the factory were well nigh impossible. Over half of the girls had been in domestic service before the war or had not worked at all, and for the majority of them it was their first experience of living and working far away from their homes. Clearly the management believed that this novelty might lead to promiscuity, but sex was not the only issue facing the Women's Police Service: in the early days their main task was breaking up fights between rival Scottish and Irish munitions workers.

The Women's Police Service was not the only organisation concerned with maintaining high moral standards. At the outset of the war the National Union of Women's Workers of Great Britain (NUWW) had come into being and it quickly spawned a Scottish committee, convened by the Countess of Aberdeen. The title of their organisation was somewhat misleading as the membership were hardly 'workers' but middle-class and upper-class women who were concerned to do good work for the lower orders, particularly for 'fallen women'. Following an initiative by the English body to establish a volunteer women's police force to protect women from men and from themselves, the Scottish committee wrote to the Scottish secretary on 29 October 1914 asking him to direct chief constables to recognise the Scottish NUWW as 'a body of trained women to work in the neighbourhood of camps and other places in Scotland where troops are being trained, with the object of meeting as far as possible the difficulties caused by the presence of women and girls of loose behaviour.' Those involved would wear a special armlet or badge, but, as the Scottish committee explained, it was necessary for the patrols to carry the authorisation of the local chief constable.

Although the scheme had received the blessing of the Home Office the Scottish Office preferred to be cautious and before deciding anything they sounded out the chief constables of Edinburgh, Glasgow, Lanarkshire and Stirlingshire, sending out a draft on 5 December which explained the reasons for the proposed women's patrols:

It should be understood that this work is not designed to relieve the police of their duties with respect to disorderly or illegal conduct on the part of prostitutes or others, but that its object will be mainly preventative and will have more particularly in view the case of girls and women who would not ordinarily come under the notice of police but who from absence of the necessary self control may be liable to be carried away by the excitement induced by unusual surroundings.

The response was positive, with all four chief constables expressing enthusiasm for the scheme and promising their support. The only discordant note was struck by Lieutenant-General Sir Spencer Ewart, the army's senior soldier in Scotland, who warned: 'Any display of tactlessness or a want of common sense on the part of well-meaning but over-zealous people may wreck the proposals and create trouble.' However, prompted by overwhelming support from the police the secretary of state, McKinnon Wood, gave his agreement to the establishment of women's patrols and at the end of 1914 a circular letter was sent to all of Scotland's chief constables asking them to co-operate with the Scottish NUWW committee by issuing the necessary identity cards. Once again there was a wholehearted response: every Scottish chief constable agreed to co-operate with the scheme and gave it their blessing. Some went further. The chief constable of Lerwick replied that 'there are a good number of these loose girls and women here and the police will be pleased to co-operate in the manner indicated', while his opposite number in Elgin welcomed the women's patrols because in his area 'swarms of young girls are constantly molesting the soldiers, and at the request of the military officers here I have repeatedly had constables patrolling near the drill halls during the evening to send these young girls to their homes'. Curiously, the scheme worked and although the Scottish NUWW committee reported instances where their patrols were either ignored or given abuse, its annual report in 1917 noted that 'the work has justified itself, in spite of the difficulties of climate and of darkness'.[14]

The establishment of the women's volunteer police forces was not the only example of the public's desire to do something for the war effort in Scotland. Perhaps the most famous contribution was the creation of the Scottish Women's Hospitals, the inspired idea of a remarkable woman, Dr Elsie Inglis, and one of several responses to the war by women doctors and nurses across the United Kingdom. With good reason Inglis has been called one of the most inspirational women of her generation, a doughty campaigner who not only had to fight hard to achieve her aims but also had to suffer a good deal of male opposition from within her profession. She was a daughter of the empire, having been born on 16 August 1864 at the north Indian hill station of Naini Tal, the summer capital of the United Provinces. Her father, John Forbes Inglis, was a member of the Indian Civil Service and at the time of his daughter's birth was serving as the commissioner for Rohilcund. His wife had rejoined him the previous year, having stayed behind in Britain to bring up six children born earlier in their marriage. During the hot season – roughly from April to September – Naini Tal was the official retreat for the officials and administrators of the state secretariat, who escaped the fire of the plains by decamping with their families to the cooler weather in the hills. It was a pleasant hot-season residence, with a boat club beside the lake and several imposing bungalows and hotels; with their tennis parties and picnics, their fancy-dress dances and amateur theatricals, the hill stations offered a hectic social round and holiday atmosphere which was very different from the normal run of life in British India.

To Elsie and her younger sister Eva it was a happy and uneventful childhood marked by the seasonal journeying between the plains and the hills, and, as for all children brought up in that environment, it was a privileged and comfortable existence with servants and a wide variety of innocent pleasures. The first change came in 1876, when John Inglis decided to take early retirement as a result of his disagreement with British policy in India; like many others of their kind he and his family prepared to exchange 'great, grey familiar' India for the green fields of home. Unlike most, though, Inglis made a protracted journey home, staying for two years in Tasmania, where two of his sons had settled, before arriving in Edinburgh. There his young daughters were educated at the Edinburgh Institution for the Education of Young Ladies in Charlotte Square, and following a year spent in Paris Elsie enrolled at the newly formed Edinburgh School of Medicine for Women in 1886. Two years later a disagreement with the school's eminent founder, Sophia Jex-Blake, over her teaching methods, led Elsie and a number of other students to break away and, with the help of John Inglis, start a rival Medical College for Women.

It would not be the last time in her career that Elsie Inglis demonstrated a sturdy sense of independence and a refusal to kowtow to authority. In 1892, having completed her training in Glasgow, she qualified as a licentiate of the Royal College of Physicians and Surgeons and her first job was at the New Hospital for Women in Euston Road, London, which had been founded by another formidable pioneer, Elizabeth Garrett Anderson. Two years later, having also worked at the Rotunda Hospital in Dublin to gain experience in gynaecology, she was back in Edinburgh to help care for her ailing father – her mother had died of scarlet fever at the outset of her medical training. With another woman doctor, Jessie MacGregor, she established a medical practice for women and the two partners set up house together at 8 Walker Street in the city's west end, an arrangement which Elsie Inglis described as having 'all the advantages of a marriage without any of its disabilities'.[15] Their clinic was known as The Hospice and it was situated initially in George Square before moving to larger premises on the High Street in 1904. At the time this ancient part of the city was not the picturesque tourist trap that it would become in later years but a noisome quarter characterised as being 'one not only of dirt, near-starvation and chronic poverty, but almost incredible overcrowding' where people lived 650 to the acre in the grim old tenement buildings in the heart of Edinburgh's old town.[16]

By then Elsie Inglis was politically active in the growing movement to extend the franchise to women. Although the vote had been extended to women in municipal elections in 1869 and they were increasingly able to stand for local committees and education boards, they were debarred from voting in parliamentary elections, a state of affairs which led to the creation of the first women's suffrage groups to campaign for votes for women. In 1897 the National Union of Women's Suffrage Societies (NUWSS) was formed under the leadership of Millicent Fawcett, a younger sister of Elisabeth Garrett Anderson, and it soon spawned a sister organisation in Scotland, the Scottish Federation of Women's Suffrage Societies. Elsie Inglis became its honorary secretary in 1906. With a national membership of 0.5 million and an annual income of £45,000 (equivalent in purchasing power to £3.2 million in 2005) the NUWSS provided a solid political platform, but its argument that women were commonsensical rational beings made little impact in parliament, where over 30 bills in favour of women's suffrage ran into the sand between 1870 and 1914. Impatient of the slow pace of reform a new grouping was formed in Manchester in 1903 under the leadership of Emmeline Pankhurst and her daughter Christabel. Known as the Women's Social and Political Union (WSPU) its members were committed to achieving their aims through a policy of escalating militancy and, if necessary, using tactics which would see many of its members being imprisoned. In 1906, the year in which a Scottish committee of the WSPU was formed, the *Daily Mail* coined the name 'suffragette' to differentiate the Pankhurst faction from the NUWSS's 'suffragists'.

Between then and the outbreak of war the activities of the WSPU became increasingly violent and while this gave the suffragette movement a high profile in the country it also led to increasing resistance in parliament. Two attempts were made in 1910 and 1912 to give women householders the vote but both bills were defeated and the failure led to an escalation in the violence. Both the Pankhursts spent time in prison after telling the courts which tried them that they regarded themselves as prisoners of war; public buildings were attacked and politicians insulted and in the most shocking incident Emily Wilding Davison killed herself for the cause by throwing herself under the king's horse at the Epsom Derby in June 1913. Suffragettes held in prison went on hunger strikes and such was the revulsion when force-feeding was used that the government introduced the 'Cat and Mouse' Act in April 1913 which enabled hunger-striking suffragettes to be released on licence and re-arrested once they had regained their health and strength.

Scotland was not immune from the violence that became a regular occurrence in the months before the First World War. As Leah Leneman has shown in her history of the suffrage movement in Scotland, agitation for women's involvement in politics went back to the 1860s and the question of women's rights remained a feature of Scottish political life up until the outbreak of the First World War. Between 1867 and 1876 over 2 million signatures were collected in petitions for women to be given the right to vote.[17] In a move which was unique to Scotland a Northern Men's Federation for Women's Suffrage was formed in 1913 to support the campaign for women to be given voting rights and it attempted to intervene with Prime Minister Asquith by sending deputations of city councillors from Edinburgh and Glasgow. The Edinburgh branch of the federation adopted as its motto 'ye mauna tramp on the Scottish thistle'. However, Asquith refused to meet them, a snub which attracted the response from one councillor that the government was composed of 'foolish piffling pigmies'. Support also came from within the Independent Labour Party (ILP) and there were regular discussions on the issue in the radical newspaper *Forward*, which was edited by Tom Johnston. First published on 13 October 1906 it carried an appeal for women's votes written by Teresa Billington, a leading member of the WSPU, and Johnston himself launched an appeal for 'complete democracy', with 'every privilege broken, every barrier burst, every sex and social hallucination swept aside'.[18] Whenever Mrs Pankhurst spoke in Glasgow she was invariably surrounded by 'a Scotch bodyguard' of male supporters.

By 1913, following the failure of the bills to extend the franchise to women, suffragette violence had become a weekly occurrence throughout Scotland. Letterboxes were attacked with corrosive acid, windows of public buildings were smashed and telegraph wires were cut. Buildings were also attacked and in some instances destroyed: on 23 June the east wing of the Gatty Marine Laboratory at St Andrews University was burned down, the damage amounting to £500 (equivalent in purchasing power to around £33,000 in 2005). This was followed a week later by a similar attack on the nearby railway station at Leuchars Junction. (The two targets seem to have been chosen because St Andrews was home to several anti–suffragist women, most notably Lady Griselda Cheape, who based her credo on the idea that 'God made man to rule'.) On the same day, 1 July, Ballinkearn Castle at Killearn was burned down and the damage was estimated at around £100,000, equivalent to around £6.5 million today.

The attacks continued into 1914 as militant suffragettes protested against the treatment of women prisoners; one of the most daring was the attempted destruction of Burns's Cottage in Alloway on 8 July. The *Glasgow Herald* reported the incident as 'a dastardly attempt' to blow up a building of national significance – the cottage was the birthplace of the poet Robert Burns – and attested that the attack had 'roused in the locality the most intense indignation'. One of the women arrested gave her name as Janet Arthur. In reality she was Fanny Parker, who had already been imprisoned for smashing windows in Dundee and was a leading member of the WSPU. Educated at Newnham College Oxford she was also a niece of Lord Kitchener, who wrote to his sister expressing his disgust and saying that he could do 'absolutely nothing in the matter'.[19] As a result she was taken to Ayr Sheriff Court, where she refused to make any declaration and was committed to prison pending further investigation. While in Perth prison she went on hunger strike and had to be forcibly fed, a barbaric method of countering a hunger strike which caused a good deal of public indignation when the methods were revealed: food and nutrients were fed by pipes through the nose and in some cases through the rectum.[20] A week later, following the intervention of her brother 'Wallier' Parker, an officer in the Royal Sussex Regiment, Fanny Parker was released into the custody of Dr Dorothy Chalmers Smith, a remarkable suffragette medical practitioner who had suffered imprisonment herself for trying to set fire to a house in Glasgow.

The outbreak of war changed everything. The WSPU immediately called off its campaign and on 10 August the Scottish secretary announced that the truce would be reciprocated by the mitigation of all sentences involving suffragettes. As a result Fanny Parker was spared a further trial and probable imprisonment. In England the Pankhursts turned their enthusiasm for women's suffrage into support for the war effort, as did many of their supporters, but not every suffragist or suffragette was prepared to follow their lead. In Glasgow Helen Crawfurd, soon to be a stalwart of the rent strikes, resigned from the WSPU and in the following year set up a local branch of the Women's International League for Peace and Freedom with her friend Agnes Dollan. Later still, on 10 June 1916, she launched the Women's Peace Crusade, which was the first concerted effort to involve people from all social classes in a mass movement against the war. By the summer of 1917 there were branches all over Scotland and a mass meeting held on Glasgow Green attracted 14,000 protesters. That same summer Helen Crawfurd became the first secretary of the National Women's Peace Crusade, which remained active until the end of the war. Another prominent Scottish campaigner for peace was Chrystal Macmillan, an honours graduate of Edinburgh University who founded the Women's International League for Peace and Freedom and in 1915 became its first secretary. She, too, had been a prominent worker for women's suffrage, having served on the NUWSS executive committee.

Other groups and individuals threw themselves into war work while managing to retain their identities and their resolve to continue the fight for the vote. The Scottish Federation agreed to suspend its political activities for the duration of the war but that did not mean that it would take a back seat. Far from it: a week after the outbreak of hostilities Elsie Inglis put forward a proposal that the federation should involve itself in 'Red Cross work' by providing doctors and nurses for the war effort. The initial idea was to set up a hospital in an empty school building in Melville Street in Edinburgh staffed 'entirely by women'. However, even at that early stage Elsie Inglis was also looking ahead to the possibility of sending hospitals to the battle-fronts and when the Melville Street building was found to be unavailable the federation's committee put forward a fresh proposal to the War Office for the establishment of a field hospital consisting of 100 beds run by women doctors and staffed by trained nurses.[21] The response from the military was not encouraging. In a retort which was to become infamous and widely quoted by the women who worked for the Scottish Women's Hospitals, Elsie Inglis was told 'Go home and sit still.' Quite why the War Office was so stuffy is difficult to understand, given that the early months of the war saw the formation of dozens of voluntary aid committees to help the war effort. It cannot just have been the issue of women. The army already employed female nurses through the First Aid Nursing Yeomanry (FANY) and its Voluntary Aid Detachments (VAD) administered through the Territorial Force; both these voluntary and unpaid organisations supplemented their own regular medical unit, the Queen Alexandra's Imperial Military Nursing Service (QAIMNS). There may have been some residual prejudice against an all-woman unit of the kind proposed by Elsie Inglis, not least because its command structure would be dominated by female doctors, but the rejection probably had more to do with lack of resources. On 9 September the surgeon-general complained to the director-general of medical services at the War Office that the arrival of 'voluntary units at that time would only have embarrassed and therefore added difficulties to the medical administration'.[22]

Besides, four volunteer nurses were already at work in the front line at the very time that Elsie Inglis was putting forward her proposals. A 'flying ambulance column' had been established by Dr Hector Munro, 'a great feminist at a time when that wasn't popular amongst men', who had established a first-aid post close to the Belgian frontier at a small village called Pervyse. One of the nurses was Mairi Chisholm, an 18-year-old Scot who had driven to London on her motor-bicycle at the beginning of the war to work as a dispatch rider with the Women's Emergency Corps. Approached by Munro, who had been impressed when he saw her driving her racing motor-bicycle through London, she set off for Pervyse. There she worked with three other nurses until the spring of 1918, when they were withdrawn after being gassed. Being so near the front line the 'madonnas of Pervyse' were under constant fire and were forced to see terrible sights when the wounded were brought in, but as Mairi Chisholm showed in her revealing diaries and letters, the nurses refused to be unnerved by the experience; an entry in her diary for 24 October 1915 reads 'The German shells are falling quite close and it is just like hell itself – one's head is absolutely splitting with the din. Oh what a life. To think we could ever be here in the midst of things like this.'[23] The *Official History* lists another ten voluntary hospitals which offered their services at the beginning of the war, including one run by another Scot, Millicent, Duchess of Sutherland.

Not to be outdone, Elsie Inglis and her committee then approached the French and Serbian governments, who both accepted the offer in October. It had been one thing to float the idea but now that it was a reality money had to be raised to get the idea off the ground. With the support of the NUWSS, appeals were made for funds for the Scottish Women's Hospital for Foreign Service and by the end of October the first £1,000 had been raised and plans were put in place to send the first hospital unit to Serbia, where Austrian forces had been repulsed in their attempt to take Belgrade. Elsie Inglis took on the daunting tasks of fundraising and employing staff with great enthusiasm, addressing meetings in London and Edinburgh. A committee was established to oversee the operation from Edinburgh, where offices at 2 St Andrew Square had been donated to them by the Prudential Insurance Society. It was a coming together of enthusiasm, raw energy and professional acumen: by the year's end £449,000 had been raised and another unit was ready for service in France, where the French Red Cross had provided accommodation at the Cistercian Abbey of Royaumont. Founded by King Louis IX in 1229, this impressive building lay to the north of Paris, but despite its physical beauty and the unspoiled countryside one of the first members of the hospital later remembered the abbey building as being 'picturesque, impressive and most abominably chilly'.[24] Ahead lay a number of problems, some unavoidable, such as the failure to complete the transformation of the abbey into a working hospital to the satisfaction of the French authorities, and some of them petty, such as the initial hostility to the use of the word 'Scottish' and a more widespread dislike of the uniform grey jackets with Gordon tartan facings. However, by the second week of January 1915 the first patients began arriving at Royaumont.

The Scottish Women's Hospital served in France throughout the war and did not close its doors until the spring of 1919. Throughout that period it came under French direction, firstly under the French Red Cross and latterly under the French Army, and 23 members of the staff were decorated with the Croix de Guerre. All told 10,861 patients were treated in the hospital, the majority of them wounded soldiers, and being so close to the battle lines of the Western Front the medical staff were left in little doubt about the grim nature of the wounds inflicted in modern warfare, especially during the battles of the Somme and Verdun. There were also times when they came under fire themselves and the hospital's forward casualty clearing station at Villers-Cotterets was forced into a temporary evacuation during the German offensives of the spring of 1918, a period which the Royaumont historian rightly calls 'their finest hour'. At Royaumont's head was Frances Ivens, another remarkable woman, a London medical graduate, who had also been active in the women's suffrage movement before the war.

As for Elsie Inglis, the progenitor of the scheme, she found herself torn between the competing needs of fundraising and administration and her natural desire to see service in the field. She was, after all, a gifted doctor herself and there must have been times when it was difficult for her to be a visitor at Royaumont when her charges were serving there and in Serbia. Her chance came in April 1915 when Dr Eleanor Soltau, the chief medical officer of the Serbian hospital, fell ill with diphtheria and Elsie journeyed to the Balkans to take her place. It was the beginning of one of the most desperate periods which any of the Scottish Women's Hospital units had to face in the Balkan theatre. When the first doctors and nurses arrived at the Serb military hospital at Nish they were appalled by what they found: 'sick and wounded lay crowded together – men who had just undergone the amputation of limbs; men in the grip of typhoid, dysentery or frostbite; men dying – some were dead'. It took time and a great deal of resolve before they could make a difference to the chaotic situation. Elsie Inglis's arrival on 11 May helped to concentrate minds and, as noted by Lady Leila Paget, who led another voluntary field hospital in Serbia, the sheer determination and resolve of the Scottish contingents made light of the difficulties they faced: 'The Scottish Women's Units are doing splendid work all over the country, and are much appreciated by the Serbians, and what makes them especially valuable in this country is their adaptability. They are willing and able to adapt themselves to any conditions or circumstances; they never grumble or complain, are always cheerful and smiling, always ready to lend a hand to any British or Serbian unit who are hard pressed, and their courage and the way they overcome almost insurmountable difficulties is extraordinary.'[25]

They would need all that resilience and more in October 1915 when a huge army of German, Bulgarian and Austro-Hungarian troops under the command of Field Marshal von Mackensen pushed into the country over the Danube. The smaller Serb Army under Radomir Putnik provided determined resistance but Belgrade fell on 9 October and the Serbs were forced to pull back into the centre of the country, where they faced a flank attack by the Bulgarian First and Second Armies. By the end of the month the railway line to the Allied base in Salonika had been cut and the Serbs began retreating south-westwards to the historic Plain of Blackbirds at Kosovo east of Pristina, where Tsar Lazar's Serb forces had been defeated by the Turks in 1389 beginning 500 years of Ottoman servitude. Twice Putnik managed to avoid encirclement but with winter fast approaching the Serbs were left with no option but to surrender or retreat over the high mountains into Montenegro and Albania and then on to the safety of the Adriatic coast. Caught up in all this were the Scottish Women's Hospital units at Kragujevac, Valjevo, Lazarevac and Mladenovac. Unlike their hosts, who were accustomed to long years of warfare, seasonal privation and the depredations of winter, the doctors and nurses of the Scottish Women's Hospitals found themselves having to make grim choices. Having decided to remain with the Serb forces, the doctors and nurses either stayed put with their charges or accompanied the rump of the Serb Army as it made its way over the mountain passes in one of the epic journeys of the war. Sixty members of the Scottish Women's Hospitals set off on that long trek, which lasted seven weeks and took them over 500 miles of daunting terrain. As recalled by their transport manager, William Smith, the experience was not for the faint-hearted: 'By this time our food-supply was running out and we were passing through a country where food, even in times of peace, is never plentiful. During this part of the march I fear we often forgot Serbia, and the tragedy and death that was going on round us. Our only thought was of food, and our talk was of food, and to recall any delicacy would bring our hearts to our mouths.'[26]

With the Serb's leader, King Peter, marching alongside his men they struggled through the winter snows taking with them 25,000 Austro-Hungarian prisoners and refugees and, symbolically, their now useless artillery. Of the 200,000 who set out, only 140,000 survived the march to the Adriatic coast where Allied ships, mostly Italian, picked them up and took them to the island of Corfu. From there the Scottish Women's Hospital staff were redeployed in support of the Allied campaign in Salonika. When they arrived the Scottish Women's Hospitals were already established: the so-called Girton and Newnham unit which had served earlier at Troyes in France. On alighting at Salonika one of the cooks, Ishobel Ross, thought that the scenery 'looked just like Skye, but very parched and dry looking'. Others thought they heard a resemblance with Gaelic in the local tongue as they started making friends in the huge multilingual garrison. Before too long the unit had earned the name of 'the Skittish Widows'.[27]

Amongst those captured with the Serb forces was Elsie Inglis, who was interned at Krushevatz and was not repatriated to Britain until February 1916. The experience clearly marked her, because for reasons which remain unclear she unexpectedly tendered her resignation that summer on the grounds that she felt that her original aims were being overlooked by the organising committee and that in some way she was being sidelined. By then she was in middle age, the war was in its third year and the hard work to create the Scottish Women's Hospitals plus her own experiences in the Balkans must have taken their toll. It is also possible that she had discovered that she was suffering from the cancer that would kill her just over a year later. Whatever her reasons, the decision caused consternation in Edinburgh. 'What a fiasco for the public to gloat over,' was the view of one committee member, 'how it will thrill them to think that when women cannot get their own way in every detail, they must needs threaten resignation.'[28] At that stage in the war the Scottish Women's Hospitals could not afford the public scandal of the resignation of their guiding light and Elsie Inglis was eventually persuaded that her decision would damage the cause. She decided to remain with the organisation and take a new unit to the southern Russian front, where two Serb divisions were fighting in support of the Romanians who had entered the war on the Allied side on 27 August 1916.

This was one of the most forlorn campaigns of the war: from the start it was a lost cause. Although the Romanians had a huge army it was poorly equipped and badly led and despite the bravery of the soldiers it proved to be no match for the opposing forces. The Romanians were soon outnumbered and outflanked. By the beginning of December von Mackensen's forces were in Bucharest and the Romanians were forced to retreat eastwards towards the province of Moldavia close to the Russian border. With them, once again, went the Scottish Women's Hospital unit, who refused to abandon the Serb divisions until there was agreement for them to be transferred out of Russia. This was a necessary precaution as many of the soldiers were Serb volunteers from Austro-Hungarian territories and their future would have been bleak had they gone into captivity.

Once again Elsie Inglis and her unit were repatriated, this time making a long and arduous journey across Russia to the port of Archangel, where a ship took them back to Britain. After a hazardous voyage it reached Newcastle, but by then Elsie Inglis was dying, and although she found the strength to put on her uniform, complete with decorations, to say goodbye to the Serb commanders, she was clearly in great distress and died before she could return to Scotland. Her death caused a great shock not only to the Scottish Women's Hospital movement but also across Scotland, where her deeds were a great source of national pride. She was buried in Edinburgh's Dean Cemetery on 29 November 1917 after a service in the High Church of St Giles taken by the Dean of the Order of the Thistle, who described her as 'an immortal link between Serbia and Scotland, and as a symbol of that high courage which will sustain us, please God, till that stricken land is once again restored'.[29] Her coffin was draped with the Union flag and the flag of Serbia and the army in Scotland gave her full military honours with high-ranking Scottish and Serb officers attending the service. Crowds lined the funeral route as many ordinary Scots wanted to pay their last respects to this extraordinary woman and the contribution she had made to the Allied war effort. Later, she was described as being the equal of Florence Nightingale in raising the profile of women in medicine, and in Edinburgh the Elsie Inglis Memorial Maternity Hospital was founded in her honour in 1925. But for all that she emerged next to Haig as one of the best-known Scots of the First World War, history has not remembered her as well as it might. In October 1988 'Elsie's' as it was known in Edinburgh was partially closed, finally shutting its door four years later in a reorganisation of local hospital services. Today it houses a nursing home and a nursery. As for Elsie Inglis herself, although she has been well served by her biographers, neither her name nor the Scottish Women's Hospitals are mentioned in the most recent histories of twentieth-century Scotland.[30]

It's tempting to think that Elsie Inglis's Scottish Women's Hospitals made a great breakthrough, but it would take time for women to become completely accepted within the medical profession. The Women's Hospitals were the product of the suffrage movement and during the war they and other voluntary women's hospitals showed that not only could women cope with the demands of military medicine, they were also able to work under stressful and trying conditions. One of the doctors at Royaumont said later in life that they had shown the government 'what women could do' and initially the signs were encouraging. By 1919 the number of women entering medical school had doubled to 3,000 and several of the female doctors went on to carve out distinguished medical careers, mainly in public health and obstetrics and gynaecology. As they had done prior to 1914, the Scottish universities continued to admit female medical students, but in stark contrast all the London teaching hospitals, with the exception of University College Hospital, closed their doors to female medical students after the war. Although some prejudices died hard, the experience of the voluntary women's hospitals during the First World War showed that in dealing with the wounded and the sick women were the equal of their male colleagues.

On that score the small number of women doctors fared better than the vast army of female munitions workers that had been brought into being after 1915. Six years later the numbers working in the latter area had fallen to 0.1 per cent of the population of working women in the UK, and at 26.4 per cent the number working in domestic service was slightly higher than the pre-war level. After the armistice the implementation of the Restoration of Pre-War Practices Act meant that returning soldiers were given back their jobs, and cutbacks in the arms trade meant that women were no longer needed in that particular workplace. At the 'university for women engineers' at Tongland returning servicemen were aghast to discover women doing men's work and threatened to boycott the Kirkcudbright Peace Pageant held in the summer of 1919 in protest at not being given jobs. They relented, but only on condition that the Tongland women marched at the rear of the parade, and the row about the employment of the women continued to cause divisions in the locality. In an attempt to keep this modern facility open Arrol-Johnston returned to motor-car production but a small two-seater model, the Galloway, was a failure at a time when mass production was coming into its own and the Tongland factory closed its doors in March 1922. However, as their historian points out, many of the women engineers continued in the profession or went on to study for degrees at technical college.[31] That option was not open to the vast majority of women munitions workers who were paid off with little more than a letter of appreciation from the ministry. In their case the wartime experience had been a temporary change and the post-war years meant a return to women doing 'women's work', usually low paid and repetitive, while the men held on to the skilled trades. In an increasingly cold economic climate dominated by wage cuts, strikes, inflation and recession, many of them would soon be struggling to hang on to even these jobs.

One thing did change permanently for women during the war. In August 1916 the coalition government began taking steps to give the vote to women, and despite fears that the extension of the franchise would cause an electoral imbalance, women being a majority, the Representation of the People Act was passed in the summer of 1917. It gave the vote to female householders and the wives of householders, with a minimum age of 30 and it became law the following year. At the same time another bill was passed permitting women to stand as members of parliament, and the first woman to be elected was Lady Astor during the 1919 post-war election. In 1928 the voting age was lowered to 21, on the same terms as men. In the course of 15 years women had been given the vote and achieved more than the pre-war militant suffragettes ever hoped to achieve (it is possible that the suffragette campaign did more harm than good, for all that it kept the issue in the public eye). The real change came with the war.

In the summer of 1914 Asquith's government had made it clear that it would not yield to the militants' terror tactics and the wartime truce allowed many of the main participants in the debate to change their positions. Fears about the way women would vote had also receded; there had been a widespread belief in Scottish socialist circles that the grant of the vote to propertied women would strengthen the Conservative Party and would not help working-class women.[32] Politicians were careful to insist that the enfranchisement was not a reward for their efforts during the war, but there is a touch of sophistry in that argument. Throughout the war, especially in Scotland, women were highly visible in the community, working as munitions workers or managing the voluntary hospitals or playing leading roles in the many voluntary movements set up to assist the war effort. Through organisations like the WSPU they had also been politicised and the debate had been opened up to include those outside the women's suffrage movement. By the end of a war that had been fought in large part to maintain the rights of small countries, votes for women was an idea whose time had finally arrived.

9 Red Clydeside and Opposing Armageddon

The story of Red Clydeside, as more than one historian has noted, has become such a phenomenon that not only has it produced its own extensive historiography it has also created its own mythology. It has also been the cause of fierce arguments and deep divisions. At one extreme 'Red Clydeside' is shorthand for the period between the summer of 1915 and January 1919, when Glasgow and Clydeside seemed to be on the brink of revolution as a series of strikes and bad-tempered demonstrations convinced the government that militant Bolsheviks in Scotland were about to rise as one and bring down capitalism. The evidence to support that view is compelling. During the war women had taken to the streets to protest against rent increases. Skilled workers in essential wartime jobs had threatened strike action for more pay and to protect their livelihoods. A number of articulate radical leaders, such as John Maclean, had emerged to call for a Marxist revolution and an immediate armistice to end the war. In an attempt to control the situation the government responded by cracking down with arrests, prison sentences and internal exile for those considered to be enemies of the state. And in the grand culmination three months after the war ended, red flags were flown in Glasgow's George Square and troops were deployed to prevent further confrontations between strikers and police. Six tanks were prepared for action in the Cattle Market in a grim foretaste of other revolutions which would be crushed by armoured vehicles later in the century. On that level Red Clydeside could be viewed as the prelude to revolution and there is sufficient contemporary evidence to show that many people in authority were convinced that in the aftermath of the war Scotland was about to be plunged into a Bolshevik-style uprising.

At another extreme Red Clydeside has been described as a series of unrelated episodes involving strike actions for increased wages and to preserve skilled jobs which took place against an unfocused political background. In this version it is emphasized that while it was true that activists created a worrying breach in public order at the beginning of 1919 and ugly rumours produced an alarming degree of public uncertainty at a time of widespread political unease in Europe, there was no revolution, the tanks were never deployed, the guns remained silent and the movement 'masked a fundamental defeat' for its leaders and participants. Later, one of its leading lights joked that the most revolutionary occurrence of the period came about when one of his comrades, the trade union leader David Kirkwood, was forced to wash the dishes, 'which he'd never done before'.[1]

And yet, for all that it has been claimed as a seminal moment in Scotland's political history or written off as a damp squib, Red Clydeside, or the 'Revolt on the Clyde' as it was also known, is central to Scotland's experience during the First World War. For a start the events did take place and although the strikes and the related disturbances never looked like breaking out into an organised and coherent political revolt, they did cause sufficient concern to make the government respond. All too often the authorities over-reacted, especially in 1919, when faulty military intelligence suggested that Glasgow was on the brink of going the same way as Petrograd; historians investigating official papers dealing with the period have expressed their alarm at uncovering evidence of 'the nastiness, ruth-lessness, and mendacity revealed by some of the agents of the state in their dealings with the Clydesiders'.[2] A particular target for state interference was the Clyde Workers' Committee (CWC), an un-official confederation of shop stewards and other workforce delegates which came into being to protect the rights of engineering workers at Beardmore's, Weir's, Albion Motors and Barr and Stroud. In William Weir the government had a forceful and confrontational controller of munitions who seemed to delight in provoking the trade unions by driving through measures aimed at breaking their power. Even if Red Clydeside ultimately failed in revolution, the strikes and upheavals associated with its name still produced a major upheaval in Scotland's political history at a time when the nation's industries were involved in the great work of producing the munitions needed to win the war.

There were two distinct phases to Red Clydeside: the incidents which took place during wartime and the post-war strikes and confrontations in early 1919 which culminated in the return of ten Labour members of parliament from Glasgow in the 1922 general election. Many of the issues and personalities were common to both and there is sufficient linkage to give cohesion to the movement, but what happened in Glasgow and Clydeside during the war was very different from what happened in the war's aftermath. The first 'Red Clydeside' was triggered in 1915 by the confrontation between engineers and the Ministry of Munitions over the issue of dilution and by the rent strikes, but it also took place against the wider context of the emergence of an anti-war and pro-peace movement within the city. The first stirrings had been heard a few days after the declaration of war with a demonstration on Glasgow Green, and the city soon became the focus for the largest and most vocal working-class opposition to the war experienced in wartime Britain. Many of those who spoke out against the conflict were also involved in the heavy industries either as workers or trade union leaders, so that when the term Red Clydeside came into common usage in 1919 it embraced both the anti-war campaigners and the trade unionists who were agitating for higher pay and to preserve their trades. Very often their aims and ambitions overlapped, although as with any informal political grouping there were differences of approach. For example, few fought harder for workers' rights (including women's rights) than David Kirkwood, yet he was by no means anti-war in outlook: early on in the conflict he 'resolved that my skill as an engineer must be devoted to my country'. At the other extreme John Maclean, a teacher by training and Marxist by evolution, was totally against the war: following his first arrest in October 1915 on the charge of 'making statements likely to prejudice recruiting' he made no secret of his opposition to the war, claiming in court that he had 'enlisted in the Socialist army fifteen years ago, the only army worth fighting for'.[3]

Under the terms of the Defence of the Realm legislation and the Munitions of War Act strikes were officially forbidden during the war but that did not prevent confrontations between management and the workforce and the subsequent withdrawal of labour. (A strike by 200,000 South Wales miners had gone ahead in March in spite of the new laws and the Miners' Federation's full demands were met by the employers.) In January 1915 engineers in Glasgow threatened to go on strike unless their claim for an additional two pence an hour was met. The rise in the cost of living was one reason for their action, and fear of losing their position as skilled workers was another, but the trigger was Weir's decision to introduce American engineers who were paid at higher rates. A strike was called on 15 February and although it was settled a fortnight later, Clydeside found itself saddled with a reputation for militancy and battle lines had been drawn between the workforce and the government. Weir did not help matters by suggesting that the strikers were being unpatriotic. A pamphlet was produced accusing the workers of aiding the enemy; both Weir and the munitions minister, Lloyd George, sneered that the Clydesiders were idle drunkards – this was a falsehood as the leadership was mainly teetotal – and there was talk of introducing martial law to prevent future strike action. Then, later in the year, came the rent strikes (see Chapter 7) which culminated in wildcat industrial action in support of those being prosecuted. The action had the broad support of several groups on the left – the Independent Labour Party (ILP), suffragettes, the Glasgow Trades Council and the various peace movements – and paved the way for further confrontation.

The next flashpoints were caused by dilution and the question of leaving certificates, both of which were imposed by the Munitions of War Act. The first involved the employment of non-skilled workers, mainly women, and the position was put bluntly in a resolution passed by the union concerned, the Amalgamated Society of Engineers (ASE), following the introduction of female labour at Lang's of Johnstone, a factory manufacturing shell lathes: 'no woman shall be put to work a lathe, and if this were done the men would know how to protect their rights'.[4] This was not bloody-mindedness on the part of the engineers but a determined attempt to safeguard their privileges as skilled workers. Men of that ilk were extremely conscious of their position in society and proud of the fact that they had worked long and hard to attain their status as craftsmen. While most were keen to support the war effort, they were not prepared to see their role eroded by the wartime introduction of unskilled and semi-skilled workers, many of them women. Not only did this threaten their privileged positions within the workplace, there were well-grounded fears that the wartime emergency measures would be continued in peacetime and that in the long term they would be the losers.

In the summer of 1915 there were two strikes at the Fairfield yard over the leaving certificate system, which regulated workers leaving one job and getting another. Those striking against the measure believed that the system could be used to penalise them by giving management the means to prevent free movement of labour. The strike leaders were punished with £10 fines. When three refused to pay they were sent to prison and the decision created further tensions between the Clyde workforce and the government, not least because, as Charlie McPherson, one of the imprisoned men remembered, they were treated as common criminals in Glasgow's Duke Street prison: 'They put me into a cell that must have been meant for some dangerous criminal, because the pot was made o' papier mâché and the stool was fixed to the ground. There was nothing I could kill anybody with! In the morning we were taken out and got our clothes and so on, and settled down to prison life. There was no distinction between prisoners – there were no political prisoners in those days. Porridge in the morning, soup at dinnertime, and porridge at night again.'[5]

Before long a confrontation had become inevitable: the CWC leaders feared that workers' rights were being eroded while the Ministry of Munitions believed that they were dealing with political hotheads whose activities could interfere with the production of munitions needed for the 1916 offensives on the Western Front. The stoppages at Lang's and Fairfield's were resolved through conciliation but the deadlock over dilution remained a stumbling block and it was clear that sooner or later the confrontation between the CWC and the government would come to blows. As 1915 drew to a close Lloyd George was under pressure to deal with the CWC, now seen as a nest of revolutionary militants, either by tightening the law or by arresting the leaders.[6] At the same time the government was grappling with the question of conscription, another unpopular policy which was attracting opposition, and there had also been a strike at the Caledon shipyard in Dundee where there had been problems over demarcation between Admiralty and private work; against that background it could hardly afford to ignore the threat of violence which was being propagated by John Maclean in his short-lived publication the *Vanguard*:

Unless the Clyde men act quickly, determinedly, and with a clear object in view they are going to be tied in a knot. We know that the

Glasgow press was threatened with the Defence of the Realm Act should it make mention of strike had one broken out. We know that the military authorities had engineers and Allied workers in the army at home ready to draft into the Clyde works in the event of a strike. We know also that, despite clamour for munitions, young men are being dismissed from all the Clyde works in order to force them into the army. When the occasion arises they will be reinstated in their old jobs, but now as military slaves – worse even than munitions slaves. Quick and firm action is needed if slavery is going to be abolished and conscription defeated. We must now fight boldly for the common ownership of all industries in Britain.[7]

This was wild talk and it was guaranteed to exasperate the authorities and prompt them into taking action. In fact by the end of 1915 Maclean was already a marked man. He went to prison for five days rather than pay the £5 fine imposed on him for making comments against recruiting and that same month, October 1915, he was sacked from his teaching post by the Govan School Board. Unabashed, he continued his Marxian education programme for working men, attracting enthusiastic audiences. Along with other activists such as Patrick Dollan; James Maxton, another remarkable teacher and evangelical socialist; and the CWC chairman Willie Gallacher, he was a regular speaker at the anti-conscription rallies which were held in Glasgow at the end of the year. One meeting in George Square on 29 November was addressed by speakers including Maclean and Sylvia Pankhurst, another of Emmeline's daughters, and attracted a lively audience despite the heavy winter rain. According to the English socialist George Lansbury, who was also a speaker, it was only with the greatest difficulty that he persuaded Maclean to give up his plans to storm the City Hall as 'the result would be considerable bloodshed'.[8] As part of the ministry's offensive to counter what was thought to be an increasingly tense situation over the implementation of dilution Lloyd George agreed to meet the Clydeside workers on their own ground in the third week of December.

The result was chaos, created by a mixture of inefficient planning and heightened passions in the Clydeside workforce. Through the intercession of Kirkwood, Lloyd George met the shop stewards at

Parkhead Forge, but at Weir's and Albion Motors he was turned away and he had to be content with a number of meetings at smaller factories. A mass meeting in St Andrew's Halls on 25 December turned out to be a disaster even though Lloyd George had agreed to compensate the workers for loss of pay (at the time Christmas Day was not a public holiday in Scotland). Attempts to get a fair hearing for the speakers were shouted down and the meeting eventually had to be brought to a premature conclusion. All this was hushed up and the official report released by the Press Association and published in the main Scottish newspapers concluded with the untruthful statement that 'the meeting was on the whole good humoured' and that the demonstrators were in a minority. That might have been the end of the matter but a reporter from *Forward* was also present and the next edition published a factual account which included Tom Johnston's comment that 'the vast overwhelming majority of the meeting was angry' and to report otherwise was wrongheaded.[9] This was too much for the government and as a result the Ministry of Munitions closed down *Forward* under regulations 2, 18 and 27 of the Defence of the Realm Act (DORA). Maclean's *Vanguard* was also closed down under the same legislation.

It was not the first time that the *Forward* newspaper had come to the attention of the authorities. Johnston had been under police surveillance and twice in 1914 the Scottish Office had dealt with complaints from outraged members of the public. One letter took issue with the 'absolutely disloyal articles and references in the recent issues of the Glasgow Socialistic weekly *Forward*' and the question of prosecution was passed to the advocate depute, who concluded that 'there is no ground for the institution of criminal or other proceedings and that any action taken by the criminal or other authorities would only serve to secure notoriety and advertisement for the newspaper without any corresponding advantage'. Further complaints received in May 1915 reached a similar conclusion and the papers were simply filed away with the comment 'nothing v. bad here'.[10] Despite the reprieve *Forward* was clearly in the line of fire and the decision to suppress it seems to have been taken both because it produced an accurate report of an incident which the government wanted to suppress and, as the *Scotsman* reported a few days later, because the editorial policy of *Forward* was critical of munitions production and the effects of dilution on the industry.[11] It was not allowed to republish until 5 February 1916. To add to the farce Maclean, Maxton, Gallacher and others were arrested in Glasgow on 29 December on the charge that they caused an obstruction in North Hanover Street by 'causing to be placed thereon a horse and a lorry and respectively delivering speeches from said lorry causing a large crowd of persons to assemble in said street, and preventing the free passage along or through the same'.[12]

No further action was taken but it was not the end of the war of words with the militants. The new year opened with the government determined to push ahead with dilution and to introduce conscription into the armed forces. That both measures were fiercely opposed in Scotland can be seen from the large number of letters sent in to the Scottish Office alleging that the military call-up would eventually be extended to industry and that the workers would lose out once again; a typical complaint to the Scottish Secretary, McKinnon Wood, read 'Such slavery will not be tolerated by the Clyde workers. All militarism must be fought.'[13] Weir in particular wanted to break the resistance to dilution, if necessary by using force, but the upshot was the appointment of three commissioners who would negotiate the introduction of dilution agreements at all the Clydeside engineering works. At the same time the ministry took measures to react swiftly and decisively against those who took any strike action against the imposition of dilution. Given the suspicions amongst the workers who feared that the government would renege on their promise to make dilution a wartime emergency measure and that in the post-war world women would take men's jobs willy-nilly because they were cheaper to employ, the negotiations dragged on into February and the delay to the timetable caused the ministry to fret.

On 7 February the first crackdown on the militants came with the suppression of the CWC newspaper the *Worker* and the arrest on charges of sedition of Gallacher along with its editor, John Muir of Barr and Stroud and Walter Bell, publisher of the Socialist Labour Press. The day before the arrests Maclean was also apprehended and taken into custody in Edinburgh Castle; the indictment against him alleged that he had made statements likely to prejudice recruiting, cause mutiny, sedition and disaffection among the civil population, and impeding the production, repair and transport of war materiel. Trial was set for 11 April in the High Court in Edinburgh. A third

tranche of arrests saw the apprehension of Maxton and James
McDougall, the former bank employee who had taken part in the
earliest anti-war demonstrations in Glasgow. As the news of the arrests
spread through Clydeside strikes took place in all the major work-
places with the exception of the Parkhead Forge, whose workers
compounded their refusal to act by entering into a dilution agreement
with the commissioners. Not that it did Kirkwood any good. The
arrival of the first women workers allowed the Beardmore management at Parkhead to sideline him from his position as convener of
shop stewards. First, Kirkwood was refused permission to speak to the
new women workers in order to advise them to 'organise and demand
higher wages' at a time when Beardmore were introducing women
munitions workers on a large scale and refusing to pay them the agreed
minimum wage. Then he was denied permission to enter the new
howitzer department where most of the women were employed and
as his privileges had been withdrawn he promptly resigned from his
position.[14] This led to strike action on 17 March and other workers at
Beardmore's at Dalmuir and Weir's joined in by downing their tools.
To the government this seemed to be 'a systematic and sinister plan' to
prevent munitions from being manufactured and a week later Kirkwood and eight other shop stewards from Beardmore's and Weir's
were ordered to leave the Glasgow area and were taken to Edinburgh.
The orders against them were not lifted until May 1917.

Although there was a moment of panic in the Ministry of Munitions that the local strike heralded a general action on Clydeside, the
trouble quickly died down mainly because other engineering works
refused to join in, a result no doubt of Kirkwood's failure to bring out
the Parkhead workers over the arrests of the militants. By the end of
March men started going back to work and only 30 of their number
had been fined for going on strike. Clearly the government's action
had made an impact. Militant leaders had been arrested and would
shortly go on trial for sedition while the rest of the leadership had been
sent into internal exile on the other side of the country. These were
harsh measures and the workers would not have been human had they
not stepped back and reconsidered their positions before taking
further action in pursuit of what were probably unattainable political
goals. The mood of the rest of the country was also against them and
the forthcoming sedition trials were welcomed by Scotland's main

newspapers: 'In every community and in every class there is a certain number of people ready to listen to the unscrupulous orator who chooses to play upon the greed, vanity, ignorance and wrong-headed selfishness of the crowd. Clyde workers have shown themselves not to be wholly exempt from this form of temptation, even at a time when their thoughts and energy should be absorbed in the work of the great war.'[15] And it was not just the leader writers who were pleased by the government's decision to crack down on the Clydeside militants. Many correspondents felt the same way and welcomed the action taken by the authorities to prosecute the ringleaders for sedition. As one letter writer put it, the strikers and their leaders had brought disgrace to the city and deserved no sympathy: 'Four thousand callous men put the lives of our brave men in the trenches in jeopardy by downing tools on that day. Such action is not new. They were plague centres on the Clyde before the war began – unwilling to work except on their own tyrannical terms. Now is the time to get rid of them. The place for them is in the army.'[16]

Similar letters greeted the outcome of the sedition trials and their publication demonstrated the depth of public unease generated by the strike action on Clydeside. There were also wild rumours of German money being used clandestinely to provoke the Clydeside workers to take action.[17] These started in the *Daily Record* and were never substantiated but they were part of the general jittery mood of the period as the effects of the war moved ever closer to civilian life: earlier in the month Edinburgh and Leith had been bombed by German airships and there had been a rash of sinkings by German submarines in home waters, including the Folkestone–Dieppe ferry *Sussex* and a New York-bound liner, the *Cymric*, both of which resulted in heavy civilian casualties. The trials of those arrested for sedition also caused a good deal of comment, most of it expressed in satisfaction that the government had finally acted against what the *Glasgow Herald* called 'a section of the community [who] have no sympathy with, even if they are not bitterly hostile to, the national cause'. The paper also argued that far from acting precipitately the government had 'displayed an amount of patience bordering on weakness' before taking measures to extirpate seditious behaviour in the west of Scotland.[18]

In common with the decision to banish Kirkwood and his associates the sentences handed down to those arrested for sedition were severe.

On 11 April John Maclean went on trial at the High Court in Edinburgh before the lord justice general, Lord Strathclyde, with the lord advocate leading the prosecution. In a packed court Maclean claimed that while he opposed conscription and the war effort in general he had not incited crowds to use violence when they took strike action. Eighteen policemen gave evidence against him, having recorded his speeches at public meetings, and their word decided the outcome when Lord Strathclyde told the jury that any verdict against the Crown would imply that the facts had been perjured. The following day Maclean was found guilty on four charges of sedition and sentenced to three years' penal servitude, first in Edinburgh's Calton Jail and then at Peterhead Prison. The next day Muir, Gallacher and Bell appeared in the same court before the same judge and despite their pleas that they were not opposed to the war they were found guilty. Muir and Gallacher were sentenced to twelve months' imprisonment while Bell received the lesser sentence of three months. A month later Maxton, McDougall and Jack Smith, an English radical living in Glasgow, also appeared before Lord Strathclyde on charges that they had incited workers to take strike action at a meeting on Glasgow Green called to oppose the Military Service Act and to protest against the banishments. Although all three pleaded guilty Smith was sentenced to eighteen months' imprisonment while Maxton and McDougall were sent to jail for a year. Maclean had prophesied that harsh sentences would be met with public outrage but as his biographer noted the protests failed to materialise: 'All the most militant leaders of the Scottish workers were now in jail and calm descended on the troubled waters of the Clyde, at least temporarily.'[19]

The calm lasted for most of the rest of the war, although there were isolated strike actions such as a long-running dispute following the unfair sacking of women munitions workers at Beardmore's East Hope Street works in the winter of 1917–18. Clydeside remained quiet when English munitions factories in London, the Midlands and the North went on strike in May 1917. The dilution commissioners finally brokered agreements in all the main factories, the CWC went into decline and there was no repetition of the militancy which had made the government fear that they were dealing with a potential revolt during the winter of 1915–16. Maxton, McDougall, Muir and Gallacher were all released from prison in February 1917 and Kirkwood was allowed to return to Glasgow three months later. Before being allowed to return to work the deportees had to sign a declaration drawn up by General Ewart, the senior army officer in Scotland, promising that they would remain on the right side of the law: 'I (name and address) hereby undertake that if I am permitted by the military authorities to reside in or near Glasgow, I will, while there, remain at work at my trade, provided that suitable work is available, and will during the continuance of the war, take no part, directly or indirectly, in any stoppage, or in any other action which is likely in any way to delay or interfere with the manufacture or supply of munitions, or any other work required for the successful prosecution of the war.'[20]

With the exception of Kirkwood, who was initially sidelined from seeking further employment, the men were offered jobs at the National Projectile Factory at Renfrew. After some initial difficulties Beardmore eventually gave Kirkwood a job as foreman at their Mile-End Shell Factory where Gallacher was now a shop steward, and between them these much-feared revolutionaries quickly broke records for munitions production. 'What a team!' noted Kirkwood in his memoirs. 'There was never anything like it in Great Britain! We organised a bonus system in which everyone benefited by high production. Records were made only to be broken.'[21] There were also rewards: in return for those efforts, which must have boosted the firm's profits, Sir William Beardmore bought Kirkwood 'the best hat in Glasgow'. As T. C. Smout tartly notes in his study of that period, 'this was no way to bring the capitalist system to its knees'.[22] Only Maclean remained in jail, and despite protests about the unfairness of the sentence and his own declining mental and physical state he was not released until July 1917 when friends like Gallacher found that he was 'more revolutionary than ever'.

The Bolshevik revolution in Russia in the summer and autumn of 1917 came as a great fillip to Maclean, who believed that it was the prelude to a wider global workers' revolt and that the time had finally arrived for the proletariat to act in concert to bring down capitalism. In Glasgow a flurry of moves to establish Workers' and Soldiers' Councils along Soviet lines thoroughly alarmed the authorities and the new Scottish secretary, Robert Munro, faced calls for their meetings to be banned. The coalition government in London, led by Lloyd

George since December 1917, agreed that the meetings should not take place and as a result the attempts to create Soviet-style councils in Glasgow were all stillborn. But that was not the end of the matter.

At the beginning of January 1918 Maclean was appointed by Lenin as the first Bolshevik consul for Scotland and with some difficulty he opened consular offices at 12 South Portland Street. Not unnaturally, given the alarm caused by the events in Russia, Maclean's appointment was not recognised by the government and he suffered a good deal of harassment through police raids and interference with his postal deliveries. Throughout that period he kept up a steady schedule of addressing meetings in the west of Scotland and the north of England, attacking the war and praising the success of the Bolsheviks. Such behaviour could not go unnoticed and inevitably Maclean was re-arrested, on 15 April, and charged with sedition, with the trial set to begin in Edinburgh on 11 May. Shortly after his arrest Glasgow witnessed a huge May Day demonstration, attended by around 100,000 people, many of them women calling for an end to the war. At that critical stage in the conflict, when the submarine war had not yet been won and a German offensive on the Western Front had almost succeeded in breaking the Allied lines, the last thing the government needed was a prophet in Glasgow preaching revolution to the masses and they acted accordingly to silence him.

Maclean's trial turned out to be a great piece of political theatre. Crowds queued to gain entrance to the public gallery of the High Court in Edinburgh, some of whom were workers who had marched overnight from Glasgow (the *Scotsman* claimed that they had to finish their journey by bus) and there was a great sense of expectation when Maclean appeared in court. Evidence was given by 28 witnesses, most of them special constables or police shorthand writers who had attended his meetings between 20 January and 4 April that year. It was a damning indictment: according to the evidence Maclean had advocated strike action and the seizure of industry along the lines of the Bolshevik revolution; he had urged workers to take over the city and had ordered them 'to throw themselves at the throats of the capitalist class'. Leading the prosecution the lord advocate stated that there were no laws to prevent anyone promoting socialism but there came a stage when that discussion took on a different character: 'At that point there came the deliberate and persistent attempt to plant seeds of disunion, disloyalty, sedition and mutiny among the people. They could not afford at the present time to have the people incited to active violence and rebellion while the enemy was at their gates.'

In response Maclean delivered a lengthy, impassioned and at times rambling speech in which he rehearsed his political motives and analysed his response to the war and the Bolshevik revolution. Much of it was highly personal, all of it was directed at criticising capitalism as an 'infamous, bloody and evil' system and it included a ringing defence of his own principles in words which were very much the measure of the man: 'I wish no harm to any human being, but I, as one man, am going to exercise my freedom of speech. No human being on the face of the earth, no government is going to take from me my right to speak, my right to protest against wrong, my right to do everything that is for the benefit of mankind. I am not here then, as the accused; I am here as the accuser of Capitalism dripping with blood from head to foot.'[23] It was to no avail. Maclean was sentenced to five years' penal servitude and incarcerated once again in Peterhead.

During his previous imprisonment he had claimed that his food was being 'doped' (drugged) and had complained about that abuse in the course of his address to the court, at the same time giving notice that he would not eat prison food 'because of the treatment that was meted out to me'. When he was interviewed by the prison medical service at the Perth Prison Hospital he demanded to have his own food supplies, and when this was refused on arrival at Peterhead he went on hunger strike. The officials who examined him, prison commissioner Dr James Devon and the Perth prison medical officer Dr H. Ferguson Watson, reported that they were 'dealing with a man who is insane, but not certified' and so began a lengthy process to have that matter rectified. With the connivance of the Scottish secretary they attempted to have Maclean certified so that he could be treated as a criminal lunatic and incarcerated indefinitely. Munro certainly thought that Maclean was insane, telling the War Cabinet that he was 'more or less a lunatic', and Maclean's prison records show that a concerted attempt was made by the prison medical service to demonstrate his insanity as a medical fact.[24] Devon also turned his attention to James Maxton and tried to prove that he was 'half daft'.

Following Maxton's prison sentence for sedition he was re-arrested after refusing to be conscripted into the army and was sent to Perth jail where he was interviewed by Devon. The findings were reported by Devon to the Scottish Office: 'The creature is mooning over books in the name of education and muddling his brains still further. He never knew the difference between being subtle and being obscure and he is a pitiful sight. His mind has lost grip to a large extent. That such a man should have been a teacher is a marvel and a mystery.'[25] Maxton was later released to take part in work of national importance on a road-building project at Ballachulish but was sent back to prison in 1917 after he took unapproved leave in Glasgow over the Christmas period. Again Devon tried to prove that he was 'not quite sane' and argued that Maxton should remain in prison as he 'might be a cause of trouble in these times'.

The plot against Maclean came to nothing when Dr Gilbert Garry, the Peterhead medical officer, declined to take part in the sectioning process as he contended that Maclean was perfectly sane. However, that was not the end of the matter. As Maclean feared, he was forcibly fed from July onwards and when his wife Agnes was allowed to see him that October she was so shocked by what was happening that she wrote to Munro complaining about the treatment:

> He told me that he tried to resist the forcible feeding by mouth tube, but two warders held him down, and that these men never left him thereafter, night or day, till he was forced to give in. I was shocked beyond measure by these statements (made to me in presence of the prison Doctor and two warders) and by the evidence of their truth supplied by his aged and haggard appearance. They contradict entirely the assurances given to me and his other friends by the Authorities that he was in good health.[26]

Like the force-feeding of the suffragettes, this was a beastly business and Maclean suffered accordingly. There is no evidence to suggest that Maclean's food was being doctored in any way and his complaints to that effect seem to have been the product of a growing paranoia while he was in prison, hence the prison doctors' references to his complaints as 'the ravings of a lunatic'. However, that cannot excuse the treatment meted out to him and from his wife's evidence it is obvious that Maclean did suffer physical and mental torment which badly scarred him. Throughout the remainder of 1918 efforts were made to have Maclean released – letters of complaint were received from organisations and individuals from all parts of the United Kingdom – but the government remained obdurate even when Ramsay MacDonald intervened on his behalf on 5 July 1918 to have him moved to a prison closer to Glasgow. Nothing happened. The Scottish Office stuck to its line that Maclean was not 'haggard and aged' and produced menus of the food available to him: typically soup, meat and potatoes at lunchtime and eggs, meat extract and sweetened milk in the evening.[27] It was not until after the armistice that Maclean was no longer considered to a serious danger to the public and on 29 November the War Cabinet took the decision to release him from Peterhead.

On his return to Glasgow on 3 December he was given a hero's welcome: a huge crowd gathered to meet him at Buchanan Street Station and his carriage was pulled through the streets to take him to his home in Newlands. However, the experience of six months in prison and the forced feeding had clearly damaged him, and friends like Dora Montefiore, a member of the executive of the British Socialist Party, could not help noticing that he emerged from prison a changed man: 'His thoughts were now disconnected, his speech was irresponsible, his mind from solitary confinement was absolutely self-centred. In a word prison life had done its work on a delicately-balanced psychology, and our unfortunate comrade was now a mental wreck.'[28] The authorities had failed in their attempt to section Maclean but it was not surprising that six months of a harsh prison regime had taken a toll on his physical and mental health.

The Clydeside militants were not the only people to suffer imprisonment and vilification for voicing opinions which went against the national interest. Following the introduction of conscription in 1916 those who refused to do military service on grounds of conscience found that they too could be imprisoned for their beliefs. Although the exemption satisfied Liberal doubts about forcing men to join the armed forces, the two Military Service Acts of 1916 failed to give a satisfactory definition of what constituted grounds for conscientious objection and this omission was the cause of a good deal of heartache and bad feeling. Most conscientious objectors had solid grounds for refusing to serve and many suffered as a result, either by being imprisoned or having to face the contempt of serving men.

Those who wished to object to military service had to register their reasons and then appear before a tribunal consisting of local dignitaries, such as town clerks and justices of the peace, together with a military representative. All told, 16,500 men registered as conscientious objectors between 1916 and the end of the war. Of that number 6,000 were exempted from any kind of military service, 5,000 were granted exemption from active service as a combatant but were forced to do non-combatant service and some 3,000 had their objections to military service overruled and were conscripted into the armed forces. A hard core of 2,425 'absolutists' refused even to apply for exemption and inevitably they ended up in prison.

To put those figures into perspective, the number of conscientious objectors has been computed as a third of a per cent of those who served in the armed forces during the war. During the same period, 1916–18, some 3.5 million men were conscripted into the army and a similar number remained in reserved occupations. Even so, despite contemporaneous allegations that the objectors were taking the easy way out by refusing war service, to be a CO or a 'conchie' was not for the timid or those delicate in mind or body. Quite apart from the social obloquy of not wearing a uniform and refusing to fight, the process of entering an objection and then pursuing it through the system required a good deal of physical and mental stamina. Their only support came from the No-Conscription Fellowship, which had been founded by pacifists to protect the rights of those who refused to take part in the fighting, and its powers were limited. If a local tribunal decided against the objections it was possible to take the case to an appellate tribunal presided over by a senior legal official. In Edinburgh the appellate tribunal was chaired by Sheriff C. C. Maconochie, who was considered by one applicant to be 'a judge of the brand of Jeffries or Braxfield [both were notorious as "hanging judges"]'.[29] If the appellate tribunal turned down their appeal they either had to accept the decision and join the armed forces as a conscript or ignore the call-up papers and face the consequences.

The majority chose the latter option, were arrested and, after appearing in court, were handed over to the military authorities, usually the local infantry depot, where they were given the choice of being court-martialled as deserters if they continued to refuse to serve, or joining the Non-Combatant Corps (NCC). Created in March 1916, the corps consisted of 32 companies, each one containing 100 men who were forced to drill but were not given any weapons training. Although the men of the NCC served as infantry privates, with eight companies seeing service in France, they were kept well away from the front line and generally performed useful services. The army's response to them was mixed. For every soldier who cursed them as 'cowardly conchies' there were those who admired them for taking a principled stand and sticking to it. The official view was that the NCC did good work but in an echo of the attitudes to Maxton and Maclean the army's director of labour believed that 'they were mostly men with some mental derangement'.[30]

However, not everything ran smoothly. Some conscientious objectors agreed to join the NCC, or were coerced, but then refused to carry out orders, with the result that they were court-martialled and sent to prison. In September 1916 there were 121 conscientious objectors in Scottish prisons and most of them were members of the ILP.[31] After a lengthy battle with the authorities to convince them of his objections to being conscripted – 'socialists had no business getting involved in the struggle' – J. P. M. Miller from Edinburgh, a member of the ILP, found himself serving in the NCC at Aldershot, where he refused to take part in any duties. Sent for court martial he was reprieved due to irregularities in his call-up procedure but the stay of execution was short-lived. He was sent back to Edinburgh, where he was sentenced in the High Court to the statutory three months' hard labour in London's Wormwood Scrubs prison, where he was set to work sewing mail sacks, 'a very unpleasant job because the canvas was very thick and hard and it was no joke trying to push a needle through it'.[32] The grim London prison was the main centre for punishment and as another Scottish conscientious objector, Eric F. Dott, found when he was imprisoned there in 1917, it was something of a home-from-home for Scots:

One thing that's very vivid to me: I can remember that there must have been a number of conscientious objectors from Scotland within the neighbourhood of the block where I was. In the hours of the day, and even more in the hours of the evening and night I would hear these men whistling Scottish tunes to each other. One would take it up from another. One of them would whistle 'The

Banks of Loch Lomond' or something like that. And away from the other end of the corridor you would hear it replied to by some other tune – 'Annie Laurie', or something like that, coming from one cell to another. The warders didn't like it – they were furious! They felt this was communicating between prisoners. But they couldn't do a thing about it. So there was this camaraderie that somehow got going even in that place.[33]

Dott, a recent school leaver, whose father was the proprietor of the Edinburgh picture dealers Aitken Dott & Son, found that his fellow Scots enjoyed one other advantage. The standard diet at Wormwood Scrubs was porridge, but as it was cooked unsalted most prisoners found it so unpalatable that they refused to eat it. As Dott found, only the Scottish prisoners knew to salt it; 'the English didn't know what to do with it' and went hungry. For Dott, a quiet and studious young man whose objection was based on his Christian beliefs, it must have been a tough experience finding himself far from home in a harsh prison environment; later he admitted that it 'wasn't a great experience' and that only the resilience of youth made it bearable.

Wormwood Scrubs was used as a punishment centre for conscientious objectors as a result of an army order of 25 May 1916 which attempted to bring some cohesion to a confused situation. Originally the army itself took responsibility for punishing conscientious objectors who refused to accept orders or who ignored their call-up papers. Although some senior officers found the system both unworkable and upsetting for all concerned, members of the NCC in France and Flanders could not expect any leniency and, being at a war front, they were liable to the full force of military discipline. Following the revelation of an incident in which 34 NCC members were sentenced to death for refusing to obey orders the War Office agreed that to prevent further problems of this kind conscientious objectors refusing military discipline would serve their sentences in civil prisons. The news of the incident had caused uproar when it became known at home and as a result of the intervention of the No-Conscription Fellowship the sentences were commuted to ten years' penal servitude.

A further refinement was a new Home Office scheme which overhauled the system of registration and appeal and introduced Work of National Importance for those given exemption. It also applied to those in prison. At the end of their prison sentences conscientious objectors were given the option of being sent to centres at Dartmoor, Knutsford and Wakefield, where they would be employed on building projects or agricultural and forestry work for the duration of the war. There were also opportunities for the work to be carried out elsewhere under supervision. After spending time at Dartmoor Eric Dott was allowed to return to Edinburgh, where he worked in a nursery garden under the supervision of a local man who shared his beliefs. Others were less lucky. Before the war Dr John C. MacCallum won 27 international caps playing for Scotland's rugby XV between 1905 and 1912, five times as captain, but his fame counted for nothing when he declared himself a conscientious objector. Under the Work of National Importance scheme he found himself labouring in a noxious reduction plant at Broxburn in West Lothian which manufactured fertiliser from animal remains.[34]

Another scheme for the diversification of treatment of conscientious objectors was the creation of a number of outside work centres which provided jobs for those capable of undertaking hard labour. There were two centres in Scotland: at a granite quarry at Dyce outside Aberdeen and at Ballachulish in Argyll, where a new road was being built along the loch side to connect it with the munitions works at Kinlochleven. Amongst those who worked on the Ballachulish scheme there was a group of 200 from Wakefield, including James Maxton and J. P. M. Miller, who thought it 'a God-forsaken place' miles away from anywhere. It consisted of a hutted camp at Caolasnacon, originally built to house German prisoners-of-war, which was served by a steamer but it was all very basic. A Home Office agent oversaw the project with an assistant and the work parties were assisted by experienced roadmen who laid the charges to demolish the rocks. Conditions at Dyce were even more primitive, consisting of a tented encampment of old army bell tents for 250 men and a number of derelict bothie cottages. Following the death of one of the workers the No-Conscription Fellowship complained about the lack of decent sanitation, reminding the Scottish Office on 12 September 1916 that the conscientious objectors, many of them from England, had been sent to 'an exposed part of the north of Scotland where the climate is exceedingly severe'. When the letter was made public it received little sympathy: a local Aberdeen newspaper retorted that there had been no severe weather of late and that the Dyce shirkers were 'degenerate or worse' and were well treated in comparison to the men in the front lines who had been 'fighting and dying for the safety and liberty of those conscientious objectors'.[35] Amongst the labour force at Dyce was the much-prosecuted English political activist Guy Aldred, who had been a popular speaker in Glasgow before the war.

The best that can be said about these schemes is that they served a national purpose and were preferable to incarcerating able-bodied men in prison, but like any correction facilities they also hardened attitudes. Many of the conscientious objectors were socialists or members of sects such as the Plymouth Brethren or Seventh Day Adventists and the prisons and work centres provided opportunities for education and debate. While at Dartmoor young Eric Dott came into contact with a number of ILP members and found that his political views were slowly changing. From being an objector to the war on religious grounds he gradually moved over to socialism and by the time of his discharge he found that he was 'a convinced socialist and something of a free thinker towards religion'.

One of the highest profile objectors to war was not a Scot, but he was connected to Scotland through the work of Dr W. H. R. Rivers, a distinguished psychologist who practised at Craiglockhart Military Hospital in Edinburgh, one of a number of major military medical institutions which had been established to deal with the war wounded. This was Siegfried Sassoon, an officer in the Royal Welch Fusiliers, a winner of the Military Cross and a well-connected poet whose war poems had been praised for their bleak realism and contempt for those who did not do the actual fighting. During the Battle of Arras he was wounded and invalided home and while recuperating in London and Sussex he seems to have undergone a profound conversion. From his letters and diaries it is clear that he wanted to make a public objection both about the direction of the war and the attitudes of the men running the war who 'glory in senseless invective against the enemy' and 'regard the progress of the war like a game of chess, cackling about "attrition", and "wastage of manpower" and "civilisation at stake".'[36] It had also become clear to him that while his poems, published that year as *The Old Huntsman*, had been praised in literary circles, their anti-war message had been ignored.

Something more vocal was required and after visiting Garsington, the home of Philip and Lady Ottoline Morrell, both influential and well-connected pacifists with links to the No-Conscription Fellowship, Sassoon decided to publish a statement of protest, which was published in a number of newspapers, including *The Times*, on 31 July 1917. In it he claimed that the war was being deliberately prolonged and that what had been 'a war of defence and liberation' had become 'a war of aggression and conquest'. Having made clear his credentials as a front-line soldier and having acknowledged his 'wilful defiance of military authority' he said that he could no longer be a party to the continuation of the war or the sacrifice of soldiers' lives: 'On behalf of those who are suffering now, I make this protest against the deception which is being practised on them. Also I believe that it may help to destroy the callous complacence with which the majority of those at home regard the continuance of agonies which they do not share, and which they have not sufficient imagination to realise.'[37]

Before the statement was published Sassoon sent a copy to his commanding officer with a covering letter informing him that it was his intention 'to refuse to perform any further military duties'. This was mutiny and Sassoon fully expected to be court-martialled when he returned to the regimental depot at Litherland near Liverpool. His friends and regimental colleagues certainly thought that he had over-stepped the mark and would have to bear the consequences: one fellow officer warned him that he would have to face a court martial where he would be reduced to the ranks and would then face conscription 'unless you become a Conscientious Objector, which pray Heaven you never will'.[38] Not only had Sassoon criticised the higher direction of the war but he had given public utterance to his refusal to take any further part in the war. It was not dissimilar to the stance taken by conscientious objectors such as Dott and Millar who were sent to prison for refusing to obey a military order and had made public their opposition to the war, but there was, of course, a difference. Sassoon was a well-known public figure who had been decorated for bravery on the Western Front; he was also a published writer who came from a wealthy family and, above all, he had influential friends including the writers Thomas Hardy, Arnold Bennett and Bertrand Russell. He also had a close friend in his brother officer and fellow poet Robert Graves, who used his extensive political contacts in mounting what might be called a damage-limitation exercise. The War Office was persuaded not to courtmartial Sassoon but to examine him before a medical board to judge his state of mind. Graves played a further part by giving evidence in Sassoon's favour and by telling his friend, untruthfully, that the army intended to declare him insane and to incarcerate him for the duration of the war. As a result, and with some hesitation, the medical board decided that Sassoon was suffering from neurasthenia and sent him to Craiglockhart for treatment.[39]

The building, which still stands, was built in 1865 as a poorhouse before being transformed fifteen years later into the Craiglockhart Hydropathic Institution. In the summer of 1916 it was brought into use as a major military hospital with several out-stations, including one on the Earl of Selkirk's estate at Bowhill in the borders. Sassoon wrote disparagingly of the place as possessing 'the melancholy atmosphere of a decayed hydropathic' and in letters to his friends called it 'Dottyville'. He was equally judgemental about the 160 inmates, describing them as 'degenerate-looking' and complaining about the constant noise at night as 'wash-outs and shattered heroes' cried out in their sleep from their 'underworld of dreams'. It is difficult to avoid the impression that Sassoon was snobbishly shocked by his fellow inmates. He shared a room with a Scottish officer who clearly irked him, and his letters to his English friends betray an amused condescension about his experiences: one dated from the Central Hotel in Glasgow stated that 'a man has motored me over to this large city and I have lunched ponderously'.[40] At the same time life was reasonably tolerable, with long walks over the nearby Pentland Hills and endless games of golf on the city's many courses. Another bonus was his growing friendship with Rivers, a gifted psychologist who was the leading specialist in dealing with 'war-neuroses' which he believed were quite different from the mental disturbances of peacetime. Rivers's philosophy was that it was his duty to deal with his patients by helping them to overcome their fears and return them to active service.

The relationship between the two men was intensely productive and has been much studied for its effect on Sassoon's literary growth.[41] The 'treatment' consisted largely of lengthy discussions and Rivers quickly came to the conclusion that Sassoon was not suffering from shellshock but was in hospital because of his 'adoption of a pacifist attitude while on leave from active service'. To Sassoon he simply said that he was suffering from 'a very strong anti-war complex' and an interesting aspect of the doctor–patient relationship is that Rivers spent much time and energy trying to discover the impulse for that complex. So powerful was the fascination that Sassoon made an appearance as 'Patient B' in Rivers's account of war neuroses which was published after the war.[42] The softly-softly approach seems to have worked: four months after arriving at Craiglockhart, Sassoon was returned to general duties and the records show that he only underwent a total of 14 days' treatment while two officers admitted at the same time underwent 127 days and 218 days of treatment respectively.[43] By the spring of 1918 Sassoon was back in action again, this time serving with 25th Royal Welch Fusiliers in Palestine, which he found to be 'an antechamber to the real hell of France'.[44] Craiglockart had been a productive period for him: he wrote some 20 poems, which were published in the hospital's magazine *The Hydra* and formed the basis for his next volume, *Counter-Attack*. He also gave encouragement to Wilfred Owen, a genuinely shellshocked officer who emerged as one of the finest poets of the war. Although Sassoon tended to patronise 'little Owen' he did help him by redrafting and criticising his early poems and, just as importantly, was able to give him a valuable introduction to the wider literary world.

While Owen returned to frontline service and was killed in action shortly before the armistice, Sassoon survived the war and died in 1967. He never really fulfilled his promise as a poet, although his memoir *Memories of an Infantry Officer* can be counted amongst the best personal accounts of the war. In contrast to the treatment handed out to the conscientious objectors Dott and Millar and to anti-war protesters such as John Maclean, all of whom were badly treated in prison, Sassoon got off reasonably lightly. Having made an articulate anti-war statement, he refused to perform any military duties in protest at the government's policy; effectively he gave up the right to be treated as a soldier. Sassoon's argument that 'the war is being deliberately prolonged by those who have the power to end it' is not so different from Maclean's statement that 'the great Powers are not prepared to stop the war until one side or the other is broken down', yet by virtue of his standing and his social and political connections Sassoon was let off the hook by being sent to Craiglockhart to be treated for shellshock while Maclean faced the hardships of prison. Neither man was insane but while Sassoon was able to use it as a mask to prevent further punishment the authorities went to great lengths to try to section Maclean, and even though they failed they certainly brought on a decline in his mental health. It can be argued that Sassoon had already 'done his bit' by serving in the trenches where his bravery earned him the nickname of 'Mad Jack' while Maclean had a reputation as a political troublemaker, but it is hard to avoid the impression that they were treated by very different rules.

10 Haig: Architect of Victory 1918

On 17 April 1918 the convoy carrying the 52nd (Lowland) Division from Palestine entered the harbour at Marseilles carrying much needed reinforcements for the Western Front, where the Germans had mounted a major offensive against the Allied lines. It proved to be an unpleasant surprise for the men on board the transports: after the heat and dust of the Middle East they found themselves back in the familiar cold and wet weather of northern Europe and ahead lay a long and tiring journey by train to their ultimate destination at Abbeville. Once there, they went into theatre reserve in General Sir Julian Byng's Third Army and began a period of intensive training for the very different conditions of warfare on the Western Front. The division's machine-gun companies were reorganised into a machine-gun battalion and, as happened throughout the army, to meet the shortfall in manpower there was an internal reorganisation in the order of battle, thus spreading the Scots contingents throughout the division. Soon after arriving, the division's strength was reduced by three battalions which were sent to reinforce the badly depleted 34th Division. These were $1/5^{th}$ King's Own Scottish Borderers, $1/8^{th}$ Cameronians and $1/5^{th}$ Argyll and Sutherland Highlanders. During this period of enforced reorganisation a total of 147 under-strength Territorial and New Army battalions were either disbanded or amalgamated, as happened for example to the $4/5^{th}$ Black Watch and $7/8^{th}$ King's Own Scottish Borderers in the 15th (Scottish) Division. On 6 May the 52nd (Lowland) Division moved back into the line at Vimy Ridge, where it was held as general headquarters reserve.

The division's return to France came as a result of a major German initiative to win the war before US forces were able to deploy in strength in Europe, and at a time when the British and French armies had been badly weakened by the previous year's offensives.

Codenamed 'Michael' (Germany's patron saint), the offensive plan was adopted on 21 January 1918 and it called for a massive rolling 'hurricane' artillery barrage followed by a rapid and aggressive advance by the infantry which in Ludendorff's words would 'punch a hole' in the British defences and lay the foundations for defeating the enemy in Flanders. Strong points would be bypassed to be dealt with later by mop-up operations.

The plans were advanced in great secrecy and there was an intensive training programme for the assault formations, which were composed of lightly equipped but heavily armed 'shock' or 'storm' troops. Their orders were to press on quickly and assertively, to take ground without thinking too much about the safety of their flanks and above all to maintain the momentum of the assault, regardless of casualties. It was a bold policy and in adopting it Ludendorff had high hopes that it would succeed in pushing the British back towards the Channel, opening the way to Paris. In addition to enjoying numerical superiority, he also knew that the British lines were unbalanced in their deployment and were in a state of flux following the decision to reorganise the order of battle as a result of the manpower shortages. Particularly affected in this respect was Gough's Fifth Army, which had been weakened by the changes yet was committed to extending its line to the south of the Somme to reinforce the French sector. From the available intelligence Haig knew by the middle of March that the Germans had 'concentrated already adequate means for a large attack' and that it had to be expected 'at short notice', but he was in the dark about Ludendorff's precise intentions.[1] Fearing that the weight of the German attack would come in the Ypres sector and being desperately short of combat troops Haig had reinforced Byng's Third Army, leaving Gough to defend 42 miles of front with only 12 divisions, some of them badly undermanned. Haig reckoned that he could afford to lose ground on the Somme but it was a gamble. The Germans would be attacking with 43 divisions and a total of 2,508 heavy artillery pieces, and as the *Official History* noted later, 'never before had the British line been held with so few men and so few guns to the mile'.[2]

The storm broke in the early hours of the morning of 21 March, when the German artillery produced a huge bombardment which lasted for five hours and left the defenders badly shaken and disorientated. Gas and smoke shells added to the confusion, which was increased even more by an early morning mist, leaving commanders with no exact idea of where and when the infantry attack was coming. In their defensive positions in the Cambrai sector near Beaumetz the 51st (Highland) Division had their first inkling that something was afoot when scouting parties from 1/7th Black Watch observed thousands of German infantrymen entering the frontline trenches carrying weapons but leaving behind their heavy packs, clearly preparing for an assault. When it came, the German attack was as intense as anything the Scots had experienced during their three years on the Western Front.[3] By then Harper had left the division to command a corps and the new divisional commander was Major-General George Carter-Campbell, who had been a company commander with the 2nd Scottish Rifles at the Battle of Neuve Chapelle and was described by a fellow regimental officer as 'an outstanding officer, small and neat in appearance with a rather dry, incisive manner'.[4]

In the Arras sector, held by XVII Corps, the brunt of the German attack fell on the 15th (Scottish) Division south of the Scarpe and the divisional commander, Major-General Hamilton Lyster Reed VC, a gunner, was told by his superiors in no uncertain terms that there was to be no withdrawal and no surrender: 'The Division is now in a point of honour. The ground it holds is of the utmost importance and it is to be held at all costs.'[5] The War Diary of one of the division's battalions, 7/8th King's Own Scottish Borderers, put it more prosaically, describing the German assault from the soldier's perspective as 'the lid being taken off hell'.[6] Also heavily involved in the fighting were eight battalions of the Royal Scots, five with the Third Army (2nd, 1/8th, 13th, 15th, 16th) and three with the Fifth Army (1/9th, 11th, 12th). One company of the 1/9th Royal Scots suffered huge casualties while covering the withdrawal of the 20th Division at Le Quesnoy: out of 100 men there were only 11 survivors.[7] Later, two further Royal Scots' battalions (5/6th and 17th) were rushed into action as reinforcements.

The intensity of the attack took the British commanders by surprise and by the end of the first day their forces had sustained 38,000 casualties, the majority in the Fifth Army. To the south of the British sector von Hutier's assault troops had broken through a 19-mile stretch of Gough's lines and the defending divisions were forced to surrender ground. In the confusion large numbers of guns were lost to enemy shellfire or were captured when their positions were overrun. Even experienced divisions found themselves in difficulties: as the 9th (Scottish) Division withdrew from its position in front of Gou-zeaucourt it lost touch with the neighbouring 47th Division, allowing the left flank to be exposed. The retreating divisions were particularly bothered by air attack and lost many casualties to 'throngs of aero-planes flitting above them'. The casualties were not just the rank and file – the 51st (Highland) Division lost three out of ten battalion commanders – and over 20,000 soldiers went into captivity. Amongst them was Captain C. J. Lambert, 16th Royal Scots, who was fortunate enough not to be shot out of hand after fighting to the last round against overwhelming odds on 22 March:

> Running was useless so we lay flat on our back with our hands in the air till the firing stopped. Germans then rushed up to us and signed for us to throw off our equipment, this we did fairly quickly. A man then waved a bayonet around my middle and led me over to the last two men I had killed, loosing off a tremendous flow of German and waving the bayonet with great effect in front of me. I shrugged my shoulders as there was nothing else I could do, and an officer came up, shook me warmly by the hand and told me to go towards their lines.[8]

Lambert was lucky. All he lost was his watch and his cigarettes to the bayonet-wielding German soldier. Earlier in the fighting Lambert had been knocked unconscious and on recovering found himself in a trench with five survivors as the enemy began closing in on the position. In other circumstances, having killed enemy soldiers im-mediately before surrendering he could have faced summary execu-tion. By the time his battalion was pulled out of the line two days later it had lost 11 officers, killed, missing or wounded and first estimates showed the loss of 240 men, most of whom turned up later unharmed. But amidst the mayhem, when some units simply gave up the struggle and ran, there were other examples of steadfastness and courage.

A year earlier, in April 1916, the South African Brigade had come under the aegis of the 9th (Scottish) Division and it demonstrated nothing but resolve in holding its positions at Marrieres Wood and refusing to pull back in the face of a sustained German attack. As the divisional historian put it, at the bitter end 'rescue was now impossible, and the South Africans grimly set themselves to sell their lives at the highest price.'[9] The brigade's casualties were so heavy that three of its battalions had to be amalgamated and for a short time it was reinforced by 2nd Royal Scots Fusiliers and 9th Cameronians. Later, these two battalions created a re-formed 28th Brigade with the 1st Royal Newfoundland Regiment.

On the second day of the Michael offensive the Third Army's battle lines remained intact but in the south the Fifth Army came under such intense pressure that it was unable to respond to the speed and intensity of the German attack: von Hutier had made startling progress, advancing up to 12 miles and prompting fears that a huge split was about to be opened up in the Allied lines. In the Ypres sector to the north John Jackson, still serving with 1st Camerons, 'began to hear of heavy British losses, of regiments and even divisions being smashed to pieces with the Germans for ever advancing and capturing the hastily prepared positions'.[10] Jackson thought that nothing could stop the inexorable German assault, but amidst the confusion of a battle which was the British Army's first defeat on the Western Front, Ludendorff's plan was beginning to unravel. By the beginning of April the Germans had advanced 20 miles along a 50-mile front, creating a huge bulge in the Allied line, and had pushed themselves to within 5 miles of Amiens. If this key city and railhead had fallen it would have been a disaster for the Allies. The French would have been forced back to defend Paris and the British would have been left with little option but to do the same in order to defend the Channel ports; the war would have hung in the balance.

However, despite the obvious danger and the need to check it, the Germans had failed to concentrate the main thrust of their assault and had dispersed the effort to take their targets. As the *Official History* put it, 'these manifold objectives required more troops than Ludendorff had at his disposal'.[11] While attacking along the Scarpe valley in front of Arras they met determined resistance and took heavy casualties. Now involved in fighting an organised defensive battle, the 15th (Scottish) Division dug in and refused to budge; with accurate artillery fire to support them the fighting soldiers grew in confidence as they saw the enemy falling to their fire. Following one heavy attack an officer in the 11th Argylls noted with some satisfaction that the enemy were no longer regarded as supermen but as ordinary soldiers who could be beaten: 'There is no doubt that this day's shooting was very valuable to the battalion, and really demonstrated to the men the value of the rifle and its effect when firing on large parties of men who have been scattered by artillery fire.'[12]

The German attack also brought about a change in the Allies' command structure, giving General Foch the authority to co-ordinate the operations of all Allied forces on the Western Front. Although Haig had been opposed to such a move he now welcomed the appointment as the only reliable means of directing Allied strategy while preserving national interests. The appointment of an overall commander came at the very moment when the initial German attack was faltering, and the Michael offensive was finally called off on 5 April without Amiens coming under threat of attack. The German break-in battle had succeeded in capturing a large salient, but the expected breakthrough to split the Allies had failed to materialise and the position would prove difficult to hold. There had also been heavy German casualties – some 250,000 killed, missing or wounded – and morale within the assault formations had been shattered by their failure to produce a decisive blow in the so-called 'Kaiserschlacht' (Kaiser's Battle) which was supposed to win the war. Even so, Ludendorff was not quite done with his offensive. Four days later, on 9 April, he launched Operation Georgette, a second attack aimed along a narrow front south of Armentières in the Ypres sector. An understrength Portuguese division was brushed aside in the Aubers– Neuve Chapelle sector, allowing the Germans to advance towards the defensive line of the rivers Lawe and Lys, which was eventually shored up by British XI Corps. Amongst those taking part in this period of bitter fighting, which the British called the Battle of the Lys, was the 40th Division, which included 10/11th Highland Light Infantry and 14th Highland Light Infantry. Both battalions lost so many casualties that they almost ceased to exist as fighting formations.

The 14th had been raised in Hamilton in 1915 as one of the army's 'bantam' battalions, which had been created to recruit men who were below the regulation height of 5 feet 3 inches but above 5 feet and otherwise physically sound. The bantam concept caught on and a complete bantam division was formed, the 35th, with its distinctive rooster divisional sign. However, the experiment came at a price: many of the recruits were not only undersized but also physically unsound and became a liability in the front line. When the 14th Highland Light Infantry joined 40th Division at Aldershot in the spring of 1915 it had to absorb another bantam battalion, the 13th Cameronians, which had been reduced to 200 men after a series of stringent medical examinations had ruled out over 800 bantam recruits from the Glasgow area.[14] (One soldier who survived the purge was sentenced to death in the aftermath of the German offensive in April 1918 when he deserted and was involved in the murder of a military policeman near Calais: John Dewar had enlisted in February 1916 in another bantam battalion, 18th Highland Light Infantry, while still under-age and this fact seems to have been taken into account when his sentence was commuted to hard labour.[15] The first bantam soldier to be executed – for desertion – was Private James Archibald, 17th Royal Scots, who was shot at Loisne on 4 June 1916.) By the beginning of 1918 the bantam experiment was all but over and original formations were bantam in name only.

By then, too, the War Office had addressed the problem of underage boy soldiers who had lied about their ages when joining up. An estimated 250,000 soldiers managed to enlist when they were still under the regulation age of 18, and they suffered proportional casualties. In June 1916 War Office Instruction ACI 1186 allowed parents to reclaim their sons from frontline service; they would be returned home and discharged. Given the imprecise nature of the instructions and the fact that the policy was not widely publicised, many families either remained ignorant of the terms or failed to act on them. Sometimes too the boy concerned refused to accept the offer and stayed on, or there was a certain amount of complicity within the battalion to keep him. That seems to have been the case with one soldier in the 1/5th Gordons to whom Alick Buchanan-Smith spoke while waiting to go into the attack at Buzancy during the Second Battle of the Marne in July 1918, when the Scots were under the command of the French general Mangin:

> They were magnificent men in the bloom of youth. Again there was little or no personal anxiety in their faces or in their actions. In part perhaps this may have been because, by then, the war had become accepted almost as a way of life.

I remember one of them vividly, partly because I had occasion to tick him off. He was a great strapping chield, bigger and broader than myself. His kilt still retained its pleats. Something stirred in me to ask him his age. 'Fifteen,' was his reply as he looked me straight in the eye. After Buzancy I never saw him again.[16]

Before the decisive summer battles which signalled the beginning of the final Allied offensive against the German lines the British forces still had to deal with the Georgette Offensive. Following the attack against the Lawe-Lys sector the Germans had mounted a pincer movement on the north and south of the Ypres salient, pushing their forces strongly towards Langemarck and Wytschaete and threatening the British reserve line. So desperate was the situation, with most of the gains of the previous year's Battle of Third Ypres (Passchendaele) having been lost, that on 11 April Haig issued the famous Order of the Day for which he is probably best remembered: 'There is no course open to us but to fight it out. Every position must be held to the last man: there must be no retirement. With our backs to the wall and believing the justice of our cause each one of us must fight on to the end. The safety of our Homes and the Freedom of Mankind alike depend upon the conduct of each one of us at this critical moment.'[17] Coming from such a reticent man as Haig it was an extraordinary document, although for some reason he made no mention of it in his diary. While some of his staff feared that Haig's sombre tone would dent morale by appearing defeatist his words captured the mood of the moment when backs were almost literally against the wall and defeat was a strong possibility. As far as the outcome of the battle was concerned, Haig had secured the support of French reinforcements to stem the German attack towards Hazebrouck, but his Order of the Day still hit the right note. It was only by standing firm and refusing the urge to retire that positions in the field could be held. It was only by fighting stubbornly and showing raw courage that the attacking German storm troops could be stopped in their tracks. As General Sir Henry Horne, commanding First Army, put it in his message of thanks to the 51st (Highland) Division, the British soldiers had shown their mettle 'not only against superior numbers but under particularly trying circumstances'.[18]

While some units and their men failed that test, the outcome of operations Michael and Georgette was decided by those who stood firm in the face of the heavy onslaught, men like Lieutenant A. E. Ker, 3rd Gordons, attached 61st Battalion Machine-Gun Corps, who was awarded the VC after holding up a German attack for ten hours. When his machine-gun post near St Quentin ran out of ammunition he and his sergeant and the badly wounded survivors continued the battle with small arms, fighting to the last round and refusing to surrender until overwhelmed by the superior odds. In the same action, near Maricourt, Lieutenant-Colonel W. H. Anderson, 12th Highland Light Infantry, was awarded the VC posthumously after leading a determined counter-attack which resulted in the capture of 12 machine guns and 70 German prisoners. A third Scottish VC was won by 2nd Lieutenant J. C. Crawford, 2/8th Argyll and Sutherland Highlanders, who found his position near Marteville surrounded and was called on to surrender. His last words as he led the counter-attack were 'To hell with surrender!' All three actions took place at the height of the first German offensive between 21 and 25 March.

The stand on the River Lys took the sting out of the German attack and although the enemy advanced beyond Merville and Bailleul to come within sight of Hazebrouck the arrival of French reinforcements from General Maistre's Tenth Army on 21 April stabilised the front. A week later Ludendorff called off the Georgette operation, bringing a degree of respite to the battered British First and Second Armies which had taken the brunt of the attack in the Ypres sector. Casualties were high: the British lost 76,000, the French 35,000 and the Portuguese 6,000; on the German side there were 109,000 casualties. During the withdrawal to Bailleul in the third week of April the 15th and 16th Royal Scots were combined and a month later, on 16 May, both battalions were disbanded when the 34th Division was suspended as a result of the losses in battle and the lack of reinforcements. By then only some 30 of McCrae's original volunteers were left in the battalion and they and the others were posted to other Royal Scots' battalions.[19] Other Scottish regiments taking part in the Lys action also suffered high casualties: at the end of the fighting the 2nd King's Own Scottish Borderers had been reduced to under 100 men; the 1st Cameronians lost a third of their men; by the beginning of June the losses in the 7th Camerons were so high that it was reduced to a cadre; in the same month as a result of the casualties caused by the German offensive the 11th Argylls was reduced in size and became the reinforcement battalion for X Corps while the 14th Argylls re-formed by absorbing the 17th Battalion.

The losses were made good by fresh drafts of conscripts from Britain who passed through one of the 13 Infantry Base Depots (IBDs) that had been established to process the men and give them a final spell of training to prepare them for life in the trenches. These were lettered A to M and the latter IBD supplied drafts to the four Scottish divisions from its base at Calais, but by that stage in the war it was proving difficult to maintain national or regional associations. By that stage of the war, too, many of the army's pre-war battalions were Regular in name only and the dilution caused problems for career army officers who found that standards had inevitably slipped.

When James Jack took over command of the 1st Cameronians in the summer of 1918, having previously commanded the 2nd West Yorkshire Regiment, there were only two surviving pre-war officers, and on meeting the brigade commander he received an unpleasant shock when he was told that the battalion was 'below form' and required 'smartening up'. Worse was to follow when Jack discovered that the battalion became 'a mob' when attempting to march at the faster pre-war 145 steps per minute common to a rifle regiment and that many of the officers were not properly turned out, wearing 'excessively light-coloured ties, collars, shirts and breeches' instead of the darker unostentatious colours preferred by the pre-war Regulars. To encourage an improvement he purchased regimental canes at his own expense to replace 'a miscellaneous collection of walking-sticks'. When Jack left the battalion in September 1918 to command 28th Brigade in the 9th (Scottish) Division he admitted that the officers and men were 'not quite first-class' but consoled himself with the thought that all ranks had done their best 'as soon as my views on soldiering had become understood'.[20] On the other hand, bucking the trend in the same period of the war, the 9th (Scottish) Division found that its drafts of replacements measured up to what was required when they arrived to replace battlefield casualties in the summer of 1918: 'They were largely composed of lads who had been taken at the age of seventeen, and were splendid examples of the beneficial effects of good training, regular exercise and military discipline on young Scotsmen.'[21]

There were other changes as a result of four years of fighting. Although the Highland regiments continued to wear the kilt, soldiers wore steel helmets instead of bonnets and officers took care to disguise their badges of rank. In Jack's battalion the officers had been indignant when told to discard their 'cream shade of breeches' but were quickly reminded that the regulation dark khaki made them less conspicuous to German snipers. Another sign of the times was that officers went into action carrying a rifle instead of a pistol or walking stick, and the swords worn by the 2nd Scottish Rifles at Neuve Chapelle were only a distant romantic memory. What did survive was the imperturbable nature of the Scottish soldier. As Buchanan-Smith had noted of his men in the 1/5th Gordons, by the summer of 1918 war had been accepted as a fact of daily life and while that produced widespread resignation and in some cases induced a good deal of cynicism, at no time did it appear that morale was waning to critically low levels. This was confirmed by a report to the War Cabinet for the period between April and July, which was based on the censorship of 84,000 soldiers' letters,[22] and it is backed up by contemporary diaries and letters. Regimental officers noted that despite the hardships their men still retained a sense of humour and could put their predicament into perspective. During the defence of Bailleul the following exchange took place between a Scottish platoon sergeant and a young soldier who had fallen to the ground apparently badly wounded:

'What are ye groaning for, laddie?'
'I've got a bullet in the fleshy part of my leg,' was the reply.
'Fleshy part of my leg!' said the war-weary sergeant, with visions of a peaceful spell at home. 'What the hell are you complaining about?'[23]

Following the failure of the attack on the British lines in the Somme and Ypres sectors Ludendorff turned his attention to the French armies along the Aisne. By 30 May they had reached the Marne, creating a salient 20 miles deep and 30 miles wide. Vigorous counter-attacks by French and US forces frustrated the German advance and British forces were also involved when the newly formed XXII Corps under Lieutenant-General Sir Alexander Godley were deployed in support of the French Army in Champagne. Amongst its four divisions were 15th (Scottish) and 51st (Highland) and both of them took part in what became known as the Second Battle of the Marne, which finally halted the German advance in the middle of July. At the end of the action the 1/6th Black Watch was given the special honour of being awarded the Croix de Guerre for its support of French forces in the field.

The battle represented the last and best chance for the Germans to win the war, but although they had won large tracts of enemy ground all the salients had vulnerable flanks which were prone to counter-attack. The Germans had also taken huge casualties and for their survivors it was dispiriting to see that so little had been gained for so much effort. At the same time, they were aware that the Americans were arriving in France at the rate of 300,000 a month and would soon produce a formidable opposition, with fresh troops and a seemingly limitless supply of weapons and equipment. The beginning of the end came on 8 August when Australian and Canadian forces attacked the German positions to the east of Amiens with a British and a French corps guarding the flanks to the north and south. The attack achieved complete surprise and the Allies were able to advance 8 miles in one day, taking over 12,000 German prisoners in the process. Writing in his memoirs the following year Ludendorff described 8 August as 'the black day of the German Army in the history of this war. This was the worst experience I had to go through . . . Everything I had feared and of which I had so often given warning, had here, in one place, become a reality. Our war machine was no longer efficient.'[24]

Haig's reaction was rather different. In a letter to his wife written that same day he claimed that he was 'only the instrument of that Divine Power which watches over each one of us, so all the Honour must be His'.[25] As a committed Christian Haig placed enormous importance on his faith and in his papers there are countless similar references to him being God's instrument, but there were many more to his management of the war than his belief that he was being directed by an infallible divine power. By the time of the successful August assault by British and Dominion forces Haig realised that the war was entering a crucial phase and that there was a strong possibility that the fighting would be over before the end of the year. He said as much to Winston Churchill, by then employed as minister of munitions, when Churchill visited him on 21 August. Churchill arrived bearing the glad tidings that he hoped to have his supply lines producing sufficient numbers of shells and tanks by June 1919 as the War Cabinet reckoned that would be 'the decisive period of the war'. Haig's reply is instructive: 'I told him we ought to do our utmost to get a decision this autumn.'[26] Throughout 1918 Haig had been carrying out his direction of operations under the suspicion that Lloyd George had lost confidence in him and was looking at ways to have him sacked from his post as commander-in-chief. The prime minister had made little secret of his disdain for Haig and his distrust of tactics which seemed to produce high casualties for no gains, but at the same time he either lacked the will to make a move against Haig or he could find no suitable candidate as a successor. As a result a state of undeclared warfare existed between 10 Downing Street and Haig's General Headquarters and the most notable casualty was Robertson, forced to resign in February 1918. His successor as chief of the imperial general staff (CIGS) was Henry Wilson, who had spent much of the war as Britain's chief liaison officer at French General Headquarters.

Such a state of affairs was bound to cause unnecessary tensions, and so it proved. Lloyd George had entertained severe reservations about the previous year's Passchendaele offensive and had come to believe that there could be no decisive breakthrough on the Western Front; Haig on the other hand entered 1918 believing the exact opposite. The former wanted to spend the year building up Britain's military strength and looking for victory in Palestine, where Allenby was enjoying a run of success against the Ottoman forces, whereas Haig was keen to continue the momentum in Flanders even though he had come to believe that the prime minister was withholding reinforcements to prevent him planning and executing offensive operations. The US entry into the war also affected the relationship: Lloyd George hoped that the use of overwhelming American force would end the war in 1919 while Haig hoped to limit US influence and retain the importance of the British Empire by winning the war a year earlier. There was also a degree of animus involved: Lloyd George seems to have viewed Haig and many of his generals as typical representatives of the upper classes while Haig sometimes found the prime minister tiresome and verbose company, confiding to his diary on 3 April following the Allied conference at Doullens, 'LG is a fatiguing companion in a motor. He talks and argues so!'[27]

There can be no better example of the strains in the relationship than the government's reaction to the aftermath of the Battle of Albert at the end of August when the Third Army attacked across the Somme and the First Army attacked on the left along the Scarpe, forcing the Germans to abandon their gains of March and April and to pull back towards their defensive positions on the Hindenburg Line. A shortage of reserves meant that the momentum could not be maintained, but Haig's armies had not only made significant gains but were finding that hundreds of Germans were surrendering without offering much resistance. Yet at the very moment when it appeared that the German will to resist was faltering, Haig received a querulous telegram from Wilson on 1 September warning him, for political reasons, to avoid unnecessary losses when continuing the attack. To Haig the inference was obvious:

> The object of this telegram is, no doubt, to save the Prime Minister (Lloyd George) in case of any failure. So I read it to mean that I can attack the Hindenburg Line if I think it right to do so. The CIGS and the Cabinet already know that my arrangements are being made to that end. If my attack is successful I will remain on as C-in-C. If we fail, or our losses are excessive, I can hope for no mercy! I wrote to Henry Wilson in reply. What a wretched lot of weaklings we have in high places at the present time![28]

Haig was right to be bullish. With the war entering its final hundred days the advantage had swung inexorably towards the Allies. America had her first experience of battle, at St Mihiel. This was followed by Foch's offensive in the Meuse-Argonne where French and US forces pushed northwards towards Sedan and Mezieres. At the same time, the British Second Army recaptured the Messines ridge while further to the north the Belgian Army Group commanded by King Albert pushed out of Ypres and over the Passchendaele Ridge towards Roulers. All along the front the Allies were making significant progress, and, applying relentless pressure, they continued their advance throughout October and into November as the Germans withdrew steadily from their positions on the Western Front. Familiar names were retaken – for the British Le Cateau, for the French the symbolic Sedan – and in common with other formations the regiments of the 15th Scottish Division found themselves fighting over ground they had last seen years earlier: 'Was it by accident or design that the last phase in its fighting career should begin around Loos and the Hohenzollern Redoubt where over three years before the Division had received its baptism of fire? There were few left in the Division who could remember those early days, but to the few the memories must have been many.'[30]

One of the last actions involved the 1st Camerons, when the British 1st Division attacked the heavily fortified village of Droninghem during the Battle of the Sambre on 7 November. Using improvised rafts they crossed the Sambre Canal under heavy German fire and, although they captured the stronghold and forced the Germans to surrender, the battalion lost around 500 casualties. For John Jackson, who had joined up in 1914 and had survived the fighting, that evening's muster was one of his saddest moments: 'When the roll was called our casualties were found to be enormous, and many old friends were no more. It was indeed hard that many of these battle-scarred warriors, having come through the entire war, should in this our last great battle, have their names included in the honoured lists of those "Killed in action".'[31]

By the time of the Battle of Sambre the war was as good as over. Turkey capitulated on 30 October, bringing to an end the fighting in Mesopotamia and Palestine, Austria–Hungary followed suit on 3 November. When the news arrived in the signals room of the 9th (Scottish) Division a visiting officer was told that 'Austria has thrown in her mitt [hand]'. As the divisional historian recorded, 'it was thus that a phlegmatic Scottish soldier announced the fall of the ancient Empire of the Hapsburgs, the oldest ruling family in Europe and the heirs of the Holy Roman Empire'.[32] On the morning of 9 November the German negotiating team arrived at the designated meeting place in the Forest of Compiègne and the terms of the armistice were decided under Foch's direction in a French railway carriage. After working on them through the night the German delegation finally agreed to the terms in the early hours of the morning of 11 November. The armistice would come into effect at eleven o'clock, when all hostilities would cease.

Although long anticipated, the announcement still caused surprise and some units were preparing to go into action when the order

arrived. The 1/5th Highland Light Infantry was making ready to attack
along the Mons–Jubise road when they received the welcome news,
but as an officer recorded it was greeted with a strange mixture of
emotions. The previous day the 52nd (Lowland) Division, in which
the battalion was serving, had lost 6 soldiers killed and 17 wounded:

> Strange to relate there was no tremendous excitement. Perhaps the
> philosopher spoke truly when he said that one always has a feeling
> of regret on doing a thing for the last time. Perhaps we had been fed
> on rumours so often that we took this for one. Perhaps we were too
> weary in mind or body to grasp the significance of this stupendous
> news. Or was it that our thoughts turned at this time to those good
> men who had given their lives for this great end? Whatever the
> reason, the fact remains that there was no enthusiasm in keeping
> with the event.[33]

Another officer in the 15th (Scottish) Division recorded similar
sentiments, overheard as two men in the King's Own Scottish
Borderers were talking in subdued tones: ' "I'd like fine to be in
Blighty the nicht. It'll be a grand nicht this at hame; something daen'
I'll bet." "Ay," said another, "an' there'll be a guid few tears, too." '
Lieutenant-Colonel the Hon. William Fraser, now back with the
1st Gordons as commanding officer, felt much the same way, experiencing great sadness leavened by a hint of optimism: 'And so ended
the last day of the Great War. One has been feeling one's way through
the dark for 4 years, and now one has come straight out in the sunlight
– and behold! one is blind, one cannot see the sun. But the blindness
will pass in time.' Showing commendable understatement Haig's diary
entry for 11 November opened with an observation on the state of the
weather: 'Fine day but cold and dull.'[34]

Any examination of the Allied prosecution of the First World War
has to consider the role played by Haig in the direction of the fighting
on the Western Front. With the possible exception of Air Marshal Sir
Arthur Harris, the architect of 'area bombing' during the Second
World War, perhaps no other commander in history has been
subjected to such obloquy and demonisation as a 'butcher and
bungler'. Although Haig ended the war on a high note, in command
of an army just under two million strong, it was his fate to be

condemned as an inept battlefield commander for inflicting heavy casualties on the British Army. At the same time he was vilified as a human being for his apparent lack of feeling and sympathy for those who suffered as a result of his decisions.

In fact this process of denunciation had already begun during the conflict. As we have seen, Haig enjoyed an uneasy relationship with Lloyd George, who had written him off as an old-fashioned cavalry-man with limited experience and few brains. Ideally Lloyd George would have liked to sack him in 1917, and in private discussions and policy papers he was critical of Haig's strategy and general direction of the war. In particular he was horrified by what seemed to be the unacceptable number of casualties during the battles of the Somme, Arras and Passchendaele. However, although he tried hard to get rid of Haig and on several occasions made the effort to replace him, it proved impossible to find a satisfactory alternative. Even when Lloyd George did give him credit for any success, not least during the final hundred days of the fighting when victory looked inevitable, he still managed to cause offence by damning with faint praise or failing to understand the full significance of what was happening. And following the conclusion of hostilities further affront was caused on both sides when Lloyd George proposed a victory parade on 30 November which would have seen Haig relegated to the fifth carriage, an insult which the field marshal refused to accept as he had no intention of taking part in 'a triumphal procession with a lot of foreigners through the streets on a Sunday!'[35]

Worse followed in 1936 when Lloyd George published his *War Memoirs*, which contained an unremitting attack on Haig as a man and soldier. Few books have done more damage to a leading figure's reputation and by the time it was published Haig was no longer alive to defend himself from his leading traducer: he died on 29 January 1928 as the result of a heart attack, probably brought on by overwork. By the time of his death the first books chronicling their authors' disillusionment with the war had begun to appear and the name Haig began to be associated with bad generals who had sent a generation of young men to horrific deaths without even knowing or caring about the effects of their decisions. The name of Haig almost became a convenient shorthand description for the entire general staff: red-tabbed aristocratic blimps who never visited the front lines and who in the words of one recent historian 'must be indicted not for incomprehension but for wilful blunders and wicked butchery'.[36] From being the highly respected commander-in-chief who had won the war Haig was slowly transmogrified into an incompetent and stupid figurehead who had on his conscience the lives of thousands of men. It mattered not that he had spent his short years of retirement fighting for the rights of ex-servicemen or that in his prime he was regarded as a proficient soldier and resourceful commander; his legacy was thought to be the serried ranks of dead soldiers' headstones in France and Flanders.

Naturally he had his supporters. Memoirs by his staff officers, such as Major-General Sir John Davidson (*Haig – Master of the Field*, 1953), praised his 'unswerving loyalty and imperturbability throughout adversity and good fortune alike' and in general the *Official History* was kind to him, despite complaints that the material used was selective. By the 1960s, though, as more official documents from the war were released into the public domain, there was a second wave of attacks against Haig and his military reputation. Chief amongst these were Leon Wolff's *In Flanders Fields* (1958), a searing indictment of the handling of the Third Battle of Ypres, and Alan Clark's *The Donkeys* (1961), which thoroughly condemned Haig for his direction of the higher war strategy. Clark claimed that the title came from a conversation between Ludendorff and General Max Hoffman in which the latter stated that the British soldiers were 'lions led by donkeys'. No attribution was given but the phrase had certainly been used before: by *The Times* in 1870 to describe the French soldiers in the Franco-Prussian War and by *Punch* in 1855 to describe the British soldiers fighting in the Crimea. However, its pithiness meant that it soon had a wide currency and added to the belief that not only had Haig been responsible for the unnecessary deaths of an entire generation but also that the war itself was an exercise in futility. A much-needed balance was struck by John Terraine's *Douglas Haig: The Educated Soldier* (1963), which put forward a robust defence of the man and his methods by arguing that Haig's tactics wore down the Germans and were the main reason why they were finally defeated. As Haig himself expressed it in his Final Despatch, which was published on 21 March 1919, 'It is in the great battles of 1916 and 1917 that we have to seek for the secret of our victory in 1918 . . .

The moral effects of those battles were enormous, both in the German Army and in Germany. By their means our soldiers established over the German soldier a moral superiority which they held in an ever-increasing degree until the end of the war, even in the difficult days of March and April, 1918.'[37]

Although Terraine, who died in December 2003, was himself criticised for taking an overtly polemical stance in his revisionist work, at least he 'restored Haig to the position of serious commander rather than a pantomime villain'.[38] That is an important consideration in coming to terms with Haig's role, because in his critics' impatience to land decisive blows on their target they either exaggerated or chose their facts selectively, with the result that Haig was all too often treated as a cardboard cut-out and not as an all too fallible human being. According to the stereotype Haig was a dull-witted cavalry officer devoid of any interest in military innovations who stubbornly continued fighting the war with the debased tactics of attrition because he lacked the ability to find any other way of winning battles. Owing his position to influence he back-stabbed his way to power and held onto it with a ruthlessness that matched his indifference to high casualty figures and then recast the record in his diaries to put himself in a good light. Even the fact that he was a serious-minded Christian has been held against him, as if there was something immoral or unusual in the fact that he prayed regularly and was a devout member of the Church of Scotland. Add on his legendary silences, his frequent inability to express himself clearly, his occasionally awkward public persona and the caricature is complete. In the words of an old army joke, here was a cavalryman who was so stupid that even his brother officers noticed.

So much for the mythology: the reality was rather different. While it is true that Haig had been commissioned into a cavalry regiment and to the end of the war retained a belief that his cavalry arm could play a decisive role in smashing the German front line and sweeping into the open green fields that lay beyond it, he was not an out of touch relic from the past: he was, in Terraine's words, an 'educated soldier'. A product of the Staff College, he served as director of military training and then as director of staff duties during the pre-war period of army reforms and was at the centre of the thinking which created the British Expeditionary Force. He also had operational experience, albeit in minor wars, from serving under Kitchener in the Sudan in the late

1890s and in the Boer War which followed. For the three years prior
to the war he had command of the Aldershot garrison in the rank of
lieutenant-general and was responsible for training the troops which
went to war in 1914 as I Corps. If he was ambitious and used his and
his wife's connections to keep his name prominent in social circles he
was no worse than many other senior officers in doing everything
possible to shin up the ladder of promotion. On operational matters, it
cannot be held against him that he lacked experience of commanding
large numbers of soldiers when he became commander-in-chief in
succession to French: so, too, did every other British general of the war.

That is the crux of any consideration of Haig as a commander. The
situation he inherited was unique in warfare. The deadlock on the
Western Front left no room for manoeuvre yet his instructions from
Kitchener on assuming command on 28 December 1915 made it
abundantly clear that his primary objectives were 'the defeat of the
enemy' and the expulsion of the 'German Armies from French and
Belgian territory', all this to be done in conjunction with the coalition
forces.[39] To execute this order Haig had to engage the numerically
stronger German forces with an army which at the time was not only
the nation in uniform but was having to pick up most of its experience
as it went along, in battles against an enemy which initially held the
strategic advantage. That meant mounting a succession of attacks in
the form of the great battles of attrition of 1916 and 1917 with artillery
that lacked sufficient amounts of the right kind of ammunition and
using large numbers of men in the attempt to break the enemy's lines.
The only other way of dealing with the strategic stalemate would have
been sporadic 'bite and hold' attacks but these, too, would not have
been effective and would still have resulted in high casualty rates. In
short, Haig and his fellow commanders had to wage war as they found
it and not as they might have wished to fight it.

Of course the policy frequently produced unacceptably high
numbers of casualties, many of whom died as a result of mistakes
or sheer bad luck – the first day of the Battle of the Somme is an
example – and Haig was not immune to falling prey to those failings.
As Marshal Turenne put it a century earlier, 'Speak to me of a general
who has not made mistakes, and you speak of one who has seldom
made war.' If anything, Haig was recklessly over-optimistic in believing that the battles of 1916 and 1917 would achieve the hoped-for

breakthrough. His armies lacked the reserves and the firepower to inflict a heavy defeat on the Germans and all too often attacks were continued far longer than necessary in the attempt to achieve a result. It is also true that some offensives, such as the latter stages of the Somme, were continued in the interests of shoring up the coalition in which Britain was the junior partner and Haig was certainly alive to that necessity.

As to the man himself, recent commentators are right when they say that there is no need for further examinations of Haig's personality and any of his perceived personal failings. What counts is his conduct as a soldier and a senior commander. As with any other public figure, he was not perfect. His diaries and private correspondence betray his dislike and distrust of his French colleagues although when it mattered, as in the spring of 1918, he was prepared to trim his views for the good of the coalition. Lloyd George was a particular bugbear but not all the problems in the relationship can be attributed to the prime minister. Under pressure Haig was often difficult and touchy, especially when he felt that his professionalism was being impugned. It is also clear that there were occasions when he could be less than generous towards his colleagues and he was not above scheming to get his own way. But against that he took a great deal of interest in his troops and visited them as often as was practicable. Inevitably the huge size of the army meant that he was seen as a remote figurehead – by 1918 he had almost two million men under his command – but that did not stop him visiting the front lines. It simply is not true that he hid in the safety of his headquarters at Montreuil or that he had no inkling of what life was like in the forward trenches. If that were the case he would never have been able to express the following sentiments about the British soldier after visiting the front lines in March 1917:

No one can visit the Somme battlefield without being impressed with the magnitude of the effort of the British Army. For five long months this battle continued . . . To many it meant certain death, and all must have known that before they started. Surely it was the knowledge of the great stake at issue, the existence of England [*sic.* – like many Anglo-Scots Haig used England for Britain] as a free nation, that served them for such heroic deeds. I have not the time to put down all the thoughts which rush into my mind when I think of all those fine fellows, who either have given their lives for their country, or have been maimed in its service. Later on I hope we may have a Prime Minister and a Government who will do them justice.[40]

These are not the words of a callous butcher but the private thoughts of a man who knew exactly what he was doing when he committed his troops to battle. He might not have exposed his innermost feelings to public show – that is one reason for his mask of command – but he had the mental toughness to take decisions which he knew would result in death, maiming and physical and mental horrors. And then there was his post-war work, which he undertook with such energy and commitment that it helped to shorten his own life. That Haig was in tune with the feelings of ordinary soldiers was shown by his central role in the creation of the British Legion and the Earl Haig Fund, both of which were founded to serve the best interests and welfare of ex-servicemen. He proved to be no figurehead, but emerged as a tireless promoter of the Legion's interests. Critics dismissed his work as guilt for the thousands of soldiers who had died under his command, but that was to miss the point. Like any other soldier who has been involved in the dirty business of warfare, Haig knew that battles could only be won by careful planning and the determination and resolve of the men who fought them.

11 A Bitter Hairst: The Reckoning

Shortly after the signatures were placed on the armistice documents in the early hours of 11 November in distant Compiègne the news was relayed back to London that the war would finally end at 11.00 that morning. Rumours of impending peace had been in common currency for some days and the news spread quickly; in most parts of the country the news was greeted with wild scenes of enthusiasm as people took to the streets to celebrate a day which many had thought might never arrive. After 1,564 days the worst war in history had come to an end. Church bells, silent since August 1914, were rung and as winter darkness fell streetlights continued burning and shop windows blazed with light in defiance of the long months of blackout. In Edinburgh searchlights played on the Scott Monument, and Princes Street was thronged with excited crowds, although it was noted that 'with the public houses closed early in the evening cases of intoxication were very rare. The early retiring habits acquired during the war period began to show their sedative influence by ten o'clock, after which the city quietened down.'

On the other hand Glasgow was more boisterous: Union flags were flown from office windows as crowds pushed through the streets dancing and cheering behind pipe bands. In Aberdeen ships' sirens sounded and in Dundee bunting decorated the ships lying in the harbour but, as the *Glasgow Herald* reported, the celebrations throughout Scotland were tempered by 'a marked restraint – an inclination, while expressing heartfelt gratitude, to remember the days of suffering and loss through which the way to victory had led'. Inevitably perhaps, the high spirits were tempered by the memory of lost loved ones and by the sobering thought that the jubilation masked much sadness in many homes.

The magazine *Punch*, which was no stranger to making fun of Scottish dourness, caught the moment in a cartoon entitled 'Armistice Day in the

North' in which two elderly bewhiskered men (a well-known stereo-type) pass the time of day: 'The news is nae sae baad the day,' says one. 'Aye,' replies the other, 'it's improvin'.' As it turned out, *Punch* probably captured the overall tone of the national mood. In Lerwick the announcement of the armistice had been passed to the editor of the *Shetland Times* by the senior naval commander and a notice was duly placed in the office window telling the people of the Shetland Islands that the war was finally over. As the editor noted, it was not a moment for rejoicing but for the expression of quiet satisfaction and gratitude: 'The news was received with deep, unspeakable pleasure by all, but there were no indications of hilarity. The strain had been too great, the tensions too strong to permit of levity. There was no pretence at what is commonly called popular rejoicings. It was with subdued feelings, a sensation too deep for words, that people met each other, and with genuine hand clasps congratulated each other that the maiming and the killing were at an end.'[1]

The killing had come to an end on the war's main battle-fronts but in many other parts of the globe it went on. In northern Russia on the banks of the River Dvina the 2/10th Royal Scots spent Armistice Day repelling an attack by Bolshevik forces which left nineteen Scottish soldiers dead and four injured. One soldier, Private John Stewart, endured the horrible experience of being wounded in the chest and then witnessing the death by sniper fire of one of his comrades who was trying to help him by applying a field dressing. As darkness fell Stewart feared that he might freeze to death but he managed to crawl to the distant light of a US army casualty-clearing station where he received treatment plus 'a Dixie of hot bully stew and a good tot of rum'.[2] The battalion was in the area together with 2nd Highland Light Infantry and 2[nd]Cameron Highlanders as part of an ill-starred Allied attempt to reinforce local Social Revolutionary forces opposed to the Bolshevik regime, but despite some local successes the campaign was an expensive sideshow which achieved nothing apart from alienating the new Soviet regime. In the summer of 1919 2/10th Royal Scots were withdrawn and arrived back at Leith on 18 June, but it was not the end of Britain's involvement in Russia. At the beginning of 1920 the 2nd Royal Scots Fusiliers were deployed to Novorossiysk on the Black Sea in support of a French military mission to the Crimea to shore up Admiral Kolchak's anti-Bolshevik White Army forces, but no sooner had they arrived than they had to assist in a rapid evacuation.

Seven Scottish battalions found themselves on garrison duty in post-war Ireland during the war of independence which accompanied the transfer of power and were not finally withdrawn until 1922. These were 1st Royal Scots Fusiliers, 1st Highland Light Infantry, 1st Seaforth Highlanders, 2nd Cameron Highlanders, 1st Gordon Highlanders, 2nd Gordon Highlanders, 2nd Argyll and Sutherland Highlanders and 2nd Royal Scots. Other soldiers were not demobbed until well into 1919: the 9th (Scottish) Division was given the honour of being the only New Army division to march into Germany at the conclusion of hostilities, their pipes and drums playing the march of The King's Own Scottish Borderers, 'Blue Bonnets Over the Border'.

The dying also continued at home. In the autumn of 1918 the world had been hit by a disastrous influenza pandemic against which there was no medical defence and doctors were powerless to deal with it. By October it was claiming an average of 7,000 victims a week in Britain alone and by the time it had finally run its course in 1919 it had claimed some 30 million victims worldwide. Known at the time as 'Spanish Flu' or '*La Grippe*' it was most deadly in the 20 to 40 age group and its virulence meant that it spread quickly through areas where troops were concentrated: in camps, trenches, hospitals and transport systems. As helpless doctors noted at the time, the year ended with 'the termination of the most cruel war in the annals of the human race' and the beginning of a new struggle to keep men alive: 'Medical science for four and one-half years devoted itself to putting men on the firing line and keeping them there. Now it must turn with its whole might to combating the greatest enemy of all – infectious disease.'[3] The total death toll in Britain was 228,000, the highest mortality rate since the great cholera outbreak of 1849, and the first city to be affected was Glasgow, where cases started to be reported in May 1918. Desperate measures were taken to control the epidemic. Schools were closed, streets were sprayed with disinfectant, people started wearing masks and several factories rescinded their no-smoking policy in the belief that tobacco fumes would kill the germs. Other precautions included the encouragement of energetic walks, washing the inside of the nose with soap and water and eating plenty of porridge.[4] Unknown numbers of young men returned safely home from the war only to succumb to influenza, and during the winter of 1918–19 the death columns of the *Scotsman* and the *Glasgow Herald* were suddenly full of the names of loved ones who had survived the war only to fall victim to the dreaded disease.

One other poignant group of servicemen encountered unexpected death within sight of their own homes when the Admiralty Yacht *Iolaire* foundered on rocks outside Stornoway harbour in the early hours of the morning of 1 January 1919. On board were 260 naval ratings and 24 crew who were returning home on leave, and of that number 205 were drowned when the stricken ship broke her back within 20 yards of the shore. It was one of the most tragic incidents of the war and hardly a family on the island of Lewis was unaffected by it. The men had made their way back to Scotland by special trains which took them north through Glasgow, Stirling, Perth and Inverness where 530 Skye and Western Isles liberty-men were taken onwards to the railhead at Kyle of Lochalsh. They travelled in two special trains provided by the Highland Railway, the first of which reached Kyle at six in the evening and the second, an hour and a quarter later. Two ships waited to take the Western Isles men on the final stage of their journey: the MacBrayne mail steamer ss *Sheila* and HM Yacht *Iolaire*, which had been built in Leith in 1881 as the *Iolanthe* and had served as a reserve patrol vessel during the war under the name *Iolaire*, Gaelic for 'eagle'. The men bound for Skye would be taken to Broadford, Raasay and Portree on board the Admiralty Drifter *Jeannie Campbell*.

When the trains arrived there was a certain amount of confusion about numbers and travel arrangements amongst the waiting naval staff, and as a result there had to be some last-minute improvisation. Men from the first train were paraded in three sections: those bound for Stornoway lined up on the right and were then ordered to board the *Iolaire*, which had arrived earlier in the day with only half a crew. At the same time, the Harris men lined up on the left and were informed that they would have to wait in the Red Cross hut until transport arrived for them. With them were the men of the Skye contingent, who also had to wait, in their case until mail was loaded on the *Jeannie Campbell*. A similar procedure was followed when the second train arrived, with the exception that 60 ratings were ordered to travel on board the *Sheila*, which would leave for Stornoway after the *Iolaire* departed. This proved too much for some of the Harris men who suddenly realised that they would be left behind, and unwilling to wait at Kyle and miss the New Year celebrations many of them slipped aboard the waiting *Iolaire*. When she left Kyle shortly before eight in the evening the glass was rising and the captain, Commander Richard Mason, expected an easy crossing.

It was not to be. The weather worsened as the ship crossed the Minch and it turned into a dirty squall-filled night with a driving southerly wind. By half past midnight the lights of Stornoway were in sight but as *Iolaire* made her approach towards the narrow entrance of the harbour – only 700 yards wide – the officer-in-charge, First Lieutenant Leonard E. Cotter, failed to alter course while passing Arnish lighthouse and without a lookout on duty the yacht headed inexorably towards a dangerous reef of rocks off Holm Island, known variously as Biaston Holm or the Beasts or Breasts of Holm. Several vessels saw the incident – the Admiralty Drifter *Budding Rose* which had been sent to escort the *Iolaire* into harbour, and the motor fishing boat *Avoca* which was following in her wake – but due to the high winds and heavy sea neither was able to render any assistance. Trapped on the rocks only 20 yards from shore *Iolaire* foundered and her back quickly broke. Thanks to the courage of John F. Macleod of Port of Ness who jumped ashore with a heaving line several men managed to clamber ashore through the heavy waters, but 205, including the three ship's officers, were drowned. By the time rescue equipment reached the scene and the islanders came to offer assistance most of the men were already dead. At 6.10 a.m. the first news reached the Admiralty by telegram informing the authorities that *Iolaire* was 'grounded on eastern shore of entrance to Stornoway' and that hopes of rescue had faded.

Feelings ran high throughout the Western Isles. These were men who had survived the war only to be drowned in home waters which many of them would have known well as fishermen, and there were inevitable recriminations which centred on the suitability of the vessel, the experience of the crew and the fact that the *Iolaire* only had 80 life jackets and boats for 100 men. Because the *Iolaire* had hit the pier on arrival at Kyle of Lochalsh earlier in the day there were also angry accusations that the captain and his crew were drunk or 'not in a fit state to perform their duties' – not an impossibility given the time of the year – but the allegations were later found to have no basis in fact. A Court of Inquiry was held a week later which produced a huge amount of evidence from the survivors but was unable to provide any satisfactory explanation as to why the captain was not on the bridge or why the wrong course was taken as the ship entered the last and most difficult stage of its journey. The main findings of the subsequent Fatal Accident Inquiry were that the officer in charge did not exercise sufficient caution in approaching Stornoway harbour, that no lookout was on duty and that there was insufficient life-saving equipment on board the doomed ship.[5]

The accident devastated the island of Lewis, which lost 174 men, all drowned within reach of their homes and at a time of year when families usually gather together to greet the new year. The townships of Luerbost and North Tolsta each lost 11 men. All their names are listed on the Lewis War Memorial, together with those of 1,151 men from the island's four parishes who were killed as a result of serving in the armed forces during the First World War, the first casualty listed being Saddler Philip Macleod of Steinish of the Royal Field Artillery, who was killed in the fighting at Mons in August 1914. Out of a population of 29,603 in the 1911 census, 6,712 Lewismen saw service between 1914 and 1919; when the figures were finally tallied the percentage of Lewismen killed during the war stood at 17 per cent of those who served, one of the highest proportions in the United Kingdom.

Built in the shape of a Scots baronial tower the Lewis memorial stands 300 feet above Stornoway on Cnoc nan Uan and it was consecrated on 24 September 1924 following a public appeal led by the island's landowner, Lord Leverhulme, who was one of the driving forces behind the memorial's construction. It was one of many monuments raised throughout Scotland during the 1920s as the country came to terms with the losses of the war and communities set about remembering and commemorating their young men who had died in uniform. The bodies lost on foreign battlefields never came back. In an attempt to bring honourable cohesion and a sense of orderliness to the task of burying its war dead Britain set up the Imperial War Graves Commission which cared for the military cemeteries which sprang up in the various war zones. Each corpse was given a separate, identical grave, the standard headstone recording name, age, rank, regiment and date of death, or, in the case of those who could not be identified, the simple words composed by the poet Rudyard Kipling, 'A Soldier of the Great War Known Unto God'.

Most of the cemeteries, some 600, are situated in France and Flanders along a line stretching from the Channel coast to the Somme, but Scottish graves are to be found around the world on all the main battle-fronts where Scottish regiments served:

France and Flanders: Royal Scots Greys, Scots Guards, Royal Scots, Royal Scots Fusiliers, King's Own Scottish Borderers, Cameronians, Black Watch, Highland Light Infantry, Seaforth Highlanders, Cameron Highlanders, Gordon Highlanders, Argyll and Sutherland Highlanders, Queen's Own Royal Glasgow Yeomanry, Lothians and Border Horse, London Scottish, Liverpool Scottish, Tyneside Scottish.

Gallipoli: Royal Scots, Royal Scots Fusiliers, King's Own Scottish Borderers, Cameronians, Black Watch, Highland Light Infantry, Argyll and Sutherland Highlanders, Ayrshire Yeomanry (Earl of Carrick's Own), Fife and Forfar Yeomanry, Lovat Scouts, Lanarkshire Yeomanry, Scottish Horse, Queen's Own Royal Glasgow Yeomanry.

Salonika: Royal Scots, Royal Scots Fusiliers, Cameronians, Black Watch, Cameron Highlanders, Argyll and Sutherland Highlanders, Lothians and Border Horse, Scottish Horse (as 13th Black Watch), London Scottish.

Egypt and Palestine: Royal Scots, Royal Scots Fusiliers, King's Own Scottish Borderers, Cameronians, Black Watch, Highland Light Infantry, Seaforth Highlanders, Argyll and Sutherland Highlanders, Lovat Scouts, Ayrshire Yeomanry (as 12th Royal Scots Fusiliers), Fife and Forfar Yeomanry (as 14th Black Watch), Lanarkshire Yeomanry (as 12th Royal Scots Fusiliers), Queen's Own Royal Glasgow Yeomanry, London Scottish.

Mesopotamia: Highland Light Infantry, Black Watch, Seaforth Highlanders.

Italian front: King's Own Scottish Borderers, Gordon Highlanders.

The precise numbers of Scottish war dead are difficult to compute exactly but it is possible to reach some conclusions about the level of the losses. At the end of the war the official figure was put at 74,000 but this was decided by the unsound method of dividing the British total by ten to reflect the fact that Scots made up 10 per cent of the United Kingdom's population. Later, when plans were being made to build a national war memorial for Scotland in the 1920s this was revised to 100,000, or 13 per cent of the British total.[6] Later still, the same memorial recorded the names of 148,218 Scots from around the world 'killed in the service of the Crown' and the figure is still being increased as new information becomes available.[7] It has also been suggested that the Scottish death rate was only exceeded by that of Serbia and Turkey: this is based on a statistic that the total Scottish casualties as a percentage of those mobilised was 26.4 per cent (the percentage in Serbia and Turkey being respectively 37.1 per cent and 26.8 per cent).[8] With a total of 690,235 Scots having been mobilised, however, this would make the Scottish total 182,222, a figure that is clearly too high.

As with all statistics from the conflict the figures obviously have to be handled with caution. The original tally of 74,000 is far too low but the higher figure which is double that amount is also suspect as it contains the names of Scots-born soldiers who served in the forces of the dominions and there may also be some duplication. Part of the problem lies in the nature of the conflict. In the first casualty lists produced during the war, men who were listed as wounded later died as a result of their injuries and the opposite was also true: missing men often turned up again unharmed and, as the wounded poet Robert Graves discovered, it was also possible to be mistakenly listed amongst the dead. There are other unknowables: men who died of wounds after the war ended or who had premature deaths as a result of their experiences are not counted and the names on the regimental rolls of honour also include soldiers who were not Scots-born but died wearing Scottish uniforms.

Although it is impossible to get absolute agreement on the exact number of Scottish casualties suffered during the war, the available regimental and municipal figures suggest that the total is probably higher than the generally accepted 100,000. One regiment alone, the Royal Scots, suffered 11,213 casualties, most of whom came from Edinburgh and the east of Scotland; The Black Watch lost 10,000 as did The Highland Light Infantry; and The Gordons lost 9,000. Of the

13,568 men who volunteered from Scotland's four universities, 2,026 were killed on active service. In Glasgow 18,000 young men, or 1 in 57 of the city's population, did not come back from the war, while Dundee's death toll was 4,213 out of a population of 180,000.[9] Rolls of honour produced by organisations such as educational establishments and the professions help to put the cold statistics into perspective by recording individual losses. In his account of the war service of the clergy of the Church of Scotland Duncan Cameron revealed that 'not a few ministers, notwithstanding their exemption from conscription, enlisted in the Armed Forces of the Crown' and that 24 died on active service. Amongst their number was a son of the manse, James Cook Macpherson, of Elgin, Hunter Gold Medallist and Gladstone Prizeman at Aberdeen University, killed at Loos on 29 September 1915. He served as a 2nd lieutenant in the Gordons and was one of the 317 Aberdeen graduates or undergraduates who lost their lives during the war.[10]

Unwittingly, the Rev. Robert J. Thompson, the minister of Coldstream who served as the bombing officer with the 1st Black Watch, gave voice to the concept of the poppy as a symbol of sacrifice when he wrote to Lady Clementine Waring on 22 October 1915 in the aftermath of the Battle of Loos. His letter was written a few weeks before John McCrae's poem 'In Flanders Fields' was published in *Punch* with its famous line 'In Flanders fields the poppies blow', which helped to cement the post-war symbolism of the red poppy as a means of commemorating the dead. ('In Flanders Fields' was written on 3 May 1915 and published anonymously on 8 December 1915. Lieutenant-Colonel John McCrae, the son of a Scottish emigrant, served as medical officer with the Royal Canadian Army Medical Corps at a field dressing station at Essex Farm near Boezinge. He died of pneumonia in January 1918.) Like McCrae, Thompson was deeply affected by the sight of the red poppies which flourished in the lime-rich soil of Flanders:

The sun shone beautifully, but on what a sight! The ugliest of German barbed-wire rusted with the blood of heroes; two dead bodies entangled therein, their faces masked in hideous smoke helmets. There were two redeeming features in the landscape – two that reminded us of something other than the brutality of war. Two red poppies grew out of the side of the parapet, while a church spire was silhouetted against a golden sky away in the South. I felt like plucking the poppies and planting them beside the corpses among the wire. What could have been more symbolical and fitting! The 'flower of dreams' as Francis Thompson calls the poppy.[11]

Sport, too, paid a price. The roll of honour of the Heart of Midlothian Football Club contains 31 names, 11 of whom were killed in action. Of them five served with 16th Royal Scots, 'McCrae's Battalion', and their historian records the names of 74 other football clubs who had members serving in that particular battalion.[12] By the middle of 1915 the secretary of the Scottish Football League had compiled the names of 168 professional footballers who were already serving in the armed forces. Also in Edinburgh, the entire Watsonian first XV took the plunge by joining up together in the 1/9th Royal Scots. Amongst them were three international players, who were all killed in action: J. Pearson who won 12 caps between 1909 and 1913, E. Milroy who won the same number during the same period and J. Y. M. Henderson who won his solitary cap against England in 1911.

During the First World War a total of 30 Scottish international rugby players were killed in action, the highest casualty rate amongst the home unions, and it was an indication of rugby's small base and social status in Scotland that the majority came from four clubs, three of which play in England: London Scottish (7), Cambridge University (5), Oxford University (4) and Watsonians (3). The giant amongst them was undoubtedly David Revell Bedell-Sivright, who won 22 caps between 1900 and 1908 and who captained both Scotland and the British Lions. A product of Fettes College, Bedell-Sivright won blues at Edinburgh and Cambridge and also found time to win the Scottish Amateur Heavyweight Boxing Championship in 1909. Known as 'Darkie' as a result of his complexion, he was considered to be one of the finest forwards of his day and off the field Bedell-Sivright was no shrinking violet. After one international match he rugby-tackled a carthorse in Edinburgh's Princes Street, and so obstreperous was his behaviour after another post-match celebration that the police dared not intervene. He died of septicaemia in 1915 while serving as a medical officer with the Royal Naval Division in Gallipoli.[13]

The rugby players are commemorated by a simple stone arch at Murrayfield Stadium in Edinburgh, not far away from the memorial to the Heart of Midlothian footballers at Haymarket, a clock tower in the form of an obelisk. All over Scotland similar memorials were erected, some of them incorporating the figure of a kilted Scottish soldier or the symbolic figure of peace or a plain Celtic cross. The bronze statue of a border reiver commemorates the war dead of Galashiels; an attacking soldier, rifle in hand, alongside a machine-gunner, does the same for the Cameronians in Glasgow's Kelvingrove park; a child with flowers in hand sits on the walled memorial at Darvel in Ayrshire; Aberdeen's memorial takes the form of an austere granite-clad court next to the city's art gallery while Dundee's memorial is a simple but imposing granite obelisk on the Law overlooking the city and the Tay estuary. In the village of Edzell the memorial lists 24 men of the parish with the solemn injunction 'We owe more tears to these dead men than time shall see us pay', while a winged angel watches over the names of the dead in nearby Montrose. Although some of the memorials have deteriorated with the passing of the years, especially those constructed as towers, they remain as constant reminders of the loss of thousands of young Scots during the war.

There were also moves to commemorate the names of the dead nationally and as early as 1917 a decision had been taken to create a memorial stone in London and to establish a museum which would reflect the role played by the armed forces. The results were the Cenotaph, which was designed by the architect Sir Edward Lutyens and which stands in Whitehall in the heart of London, and the Imperial War Museum, which was established in the London borough of Lambeth. Both projects were supported within Scotland but at the same time there was a widespread view that the country should have its own distinctive memorial and museum to commemorate the part played by Scots in the conflict. From the outset it was agreed that Edinburgh Castle would be the best site for the project even though it would require a great deal of sensitivity, being a highly regarded historic building, a major tourist attraction and a working military barracks. The guiding light behind the idea was the Duke of Atholl who argued that 'if the Scottish nation wanted a memorial they would put it up with their own hands in their own country and with their own money'. To push the scheme forward, at the end of 1917 General Ewart, the General Office Commanding (GOC) Scotland, wrote to all regimental colonels asking for their support and urging the use of Edinburgh Castle to house the proposed memorial and museum as 'no nation in the wide world has in its capital a finer and more natural monument of war'.[14]

A year later a Scottish National War Memorial Committee of 28 leading Scots was appointed by the secretary of state for Scotland with the brief 'to consider what steps should be taken towards the utilisation of Edinburgh Castle for the purposes of a Scottish National War Memorial'. Its members were: the Duke of Atholl; Lord Carmichael, Admiral Commanding-in-Chief at Rosyth; the General Officer Commanding-in-chief Scottish command; the Lord Provosts of Edinburgh, Glasgow, Aberdeen, Dundee and Perth; the Rt. Hon. William Adamson MP (Labour, West Fife); Lord Balfour of Burleigh; the Rt. Hon. James Brown MP (Labour, South Ayrshire); Sir John Burnet, consultant architect; Lieutenant-Colonel D. W. Cameron of Lochiel; David Erskine of Linlathen, Chairman of the Board of Trustees of the National Galleries of Scotland; Lieutenant-General Sir Spencer Ewart; Sir John Findlay, proprietor of the *Scotsman*; Lord Glenconner; Lord Justice-Clerk Kingsburgh; Sir Herbert Maxwell, Chairman Royal Commission on Scottish Historical Monuments; Sir Hector Munro of Foulis; Lord Newlands; Sir William Robertson, Vice-Chairman the Carnegie Trust; the Very Rev. Sir George Adam Smith; the Rt. Hon. Eugene Watson; the Very Rev. A. A. Wallace Williamson; J. Lawton Wingate, President of the Royal Scottish Academy; Sir George Younger MP (Conservative, Ayr Burghs) and Captain George S. C. Swinton, the Lord Lyon King of Arms, who was appointed secretary. Their chosen architect was Sir Robert Lorimer, who had designed the Thistle Chapel in the High Church of St Giles and who was a leading exponent of the Arts and Crafts school. He was also responsible for the design of several military cemeteries and a number of civic and institutional war memorials.

Lorimer's solution was to place the memorial on the north side of Crown Square, which was occupied by a barrack block known as Billings' Building. It would incorporate a shrine and cloisters with stained-glass windows, the intention, according to Lorimer, being to create a building which would be of 'a dedicatory character without actually being church or chapel'. The projected total cost was £250,000 (equivalent in purchasing power to £7.5 million in 2005), an immense sum in 1919, when the committee's deliberations were finally published together with Lorimer's design.[15] But it was not just the cost which created concern. From the outset the project was mired in controversy: there were protests that the edifice would deface the skyline of a familiar and much-loved Edinburgh building, there was concern that the shrine and cloisters would resemble a church or chapel and there were even complaints that the whole project smacked too much of a celebration of militarism. The publication of the committee's findings sparked a mass outbreak of criticism and for months the correspondence page of the *Scotsman* was filled with angry letters condemning the project. One of the principal and most influential opponents was the Earl of Rosebery, a former Liberal prime minister, who compared Lorimer's design to a 'huge jelly mould' and argued that the castle was already 'a noble monument of all Scottish history and to bastardise this with a view to connecting it with the recent war would surely be a mistake from every point of view'.[16] Worse followed when the Ancient Monuments Board opposed the scheme on the grounds that Lorimer's drawings underestimated the effect on the skyline, and the construction of a full-size mock-up in November 1922 seemed to prove their point.

Amidst the criticism and a spate of resignations from Atholl's committee Lorimer was forced to rethink the design and as a result the final plan retained the shell of Billings' Building, which would be transformed into a Gallery of Honour containing memorials to the twelve Scottish regiments. On the north side he proposed a deep apse for the shrine, where a steel casket would be placed on a stone of remembrance to house the rolls of honour, and, mindful of earlier complaints about scale, its roof would be no higher than the existing Billings' Buildings. At the same time, Atholl abandoned a grandiose plan for the proposed museum and agreed that it should be housed in the existing officers' quarters in Crown Square and in the rooms adjacent to the Crown Jewels of Scotland. All the time fundraising went on, albeit at a slow pace: the first contribution was £500 from a prominent businessman, the second half-a-crown from a Black Watch soldier who had started life as a tinker, and by August 1922 £120,000

(£4.4 million) had been found, thanks largely to a magnificent single contribution of £50,000 (£1.8 million) from A. P. Lyle of Glen Delvine. Exactly a year later, following the approval of the War Office and the Ancient Monuments Board, work began on the project under Lorimer's direction.

The intention was that on entering the memorial people would be overwhelmed by the total effect and that they would find themselves in an ancient and hallowed location. The execution gave substance to those hopes. Lorimer insisted on extremely high standards from the artists and craftsmen employed on the project and the end result fully justified the description given to it by the novelist Ian Hay: 'a coronach [funeral lament] in stone'. The centrepiece was and is provided by the bays commemorating the regiments and their battle honours. Eight stained-glass windows let in blue-grey natural light, the effect being to recreate a Scottish sea and sky in summer weather. The windows of the memorial also add their voice to the story of the war with representations of departing troopships, leave trains and munitions workers. A huge figure of Archangel Michael is suspended over the casket and remembrance stone of green Corona marble, and around it, on the walls of the shrine, a bronze frieze contains a hundred figures representing the different ranks and types of service personnel who fought in the war: infantry soldiers, engineers, pilots, sailors, nurses, a Camel Corps trooper in shorts and a warmly wrapped soldier from the Russian front of 1919 in snowshoes. Space was also found to commemorate every formation which fought in the war, from the Royal Naval Reserve to the Mercantile Marine, and from the chaplains to the medical services. The role played by women is also remembered, with a memorial to the honour of all Scotswomen surrounded by the titles of their units, including Elsie Inglis's Scottish Women's Hospital. There is also room for the 'Humble Beasts that served and died': horse, mule, camel, reindeer, elephant and dog, as well as a panel for 'The Tunnellers' Friends', the canaries and mice which gave sappers warning of the presence of dangerous gases.

Nothing was left to chance and nothing was omitted. This was the only opportunity to memorialise Scotland's contribution to the war and the result is a striking mixture of raw beauty and restrained reverence. Over 200 craftsmen and craftswomen were employed on the project and their professional skills helped to turn the memorial into a sacred place which justified the effort put into its creation. Amongst them were Gertrude Alice Meredith Williams, who sculpted the statue of Michael and created the bronze frieze from her husband's drawings of soldiers during his wartime service on the Western Front. Other sculptures were executed by Alexander Carrick, George Salvesen, Phyllis Bone and Pilkington Jackson, who made sure that military details were correct. Responsibility for the stained-glass windows was in the hands of Douglas Strachan, who had collaborated with Lorimer on earlier projects, and the heraldic artistry work was controlled by John Sutherland, 'a striking figure from Shetland, six foot tall, with long grey hair which he bobbed and he had a yellow complexion from working too much indoors.'[17]

The grandeur created by them deserved a solemn reception and that was certainly the case when the memorial was officially opened on 14 July 1928 by the Prince of Wales with dignitaries representing the armed forces and all corners of Scottish civic and public life in attendance. Once the service of dedication had come to an end the colonels of the regiments marched slowly into the shrine carrying their regimental rolls of honour which were to be placed inside the casket later by the King and Queen, the memorial's first visitors. The roll for the Women's Services was carried by the Duchess of Atholl, wearing the nursing uniform of the Voluntary Aid Detachment. Outside, in Crown Square, the pipes played Scotland's traditional lament, 'The Flowers of the Forest', and the entire proceedings were broadcast by loudspeakers to a huge crowd standing on the castle esplanade. *The Scotsman* reported the following day that many of them were in tears and after the main service was over they queued patiently to leave their wreaths and flowers in Crown Square outside the memorial. It was a sombre and unforgettable moment. As Ian Hay put it in his history of the project, this was Scotland's way of paying its respects in a dignified and, above all, communal manner: 'Still, the appeal of outward beauty must take second place: it is what lies within that matters. Nearly everybody in Scotland has a proprietary interest in the contents of that casket.'[18] He added the momentous thought that it was right that Scotland should have a national memorial as the country was 'small enough to know all her sons by heart' and the mourning was both general and particular. Significantly there was no triumphalism in the memorial; the word 'victory' only appears once.

The other means of memorialising the war came through an outburst of literary endeavour. In common with all the combatant nations of the First World War Scotland produced its own quota of war poetry, most of it written during the conflict. Much of the outpouring was humdrum stuff either reflecting the extreme patriotism which sent men off to fight for their country in the early days or the dehumanising and demeaning effects of battle, but the fighting also produced at least two Scottish poets whose work can stand alongside English war poets of the calibre of Siegfried Sassoon, Wilfred Owen and Isaac Rosenberg. Inevitably the writing of the war poets coloured the pessimistic view of the war which was accepted by later generations – the futility, the cruelty, the mismanagement and the horror – but there was also a belief that the experience was a privilege, a rite of passage that had been denied others and that they had lived through a time when, to use the words of the Spanish writer Jose Ortega y Gasset 'Everything is possible, everything is possible!' The response was complex and parti-coloured and in that respect the work of the Scottish poets is little different from the work produced by poets from other parts of Britain and Ireland. And just as the war paved the way for modernism and created a climate for the diffusion of culture throughout Europe so too was Scotland's literary culture changed utterly by the rejection of older values made archaic by the experience of war.

Of the Scots who wrote poetry based on their experiences of war Charles Hamilton Sorley and Ewart Alan Mackintosh are perhaps the best known and best remembered. Sorley's poetry has featured prominently in the main anthologies of British war poetry and Mackintosh's work has been put into the context of his time as a frontline infantry soldier. Both poets were similar in that they were born into Scottish families but were brought up and educated in England and stand, therefore, somewhat outside the contemporary Scottish literary tradition, which had seen a revival of verse written in the vernacular. Both, though, were intensely aware of their heritage: Mackintosh was a Gaelic speaker and Sorley admitted that he felt no sense of patriotism towards England. In fact, as we have seen, Sorley had an ambivalent attitude towards the war and towards Germany. He realised that he had to serve his country but he refused to take the sentimental approach of the jingoist, preferring the hard-eyed vision of the realist. There is a delicate sense of irony in the refrain of one of his earliest war poems, 'All the hills and dales along', which he wrote shortly after enlisting and which reveals a subtle understanding of the brutality of military life and the fate that lay ahead for many fighting soldiers:

> On marching men, on
> To the gates of death with song.
> Sow your gladness for earth's reaping,
> So you may be glad though sleeping.
> Strew your gladness on earth's bed,
> So be merry, so be dead.[19]

There is a good deal of moral indignation in the focus of Sorley's poetry, much of which was written while he was at the front line and by the time of his death at Loos he regarded war as a nightmarish activity, quite separate from the experiences of everyday life. In one of his last letters, to his friend Arthur Watts, he admitted that the constant casualties and the sight of mutilated men had gnawed at his humanity, leaving an empty shell: 'One is hardened by now: purged of all false pity: perhaps more selfish than before. The spiritual and the animal get so much more sharply divided in hours of encounter, taking possession of the body by swift turns.'[20] In that sense, there is a strong feeling in Sorley's work of the poet as witness. Like many other war poets, he believed that he had to come to terms with the experience of battle and then record it so that others could understand that there was no glory in violent death and no victory in the demise of the individual.

Mackintosh, too, refused to be taken in by any feeling that war was a glorious adventure. Some of his earlier poems, such as 'Cha till McCruimen: Departure of the 4th Camerons', exulted in the excitement of impending battle insisting that the volunteers were marching off to war 'with merry hearts and voices singing', but his exposure to battle soon changed his tune. There is a world of difference between his initial exuberance and a poem like 'Recruiting' which voices Mackintosh's sarcastic opinion of 'fat civilians' and 'girls with feathers' who push young men into uniform while taking no risks themselves. It was prompted by a recruiting poster which Mackintosh saw in a railway carriage; he found the patriotic sentiments vulgar and realised that the gulf between 'washy songs on England's need' and the reality of war was almost unbridgeable:

> 'Lads, you're wanted! Over there,'
> Shiver in the morning dew,
> More poor devils like yourselves
> Waiting to be killed by you.[21]

Mackintosh also wrote a number of deservedly popular songs and parodies, such as 'High Wood to Waterlot Farm' and 'The Charge of the Light Brigade brought up to Date', but his reputation rests on the much anthologised poem 'In Memoriam, Private D[avid] Sutherland', which is a bitter reflection on the anguish felt by soldiers following the deaths of men under their command. The incident which prompted the poem was a raid by 1/5th Seaforths on a German trench in May 1916 which resulted in four deaths, including that of Private Sutherland who, to Mackintosh's great grief, had to be left behind during the attack.[22]

Other notable Scottish poets of the First World War included W. D. Cocker, Roderick Watson Kerr, Joseph Lee and J. B. Salmond, but all have been largely forgotten despite recent work to draw attention to their contribution.[23] More enduring was the work of poets who wrote in Scots and whose pre-war and wartime poems prefigured the Scottish Renaissance movement brought in by Hugh MacDiarmid in the 1920s: Charles Murray, Violet Jacob and Marion Angus.[24] Salmond also wrote most of his poetry in the vernacular and is easily identified as a Scottish writer, but there is another aspect to his work which makes it different from the English experience: his use of the reductive idiom which allows the writer to cock a snook at those in authority. Salmond was an establishment figure who was commissioned in the 7th Black Watch and who went on to edit the *Scots Magazine* but his poem 'Any Private to Any Private' savagely underscores the antipathy towards war felt by many ordinary soldiers:

> I canna mak' it oot. It fair beats a',
> That Wullie has to dee for God kens what.
> An' Wullie's wife'll get a bob or twa,
> Aifter they interfere wi' what she's got.

They'll pester her, and crack a dagoned lot;
An' Heaven kens, they'll lave her awful' ticht.
'A burden to the State.' Her Wullie's shot.
I kenna, hoo I canna lauch the nicht.[25]

There are echoes in this poem of the conversational style of much of
Sassoon's poetry, especially his 'Base Details', but here Salmond is
taking the point of view and adopting the voice of a private soldier
sickened by the death of a school friend and angered by a newspaper
report that the death of so many young married soldiers meant that
war widows would become a burden on the state. Kerr created the
same effect in his poem 'The Corpse' in which he introduces the still
figure of a dead soldier – a common First World War image – and
then brings the poem to a close with the chilling lines 'Thank God! It
had a sack/Upon its face.' Three poets who wrote in Gaelic also
deserve mention: Donald MacDonald (Dòmhnall Ruadh Chorùna),
John Munro (Iain Rothach) and Murdo Murray (Murchadh Moir-
each). All came from the Western Isles and all served in France and
Flanders either in the Seaforth Highlanders or the Cameron Highlanders.

Although Ian Hay's *The First Hundred Thousand* achieved widespread
popularity during the conflict, by far the best Scottish novel to emerge
from the war was John Buchan's *Mr Standfast*, which features the
character of Richard Hannay and was a sequel to an earlier novel,
Greenmantle (1916). A spy thriller (or 'shocker' as Buchan called the
genre) it contains some of the best descriptions of the fighting on the
Western Front during the German breakthrough in spring 1918 as well as
a surprisingly sympathetic account of the industrial unrest in Glasgow
and the west of Scotland. On its publication in 1919 the *British Weekly*
hailed it as 'a peerless tribute to the British Army'. Amongst the better
personal accounts of the war three were written by well-known Scottish
writers: James Bridie's *Some Talk of Alexander*, Compton Mackenzie's
Gallipoli Memories and David Rorie's *A Medico's Luck in the War*.

If the poetry and fiction produced by Scottish writers during the
war was not all of lasting quality the war itself made a huge impact on
the development of modern Scottish literature. Twenty years after the
outbreak of the war Hugh MacDiarmid addressed his fellow Scots in
his poem 'Towards a New Scotland' and posed the question:

> Was it for little Belgium's sake
> Sae mony thoosand dee'd?
> And never ane for Scotland fegs
> Wi' twenty thoosand times mair need![26]

In a sense he had already answered the question himself. On his demobilisation from the army in 1919 the poet had been transfigured literally and metaphysically from the Christopher Murray Grieve who had served on the Salonika front as a quartermaster-sergeant into the poet Hugh MacDiarmid who would go on to lead a cultural revolution aimed at transforming Scottish literature. As his biographer Alan Bold put it, he had lost faith with the Independent Labour Party and Fabian socialism and 'having seen men die for "gallant little Belgium" and the "honour of England" he now held firmly nationalistic opinions about the economic state and inferior political status of Scotland'.[27] MacDiarmid began writing poetry in Scots and from those early efforts he evolved the idea of a Scottish renaissance movement whose aim was to dissociate Scottish writing from the vernacular-based poetry of the late nineteenth century and to bring it into line with contemporary political thinking. His first collection, *Annals of the Five Senses*, appeared in 1923, a second collection, *Sangschaw*, in 1925, and *Penny Wheep* appeared in 1926, the same year as he produced his influential long poem 'A Drunk Man Looks at the Thistle'.

Like Yeats, Eliot and Pound he was aware of the post-war exhaustion of English culture and of the need to explore a new means of self-expression, claiming in his long poem 'Talking with Five Thousand People in Edinburgh' that 'most of the important words were killed in the First World War'. Turning his face against popular vernacular poetry of the kind written by, amongst others, Charles Murray, he put forward the idea of a 'synthetic Scots', an etymologically based language which would 'adapt an essentially rural tongue to the very much more complex requirements of our urban civilisation'.[28] MacDiarmid also understood that the war had changed the cohesion of European civilisation in general by breaking up the old and laying the ground for the new. In those circumstances it would be the duty of countries like Scotland to redeem European cultural values, and, like many others writing at that time, he realised that the First World War had been fought in some measure to protect the rights of small nations. In that respect his campaign for the revival of Scottish letters also had a political context: he was one of the founder members of the Scottish committee of International PEN and in 1928 he joined the National Party of Scotland which campaigned for Scottish independence.

Perhaps the greatest literary evocation of Scotland's wartime experience is to be found in Lewis Grassic Gibbon's *Scots Quair* trilogy (1932–34), most notably in the first part, *Sunset Song*, which is set in the war years. Although the author (real name, James Leslie Mitchell) was a teenager at the time, his fictionalisation of the experience of the war in his native Mearns provides a telling account of the destruction of the locality's communal identity. Everyone in Kinraddie is affected by the war. The central character, Chris Guthrie, has married Ewan Tavendale, who as a farmer is exempted from war service. However, unable to endure taunts that he is a coward, Ewan joins the army and is brutalised by life as a soldier. On leave before embarking for service in France he behaves brutally towards Chris and their child – a fitting motif for the violence of war – and leaves for the front without making amends. Later it transpires that he has been shot after deserting in a vain attempt to get back to Kinraddie to make good what he had done to his family. Two other main characters are also killed in the war: Long Rob of the Mill, a conscientious objector who eventually joins up after spending time in prison, and Chae Strachan, a socialist who has no truck with the war but nevertheless enlists. After the war Chris marries Robert Colquhoun, a minister who has been gassed in the war, and the novel ends with a moving description of the consecration of Kinraddie's war memorial, which is based on 'the old stone circle by Blawearie loch raised up and set all in place, real heathen-like, and a paling set on it'. On one of the standing stones are cut the names of four men of Kinraddie who lost their lives in war, amongst them a socialist, a freethinker and a deserter.[29] As for Kinraddie, it has been torn apart by the war: the land is sold off and the profiteering of wartime farming and tree planting helps to destroy the last of the old peasant crofting culture and economy.

The war left other long shadows. Given the length and bitterness of the conflict it was understandable that some soldiers found it impossible to forget what had happened to them. This was particularly true of those who had suffered physically or mentally but it also

affected men who felt that they had been wronged or that their
honour had been impugned as a result of being let down by others. In
the first weeks of the war the 1st Gordons had been forced to surrender
during the retreat from Mons and some 500 officers and men had been
taken into German captivity (see Chapter One). A handful managed
to escape but the rest were taken to Sennelager in Westphalia, a
German army-training centre which rapidly became a large prisoner-
of-war camp. From there they were sent to other camps, where
conditions varied according to the numbers of prisoners and the
attitudes of the prison guards. Not unnaturally, most prisoners of war
(PoWs) felt degraded by their position. However, although there
were several ingenious escape attempts, (one of the most successful
being a breakout by three soldiers captured at Loos – one Canadian
and two Scots, Private James McDaid, 10th Argylls, and Private
Johnny Anderson, Black Watch – who disguised themselves and
calmly walked out of their camp at Münster in the summer of
1917 and made their way to the Dutch border) for the majority
being a PoW meant sitting it out until the war was over. Inevitably,
that gave men, including the 1st Gordons, time to brood and to relive
the moments that had led to their capture.

   That was certainly the case with Brevet Colonel William Eagleson
Gordon, who found himself incarcerated at a camp in Torgau. Having
accomplished a great deal in his military career – he had won the Victoria
Cross in the Boer War and had been appointed an aide-de-camp to the
king – he would have liked to add to his achievements while in France
yet within a few days of arriving at the battle-front he was in captivity. In
his mind, at least, the surrender had been unnecessary and there was only
one man to blame for that action: Lieutenant-Colonel F. H. Neish, the
commanding officer of 1st Gordons. Determined to set the record
straight Gordon wrote a lengthy deposition on 16 September 1914
and handed it to the War Office when he was exchanged for a German
prisoner early in 1916. In it, he placed the blame squarely on Neish's
shoulders, describing his behaviour as that of 'a wayward child determined at all costs to give trouble':

   In the action before Berthy it was Lt Colonel Neish who made no
   attempt to act. Until the end I never set eyes on him and have no
   idea where he got to. I, however, at intervals heard his voice. It was

Lt Colonel Neish who shouted 'I am not in command of this column. I call this slaughter.' It was he who said to me 'the men are to hold up their hands' and it was he who asked the Master of Saltoun [Captain Alexander Fraser] to tell the Germans that the column would surrender.[30]

Later in 1916 Neish was also repatriated, in his case as a result of illness, and on his return he too wrote an account of the action in which he made no mention of ordering his men to surrender and claimed that it was his duty to look after his men's best interests. Gordon was intent on clearing his name and, after the war, in the summer of 1919, the army held an inquiry into the 1st Gordons' surrender to establish if the officers' actions were justified. This was a standard military procedure following any surrender but given Gordon's allegations an investigation was certainly necessary.

In the normal scheme of things the inquiry would not have prompted much public interest, but it coincided with a court case involving the same incident and had to be postponed to allow the legal process to continue. A soldier of the 1st Gordons, Corporal George Mutch, had managed to escape from Sennelager and on his return to Scotland in December 1917 he had been interviewed by Cedric Fraser, a journalist from the *People's Journal*, whose subsequent report insisted that Gordon had given the order to surrender. On learning of its publication Gordon sued the publishers, John Leng and Company, for damages of £5,000. Not only was he anxious to protect his name and set the record straight but he was convinced that there was a plot to ruin him as Neish was a shareholder in John Leng. (Neish, by then retired from the army, retorted that it was a financial relationship and that he had no knowledge of newspapers.) The case was heard in the Court of Session and it caused a great deal of publicity in Scotland, with soldiers and friends of the Gordon Highlanders finding themselves divided in their sympathies.[31] At the conclusion of the trial the jury agreed with Gordon's assertion that he had not given the order to surrender and his case was given weight when Mutch claimed that he had been misrepresented in the offending article, with words being put into his mouth by the journalist after the interview. Gordon was awarded damages of £500 but he was still determined to clear his name within the army.

During the military court of inquiry which followed at the conclusion of the trial Gordon repeated his allegation that Neish was to
blame for the surrender and expected to be exonerated. However, on
7 August the court reached the conclusion that 'the column was
captured owing to the chances of war' and 'considered that both
Gordon and Neish deserve every sympathy'. That should have
concluded the matter but as late as 1923 Gordon was still attempting
to persuade the War Office to reconsider the decision taken by the
'bastard court'; his ire was compounded by a story spread by an officer
in the Oxfordshire and Buckinghamshire Light Infantry who claimed
that during their captivity Gordon had 'practically ordered us not to
escape'. It was left to Lord Saltoun, whose eldest son, the Master of
Saltoun, was involved in the incident, to give Gordon much-needed
solace when he wrote to him in March 1923 saying that the case
'makes one understand the bitter contempt with which real fighting
soldiers always speak of the War Office'.[32]

As with countless other soldiers from the warring nations, thousands of Scots returned home, picked up the pieces and got on with
their lives as best they could. Later in life, in his autobiography *Lucky
Poet*, MacDiarmid spoke of the returning soldier bringing back to
civilisation 'an ardour of revolt, a sharp bitterness, made up partly of
hatred and party of pity' but there were also those who had experienced satisfaction from their service, knowing that they had survived
unimaginable dangers. Sergeant Francis Halcrow Scott, who served
with the 16th Royal Scots, answered a query from his parents about
the dangers on the front line with the thought that coming under
artillery fire was well-nigh impossible to describe: 'Well I can't say I
felt "fear" exactly but it was more a feeling of "awe" that came over
me as naturally you are pretty helpless and can't do anything while
these things are coming over.'[33] There was, of course, a darker side.

Many of the four million survivors were disabled (at least 10 per
cent of these would have been Scots), while other survivors could not
find work, or became homeless. There was an overwhelming need to
tackle the problems faced by ex-servicemen on their return to civilian
life. A number of associations and ex-servicemen's clubs already
catered for the veterans but being independent of each other they
lacked political and financial cohesion and the different factions were
often at loggerheads over the best way forward. It was not until 1920

that the first steps were taken to forge some unity and the guiding figure was Haig, who had retired from the army in January 1919 and who had long insisted that the needs of former service personnel warranted urgent attention. His experience, and the respect in which he was held, led to the creation in 1921 of the British Legion and the British Legion Scotland (in 1971 the queen granted the organisation the title of the Royal British Legion Scotland). The latter came into being in March 1921 although the official founding date is 18 June following the first 'Unity Conference', held in the Usher Hall in Edinburgh. By the end of the following year the British Legion Scotland was able to report that it had dealt with 7,645 cases in respect of pensions, medical claims and arrears of pay, recovering some £3,500 in the process.[34] That year also saw the first 'poppy' appeal, raising funds for ex-service personnel (in Scotland this is the responsibility of the Earl Haig Fund), and in 1919 the first Armistice Day commemoration had been held as the nation kept two minutes' silence on 11 November at 11 a.m.

In Muriel Spark's novel *The Prime of Miss Jean Brodie* (1961), the eponymous heroine, a schoolteacher in Edinburgh in the 1930s, plays on the emotions of her young girl pupils by telling them the story of Hugh Carruthers, her fiancé who was killed in action a week before the armistice. The sentimental account of their doomed love is bound up in Brodie's mind with the story of the Battle of Flodden in 1513 and this is reinforced by the references to the 'Flowers of the Forest', the great song of national mourning written by Jean Elliot of Minto to commemorate the dead in one of the worst tragedies in Scotland's history. The effect was to reinforce the notion that there was a 'lost generation' and that the young women of Scotland were left bereft by the loss of so many potential partners. But just as the reader is never sure if Hugh actually existed or if Jean Brodie is using the story to influence her young girls, so is the idea of a lost generation largely myth. While the majority of the male casualties were in the 16 to 34 age group (some 45,000) and scarcely a part of Scotland was spared losses, the census figures for 1921 showed an increase in the number of males in Scotland, from 2,308,839 in 1911 to 2,347,642 three years after the war. The overall increase in the size of the post-war Scottish population in those same ten years was 121,593. The same census also reveals a slight reduction in the numbers of unmarried women in the

20 to 44 age group and a higher proportion of married women, although this may have been due to the war's effects on marriage patterns and 'a trend towards more universal marriage at younger ages'.[35]

And yet, mere numbers cannot tell the whole story. As elsewhere, Scotland was no stranger to the after-effects of war. Although this was an age when men were supposed to suffer in silence and to show a stiff upper lip, the repression of war experiences could not disguise the fact that many veterans were condemned to spend the rest of their lives suffering in smaller or greater measure from the effects of the war. It is undeniable that former soldiers continued to die in their hundreds after the Armistice as a result of war-related injuries or illnesses: the total listed as wounded in the British armed forces was 1,676,037, at least 10 per cent of whom would have been Scots, and until 1939 the annual reports of the Registrar-General for Scotland recorded the numbers of former servicemen who had died as a result of their war wounds. All over the country charitable organisations such as the British Legion Scotland catered for the needs of the veterans, but theirs was largely a hidden sorrow, usually out of sight and out of mind. There was also the continuing pain of those who had lost loved ones: women made unseasonal widows, children who would never know their fathers and parents denied the opportunity of seeing their teenage sons become men. For them, men like Sir Harry Lauder who had lost his only son in December 1916, the war would never end: 'Everything was unreal. For a time I was quite numb. But then, as I began to realise and to visualise what it was to mean in my life that my boy was dead, there came a great pain. The iron of realisation slowly seared every word of that curt telegram upon my heart. I said to myself over and over again. And I whispered to myself, as my thoughts took form, over and over, the one terrible word: "Dead!"'[36] Those words of anguish could have been written for thousands of other Scottish families for whom 'the Great War', as it was generally known, had been won at a terrible personal price.

12 Aftermath

The end of the war meant a return to domestic politics and a general election was called for December 1918. It was long overdue. The parliament elected in December 1910 had perpetuated its existence by wartime legislation and at the conclusion of hostilities Lloyd George's coalition government held the reins of power. It was also destined to continue to do so for the next four years as Lloyd George was determined to fight and win the election on the coalition's wartime record. Here he enjoyed the support of most of the Liberal Party and the Conservatives, whose leader, Andrew Bonar Law, had been a staunch supporter (if occasional critic) in his position as chancellor of the exchequer. At the same time, Labour left the coalition, as did the supporters of Asquith, who had been out of office since the formation of Lloyd George's War Cabinet in December 1916; they had lost further ground by forcing a vote of no confidence in March 1918 over the government's handling of military manpower resources. The attempted coup had failed but in the longer term it spelled eventual electoral ruin for the Liberal Party. Known as the 'Coupon Election' – coalition candidates were endorsed by a letter signed jointly by Lloyd George and Bonar Law that Asquith dismissed as a 'coupon' – the coalition won easily, taking 474 seats, 338 being Conservatives and 136 being 'coupon' Liberals. Labour returned 57 members while Asquith's followers were reduced to 26 seats. In Scotland the figures mirrored the national trend: Conservatives 32, Coalition Liberals 19, Asquith Liberals 8, Labour 8 (including one coalition member, George Barnes in Glasgow Gorbals). The Liberals' discomfort was increased with two high-profile casualties: in East Fife Asquith lost the seat to the Conservative Captain Alex Sprot, and the former Scottish secretary, McKinnon Wood, was unseated at Glasgow St Rollox, a seat he had held since 1906.

Although the Liberals were not yet out of political contention –

Lloyd George remained as prime minister – the divisions created by the election had a lasting effect on party solidarity. Coalition Liberals found themselves fighting their former colleagues or supporting the Conservative candidate and the split between the two factions became formal in 1920. That same year Asquith enjoyed a spectacular triumph when he won the Paisley by-election, but with the coming of the peacetime years the once all-powerful Liberal Party was on the wane. The split in its ranks had damaged party unity, it had been criticised for its handling of the war, not just on the war fronts but also in its treatment of labour disputes, and there was widespread dislike of the party's traditional support for Irish home rule. (By 1920, with the partition of Ireland and the creation of the Irish Free State, the latter issue had become academic.) The chief beneficiaries in Scotland were the Conservatives who not only won the most seats but attracted 30 per cent of the vote. From being a party whose members of parliament 'could fit into two railway carriages' they emerged from the war as a significant political power in the land.[1] Labour, too, emerged with credit from the election, winning as many votes as the Conservatives but losing out on seats due to the vagaries of the 'first-past-the-post' system. Following the 1918 Representation of the People Act the franchise had been extended to all male adults over the age of 21 and to females over the age of 30. This increased the size of the electorate from 779,000 to 2,205,000 but problems with registration, including the absence of servicemen, meant that the turnout was only 60 per cent of those eligible to vote. Labour probably suffered as a result: although it took votes from the Liberals the lack of cohesion in the party's organisation meant that it failed to build on the potential offered by its working-class support, many of whom had been involved in the wartime agitation. Those Labour candidates elected were also respectable and middle-of-the-road: Alex Wilkie (Dundee) and William Adamson (West Fife) had supported the war, and of the five newcomers F. H. Rose (Aberdeen North), James Brown (Ayrshire South), and Duncan Graham (Hamilton) were also supporters. Consoling its readers that 323,000 votes for Labour would have been 'inconceivable' in 1914 *Forward* had to concede the harsh reality that 'so much had been expected and so little gained'.[2]

Nonetheless a pattern was beginning to emerge in Scottish politics. Both the Conservatives and Labour picked up support from the

Liberals, but each benefited in different ways. Increasingly the middle classes were seen as the preserve of the Conservatives, who worked hard to build up core support in country areas and amongst young people who wanted to 'get on in life'. Labour looked for support from the industrial working class but also got backing from moderates and free thinkers who saw them as the coming party and an engine for social change. However, there were subtle differences in Scotland. The Scottish Divisional Council of the Independent Labour Party (ILP) embraced a more radical brand of socialism – in 1920 it voted for affiliation to Lenin's Third International – and leading activists such as Willie Graham (Edinburgh Central) and Neil MacLean (Govan) were well to the left of their English counterparts.

In the midst of this change the main casualty was the cause of Scottish home rule, which began a slow but gradual decline. At first it was not apparent and for the next six years it was a live political issue, culminating in two further attempts to introduce home rule bills in 1924 and 1927. In 1918 the Scottish Home Rule Association was revived by Roland Muirhead, the secretary of the ILP's Lochwinnoch branch, and it attracted the support of many other ILP members, including Maxton and Johnston. Both the Scottish Council of the Labour Party and the Scottish Trade Union Congress (STUC) passed resolutions in favour of home rule and for Scotland to be represented at Versailles as an independent country, and the following year the Executive of the Scottish Council of the Labour Party adopted a draft bill which stated that 'a determined effort should be made to secure Home Rule for Scotland in the first Session of Parliament, and that the question should be taken out of the hands of place-hunting lawyers and vote-catching politicians by the political and industrial efforts of the Labour Party in Scotland which should co-ordinate all its forces to this end, using any legitimate means, political or industrial, to secure the establishment of a Scottish Parliament'.[3]

As we shall see, the home rule issue continued to exercise minds in the next election in 1922 and it remained a burning issue for some time thereafter, but it was already causing problems for its supporters. The Labour Party as a whole was lukewarm about the idea as any breakaway would dilute its support across the United Kingdom and, in any case, they were not yet in a position to implement such a measure. There were also fears that support for home rule played into the hands of the Conservatives, who were able to claim that those who advocated any form of independence or devolution were no better than Sinn Feiners or Communists only interested in starting a Russian-style revolution. Within three months of the end of the war this apprehension was given new emphasis when the political unrest which was lying below the surface of Scottish life bubbled up in a spectacular way in Glasgow's George Square. While the cessation of hostilities had been welcomed, the end of the war meant that there would be immediate and perhaps unwelcome changes in the patterns of work in the heavy industries. During the war years manufacturing techniques had been improved to ensure maximum production; women had been employed in factories, and skilled workers had been forced to give up some of their privileges, but with inevitable cutbacks in production there was now the spectre of mass unemployment. These factors threatened to erode the collective bargaining power of skilled craft workers, who were the only sector of the workforce capable of defending themselves against the employers' ability to control the labour process and drive down manufacturing costs.[4] Now there was further change in the air.

Demobilised servicemen would soon be returning and as Lloyd George had made an election pledge 'to make Britain a fit country for heroes to live in' they expected to find employment, a living wage and decent housing. The revolutions in Russia and Germany had also fostered the idea that the old order was changing, and depending on the political perspective the contemporary upheavals were either a force for improvement or something to be resisted. This was both a challenge and an opportunity for the workers' leaders. For the powerful engineering unions the immediate post-war period offered the first chance for them to regain the initiative to protect their workers' rights after the wartime years of bending their collective will to the restrictive legislation of the Munitions of War Act. As the Marxist activist Harry McShane put it in his memoirs, the moment had to be grasped: 'We had known only working-class revolt. Now we could talk about working-class power.'[5]

The first step was a renewal of demands to reduce the number of hours in the working week and in a national ballot organised by the Amalgamated Society of Engineers there was a two-to-one majority for accepting a 47-hour week. However, the figures in Scotland were not so encouraging: there was considerable opposition to the measure as it would entail a long morning shift, from 7.30 a.m. to noon without any break. The alternative was the adoption of a 40-hour week, which would also ease unemployment by reducing working hours. As this was opposed by the employers but had the support of the Labour Party and the ILP in Scotland, as well as the STUC and the Glasgow Trades Council, there was clearly room for the demand to spill over into confrontation.[6] By the middle of January 1919 strike action seemed inevitable, and when it came Glasgow hovered on the brink of anarchy. On Monday 27 January 40,000 shipyard workers went on strike and by the following day the number had almost doubled. Although the strike was not universal – municipal workers refused to join it – the stoppages caused consternation in government and, as had happened in 1916, there was a massive overreaction by the authorities.

At the end of the week, on 31 January, soon to be remembered as 'Bloody Friday', a mass demonstration of 100,000 strikers assembled in George Square to support the call for a 40-hour week and to protest at the ending of wartime rent restrictions. While their leaders were inside the City Chambers, tempers became frayed in the square and a series of clashes with the police led to scuffles which quickly became bad tempered. At that point the police panicked, drew their batons and charged the crowd. Bottles were thrown, windows were smashed, heads were broken, the leaders were arrested and the Riot Act was read by the Sheriff of Lanarkshire. That same afternoon the Cabinet discussed the incident and agreed with Robert Munro, the Scottish secretary, when he denounced the confrontation, not as strike action but as 'a Bolshevist rising'.[7] An earlier decision to use troops in support of the civil power was put into immediate effect: 12,000 English troops were deployed to Glasgow and 6 tanks and 100 army trucks were sent north by overnight trains. Within a day Glasgow had come under military control, and although the tanks did not leave their base at the Cattle Market, troops appeared on the streets and machine-gun posts were established at key points in the city centre.

Whatever else the riot accomplished, it lanced the boil of dis-affection and over the next few days the strikers started returning to work as nerves became calmer. Ten days later the strike committee advocated 'a full resumption of work by all strikers', the demand for a

40–hour week was dropped and the militancy was as good as over. But there were repercussions. Twelve strike leaders who had been arrested were prosecuted for inciting a riot and faced trial in the High Court in Edinburgh that April. Two of them, William Gallacher and Emanuel Shinwell, received prison sentences, a result which the *Glasgow Herald* justified as a blow against 'that squalid terrorism which the world now describes as Bolshevism'.[8] The sensationalist language matched the mood. At the time it seemed that justice had triumphed and that a potential revolution had been nipped in the bud so that decent citizens could sleep easily at night. It is easy to see why such a view prevailed. Most of the reporting of Bloody Friday was inaccurate and incendiary and the Cabinet had been given wild evidence by Special Branch about the strike being the precursor of a wider and more damaging revolution. Russia had already succumbed to violent change, there was political unrest in Berlin, Vienna and Budapest and there were still memories of the 1916 Easter Rising in Dublin when Irish republicans had attempted to seize power. Against that background it is obvious why the authorities took such a firm stance, although the deployment of tanks was excessive and under different circumstances could have been provocative. With red flags flying in George Square and some demonstrators talking of bringing the city to a standstill, the security measures clearly erred on the side of safety-first. Only later did it become clear that the incident was a mass workers' demonstration, which, although unruly and potentially dangerous, only got out of control when the police overreacted by charging the crowd with drawn batons. Contemporary evidence also shows that the strike leaders were badly shaken by the incident and shocked by how quickly the violence had escalated.[9]

However, this latest episode in the Red Clydeside saga had consequences which suggest that it was more than a squabble between the authorities and disaffected workers, or a riot which got out of control. Labour benefited, picking up support amongst disaffected workers who believed that they were under attack from a repressive government and had to take steps other than direct action to improve their lot. As talk of revolution died down it was replaced by the gradualism preached by Labour leaders like Johnston, Maxton, Kirkwood and Wheatley. Progress, they argued, lay in political change and rational argument; there was no New Jerusalem to be found under the red banner. The policy seemed to work, too: in the 1919 municipal elections Labour made significant gains in Fife and Glasgow, allowing one activist to claim that the latter had become 'a red city'. Labour's ability to build on the events of 1919 gives credence to the claim that the movement in Scotland was 'reformist rather than revolutionary',[10] reinforced by the no-nonsense non-conformist approach of the Labour leadership as they kept up their arguments for social justice and fair play. Perversely, the unrest of January 1919 also had a useful impact for Conservatives, who were seen as the one party capable of dealing with this 'Bolshevik threat'. Those who had been alarmed by the events in George Square now looked to the Conservatives as the natural party of law and order and a bulwark against the radicals.

Amongst the losers were the trade unions, who had had their fingers badly burned and were for the time being unwilling to involve themselves in further strike activity, and those on the extreme left, who believed that Scotland was on the cusp of revolution. The main casualty was John Maclean, who found himself increasingly isolated after the war. His behaviour continued to be paranoid (he never stopped believing that he was being 'doped' by government spies and he blamed the collapse of his marriage on the interference of the security services) and his beliefs were frequently perverse (he claimed that Lord Leverhulme's land improvement schemes in the Western Isles were driven by the need to supply the Royal Navy with new bases for a future war against the USA). Astutely, though, he recognised that the Bloody Friday demonstration and the related strike activity could have provided the momentum for revolution from within, but he lacked the leadership skills and the organisational ability to harness the energy. His big message was also misunderstood or ignored, namely that the proletariat alone had it in their power to bring down capitalism and destroy the machinery of state. Above all he lacked a power base and his isolation was increased by his failure to form a separate Scottish Communist party in 1920: acting on the orders of the Comintern in Moscow, it was decreed that the Communist Party in Britain should be a British national party and as a result the Communist Party of Great Britain (CPGB) was formed. Later, Maclean's refusal to support it was ascribed to his mental state but the real reason was his belief that the CPGB would be a brake on radical socialist progress in Scotland.[11]

Three years later, in February 1923, Maclean founded the Scottish Workers' Republican Party (SWRP) 'within which the workers in control can evolve present-day capitalist property into working-class property as a stage on the road to communal use of all the wealth produced.'[12] By then he had been in prison again, having been tried on a charge of sedition in May 1921 and sentenced to three months' incarceration in Barlinnie. On his release he was rearrested on a similar charge and sentenced to a year's imprisonment in the same prison and was not released until 25 October 1922. He would not have been human if the six terms of imprisonment and the constant police harassment had not affected him, physically and mentally, and it stands to reason that his lack of political progress must have been a grave disappointment to him personally. Although he stood as an SWRP candidate in municipal elections and contested the Gorbals constituency in the 1922 general election, he failed to muster much support, polling only 4,027 votes compared to the 16,479 cast in favour of the Labour candidate, George Buchanan. (Typically Maclean advised voters to vote Labour if they were not 100 per cent behind him.)

Partly, Maclean was damned by his refusal to compromise or to offer policies which were achievable. Put simply, his rhetoric might have been challenging and impressive but it was out of kilter with the times and the aspirations of the people who listened to him. As Tom Johnston put it at the time of the 1918 trial, Maclean advocated change through revolution but 'the bulk of the workers do not want a Social Revolution by any method, but go on rivet-hammering competitions, and scrambling for overtime, and regard John Maclean as "decent enough, but a bit off".'[13] People might have respected Maclean and his principles but the fact remained that they did not want to vote for a man whose last election address asked them to declare a republic and to transfer land and the means of production to the working classes. Exhausted by his efforts to make an impact Maclean caught a cold while electioneering; it quickly developed into pneumonia and he died on 30 November 1923 at the age of 44.

With his death he achieved a lasting immortality. The poet Hugh MacDiarmid called him the greatest Scot of his generation, 'a flash of sun in a country all prison-grey', while the Gaelic poet Sorley MacLean admitted his influence, 'the great John Maclean, the top and hem of our story'; Hamish Henderson's song 'The John Maclean March', written in 1948, became an alternative national anthem and for many political activists on the left Maclean became an inspiration, hailed variously as a socialist, an internationalist and a Scottish nationalist (albeit of a republican hue).[14] Of his integrity there can be no doubt. Maclean belongs to that breed for whom black was black and white was white and compromise was the work of the devil. Even when it became clear in the post-war years that his brand of Marxist revolutionary socialism had little popular support he never wavered in his beliefs. Immoderate of language and occasionally reckless in his behaviour he refused to take the easy way even though he knew that his actions would lead to imprisonment. As an internationalist, he sensed the revolutionary momentum which was at work in the aftermath of the Russian revolution, and even though this failed to spread through Europe as he anticipated, he clung to his belief that only the working class 'can bring about the time when the whole world will be in one brotherhood, on a sound economic foundation'.[15] In that respect he was an idealist whose political convictions made him an uneasy companion, singular in his approach and unyielding in his actions and beliefs. Inevitably, his public actions came at a price to his private life and there is more than a hint of the martyr in his courting of retribution from the establishment. But, for all that his reputation is still the subject of intense disagreement, Maclean remains a man of principle, a tragic hero whose death and subsequent elevation as a Scottish political icon gained him the fame and attention that failed to materialise during his lifetime.

The year before his death Maclean had witnessed the inexorable rise of Labour, which also signalled the end of his own ambitions. In 1922 the Conservatives ended their coalition with the Liberals and went into a general election which secured them a majority with 347 seats. Once again the Liberals lost heavily but the Labour Party made a sensational advance, winning 142 seats. Of these, 29 were won in Scotland and 10 of that number represented Glasgow constituencies. Amongst these Glasgow MPs were Wheatley, Maxton, Kirkwood and Buchanan, all pictured in the public mind as 'Red Clydesiders', and when the new Labour MPs left for London on 19 November their carriage of the night train resounded to the singing of the 'Internationale' and Psalm 124, with its confident opening line 'Had not the Lord been on our side'. There was something noble and visionary in the hopes of those Scottish founding fathers of the Labour movement as they made their way south to what they hoped was a new beginning. Shinwell recalled the crowds at St Enoch Station whose eyes 'once again had the gleam of hope where despair had so long held sway', while Wheatley came to believe that the huge number of well-wishers 'proved to me beyond doubt that people were ready to respond to a bold Socialist lead'.[16] All were convinced that change was possible and amongst the hopes they carried south with them was the dream of home rule. Maxton spoke of 'the atmosphere of the Clyde getting the better of the House of Commons' and by the following year he was telling his supporters in Glasgow that he wanted 'to make English-ridden, capitalist-ridden, landowner-ridden Scotland into the Scottish Socialist Commonwealth' and to create a Scottish parliament with 134 seats.[17]

However, home rule did not become a direct political issue until the early summer of 1924, following the previous year's general election, which was fought on the issue of Tariff Reform. Once again Labour in Scotland did exceptionally well, winning 34 seats and 35.9 per cent of the total votes cast. Reunited, the Liberals enjoyed something of a comeback, winning 158 seats in the United Kingdom (23 in Scotland), but it was to be short-lived. The Conservatives slumped to 258 seats and, crucially for his party's future, Asquith decided to throw in his lot with Labour, who had won 191 seats. As a result the first Labour government came into power with Ramsay MacDonald as prime minister, but its ability to pursue socialist policies was hampered by its need for Liberal support. One of its most radical initiatives was the Housing Act, which was ushered in by John Wheatley, who served as minister of health. The legislation produced funding from central government for local council housing and in Glasgow resulted in the construction of 21,586 badly needed and spacious new houses. Although the scheme was later attacked on the grounds that 'rent control caused housing stock to deteriorate because nobody was paying for its upkeep' and therefore created more slums,[18] at the time Wheatley's act justified his own description of the legislation as 'the red cross work of the class struggle'.[19]

The government also allowed the introduction of a Government of Scotland Bill which was sponsored by Buchanan, who claimed that his 'mild meagre measure' was 'representative of Scottish Labour opinion'. The bill would have provided devolution to a single assembly which would have had modest tax-raising powers and an annual subsidy from the imperial budget starting at £500,000. It was based on the Liberals' 1914 bill but it had one built-in problem which later became known as the 'West Lothian Question', namely what would be the position of Scottish members of parliament following devolution, would they continue to be able to cast their votes on purely English matters? (The matter had first been raised in 1914 by Arthur Balfour, who asked, 'Are you going to leave the whole of these 72 Scottish members here to manage English education?' Later, during the devolution debates of the 1970s the same point was raised by Tam Dalyell, member for West Lothian, in the course of the debates on the Scotland Bill.) The question was further complicated by the fact that Labour depended on the Scottish members for their parliamentary majority and could hardly propose any measure which would take Scottish MPs out of Westminster. Buchanan's ingenious solution was a proposal that the problem need not be addressed 'until separate provision is made for devolution in England and Wales' – an unlikely eventuality – but as it turned out the issue was academic. At the end of a lengthy and prolix debate the Speaker ruled that the bill had lapsed due to lack of available time, and despite angry protests by the Scottish Labour members Buchanan's bill was not given the opportunity of being put to the vote.

In other respects the first Labour government turned out to be a moderate administration, almost as if MacDonald were determined to disprove Churchill's gibe that Labour was 'not fit to govern'. It was also shortlived. In September 1924 the government fell, following Conservative moves for a vote of censure over the failure to prosecute a Communist newspaper editor, J. R. Campbell, who had published an article allegedly inciting the armed forces to mutiny. The Liberals' compromise suggestion of a Select Committee was unacceptable to MacDonald, with the result that the government was defeated and a new general election was called for the following month. This time the Liberals paid in full measure for supporting Labour, as the electorate clearly believed that their choice lay between Conservatives and Labour. Under Stanley Baldwin the Conservatives picked up votes from the Liberals and won a total of 415 seats, 38 of them in

Scotland. Labour dropped to 152, with 26 in Scotland, but the biggest losers were the Liberals, who ended up with only 42 seats, and only 9 of these were in Scotland. Baldwin remained in power until 1929 and during the course of his government another home rule bill for Scotland was introduced, this time by the Rev. James Barr, who proposed to answer the West Lothian Question with the suggestion that Scottish MPs would quit Westminster for their own parliament in Edinburgh. Although it was backed by a Scottish Convention, composed of MPs, trade union leaders and local authority represen-tatives, it fared no better than Buchanan's bill and once again the debate was cut short due to lack of parliamentary time. Thereafter home rule slipped down Labour's agenda as the country began to face more pressing economic and social problems.

By then ten years had passed since the war ended and the story in Scotland had been one of general decline and a gradual collapse in confidence. In the immediate aftermath of the conflict the economy remained reasonably buoyant, mainly as a result of the wartime boom and the confidence generated by the end of the war, but by the early 1920s the alarm bells were ringing. Between 1921 and 1923 ship-building on the Clyde dropped from 510,000 tons to 170,000 tons as a result of cancellations, delayed orders and the effects of the Washing-ton Treaty of 1921 which limited the size and extent of Britain's future warship construction. Industrial unrest also added to the problems − a dispute with the boilermakers in 1923 and the effects of the general strike three years later − but the Clyde was already beginning to pay for the artificial boom which had rescued it during the war. On 5 January 1931 the unthinkable happened when the last ship to be built at Beardmore's left the Clyde and the shipyard at Dalmuir was put up for sale. Other heavy industries also suffered, with production at the North British Locomotive Company dropping off by two-thirds during the same period due to falling orders.[20] The railway merger of 1923 also affected the industry when the London Midland and Scottish railway absorbed the Caledonian and Glasgow and South-Western while the London and North-Eastern took over the North British and its subsidiary companies. Direction of both companies was moved to London and there was a resultant scaling down of engineering work in Glasgow and Kilmarnock. Coal pro-duction suffered as a result of falling international markets, especially in eastern Europe, and the same fate for the same reasons was visited on the fishing industry, which saw its numbers decline from 33,283 fishermen in 1913 to 26,344 in 1926.[21] Jute production in Dundee was affected adversely by declining orders and workers' strikes and the production of textiles also suffered from ever-shrinking markets. There was also a sharp reduction in the numbers of people working on the land: in 1921 the census carried out by the Board of Agriculture showed that the number of male workers had fallen from 175,651 in 1911 to 169,984 ten years later. According to the board's findings the decline was not restricted to any particular part of the country but was widespread throughout Scotland. In the Borders one investigator reported that 'an old shepherd, who has passed all his days in the Cheviot country, stated that for every five persons employed on the land in his district, there was now only one'. Only in the Lothians had there been no decline.[22] Soon machine-age farming would replace the draught beasts and with them went the cottars' tied houses as the face of farming changed forever, leaving Lewis Grassic Gibbon to mourn that 'the ancient, strange whirlimagig of the generations that enslaved the Scots peasantry for centuries is broken.'[23]

In the seven crofting counties of the Highlands and islands – Argyll, Inverness, Ross and Cromarty, Sutherland, Caithness, Orkney and Shetland – there was a steady and worrying haemorrhage in population, falling from 341,535 in 1911 to 325,853 in 1921. Emigration accounted for some of the losses; wartime casualties undoubtedly took a toll but they were also aggravated by a decline in arable cultivation. As a result, fewer people were employed on the land and smaller wages meant a lower standard of living and a subsequent deterioration in the available housing stock. Wartime taxation and a post-war increase in rates affected estate owners and in 1921 the Deer Forest Committee reported that high running costs had brought 'most Highland estates to the brink of bankruptcy'. Those which survived lacked investment and the general trend was to turn cropping over to grass and to allow pasture to become rough grazing.

Only in land settlement – the granting of small-holdings to ex-servicemen – had there been a modest improvement, although shortage of available land in the Highlands and Islands continued to be a headache. Since 1886 crofters had enjoyed security of tenure, and the passing of the Land Settlement (Scotland) Act in 1919 produced more funds, £2.75 million (equivalent in purchasing power to £84 million in 2005), and gave the Board of Agriculture the authority for the compulsory purchase of privately owned land. In time, this process of state intervention would undo many of the injustices perpetrated within the crofting community during the previous two centuries, but the complexities of the legal system meant that compulsory purchases did not solve the problem of land ownership overnight. As a result land raids became a popular solution and the outraged feelings of dispossession were increased by the fact that men returning from the war felt that they should be rewarded with land. One man of Harris spoke for many when he said: 'When we were in the trenches down to our knees in mud and blood we were promised all good things when we should return home victorious.'[24]

Land raids had begun in Skye in the 1880s to recover lost grazings and had continued into the new century, with raids taking place on South Uist and Benbecula. In 1911 the first steps towards compulsory purchase had been taken with the establishment of the Board of Agriculture, but its powers and its budget proved to be limited. Small wonder then that the 1919 act raised so many expectations, especially amongst the ex-servicemen who believed that they were about to get their just deserts. Matters came to a head in Lewis, which had a long history of economic problems, mainly due to the shortage of available land. These were now exacerbated by the post-war decline in fishing, especially the collapse of the herring trade to Russia and the Baltic countries. As a result Lewismen were denied the lucrative seasonal work which had helped to sustain them in the past, and its failure added to the clamour for land. At that critical moment Lewis was put up for sale by its owners, the Mathesons, and was bought by Lord Leverhulme, a wealthy industrialist who had made his fortune manufacturing Sunlight soap. A philanthropist by inclination and an improver by instinct, he had imaginative plans to improve the island's economy by ending the reliance on small and unprofitable crofts and introducing modern technology to harness the wealth provided by the sea. A fish-canning factory would be built at Stornoway together with a power station, a new and larger fishing fleet would come into service and the people would be able to give up their old crofting way of life and embrace the modern world. Provision was even made for the construction of a railway.

There is little doubt that Leverhulme was sincere in his intentions but his ideas were hopelessly out of touch with the times and with the situation on Lewis. Not only was he trying to introduce the improvements and modernisation at a time when fishing was in decline, but he failed to understand the islanders' attachment to the land and the importance they placed on the crofting way of life. Even when the significance of that connection was put to him in graphic terms he failed to comprehend that the islanders were not interested in 'fancy dreams that may or may not come true'. What they wanted, he was told at a public meeting in March 1919, was land. 'Is he willing to give us the land?' asked Allan Martin, one the crofters' leaders. 'And is he willing to give it now?'[25] The question had an immediate effect as there were about 800 people on Lewis who had applied for crofts before the war, and a number of farms had been considered for conversion into smallholdings. Now there seemed to be a stark choice: the islanders could accept Leverhulme's plans for improvement or they could press for land ownership under the terms of the new Land Settlement Act. In response Leverhulme put his cards on the table: in general he was vitally opposed to compulsory purchases to provide smallholdings, describing the scheme as 'a gross waste of public money', and in particular he was adamant that he needed two of the farms at Coll and Gress for the production of milk for the island. By then they had already been occupied by land raiders who had told Robert Munro, the Scottish secretary, in no uncertain terms that they were acting 'to Fulfil the promise granted by the Government to demobilised soldiers and sailors, the land ought to be in wait for us [*sic*]'.[26]

The stage was now set for confrontation and the Scottish Office was in a quandary about how to deal with it. On the one hand it was bound to implement land reform and to make good the government's promises to ex-servicemen, but on the other it did not want to clash with Leverhulme, who was spending large amounts of his own money, estimated at £200,000 (£6 million in 2005), on improvements for the island. Eventually a compromise was reached whereby the land settlement issue should be mothballed for ten years to allow Leverhulme 'an opportunity of showing whether by the development of his schemes he would convince the Lewismen that it was in their best interests to fall in with his proposals and cease their demands for smallholdings'.[27] However, it failed to change anything and at the beginning of 1920 the farms at Coll and Gress were reoccupied by raiders, who announced their intention to stay put by starting to build houses on the reclaimed land. Leverhulme responded provocatively by dismissing 60 men from the Back, Vatisker and Coll townships and stating that they would only be re-employed if the raiders gave up their holdings. He also offered to compromise by providing small allotments on common grazing land, but both offers were rejected and the only outcome was an outbreak of further land raids elsewhere on Lewis. The stand-off attracted increasing concern from Munro, who reminded Leverhulme that the government had statutory powers to meet the local demand for compulsory land purchases and that Lewis could not remain forever outwith the legislation provided by the Land Settlement Act.

Increasingly through 1920 the correspondence between the two men became more heated – Munro was a Highlander who was sympathetic to the crofters – and in May Leverhulme put further pressure on the islanders by announcing the suspension of all his works, an action which took £3,000 a week out of the Lewis economy. This led to mass unemployment and, as Leverhulme clearly anticipated, meetings were held later in the year at which the islanders agreed to support his proposals and to 'undertake for at least ten years not to take part in the illegal raiding of any farm lands in Lewis, so as to give his Lordship the necessary opportunity and support he requires to make his schemes a success'.[28] Thinking that the majority of the people of Lewis now supported Leverhulme and would stop raiding and withdraw requests for smallholdings, Munro agreed to suspend the statutory powers for Lewis on condition that there was no interruption to the development schemes. As a further concession Leverhulme announced that eight farms in the south-west of the island would be made available for settlement, but these moves did little to appease the land raiders from Back as they would not be considered for the new settlement. Further misunderstandings abounded when the raiders at Coll and Gress agreed to withdraw from the farms following a meeting with the lord advocate. In return they thought they had his guarantee that the Board of Agriculture would consider their case but later the lord advocate denied that he had given any such thing.

The end was not long in coming. Land raids broke out again in the spring of 1921 and as a result Leverhulme started running down his development programme on the island. This time there was another motive. By then he was in financial difficulties and at the end of August he announced that the works on Lewis would be suspended indefinitely to allow him to concentrate on his holdings on Harris, which he had purchased in 1919. In time the harbour at Obbe would become Leverburgh, named in Leverhulme's honour, but the grand-iose schemes for Harris were also doomed to failure following their benefactor's death in 1925. As Munro had promised (or threatened), the end of the Lewis development meant that the Scottish Office was free to commence land settlement negotiations, a measure which delighted the land raiders but left Lewis without regular employment and in receipt of only a modest grant of £38,000 for relief works such as road-building. Although land settlement schemes had dealt with the remaining farms by the end of 1924, they failed to stop emigration. By the time of the next census in 1931 the population of the crofting counties had fallen by 16,000 to 325,853, but 'the awful and glaring injustices of the old agrarian order had least been removed'.[29] In addition to the Lewis land raids, there had been similar activities in the Uists, Benbecula, Skye and Sutherland where disgruntled ex-service-men had occupied land in protest at the slow implementation of local land settlement schemes. Having been under German fire, they told the authorities, they were not afraid of the threat of imprisonment or having their names removed from the lists of those eligible for land settlement.

During the course of their dealings with Leverhulme a crofter called John Smith responded to the blandishments on offer with the reproach that the islanders might be poor and many of their homes might be wretched but they enjoyed a way of life which was beyond Leverhulme's comprehension:

You have spoken of steady work and steady pay in terms of veneration – and I have no doubt that in your view and in the view of those unfortunate people who are compelled to live in smoky towns, steady work and steady pay are very desirable things. But in Lewis we have never been accustomed to either – and strange though it might seem to you, we do not greatly desire them. We attend to our crofts in seed-time and harvest, and we follow the fishing in its season – and when neither requires our attention we are free to rest and contemplate. You have referred to our houses as hovels! But they are our homes, and I will venture to say, my Lord, that, poor though these homes may be, you will find more real happiness in them than you will find in your castles throughout the land.[30]

Smith was giving voice to a way of life which Leverhulme clearly did not understand and was determined to change. To him, many of the small single-roomed thatched houses which formed so much of Lewis's housing stock must have seemed primitive or austere, but at the time many visitors to the island remarked on the healthiness of the people and on the fact that their accommodation was superior to inner-city slums. In any case many of the houses were being replaced by larger ones with slated roofs and more were built as a result of the land settlement process. Although the 1917 Royal Commission on Housing drew attention to the poor state of much of Scotland's housing stock in rural areas, its main condemnation was centred on the appalling state of urban housing and the conditions faced by over half the population, who were forced to live in houses with only one or two rooms. The commission's members noted that 'bad housing may be fairly regarded as a legitimate cause of social unrest' and conceded that people did not live in tenement slums because it suited them (a common misconception) but because there was no other option and the wonder was that the poor conditions were tolerated. Lloyd George had promised homes fit for heroes but just as the crofter-soldiers found no land waiting for them, all too often returning soldiers were forced to put up with the cramped and unsanitary conditions which prompted James Stewart, MP for St Rollox, to tell a visiting English journalist that the city was 'earth's nearest suburb to hell'.[31] Living in such conditions required no little tolerance and fortitude. For the most part it was a long battle for survival, and although Glasgow's tenements bred a strong sense of community, it would take another world war before the first realistic steps were taken to improve Scotland's slum housing.

For the growing middle classes post-war life was rather different. Bruce Marshall's novel *The Black Oxen* describes a group of reasonably well-heeled young Edinburgh men returning to the city to pick up the pieces of their professional careers as lawyers, stockbrokers and businessmen and enjoying the pleasures that were on offer. As they dine together at the first peacetime New Year celebrations one of them looks at the ex-soldier waiting on them and sees his group as 'unexceptional young men . . . whose short and uneventful officers' war had been upholstered in a way Sandy Boyce's long and dangerous private soldier's war had never been'.[32] Men like those sitting in the smart restaurant were natural Conservatives and during the course of the novel Marshall, a soldier during the war, reveals the gulf between them and the older pre-war generation. Whereas their fathers were brought up as Liberals the young men came back from the war and flocked to the Conservative Party and its protectionist anti-Bolshevik policies. There is much to Marshall's contention. In the immediate post-war period the Conservatives in Scotland created a party administration which fought hard to win the hearts and minds of the professional middle classes and through energetic and imaginative recruiting policies quickly built up a membership of 20,000 supporters. Although by the end of the war the majority of commissioned army officers did not come uniquely from wealthy and privileged backgrounds, post-war life was different for the returning middle-class soldier. For a start, employment was more or less assured and there was a return to the old certainties of pre-war life as the professions and institutions embraced a business-as-usual philosophy. People started going on holiday again and the main Scottish resorts experienced post-war booms which saw the construction of visitor attractions and the refurbishment of hotels and guest houses. Requisitioned properties were also returned to civilian use, often in a different guise, like the Craiglockhart Hydropathic, which became a Catholic teacher-training college after its wartime use as a hospital for shellshocked officers.

Appealing to patriotism, integrity and the maintenance of Christian family values in an uncertain world, the Conservatives became a magnet for people who either upheld traditional standards or aspired to them. There might be a hint of the stereotype in the golf-playing chartered accountant who educated his children privately, who had a good war record and went to church on Sunday, but that was the type of person the Conservatives wanted to encourage. Whereas before the war the party relied on its main support from the landed classes, it needed to broaden its appeal by embracing the professional middle classes. One sign of the changing times could be found in that bastion of the Scottish establishment, the New Club in Edinburgh. Before the war the bulk of its membership had lived in the country and used the club as their base when visiting Edinburgh. By the 1920s, though, the club was attracting more city members 'in an Edinburgh that tended to be preoccupied with appearance, respectability and frugality, and which was dominated socially by the kirk, academia, and the professions of law and medicine'.[33] The club also continued its close connection with the armed forces, which by the end of 1919 had returned to their peacetime levels.

In 1920 The Royal Scots Greys were sent to the Middle East and then to India and were one of the last cavalry regiments to be mechanised. There were similar tours of duty for the other regiments, all of which served in both theatres in the 1920s and 1930s. The 2nd King's Own Scottish Borderers, for example, was out of the country for most of the period, serving in Egypt, Hong Kong and India, while in 1930 the 2nd Seaforth Highlanders found themselves involved in fierce fighting against local tribesmen on the Afghanistan border. For most Scottish soldiers, now all volunteers, imperial policing was central to army life. The size of the army was reduced to 207,000 soldiers, and successive defence cuts meant that it was soon ill-equipped to fight a major war.

The navy, too, contracted, as a result of international agreements to restrict the size of major warships, but there was still one dramatic naval part to play when Scotland was granted a last glimpse of German sea power after 74 ships of the German Navy were interred in Scapa Flow as part of the reparations laid down by Article XXIII of the armistice terms. For the Germans this was complete humiliation. Not only were they forced to surrender to the opponents whom they believed they had defeated at Jutland, but they were escorted into captivity after steaming to their rendezvous point 50 miles to the east of the Isle of May. From there they entered the Firth of Forth before sailing north to Orkney, which they reached on 27 November 1918. It was a cheerless existence and although many of the crews were repatriated, the remaining 5,000 faced a long and bleak winter in conditions which were no better than prison.

As the peace conference dragged on at Versailles it became clear to the senior German officer, Rear Admiral Ludwig von Reuter, that he would have to hand over his ships to the Allies, the date eventually fixed being 21 June 1919, at the conclusion of the Versailles conference. Unable to face such dishonour von Reuter ordered his captains to begin scuttling their ships at midday, thereby creating the biggest mass sinking in history. For a party of Orkney children enjoying an outing on the small steamer, the *Flying Kestrel*, it was an unforgettable moment as the familiar grey leviathans started sinking and keeling over in the waters of the Flow. First to go was the battleship *Friedrich der Grosse* and by the end of the day 5 battle-cruisers, 10 battleships, 5 cruisers and 32 destroyers had been scuttled and had sunk. There was nothing further the Royal Navy could do before they officially moved out of Scapa in February 1920, and it was decided to leave the ships where they were with their masts and parts of their superstructures still visible. It was not until 1923 that the first salvage operation got under way and by the end of the 1930s 38 ships had been salvaged and 327,000 tons of scrap metal had been recovered.

By then the country was on the brink of another war with Germany as a result of Germany's invasion of Poland and the failure to contain fascist aggrandisement and territorial ambitions in Europe. By then, too, Scotland had been through the general strike of 1926 and had suffered from the worldwide slump of the early 1930s which saw general unemployment rise to 30 per cent, while in jute, mining and shipbuilding it was much higher. In 1931 unemployment in Dundee rose above 70 per cent. Mass unemployment was not the only problem facing Scottish society. In the 1920s emigration had reached a new high of 550,000, or 20 per cent of the working population, many of them going to work in industrial cities in England, the rest trying their luck further afield in Canada and Australia. The lack of work and the shortage of money had desperate consequences for the workforce who remained behind. Housing, already inadequate, could not be improved, and child mortality rates rose as a result of unsanitary conditions and overcrowding. By the 1930s the combination of poverty, poor diets, lack of education and an overwhelming absence of hope had led to the creation of an underclass for whom there seemed to be no way out of the spiral of despair. Everywhere Scotland was being painted in shades of grey and the whole country seemed to be in terminal decline. In the autumn of

1931, sixteen years after the town clerk of Glasgow had expressed heady self-confidence in the ability of his 'commercial metropolis' to survive the war and to continue to prosper, the same city's Chamber of Commerce was left to bemoan the general decline in 'shipping, railways, banks, steel, manufacturing, leaching, and calico printing, the drapery and soft goods trade, chemical manufacture, and even philanthropy'.[34] In the same period, the poet and critic Edwin Muir travelled around Scotland to record what he saw and came to the conclusion that the economic and political crisis had been more severe in Scotland than in any other part of the United Kingdom and that there were few signs that things might get better:

> Scotland is losing its industries, as it lost a hundred years ago a great deal of its agriculture and most of its indigenous literature. The waste glens of Sutherlandshire and the literary depopulation of Edinburgh and Glasgow were not obvious blows at Scotland's existence, and so they were accepted without serious protest, for the general absorption in industrial progress and money blinded everybody to them. Now Scotland's industry, like its intelligence before it, is gravitating to England, but its population is sitting where it did before, in the company of disused coal-pits and silent ship-yards.[35]

Add on the fact that control of Scotland's economy seemed to have shifted southwards – three out of seven national banks were under English control – and it was hard to avoid the impression that the country was facing an inexorable decline from which it might never recover.

Perversely, perhaps, the coming of another global conflict helped to pull Scotland out of the slough of despond. Following the long years of industrial decline and the exorbitantly high unemployment rates of the early 1930s Clydeside emerged once again as a major motor of the British economy. Full order books brought work and employment to the Clyde as the shipyards responded to the need for warships and merchant ships to make good the losses in the submarine war against Nazi Germany. The battleship HMS *Duke of York* was completed at John Brown's in September 1941, followed a year later by the aircraft carrier HMS *Indefatigable* and within a year Clydeside was responsible for building an average of five merchant ships a week thanks to improvements in welded prefabrication. Engineering and armaments production also prospered, as did jute, with Dundee swinging into action to meet the bulk of the nation's demand for sandbags. By the war's end the shipyards had 65,000 workers in their employment and the heavy industries alone accounted for a quarter of the Scottish workforce. It was not all bonanza. The outputs of coal dropped, but by and large, with full employment helped by military and industrial conscription, Scotland experienced a boom similar to the one it had enjoyed during the First World War.

With the help of state intervention agriculture also blossomed. Farmers had to meet an insatiable demand for food and subsidies allowed them to increase productivity and extend the amount of acreage given to cropping and animal husbandry. To meet the demand for additional labour women were conscripted to serve in the Women's Land Army, with some 8,000 serving on Scottish farms, sometimes alongside German and Italian prisoners of war. As happened in the previous conflict, women also worked in the heavy industries: the Rolls Royce complex at Hillington outside Glasgow employed 10,000 women in the construction of aircraft engines for Spitfire and Lancaster warplanes. Dilution remained an issue, although by the time of the Second World War women were permitted to join trade unions and received equal pay. In all those respects the Scottish experience of the second conflict was a mirror image of the First World War with the exception that the demands of 'total war' involved government intervention and direction, with the result that it was very much a British war. However, the Scottish workforce prospered. Annual average wages rose from £86 (around £3,660 in equivalent purchasing power in 2005) in 1938 to £170 (£4,990), in 1944 and the gradual introduction of welfare schemes such as the provision of free milk offset some of the worst effects of food rationing, which lasted well into the post-war period.[36] One great difference was the smaller number of battlefield casualties in the second conflict: of the estimated 260,000 British war deaths, some 10 per cent would have been Scots.[37]

There was another reminder from the past in the shape of the Red Clydesider and former editor of *Forward*, Tom Johnston, the Labour MP for West Stirlingshire, who had faced arrest in 1915 for holding anti-war views but a quarter of a century later was part of the political establishment. At the outbreak of war he was appointed a regional commissioner for civil defence, charged with the responsibility of directing Scotland's air raid precautions, a post he conducted with great vigour and determination. As a result he was given the post of secretary of state for Scotland in February 1941. The British prime minister, Winston Churchill, clearly intended that Johnston should use his name and influence to prevent the kind of industrial unrest that had threatened to hamstring Clydeside during the First World War, and in that respect it was a successful appointment. Although Scotland was not strike-free during the conflict there was no repetition of the events of 1915 and 1916 and Johnston claimed that the loss of working days to strikes in Scotland was less than 1 per cent. During his period in office he ran Scotland almost as a personal fiefdom, imposing state control and introducing a number of welfare reforms, including a forerunner of the National Health Service on Clydeside. Just as importantly, although he was in favour of home rule for Scotland, he was a great supporter of the war effort in a national context and his interventionist approach helped to pave the way for Labour's ambitious plans for post-war reconstruction. Central to Johnston's philosophy was a belief that never again should Scotland be forced to return to the bad old days of unemployment, lack of investment, endemic poverty and social malaise that had followed the First World War. If that earlier conflict had been the war which had been fought to end all war, then the Second World War would be the war which ushered in a brave new world of social justice. Or, as Johnston put it so eloquently in his memoirs, in the unity of the war years lay the strength which should accompany the peace: 'if only we could lift great social crusades like better housing and health from the arena of partisan strife, what magnificent achievements could be ours'.[38] It was a bold vision certainly, but it was also a British vision. However, it stood as a reminder that for all the high hopes Johnston had expressed in *Forward* for the creation of a better and more equable society, Scotland had advanced very little since the heady days of 1919, when everything seemed possible in a land fit for heroes.

Epilogue
The Last of the Old Scots Folk

Almost one hundred years after those slightly hysterical late summer months which saw thousands of Scots volunteering to fight for the rights of another small country – gallant little Belgium – Scotland could almost be another country. The changes are many and varied. Partly they arise from the return of the Scottish parliament which introduced a measure of devolution in 1997 and in so doing changed the Scottish political landscape. Although the reforms were not as wide-ranging as those laid out in the home rule bill which was to have been introduced in 1914, the passing of the Scotland Act was broadly welcomed and allowed Scots to take control of a number of important responsibilities including health, education and the law. Partly, too, the sea change came from the demise of the heavy industries – coal, shipbuilding and engineering – which had made Scotland the power-house of the United Kingdom. Along with the closing of the south Wales coalfields and the shipbuilding yards on the Tyne, the collapse of the industries in the Clyde valley signalled the end of a way of life which was already on its last legs when it went into terminal decline in the 1970s. Attitudes to the armed services have also altered drama-tically. Visitors to Edinburgh Castle might be thrilled or impressed by the building and its associations but it presents a manicured and easily accessible version of Scotland's turbulent history and is no longer the mighty edifice which defied sieges and represented the nation's military traditions. Those soldiers who occasionally mount ceremonial guards are based at Dreghorn or Redford barracks on the city's southern side and the reduced military presence means that the castle is more of a visitor attraction than a strategic necessity. Even the army itself has changed. In 2006, in response to far-reaching defence reforms and to a declining number of Scots willing to join the army, the six remaining Scottish infantry regiments re-formed as The Royal

Regiment of Scotland with a common uniform and cap badge. And as the visitors look north from the ramparts of the castle they will look in vain for any sight of warships in the waters of the Firth of Forth. Rosyth is no longer a naval base, and apart from occasional ships coming in for repair at the privatised dockyard, the naval associations of this historic stretch of water have gone for ever.

How Scotland got to this position is the story of its progress in the so-called 'short' twentieth century, which began in 1914 and ended with the breakdown of Communism and the equally sudden collapse of Cold War confrontation in the century's last decade. That starting point – the summer of 1914 and its grim aftermath when it became clear that things would never be the same again – means that modern Scotland is rooted firmly in the years of the First World War. It is a story of gains and losses, and of some consolidation, but, more than anything else, of change and decay. In common with every other combatant country the deaths of so many young men left a lasting and painful legacy for thousands of Scottish families, especially in the years 1915 and 1916, when Scotland lost its highest number of casualties fighting in the first great battles of attrition on the Western Front. On countless memorials scattered up and down the land their names still have the power to move later generations, telling as they do a tale of young lives lost and the death of hope for those who mourned them. The memorials are particularly poignant in the remoter country areas, where the names of men from the same village, township or farm show the extent of the local suffering. If a Bavarian machine-gunner opened fire on an infantry company whose members came from the same locality in, say, Wester Ross, then the losses would be not only horrific but they would be spread thickly across a small and perhaps fragile community. That is one of the painful hardships which rural Scotland, with its menfolk fighting in tightly-knit regiments with strong local connections, had to bear, although it has to be said that the experience was also repeated in the towns and cities of the Central Belt, especially during the fighting on the Somme in 1916.

'No man outlives the grief of war', wrote the poet William Soutar in 1940 in his poem 'The Permanence of Young Men'. By then he was bedridden with a form of spondylitis contracted when he was demobilised from the Royal Navy at the end of the First World War, and there would be many more in Scotland who shared with him 'a sadness unannulled' as they remembered lost loved ones.[1] One of the great ironies was that while the Scots were fighting for the rights of small nations, the cause of home rule was one of the casualties of the First World War. It became an increasingly remote possibility in the post-war period, in spite of the creation of the National Party of Scotland in 1928 and the lingering clamour for some kind of home rule or independence. With the collapse of the Liberals home rule was doomed and while the Clydeside Independent Labour Party (ILP) members kept the flame alive, they stood little chance of pushing through the measure at Westminster where their English and Welsh Labour colleagues under MacDonald's leadership were more concerned with widening the party's base and winning more votes than the Conservatives. It was one thing to support home rule with fiery patriotism in the familiar ambience of Glasgow Green but it proved another matter at Westminster where the Clydesiders' zest in debate was frequently inspiring but changed nothing. They might have brought straight-talking exuberance into the House of Commons, but they never had any chance of putting into effect Maxton's boast that the atmosphere of Red Clydeside would get the better of Westminster. It was not until 1997 that a Scotland Act allowed the creation of a Scottish parliament with restricted devolved powers and the great 'unfinished business' of 1914 was finally realised.

The slow disappearance of the Liberals left the Conservatives as Labour's main rival; it was the party of empire and middle-class respectability while Labour became entrenched in its industrial heartlands. Gradually the battle-lines became drawn and in succeeding elections seats rarely changed hands as the two parties occupied entrenched positions in what were increasingly the politics of the United Kingdom. That was perhaps the lasting legacy of the war. In the rent strikes and industrial unrest of 1915, 1916 and 1919 Scottish socialist idealism emerged as a dominant and attractive factor in political life. In its leaders there was a moral force and vigour which was distinctly Scottish and rooted in the Covenanting principles of temperance, self-help and a high-minded desire to make the world a better place. For a time it seemed that those values would dominate the emergent Labour Party, but even by the time of their election victory in 1922 it was clear that the ambitions of the Red Clydesiders would be subordinated to the demands of British realpolitik. The decline of the ILP in the 1930s was matched by the decay of a distinctive Scottish socialist way of addressing politics, as their ideals gave way to the cautious middle-of-the-road approach taken by middle England. Even the trade unions began losing their Scottish character and became more British or internationalist in their approach to workers' rights. What bound Labour and the Conservatives, perhaps, was an unbending trust in the strength and importance of the union and a shared belief in modest state intervention: under a Conservative Scottish secretary, Walter Elliott, measures such as the Scottish Special Housing Association and the Scottish National Development Council came into being in the 1930s.

More than anything else, that was the glue which kept Scotland together and which made the union the foundation for all political discourse. It is tempting to wonder what would have happened if the Liberals had realised their home rule aspirations for Scotland and if the war had not hastened the inexorable rise of Labour, the party which came to dominate Scotland and which in time represented a certain type of Scottishness. That experience of war therefore meant that Scotland continued to exist in a kind of limbo as part of the United Kingdom, a country which was also a region, an integral part of a greater national entity which seemed to have no alternative future. That unflattering position would not have surprised the Scots who did the fighting. At the time of joining up and even after 1918 they would have accepted it. In the majority of the letters and diaries written by the young men who marched off to war the modern reader has to search long and hard to find comments which express any kind of nationalist sentiment. The volunteers might have taken fierce pride in being a Royal Scot or a Gordon Highlander and they might have considered themselves to be better than the other mob, but that was tribal and strictly personal. Instead they fought for their country, the United Kingdom, and for the king who ruled it; on a private and personal level they fought for their families, those who were nearest and dearest to them.

During the fighting the Scottish landmass had not been attacked in any appreciable way and apart from the sight of people in uniform and the growing casualty lists in the newspapers or the presence of the navy's battle fleet on the east and north coasts there had been little physical evidence of hostilities. Unlike other equally small European nations such as Belgium or Serbia, armies did not march over Scotland, there were no battles, no destruction of property and no loss of life on home ground from combat or disease; usually it was a case of 'business as usual'. Against the greater numbers of dead produced by the destruction of empires between 1914 and 1918 the Scots fatalities of 148,000 seem modest. The total for the British Empire was 908,371; French casualties were 1,398,000, the Austro–Hungarians lost 1.1 million and the Russians 1, 811,000; German losses amounted to 2,037,000; the Italians lost 578,000 the Turks 804,000 and the Serbs 278,000.[2] Yet the 'war to end wars', as it was soon hopefully known, cast a long shadow over Scotland's development and changed the way it viewed itself as a nation, for scarcely any family had been unaffected by the losses. The novelist Lewis Grassic Gibbon, the pen name of James Leslie Mitchell, captured the post-war mood when the minister of Kinraddie, himself a war veteran, addressed his flock before the unveiling of the local war memorial at the end of the novel *Sunset Song*, which is set in the Mearns, the Lowland farming area of the North-East.

They went quiet and brave from the lands they loved, though seldom of that love might they speak, it was not in them to tell in words of the earth that moved and lived and abided, their life and enduring love. And who knows at the last what memories of it were with them, the springs and winters of this land and the sounds and scents of it that had once been theirs, deep, and with a passion of their blood and spirit, those four who died in France? With them we may say there died a thing older than themselves, these were the Last of the Peasants, the last of the Old Scots folk.[3]

For Gibbon's fictional men of Kinraddie and for many more real Scots who fought in far-off places, it was a curious kind of victory.

Notes

Preface

1. NAS HH31/1/7 Official histories of the War: request from St Andrews Society, Glasgow, that distinction be made between English and British nationalities.
2. Keith Grieves, 'Early Historical Responses to the Great War: Fortesque, Conan Doyle and Buchan', Bond, *First World War and British Military History*, 16–21.

Prologue

1. Hector Maclean, 'Balnaboth 2000' in Royle, *Glens Folk*, 38.
2. Report of the Royal Commission on the Housing of the Industrial Population of Scotland, Rural and Urban (1917), para 1052.
3. Cameron, *Ballad and the Plough*, 11.
4. Baynes, *Morale*, 23.
5. Helen B. Cruickshank, 'Glen Prosen's Postie', Royle, *Glens Folk*, 34–5.

1 Your King and Country Need You: August 1914

1. Alastair J. Durie, 'The First World War and Tourism in Scotland' in *Scotland for the Holidays* (East Linton, 2003), 171–91.
2. L. J. Paterson, *Twelve Hundred Miles for Thirty Shillings* (Edinburgh, 1988), 14.
3. H. J. Hanham, 'The Creation of the Scottish Office 1881–7', *The Juridical Review,* vol. 10, 1965, 209.
4. Devine, *Scottish Nation*, 307–8.
5. Harvie, *No Gods and Precious Few Heroes*, 3–5.
6. Clive H. Lee, 'The Scottish Economy and the First World War' in Macdonald & McFarland, *Scotland and the Great War*, 11–35.
7. Kenefick & McIvor, *Roots of Red Clydeside?*, 37.
8. Bridie, *One Way of Living*, 190.
9. Charles Oakley, *The Second City* (London and Glasgow, 1946), 269.

10. Donaldson, *Language of the People*, 10.
11. Michael Lynch, 'Scottish Cultural History in its Historical Perspective' in Scott, *Scotland: A Concise Cultural History*, 35.
12. Barr, *Home Service*, 14.
13. Murray, *Hamewith*, 70.
14. Brown & Meehan, *Scapa Flow*, 228.
15. Jack, in Terraine (ed.), *General Jack's Diary*, 21
16. McConachie, *Student Soldiers*, 11.
17. Ibid., 12.
18. Rule, *Students under Arms*, 220.
19. *Scotsman*, 5 August 1914.
20. NAS HH31/2/10 German Vessels detained in Scottish Ports, August 1914.
21. Munro, *The Brave Days*, 319–20.
22. John Buchan, prefatory note in *Poems of Neil Munro*, 5.
23. Ibid., 59–60.
24. NAS GD 326/24/1 Morton of Darvel Papers.
25. *Forward*, 13 August 1914.
26. Sorley, *Letters*, 220–21.
27. Barr, *Home Service*, 14.
28. R. B. Haldane, *An Autobiography* (London, 1929), 297.
29. *Scotsman*, 12 August 1914.
30. Cameron, *Muster Roll of the Manse*, introduction.
31. Cooper, *Domi Militiaeque*, 5; Lyn Macdonald, *Voices and Images*, 27; Stewart & Buchan, *Fifteenth Scottish Division*, 3.
32. Chalmers, *Saga of Scotland*, 5; *Glasgow Herald*, 5 September 1914
33. Alexander, *McCrae's Battalion*, 54–90.
34. Corbett & Newbolt, *Naval Operations*, vol. v, Appendix J; General Annual Report of the British Army; Raleigh and Jones, *War in the Air*, appendices 35–6.
35. NAS HH 31/1/1 Records of the Scottish Home and Health Department. Suspicion aroused by Ordnance Survey officials at Dalwhinnie: police reports and correspondence.
36. NAS HH31/5/1 Dissemination of false news: report that Lord Lieutenant of Kincardine had been spreading news that the British Expeditionary Force had been annihilated.
37. NAS GD 124/15/1852/1–2 Mar and Kellie Muniments.

2   The Flower of Scotland

1. John Keegan, *Six Armies in Normandy* (London, 1983), 168.
2. Stephen Wood, *The Scottish Soldier* (Manchester, 1987), 41.
3. General Annual Report of the British Army 1913–1919; Henderson, *Highland Soldier*, 44.

4. *Journal of the Royal United Services Institution*, August 1903; Devine, *Scottish Nation*, 346.
5. Peter Corstorphine in MacDougall, *Voices from War*, 2.
6. Ibid., 6.
7. Strachan, *First World War*, vol. i, 159.
8. Correlli Barnett, *Britain and Her Army* (London, 1970), 278.
9. Baynes, *Morale*, 20.
10. NA WO 95 Part I, War Diaries, 1st, 2nd, 3rd, 5th Divisions.
11. Edmonds, *Official History 1914*, vol. i, 11.
12. Baynes, *Morale*, 168.
13. Robert Leggat, 'How it was in the Army' in *Covenanter*, February 1963, 82.
14. Ernest Parker, *Into Battle* (London, 1994), 12–13.
15. Henderson, *Highland Soldier*, 128; Robert Graves, *Goodbye to All That* (London, 1929), 131; Eric Linklater, *Magnus Merriman* (London, 1934), 52.
16. Reith, *Wearing Spurs*, 17; Ewing, *Royal Scots*, vol. i, 3–11; Ian S. Wood, 'Be Strong and of Good Courage: Royal Scots' Territorial Battalions from 1908 to Gallipoli' in MacDonald and McFarland, *Scotland and the Great War*, 108
17. Bill Hanlan in MacDougall, *Voices from War*, 13.
18. Brown, *First World War*, 35.
19. NA WO 95/1266 War Diary 1/14th London Regiment (London Scottish); Macdonald *1914*, 397–400.
20. Paterson, *Pontius Pilate's Bodyguard*, vol. i, 417–22.
21. NA WO 95/1717 War Diary 2nd Scottish Rifles; Jack, *Diary*, 22–4.
22. Anon., A Soldier's Diary of the Great War, RHQ Royal Scots, 9–10.
23. Paterson, *Pontius Pilate's Bodyguard*, vol. i, 245.
24. Edmonds, *Official History 1914*, vol. i, 87, 415–27.
25. NA WO 95/1423 War Diary 2nd Royal Scots.
26. Gillon, *KOSB in the Great War*, 36.
27. NA WO 95/1421 War Diary 1st Gordon Highlanders; Edmonds, *Official History 1914*, vol.i, 187–8.
28. Macdonald, *1914*, 417–41.
29. Buchan, *History of the Royal Scots Fusiliers*, 308–09.
30. NA WO 95/1263 War Diary 1st Scots Guards.
31. Macdonald, *1914*, 46–7.
32. Strachan, *First World War*, vol. i, 278.

3   First Blood: Neuve Chapelle, Aubers Ridge and Loos 1915

1. Sir George Arthur, *Life of Lord Kitchener* (London, 1920), vol. iii, 329.
2. C. E. Callwell, *Field Marshal Sir Henry Wilson: His Life and Diaries* (London, 1927), vol. i, 178.

3. Jackson, *Memoir*, 17.
4. Stewart & Buchan, *Fifteenth Scottish Division*, 7.
5. Jackson, *Memoir*, 28.
6. Rule, *Students under Arms*, 13.
7. Findlay, *With the 8th Scottish Rifles*, 10; Stewart and Buchan, *Fifteenth Scottish Divison*, 5.
8. McConachie, *Student Soldiers*, 33.
9. Ibid., 38–40
10. *Blackwood's Magazine*, June 1915.
11. Hay, *First Hundred Thousand*, 15.
12. Samuel Hynes, *A War Imagined: The First World War and English Culture* (London, 1990), 48–9.
13. Russell, *Diary*, 6.
14. Ibid., 10.
15. Ewing, *Royal Scots*, vol. i, 70–1.
16. Buchan, *History*, vol. iv, 81; Baynes, *Morale*, 255.
17. NA WO 95/1715 War Diary 2nd Scottish Rifles.
18. Baynes, *Morale*, 82.
19. NA WO 95/3948 War Diary 4th Black Watch; *Courier and Argus*, 24 February 1915.
20. Joseph Lee, 'The Green Grass' in *Dundee Advertiser*, 6 August 1915.
21. Ewing, *9th Division*, 60.
22. Sheffield & Bourne (eds), *Haig Diary*, 20 June 1915, 128.
23. Sheffield & Bourne (eds), *Haig Diary*, 17 August 1915, 136.
24. Sheffield & Bourne (eds), *Haig Diary*, 19 August 1915, 137.
25. John Charteris, *At GHQ* (London, 1931), 112.
26. Eric and Andro Linklater, *The Black Watch* (London, 1977), 144.
27. Terraine, *Haig*, 159.
28. Jackson, *Memoir*, 45–6.
29. Jack, *Diary*, 108.
30. *Alma Mater*, February 1917.
31. Russell, *Diary*, 35.
32. Stewart & Buchan, *Fifteenth Scottish Division*, 34.
33. Jackson, *Memoir*, 48.
34. Captain G. C. Wynne, *If Germany Attacks: The Battle in Depth in the West* (London, 1940), 77.
35. NA WO 95/1954 War Diary, 10th Scottish Rifles.
36. Hay, *First Hundred Thousand*, 47.
37. The total number of casualties from Scottish regiments on the memorial is 5,475. Appendices to Ewing, *9th Scottish Division*, and Stewart and Buchan, *Fifteenth Scottish Division*; Buchanan-Smith, *The Gordon Highlanders, Loos and Buzancy*, 17.
38. NA WO 95/1421 War Diary 4th Gordon Highlanders.
39. Sorley, *Collected Poems*, 91.

40. Catriona M. M. Macdonald, 'May 1915: Race, Riot and Representa-
    tions of War' in Macdonald and McFarlane, *Scotland and the Great
    War*, 151–4; Phillip Knightley, *The First Casualty: The War Correspon-
    dent as Hero, Propagandist and Mythmaker* (London, 1975), 80–1.
41. Inverness Courier, *Cameron Highlanders*, 14.
42. Keegan, *First World War*, 218; Inverness Courier, *Cameron High-
    landers*, 23.
43. Jackson, *Memoir*, 51.
44. Edmonds, *Official History 1915*, vol. ii, 265.
45. Stewart and Buchan, *Fifteenth Scottish Division*, 49–50.

4   End of Innocence: The Somme 1916, Arras 1917

1. Buchan, *History*, vol. iii, 452.
2. NA PRO 30/57/50 Kitchener Papers, Haig to Kitchener, 29
   September 1915.
3. Masefield to his wife, 21 October 1916 in Peter Vansittart, *John
   Masefield's Letters from the Front 1915–1917*, (London, 1984), 191.
4. Gerard de Groot, 'Douglas Haig, the Reverend George Duncan and
   the Conduct of the War 1916–1918' in Norman Macdougall, *Scotland and War AD76–1918* (Edinburgh, 1991).
5. NA WO 33/721–725 Tactical Notes, (GHQ).
6. NA WO 95/1715 War Diary 2nd Scottish Rifles, Special Order to
   23rd Brigade.
7. Quoted in Denis Winter, *Haig's Command*, 45.
8. Alexander, *McCrae's Battalion*, 306, note 39.
9. Tait, *Stones in the Millpond*, 43; Chalmers, *Saga of Scotland*, 32; Jack,
   Diary, 143; Russell, *Diary*, 39.
10. Macdonald, *Somme*, 68.
11. Edmonds, *Official History 1916*, vol. i, 492–3.
12. *Scotsman*, 15 December 1919.
13. Captain R. B. Ross, *The Fifty-first in France* (London, 1918), 221.
14. Bewsher, *51st Highland Division*, 80–5.
15. Brown, *First World War*, 61.
16. Bewsher, *51st Highland Division*, 105.
17. Ibid., 126.
18. Edmonds, *Official History 1916*, vol. ii, 514.
19. Chalmers, *Saga of Scotland*, 57.
20. Edmonds, *Official History 1916*, vol. ii, 522.
21. NA WO 95/2403 War Diary 16th Highland Light Infantry; Chal-
    mers, *Saga of Scotland*, 67.
22. The most trenchant argument is contained in Paddy Griffith, *Battle
    Tactics of the Western Front: The British Army's Art of Attack 1916–1918*
    (London, 1994), 62–78

23. Ewing, *9th Division*, 142.
24. Mackintosh, *War, the Liberator*, 25–6.
25. NA WO 95/2431 War Diary 9th Highland Light Infantry; *Memoir of Lieutenant-Colonel John Collier Stormonth Darling*, (Kilmarnock 1923), 20.
26. NA WO 95/2865 War Diary 8th Argyll and Sutherland Highlanders; William Murray in Macdougall, *Voices from War*, 92–3; Gordon Irving, *Great Scot! The Life of Sir Harry Lauder* (London, 1968), 88–91.
27. Paterson, *Pontius Pilate's Bodyguard*, vol. i, 317.
28. Stewart & Buchan, *Fifteenth Scottish Division*, 115.
29. NA WO 95/1773 War Diary 12th Royal Scots; Ewing, *9th Scottish Division*, 197.
30. NA WO 95/2458 War Diary 16th Royal Scots.
31. De Groot, *Haig*, 312; WO95/362, HQ Third Army, April 1917.
32. Anthony Clayton, *Paths of Glory: The French Army of 1914–18* (London, 2003), 130–5.
33. Bewsher, *51st Highland Division*, 163.
34. Ibid., 186.
35. Ewing, *9th Scottish Division*, 205.
36. Edmonds, *Official History 1917*, vol. i, 509–16; Stewart and Buchan, *Fifteenth Scottish Division*, 212; Bewsher, *51st Highland Division*, 174.
37. Jackson, *Memoir*, 133.
38. Lawson, *Cameronian Officer*, 113.

5 Battles Far Away: Gallipoli, Mesopotamia, Salonika and Palestine

1. Holmes, *Tommy*, 13–5.
2. David Lloyd George, *War Memoirs*, vol. iii (London, 1934), 1376; Winston Churchill, *The World Crisis*, vol. iii (Part I) (London, 1927), 187.
3. Mackintosh, *War, the Liberator*, 39.
4. NA PRO 30/57/50 Kitchener Papers Kitchener to French, 2 January 1915.
5. NA CAB 22/1, Meeting of the War Council, 13 January 1915.
6. Hamilton, *Gallipoli Diaries*, vol. i, 2; Aspinall-Oglander, quoted in James, *Gallipoli*, 53.
7. NA CAB 19/3 Kitchener Papers, Kitchener to Hamilton, 19 March 1915.
8. Ibid., 23 March 1915.
9. Hamilton, *Gallipoli Diaries*, vol. i, 96.
10. Quoted in Steel and Hart, *Defeat at Gallipoli*, 108.

11. Aspinall–Oglander, *Military Operations – Gallipoli*, vol. i , 214–15.
12. NA WO 95/4321 War Diary 7th Royal Scots; Thompson, *Fifty-Second (Lowland) Division*, 8.
13. NA WO 95/4321 War Diary 4th Royal Scots, War Diary 7th Royal Scots.
14. *Evening Dispatch*, 8 July 1915.
15. IWM SR 8342, Alexander Burnett, 4th Royal Scots Fusiliers.
16. IWM SR 8325, George Waugh, 1/4th King's Own Scottish Borderers.
17. Mackenzie, *Gallipoli Memories*, 373.
18. Thompson, *Fifty-Second (Lowland) Division*, 240.
19. NA WO 95/4321 War Diary 4th Royal Scots.
20. Aspinall–Oglander, *Military Operations – Gallipoli*, vol. ii , 486.
21. Iain Fraser Grigor, 'Gallipoli' in Kay, *Odyssey, the Second Collection*, 45–56.
22. R. W. F. Johnstone, 'Some Experiences of the Great War', unpublished material quoted in Paterson, *Pontius Pilate's Bodyguard*, vol. i, 293.
23. Palmer, *Gardeners of Salonika*, 62.
24. Alan Bold (ed.), *The Letters of Hugh MacDiarmid* (London, 1984), 16.
25. Interview with Sheila Duffy, November 1975, quoted in ibid., 95.
26. NA WO 95/4870 War Diary 10th Black Watch.
27. NA CAB 45/3 Milne to War Office, 17 May 1917.
28. Wakefield & Moody, *Under the Devil's Eye*, 99.
29. Philip Mason, *A Matter of Honour: An Account of the Indian Army, Its Officers and Men* (London, 1974) 434–41.
30. NA WO 95/5138 War Diary 2nd Black Watch.
31. Anon, *With a Highland Regiment*, 41; Brigadier-General A. G. Wauchope, 'The Battle Beyond Baghdad', *Blackwood's Magazine*, August 1917.
32. Lawrence James, *Imperial War*, 129–35.
33. Young, *With the 52nd Lowland Division*, 36.
34. NA WO 95/4608 War Diary 5th King's Own Scottish Borderers.
35. Lawrence James, *Imperial War*, 175.
36. *Scotsman*, 5 July 1915.
37. Private William Begbie, unpublished diary, quoted in Paterson, *Pontius Pilate's Bodyguard*, vol. i, 282–83.
38. *Broughton Magazine*, Christmas 1917, quoted in Alan Bold (ed.), *The Letters of Hugh MacDiarmid* (London, 1984), 17–18.
39. Young, *Forgotten Scottish Voices*, 46–60.
40. Thompson, *Fifty-Second (Lowland) Division*, 507.

6   The Land, the Sea and the Clash of the Battle Fleets

1. McShane, *No Mean Fighter*, 83.
2. Macdonald, *Voices and Images of the Great War*, 263–4; Jackson, *Memoir*, 121.
3. Reith, *Wearing Spurs*, 209; Trevor Royle, *Awa' for a Sojer: A History of the Scottish Soldier*, BBC Radio Scotland, July 1986.
4. Lauder, *Minstrel in France*, 100–6.
5. Bill Hanlan in Macdougall, *Voices from War*, 20–1.
6. NA WO71/444 Judge Advocate General, Field General Courts Martial.
7. Bill Hanlan in Macdougall, *Voices from War*, 20–1.
8. NA MUN 5/19/221/8 Defence of the Realm Consolidation Act, 27 November 1914.
9. NAS HH31/28 Recruiting, appeals tribunals, conscientious objectors, agricultural workers 1915–1924.
10. Murray, *Hamewith*, 83.
11. Paul Kennedy, *The Rise and Fall of British Naval Mastery* (London, 1976), 241.
12. Admiralty Weekly Orders 398/16 and 1943/16.
13. John Arbuthnot Fisher, *Memories and Records* (London, 1920), vol. i, 193.
14. Massie, *Castles of Steel*, 414–6.
15. Sir Roger Keyes, *Naval Memoirs* (London, 1934), vol. i, 163.
16. Trevor Royle, 'Something in the Army' in Morrice McCrae (ed.), *The New Club: A History* (Edinburgh, 2005), 98.
17. Filson Young, *With the Battle Cruisers* (London, 1921), 113.
18. James Morris, *Pax Britannica: Climax of an Empire* (London, 1968), 425.
19. Gordon, *Rules of the Game*, 27–34.
20. Alistair C. McLaren, 'Remembering the old Watson's: Edinburgh's First Air Raid', *Watsonian*, (Edinburgh, 1987), 27.
21. Cole and Cheeseman, *Air Defence of Britain*, 120–1.
22. NA ADM 137/4069 Submarine Reports: Home Waters, Reports on Enemy Submarine Activity received in NID, 4 May–July 1916.
23. Gordon, *Rules of the Game*, 65.
24. Marder, *Dreadnought to Scapa Flow*, vol. iii, 47.
25. 'By one who was there', *Scotsman*, 5 June 1916.
26. Marder, *Dreadnought to Scapa Flow*; Hough, *Great War at Sea*; Gordon, *Rules of the Game*; Massie, *Castles of Steel*.
27. Royle, *Kitchener Enigma*, 368–76.
28. Marder, *Dreadnought to Scapa Flow*, vol. iii, 192.
29. Orkney Public Library, OSA1 Orkney Sound Archive, 'First World War Interviews' by Eric Marwick; *Orkney Herald*, 21 June 1916.
30. NA ADM 137/4069 Submarine Reports: Home Waters, Reports on Enemy Submarine Activity received in NID, 1 June 1916.

31. NA ADM 137/3261 Court of Enquiry: Sinking of HMS *Hampshire*, Loss of Earl Kitchener of Khartoum.
32. NA ADM 137/3261 Brock to Jellicoe, 12 June 1916.
33. NA ADM 137/3913 Original History Sheets of U type German submarines U-41–U-80.
34. NA ADM1/7981 Beresford Correspondence 1907.
35. NAS HH31/2/2 Correspondence between Aberdeen Fish Traders Association and Board of Agriculture and Fisheries regarding Admiralty requisitioning of trawlers, 15 September 1914 and 2 October 1914.
36. Director of Naval Construction, Admiralty Trawlers and Drifters 1916–1921, Admiralty Copy 54, July 1922.
37. Jones, Duncan, Conacher & Scott, *Rural Scotland During the War*, 72.
38. Ministry of Defence, UK Defence Today, 'Battle of May Island Remembered', 30 January 2002.
39. John Terraine, *Business in Great Waters: The U-Boat Wars 1915–1945* (London, 1989), 15.
40. Jones, Duncan, Conacher & Scott, *Rural Scotland During the War*, 18–19.
41. David J. Smith, *Action Stations: Military Airfields of Scotland, the North-East and Northern Ireland* (London, 1989).
42. NAS HH31/39 St. Kilda. Damage to buildings due to a bombardment by German Submarines. Details of Damage. Parliamentary questions. Correspondence etc.

7   The Workshop of War

1. Scott & Cunnison, *Industries of the Clyde Valley*, 19; Census of Scotland 1911, vol. i, County Tables, Table XXII.
2. Campbell, *Rise and Fall of Scottish Industry*, 192.
3. NAS HH31/7/1 Liquor control: intemperance in Glasgow.
4. *Glasgow Herald*, 31 December 1907.
5. Johnston, *Beardmore Built*, 41–53; Peebles, *Warship Building on the Clyde*, 68–72.
6. Gordon, *Rules of the Game*, 7–8.
7. Peebles, *Warship Building on the Clyde*, 78–84.
8. Ibid., 89 and Appendix EIII.
9. E. L. Lewis, *The Children of the Unskilled: An Economic and Social Survey* (London, 1924), 9.
10. Johnston, *Beardmore Built*, 98–9; Johnston, *Ships for a Nation*, 141–5.
11. Melling, *Rent Strikes*, 16; McLean, *Legend of Red Clydeside*, 18–9.
12. *Glasgow Herald*, 13 October 1915.
13. *Forward*, 12 June 1915.
14. Finlay, *Modern Scotland*, 12–8; Devine, *Scottish Nation*, 541–2.
15. *Forward*, 9 October 1915.

16. Alan McKinlay, 'Technical Change and Craft Control in Shipbuilding' in Kenefick & McIvor, *Roots of Red Clydeside*, 92–8.
17. The twelve volumes of the History of the Ministry of Munitions were written but never published.
18. Cmd 7439, 7, HM Inspector of Mines for Scotland, 1913 Report.
19. Johnston, *Beardmore Built*, 80–91.
20. *Glasgow Herald*, 30 June 1915.
21. *Whitaker's Almanac for 1920*, (London, 1921), 840.
22. Clive H. Lee, 'The Scottish Economy and the First World War' in Macdonald and McFarland, *Scotland and the Great War*, 27.
23. *Dundee Advertiser*, 8 February 1918.
24. NAS HH31/2/1 Instructions from the Admiralty regarding closing of British ports to neutral fishing vessels, Admiralty to Secretary for Scotland, 28 September 1914; NAS HH31/2/5 Restrictions on fishing in North Sea and effects of fishing industry; effects of mine laying on fishing activities; Clive H. Lee, 'The Scottish Economy and the First World War' in Macdonald and McFarland, *Scotland and the Great War*, 17–9.
25. NAS HH31/2/8 Lists of fishing vessels operating from east coast ports; monitoring of movements of fishing vessels.
26. Newbolt, *Naval Operations*, vol. v, 23.
27. Dan van der Vat, *Stealth at Sea: The History of the Submarine* (London, 1994), 108–15.
28. C. J. K. Campbell, Proposal for a Maritime, Army and Airforce Museum in Balivanich, September 2004. Private consultation document.
29. *Glasgow Herald*, 31 December 1914.
30. *Scotsman*, 17 October 1916.
31. NAS HH 31/24/1 Departmental Committee on Food Production (Scotland) Report, July 1915.
32. Jones, Duncan, Conacher & Scott, *Rural Scotland During the War*, 143.
33. Ibid, 172.
34. 'Scottish Agriculture During the War' in *Transactions of the Highland and Agricultural Society* (xxxi) 1919.
35. Morrice McCrae, *The New Club: A History*, (Edinburgh, 2005), 96.
36. Jones, Duncan, Conacher & Scott, *Rural Scotland During the War*, 179–81.
37. Smout, *Century of the Scottish People*, 133–48.
38. Charles McMaster, 'The Gothenburg Experiment in Scotland' in *Scottish Labour History Review*, no. 3, Winter 1989, 4–6.
39. NAS HH31/7/6 Liquor traffic: resolutions from various organisations regarding prohibition and restriction of sale of alcoholic liquor.
40. NAS HH31/7/2 Intoxicating liquor: requests for introduction of prohibition; prohibition in Royal Household.

41. NAS HH31/7/5 Liquor traffic: consumption of intoxicating liquor by convalescent soldiers.

8 **Women's Work**

1. Scott and Cunnison, *Industries of the Clyde Valley*, 98.
2. Billy Kay, 'They Fairly Mak Ye Work' in Kay, *Odyssey I*, 38.
3. Devine, *Scottish Nation*, 532–7.
4. Clive H. Lee, 'The Scottish Economy and the First World War' in Macdonald and McFarland, *Scotland and the Great War*, 23.
5. British Association for the Advancement of Science: Credit, Industry and the War (London, 1915), 70–1; NAS HH31/2/5 Restrictions on fishing in North Sea and its effects on the fishing industry.
6. NAS 31/27/3 Civilian Work; Employment of Women; Scottish Committee on Substitutory Labour; Conditions of Clerical Employment Committee; Chartered Accountancy; Business and Commercial Occupations; Local Committees; Exemption of Accountants; Central Advisory Committee for Women's Employment; Braybon, *Women Workers in the First World War*, 45–6.
7. Andrews, *The Economic Effects of the World War upon Women and Children in Great Britain*, 33.
8. *Ministry of Labour Gazette*, September 1924; *Glasgow Herald*, 24 February 1916.
9. Georgine Clarsen, 'A Fine University for Women Engineers: A Scottish Munitions Factory in World War I' in *Women's History Review*, vol. xii, no. 3, 2003; Margaret Brooks, 'Women in Munitions 1914–1918: the Oral Record' in *Imperial War Museum Review*, no. 5, 1990; Devil's Porridge Museum, Eastriggs, Gretna.
10. *The Times*, 29 November 1916.
11. Rebecca West, 'The Cordite Makers' in Jane Marcus (ed.), *The Young Rebecca: Writings of Rebecca West 1911–1917* (London, 1982).
12. NAS HH 31/27/1 Civilian Work; Employment of Women; Scottish Committee on Substitutory Labour; Conditions of Clerical Employment Committee; Chartered Accountancy; Business and Commercial Occupations; Local Committees; Exemption of Accountants; Central Advisory Committee for Women's Employment
13. NAS HH 31/7/7 Central Control Board (Liquor Traffic): proceedings of conference held in Glasgow, 18 January 1916.
14. NAS HH 31/16 Women Patrols, Dangers to Young Girls.
15. Balfour, *Elsie Inglis*, 126.
16. Lesley Scott-Moncrieff, 'High Street, Lawnmarket and West Bow' in David Keir (ed.), *Third Statistical Account of Scotland: Edinburgh* (Glasgow, 1966), 44–6.
17. Leneman, *Guid Cause*, 12.

18. *Forward*, 20 October 1906.
19. *Glasgow Herald*, 11 July 1914; Royle, *Kitchener Enigma*, 247–8.
20. NAS HH 16/46 Criminal Case Files, Frances Gordon (Suffragette).
21. McLaren, *Scottish Women's Hospitals*, 4–7.
22. Crofton, *Women of Royaumont*, 334.
23. NLS Acc 8006, Chisholm Diary, 24 October 1915.
24. Crofton, *Women of Royaumont*, 17.
25. McLaren, *Scottish Women's Hospitals*, 100.
26. Ibid., 153–4.
27. Ishobel Ross, *Little Grey Partridge*: First World War Diary of Ishobel Ross (Aberdeen, 1988), 11; J. De Key Whitsted, *Come to the Cookhouse Door: A VAD in Salonika* (London, 1923), 158.
28. Leneman, *In the Service of Life*, 60.
29. *Scotsman*, 30 November 1917.
30. Elsie Inglis's most recent biographer is Leah Leneman; Margot Lawrence's *Shadow of Swords* deals principally with the Serb years and Eileen Crofton is the historian of the Scottish Women's Hospitals in France.
31. Georgine Clarsen, 'A Fine University for Women Engineers: A Scottish Munitions Factory in World War I' in *Women's History Review*, vol. xii, no. 3, 2003, 347.
32. Leneman, *Guid Cause*, 214.

9   Red Clydeside and Opposing Armageddon

1. Harvie, *No Gods and Precious Few Heroes*, 23; McLean, *Legend of Red Clydeside*, 239.
2. James Hinton's review of the first edition of Iain McLean's *Legend of Red Clydeside* in *Albion*, 17, 1985. It is quoted at greater length in the introduction to the revised edition, p. xx.
3. David Kirkwood, *My Life of Revolt* (London, 1935), 82; *Glasgow Herald*, 11 November 1915.
4. McLean, *Legend of Red Clydeside*, 38. Professor McLean noted that the engineers' resolution had 'a Covenanting tone all right', *Sunday Herald*, 30 January 2000.
5. Ibid, 44–5.
6. Charlie McPherson in MacDougall, *Voices from War*, 37.
7. *Vanguard*, November 1915.
8. George Lansbury, *My Life* (London, 1928), 94–6.
9. *Glasgow Herald*, 27 December 1915; *Forward*, 1 January 1916.
10. NAS HH31/5/2 *Forward* socialist newspaper: copies forwarded to Lord Advocate with expression of concern as to anti-war sentiment contained in some articles.
11. NAS HH31/5/6 *Forward* socialist newspaper: report of discussion

in House of Commons regarding its suppression; *Scotsman*, 5 January 1916.

12. *Glasgow Herald*, 30 December 1915.
13. NAS HH31/5/7 *Forward* socialist newspaper: letters protesting against its suppression.
14. Myra Baillie, 'A New View of Dilution: Women Munitions Workers and Red Clydeside' in *Scottish Labour History Journal*, vol. xxxix, 2004, 32.
15. *Scotsman*, 13 April 1915.
16. *Glasgow Herald*, 15 April 1915.
17. McLean, *Legend of Red Clydeside*, 84.
18. *Glasgow Herald*, 13 April 1916.
19. Broom, *John Maclean*, 85.
20. NAS HH31/22 Munitions tribunals; Glasgow Shipwrights; Munitions of War Act; Forms; Arrest and Deportation of Clyde Workers.
21. Kirkwood, *My Life of Revolt*, (London, 1935), 168.
22. Smout, *Century of Scottish People*, 267.
23. Trial report, *Scotsman*, 10 May 1918.
24. NAS HH16/125/1–4 Prison Commission and daily medical reports on artificial feeding; complaints and protests against forced feeding.
25. NAS HH31/29 Lists of Conscientious Objectors in Civil Custody; James Maxton.
26. NLS Acc 4251/3 Agnes Maclean to Scottish Secretary, 5 November 1918.
27. NAS HH16/125/2 Prison Commission and daily medical reports on artificial feeding; complaints and protests against forced feeding.
28. Dora Montefiori, *From a Victorian to a Modern* (London, 1927), 201.
29. William H. Marwick in MacDougall, *Voices from War*, 51.
30. NA WO95/85, War Diary, Director of Labour, 4 March 1917.
31. NAS HH31/29 Lists of Conscientious Objectors in Civil Custody; William Kenefick, 'War Resisters and Anti-Conscription in Scotland: An ILP Perspective' in Macdonald and McFarland, *Scotland and the Great War*, 66–7.
32. J. P. M. Miller in MacDougall, *Voices from War*, 62–7.
33. Eric F. Dott in MacDougall, *Voices from War*, 80–1.
34. John W. Graham, *Conscription and Conscience: A History 1916–1919* (London, 1921), 240–1.
35. NAS HH31/29 Employment of Conscientious Objectors at Dyce by National Road Board; *Aberdeen Free Press*, 12 September 1916.
36. Rupert Hart-Davis (ed.), *Siegfried Sassoon Diaries 1915–1918* (London, 1983), 176.
37. *The Times*, 31 July 1917.
38. Rupert Hart-Davis (ed.), *Siegfried Sassoon Diaries 1915–1918* (London, 1983), 176.
39. NA MH106/1887 Craiglockhart Military Hospital, British Expedi-

tionary Force to France, Officers 1916, October 27 1917–November 1917.

40. Rupert Hart-Davis (ed.), *Siegfried Sassoon Diaries 1915–1918* (London, 1983), 183–94.

41. Pat Barker's novel *Regeneration* (London, 1991) is a good example.

42. W. H. R. Rivers, *Conflict and Dream* (London, 1923), 168.

43. NA MH106/1887 Craiglockhart Military Hospital, British Expeditionary Force to France, Officers 1916, October 27 1917–November 1917.

44. Rupert Hart-Davis (ed.), *Siegfried Sassoon Diaries 1915–1918* (London, 1983), 220.

10   Haig: Architect of Victory 1918

1. Sheffield & Bourne (eds), *Haig Diary*, 18 March 1918, 388.

2. Edmonds, *Official History 1918*, vol. i, 258.

3. NA WO95/2879 War Diary 7th Black Watch.

4. Baynes, *Morale*, 21–2.

5. NA WO95/1911 War Diary HQ 15th (Scottish) Division.

6. NA WO95/1953 War Diary 7/8th King's Own Scottish Borderers.

7. NA WO95/1954 War Diary 9th Royal Scots.

8. Lambert Diary in Paterson, *Pontius Pilate's Bodyguard*, vol. i, 358–9.

9. Ewing, *9th Division*, 279.

10. Jackson, *Diary*, 154.

11. Edmonds, *Official History 1918*, vol. ii, 460–1.

12. NA WO95/1944 War Diary 11th Argyll and Sutherland Highlanders.

13. Sheffield & Bourne (eds), *Haig Diary*, 3 April 1918, 397.

14. NA WO95/2612 War Diary 14th Highland Light Infantry.

15. Charles Messenger, *Call to Arms: The British Army 1914–1918* (London, 2005), 271–2.

16. Buchanan-Smith, *The Gordon Highlanders, Loos and Buzancy*, 17.

17. Terraine, *Haig*, 432–3.

18. NA WO95/2844 War Diary HQ 51st (Highland) Division.

19. Alexander, *McCrae's Battalion*, 254.

20. Jack, *Diary*, 245–59.

21. Ewing, *9th Division*, 293.

22. Sheffield, *Forgotten Victory*, 194.

23. Bewsher, *51st Highland Division*, 323.

24. Erich von Ludendorff, *My War Memories*, (London, 1919), vol. ii, 679.

25. Haig to Lady Haig, 8 August 1918 in Sheffield and Bourne (eds.), *Haig Diary*, 440–1

26. Sheffield and Bourne (eds), *Haig Diary*, 21 August 1918, 448.

27. Ibid., 3 April 1918.

28. Ibid., 1 September 1918, 452–3.

29. John J. Pershing, *My Experiences in the World War* (New York, 1931), vol. ii, 272.

30. Stewart & Buchan, *Fifteenth Scottish Division*, 262.

31. Jackson, *Diary*, 186.

32. Ewing, *9th Division*, 382.

33. Thompson, *Fifty-Second (Lowland) Division*, 572.

34. Stewart and Buchan, *Fifteenth Scottish Division*, 277; Fraser, *In Good Company*, 333; Sheffield and Bourne (eds.), *Haig Diary*, 11 November 1918, 486

35. Haig to Sir Clive Wigram, 1 December 1919, Sheffield and Bourne (eds.), *Haig Diary*, 490.

36. John Laffin, *British Butchers and Bunglers of World War One*, (Gloucester, 1988), 168.

37. Haig, Final Despatch, 21 March 1919 in Sheffield and Bourne (eds), *Haig Diary*, 523.

38. Gary Sheffield, 'John Terraine as Military Historian', *Journal of the Royal United Services Institute*, vol. 149. no.2, April 2004, 70–5.

39. NA PRO 30/57/66 Instructions of the Secretary of State for War to the General Commanding-in-Chief, British Forces in France, 28 December 1915.

40. Sheffield & Bourne (eds.), *Haig Diary*, 31 March 1917, 42–3.

11 A Bitter Hairst: The Reckoning

1. *Scotsman*, 12 November 1918; *Glasgow Herald*, 12 November 1918; *Punch*, 13 November 1918; *Shetland Times*, 16 November 1918.

2. Paterson, *Pontius Pilate's Bodyguard*, vol. i, 379–85.

3. *Journal of the American Medical Association*, 28 December 1918.

4. *Glasgow Herald*, 17 July 1918.

5. NA ADM116/1869 Case 693 contains the evidence cited during the Court of Inquiry into the loss of HM Yacht *Iolaire*.

6. Finlay, *Modern Scotland*, 36; Harvie, *No Gods and Precious Few Heroes*, 24.

7. Information from Lieutenant-Colonel Ian Shepherd, the Scottish National War Memorial, 4 May 2005: 'We currently have 148,218 records, but I make two provisos: 1. I add several names each year as a result of information provided by families. I will be adding an Australian Scot and a Canadian Scot shortly. 2. In some instances an individual's name can appear in more than one Roll and I do not know whether the computer counts this as two people. 3. The figure includes Scots from around the world "killed in the service of the Crown" . . . we have Rolls of Honour for Australian, Canadian,

Indian, New Zealand and South African forces as well as for men in English etc regiments.'

8. Ferguson, *Pity of War*, 298.

9. Finlay, *Modern Scotland*, 36–7; Winter, *Great War*, 94–5.

10. Cameron, *Muster Roll of the Manse*, 137; J. M. Winter, *Great War*, 94.

11. NAS GD372/87/12 Waring of Lennel Papers.

12. Alexander, *McCrae's Battalion*, appendices 3 & 5.

13. Commonwealth War Graves Commission, *Gone But Not Forgotten: The Commemoration of Rugby Players Who Died in the Two World Wars* (October 2002).

14. Peter Savage, *Lorimer and the Edinburgh Crafts Designers* (Edinburgh, 1980), 134–5.

15. Cmd 279, 1922 Proposals for Scottish National War Memorial.

16. *Scotsman*, June 1919.

17. Peter Savage, *Lorimer and the Edinburgh Crafts Designers* (Edinburgh, 1980), 145.

18. Ian Hay, *Their Name Liveth*, 100.

19. Sorley, *Collected Poems*, 68–9.

20. Sorley, *Letters*, 305–6.

21. MacKintosh, *War, the Liberator*, 15.

22. NA WO95/2866 War Diary 5th Seaforths; Campbell and Green, *Can't Shoot a man with a Cold*, 120–33.

23. Alan MacGillivray, 'Land of Brave Men: Scottish Poetry of the First World War' in *Laverock*, no. 3 (Association for Scottish Literary Studies, 1997).

24. Colin Milton, 'Modern Poetry in Scots before MacDiarmid' in Cairns Craig (ed.) *History of Scottish Literature* (Edinburgh, 1987–88), vol. iv.

25. Salmond, *The Old Stalker and Other Poems*, 87–8.

26. Hugh MacDiarmid, *Complete Poems* (London, 1978) vol. i, 450.

27. Alan Bold (ed.), *The Letters of Hugh MacDiarmid* (London, 1984), 101–2.

28. *Scottish Chapbook*, vol. i, no. 3, October 1922.

29. Gibbon, *Scots Quair*, 191–4; Calder, *Meditations on Memorials*, 7–10.

30. NA WO 141/37 Inquiry into the Circumstances of Surrender, 1st Bn Gordon Highlanders on 27 August 1914.

31. *Dundee Advertiser*, 16 July 1919.

32. NA WO 141/38 Inquiry into the Circumstances of Surrender, 1st Bn Gordon Highlanders on 27 August 1914.

33. Tait, *Stones in the Mill Pond*, 48.

34. John A. Lister, *Sixty Years On: The History of the Royal British Legion Scotland* (Edinburgh, 1982), 7–14.

35. Winter, *Great War*, 256.

36. Lauder, *A Minstrel in France*, 74.

12 Aftermath

1. Finlay, *Modern Scotland*, 54.
2. *Forward*, December 1918.
3. Labour Party, Scottish Council, Report of Fifth Annual Conference (Glasgow, 1919), 20.
4. R. J. Morris, 'Skilled Workers and the Politics of "Red" Clyde' in *Journal of Scottish Labour History*, no. 18, 1983.
5. McShane, *No Mean Fighter*, 94.
6. McLean, *Legend of Red Clydeside*, 112–7.
7. CAB23/9 War Cabinet, 31 January 1919.
8. *Glasgow Herald*, 19 April 1919.
9. *Daily Record* and *Glasgow Herald*, 1 February 1919.
10. Devine, *Scottish Nation*, 314.
11. Milton, *John Maclean*, 219.
12. Quoted in Broom, *John Maclean*, 156.
13. *Forward*, 18 May 1918.
14. Hugh MacDiarmid, 'John Maclean' in *Complete Poems*, vol. i , 485–7; Sorley MacLean, 'The Clan Maclean' in *Spring Tide and Neap Tide: Selected Poems* (Edinburgh, 1977); Hamish Henderson's 'The John Maclean March' was first sung at the John Maclean Memoiral Meeting in St Andrew's Hall, Glasgow on 28 November 1948.
15. John Maclean's speech from the dock at the High Court in Edinburgh, 9 May 1918, quoted in various newspapers.
16. Emanuel Shinwell, *Conflict without Malice* (London, 1935), 194–5; John Paton, *Left Turn* (London, 1936), 150.
17. Quoted in Gordon Brown, *Maxton* (Edinburgh, 1986), 161.
18. *Sunday Herald*, 30 January 2000.
19. Wood, *John Wheatley*, 145.
20. Harvie, *No Gods and Precious Few Heroes*, 40.
21. Report of the Scottish Liberal Land Inquiry Committee 1927–1928 (Glasgow, 1928), 311.
22. Ibid., 2–6.
23. Lewis Grassic Gibbon, 'The Land' in *A Scots Hairst: Essays and Short Stories* (London, 1967), 77.
24. *Stornoway Gazette*, 28 November 1919.
25. NAS AF 67/268 Hebrides: Distress: Relief and Development Schemes, Lewis. Administration of landward part of Lewis Estate of public trust. Lord Leverhulme's proposals.
26. Quoted in Donald Macdonald, *Lewis: A History of the Island* (Edinburgh, 1978), 179.
27. NAS AF 67/252, Hebrides: Distress: Relief and Development Schemes, Memorandum on Lewis, 28 October 1920.
28. NAS AF 67/255 Hebrides: Distress: Relief and Development

Schemes, Land Question in Lewis and Harris. Lord Leverhulme's schemes. Miscellaneous representations, resolutions, etc.

29. Hunter, *Making of the Crofting Community*, 205.
30. NAS AF 67/278 Hebrides: Distress: Relief and Development Schemes Lewis. Reef Township. Road.
31. William Bolitho, *The Cancer of Empire* (London, 1924), 17.
32. Bruce Marshall, *The Black Oxen* (London, 1972), 15–6.
33. Roddy Martine, 'The New Club and Scotland's Aristocracy' in Morrice McCrae, *The New Club: A History*, (Edinburgh, 2005), 71.
34. *Daily Record*, 23 October 1931.
35. Muir, *Scottish Journey*, 243–4.
36. Devine, *Scottish Nation*, 546–50.
37. John Ellis, *World War II: A Statistical Survey* (Facts on File, 1993).
38. Johnston, *Memories*, 112.

Epilogue: The Last of the Old Scots Folk

1. William Soutar (ed.) W. R. Aitken, *Poems, a New Selection* (Edinburgh, 1988), 40–1.
2. Winter, *Great War*, 75.
3. Gibbon, *Scots Quair*, 192–3.

Bibliography

Official Papers and Records

National Archives, Kew (NA)

ADM 137 Admiralty: Historical Section: Records used for *Official History*, First World War

CAB 3 Committee of Imperial Defence: Home Defence Memoranda (A Series) 1901–1939

CAB 4 Committee of Imperial Defence: Miscellaneous Memoranda (B Series) 1903–1939

CAB 12 Committee of Imperial Defence: Minutes of the Home Ports Defence Committee

CAB 14 Committee of Imperial Defence: Air Committee: Minutes and Memoranda (AC and AP series)

CAB 15 Committee of Imperial Defence, Committee on the Co-ordination of Departmental Action on the Outbreak of War, and War Cabinet, War Priorities Committee: Minutes, Papers and War Books

CAB 44 Committee of Imperial Defence, Historical Branch and Cabinet Office, Historical Section: War Histories: Draft Chapters and Narratives, Military, War of 1914–1918

CAB 45 Committee of Imperial Defence, Historical Branch and Cabinet Office, Historical Section: Official War Histories, Correspondence and Papers, War of 1914–1918

MUN 5 Records of the Ministry of Munitions

WO 95 War Diaries 1914–1922: Part I France, Belgium and Germany, Part II Italy, Part III Gallipoli and Dardanelles, Part IV Egypt, Palestine and Syria, Part V Salonika, Macedonia, Turkey, Black Sea and South Russia, Part VI Mesopotamia, Iraq and North Persia

WO 154 First World War Diaries and Quarterly Historical Reports

WO 157 First World War Intelligence Summaries

WO 158 First World War Headquarters Records

WO 161 War Office Miscellaneous Papers First World War

National Archives of Scotland (NAS)

AF 67 Crofting Files
HH 16 Criminal Case Files
HH 31 First World War Files

National Library of Scotland (NLS)

NLS Acc 3155 Haig Papers
NLS Acc 4251 John Maclean Papers
NLS Acc 8006 Mairi Chisholm Papers

Imperial War Museum: Department of Sound Records (IWM)

Published Reports

Defeat at Gallipoli, The Dardanelles Commission 1915–1916, Parts I and II, Cmd. 371
General Annual Reports of the British Army (including the Territorial Force from date of embodiment) 1 October 1914 to 30 September 1919. P.P. 1927, XX, Cmd. 1193
Report of the Royal Commission on the Housing of the Industrial Population of Scotland, Rural and Urban, Edinburgh, 1917, Cmd 8731
War Office: Soldiers Died in the Great War 1914–1919 (War Office, London, 1921): Part 3 The Scots Guards, Part 6 The Royal Scots (Lothian Regiment), Part 26 The Royal Scots Fusiliers, Part 28 The King's Own Scottish Borderers, Part 31 The Cameronians (Scottish Rifles), Part 46 The Black Watch (Royal Highlanders), Part 63 The Highland Light Infantry, Part 64 The Seaforth Highlanders (Ross-shire Buffs, Duke of Albany's), Part 65 The Gordon Highlanders, Part 66 The Queen's Own Cameron Highlanders, Part 70 Princess Louise's (The Argyll and Sutherland Highlanders)

Newspapers and Journals

Aberdeen Daily Journal
Alma Mater (Aberdeen)
Blackwood's Magazine
Courier and Argus (Dundee)
Covenanter
Dundee Advertiser
Evening Dispatch (Edinburgh)

Evening News (Edinburgh)
Forward (Glasgow)
Glasgow Herald
Inverness Courier
Orcadian
Scotsman
Scottish Labour History Journal
Shetland Times
Stornoway Gazette
The Times

Regimental Histories, Personal Accounts and Poetry

Alexander, Jack, *McCrae's Battalion: The Story of the 16th Royal Scots* (Edinburgh, 2003)

Anderson, R. C. B., *History of the Argyll and Sutherland Highlanders, 1st Battalion 1909–1939* (Edinburgh, 1954)

Anon., *With a Highland Regiment in Mesopotamia 1916–1917, by One of its Officers* (Bombay, 1918)

Barber, Gordon, *My Diary in France: Experiences and Impressions of Active Service during a period of the War with the Central Empires: 19 September, 1914–2 November, 1914 : 1 December, 1915–2 June, 1916* (Liverpool, 1917)

Barr, James Craig, *Home Service: The Recollections of a Commanding Officer serving in Great Britain during the War, 1914–1919* (Paisley, 1920)

Baynes, John, *Morale: A Study of Men and Courage* (London, 1967)
& Hugh Maclean, *A Tale of Two Captains* (Haddington, 1990)

Bewsher, F. W., *The History of the 51st (Highland) Division 1914–1918* (Edinburgh, 1921)

Bridie, James, *Some Talk of Alexander* (London, 1926)
One Way of Living (London, 1939)

Brown, Malcolm & Patricia Meehan, *Scapa Flow* (London, 1968)

Buchan, John, *Poems, Scots and English* (Edinburgh and London, 1917)
Mr Standfast (London, 1919)
The History of the Royal Scots Fusiliers 1678–1918 (London, 1925)

Buchanan-Smith, Alick, *The Gordon Highlanders, Loos and Buzancy* (Aberdeen, 1981)

Burns, Robert, *Once a Cameron Highlander: 1914–1919* (Glasgow, 2000)

Campbell, Colin & Rosalind Green, *Can't Shoot a Man with a Cold: Lt E. Alan Mackintosh MC 1893–1917, Poet of the Highland Division* (Glendaruel, 2004)

Chalmers, Thomas, *A Saga of Scotland: History of the 16th Battalion The Highland Light Infantry* (Glasgow, 1931)
An Epic of Glasgow: History of the Fifteenth Battalion The Highland Light Infantry (Glasgow, 1934)

Clarkson, D. R., *Memoirs of a Company Runner: 1914–1918 War* (Edinburgh, 1972)

Cooper, John, *Domi Militiaeque: The Experiences of a Private Soldier during the latter half of the Great War of 1914–1918* (Glasgow, 1982)

Ewing, John, *History of the 9th (Scottish) Division 1914–1919* (London, 1921)

The Royal Scots 1914–1919, 2 vols (Edinburgh, 1925)

Falls, Cyril, *The Gordon Highlanders in the First World War* (Aberdeen, 1958)

Findlay, J. M., *With the 8th Scottish Rifles 1914–1919* (Glasgow, 1926)

Forrester, James & Watson Crawford, eds, *Dunbartonshire men at the Front: The War Diary of the 9th Argyll & Sutherland Highlanders* (Glasgow, 1978)

Fraser, David ed., *In Good Company: the First World War Letters and Diaries of the Hon. William Fraser, Gordon Highlanders* (Salisbury, 1990)

Gibbon, Lewis Grassic, *A Scots Quair: Sunset Song, Cloud Howe, Grey Granite* (London, 1946, reset 1950)

Gillon, Stair, *The KOSB in the Great War* (London, 1930)

Greenhill-Gardyne, A. D., *The Life of a Regiment: The History of the Gordon Highlanders*, vol. IV 1914–1919 (Aberdeen, 1958)

Greig, Robert M., *Doing his Bit: A Shetland Soldier in the Great War*, ed. Alex Cluness (Lerwick, 1999)

Hamilton, General Sir Ian, *Gallipoli Diaries* (London, 1920)

Hay, Ian, *The First Hundred Thousand* (Edinburgh and London, 1916)

Inverness Courier, *The Cameron Highlanders at the Battles at Loos, Hill 70, Fosse 8, & the Quarries* (Inverness, 1924)

Jackson, John, *Private 12768: Memoir of a Tommy* (Stroud, 2004)

Kemp, J. C., *The History of the Royal Scots Fusiliers 1915–1959* (Glasgow, 1963)

Lauder, Harry, *A Minstrel in France* (London, 1918)

Lawson, James Burnett, *A Cameronian Officer: Being a Memoir of Lieutenant James Burnett Lawson, Second Cameronians (Scottish Rifles)* (Glasgow, 1921)

Lee, Joseph, *Ballads of Battle* (London, 1917)

Workaday Warriors (London, 1917)

Lloyd, Mark, *The London Scottish in the Great War* (Barnsley, 2001)

McConachie, John, *The Student Soldiers* (Elgin, 1995)

MacDougall, Ian, ed., *Voices from War: Personal Recollections of War in our Century by Scottish Men and Women* (Edinburgh, 1995)

Mackenzie, Compton, *Gallipoli Memories* (London, 1929)

Mackintosh, Ewart Alan, *A Highland Regiment* (London, 1917)

War, the Liberator (London, 1918)

McShane, Harry, with Joan Young, *No Mean Fighter* (London, 1978)

Morrison, A. D., *7th Battalion, The Argyll and Sutherland Highlanders 1914–1919* (Stirling, n.d.)

Munro, Neil, *The Brave Days* (Edinburgh and London, 1931)

Poems, ed. John Buchan (Edinburgh and London, 1931)

Murray, Charles, *Hamewith: The Complete Poems of Charles Murray* (Aberdeen, 1979)

Paterson, Robert H., *Pontius Pilate's Bodyguard: A History of the First or the Royal Regiment of Foot, The Royal Scots (The Royal Regiment)*, vol I 1633–1918 (Edinburgh, 2000)

Peterkin, Millicent B., *Hospital Barges in France: Correspondence from a Nursing Sister, with the British Expeditionary Force, during World War 1*, ed. Peter L. High (Abernethy, 1997)

Reith, John, *Wearing Spurs* (London, 1966)

Rorie, David, *A Medico's Luck in the War* (Aberdeen, 1929)

Rule, Alexander, *Students Under Arms* (Aberdeen, 1934)

Russell, Jack, *Diary of a Kitchener's Recruit: Being the experience of a Gordon Highlander during the first two years of the Great War, August, 1914, to September, 1916* (Aberdeen, 1916)

Salmond, J. B., *The Old Stalker and Other Poems* (Edinburgh and London, 1936)

Sorley, Charles Hamilton, *Collected Poems*, ed. Jean Moorcroft Wilson (London, 1985)

Letters of Charles Sorley (Cambridge, 1919)

Sotheby, H. G., *The 10th Battalion, Argyll and Sutherland Highlanders 1914–1919* (London, 1931)

Spear, Hilda D., & Bruce Pandrich, *Sword and Pen: Poems of 1915 from Dundee and Tayside* (Aberdeen, 1989)

Stewart, J, & John Buchan, *The Fifteenth (Scottish) Division 1914–1919* (Edinburgh, 1926)

Story, H. H., *The History of the Cameronians (Scottish Rifles) vol. II 1910–1933* (Hamilton, 1961)

Tait, Christian S., *Stones in the Millpond* (Lerwick, 2001)

Thompson, R. R., *The Fifty-Second (Lowland) Division 1914–1918* (Glasgow, 1923)

Wauchope, A. G. ed., *A History of the Black Watch (Royal Highlanders) in the Great War 1914–1918*, 3 vols (London, 1925–26)

Young, Derek, *Forgotten Scottish Voices from the Great War* (Stroud, 2005)

Young, James, *With the 52nd Lowland Division in Three Continents* (Edinburgh, 1920)

Secondary Sources

Scotland

Anthony, Richard, *Herds and Hinds: Farm Labour in Scotland 1900–1939* (East Linton, 1996)

Balfour, Lady Frances, *Dr Elsie Inglis* (London, 1918)

Bold, Alan, *MacDiarmid: A Critical Biography* (London, 1988)

Broom, John, *John Maclean* (Loanhead, 1973)

Calder, Angus, 'Meditations on Memorials' in Angus Calder (ed.) *Disasters and Heroes: On War, Memory and Representation* (Cardiff, 2004).

Cameron, David Kerr, *The Ballad and the Plough: A Portrait of Life in the Old Scottish Ferm Touns* (London, 1978)

Cameron, Duncan, *Muster Roll of the Sons of the Manse 1914–1919* (Edinburgh and Glasgow, 1919)

Campbell, R. H., *The Rise and Fall of Scottish Industry 1707–1939* (Edinburgh, 1980)
  Scotland since 1707: The Rise of an Industrial Society (Edinburgh, 1985)

Crofton, Eileen, *The Women of Royaumont: A Scottish Women's Hospital on the Western Front* (East Linton, 1997)

Devine, T. M., *The Scottish Nation 1700–2000* (London, 2001)

Donaldson, William, *Popular Literature in Victorian Scotland* (Aberdeen, 1986)
  The Language of the People: Scots Prose from the Victorian Revival (Aberdeen, 1989)

Finlay, Richard, *Modern Scotland 1914–2000* (London, 2004)

Gordon, Eleanor, *Women and the Labour Movement in Scotland 1850–1914* (Oxford, 1991)

Gordon, Eleanor & Esther Breitenbach eds, T*he World is Ill Divided: Women's Work in Scotland in the Nineteenth and Early Twentieth-Century Scotland* (Edinburgh, 1990)

Out of Bounds: Women in Scottish Society 1800–1945 (Edinburgh, 1992)

Harvie, Christopher, *Scotland and Nationalism: Scottish Society and Politics 1707–1977* (London, 1977)
  No Gods and Precious Few Heroes: Twentieth-Century Scotland (Edinburgh, 1998)

Hay, Ian, *Their Name Liveth: The Book of the Scottish National War Memorial*, rev. ed. (Edinburgh, 1985)

Henderson, Diana M., *Highland Soldier 1820–1920* (Edinburgh, 1989)

Hinton, James, *The First Shops Stewards' Movement* (London, 1973)

Holford, J., *Reshaping Labour: Organisation, Work and Politics – Edinburgh in the Great War and After* (London, 1988)

Hunter, James, *The Making of the Crofting Community* (Edinburgh, 1976)

Hutchison, I. G. C., *A Political History of Scotland: Parties, Elections and Issues 1831–1924* (London, 1986)
  Scottish Politics in the Twentieth Century (Basingstoke, 2001)

Johnstone, Ian, *Beardmore Built: The Rise and Fall of a Clyde Shipyard* (Clydebank, 1993)
  Ships for a Nation: John Brown & Company Clydebank (West Dunbartonshire, 2000)

Johnston, Tom, *A History of the Working Classes in Scotland* (London, 1944)

Jones, D. T., J. F Duncan, H. M.Conacher & W. R. Scott, *Rural Scotland during the War* (Oxford, 1926)

Kay, Billy ed., *Odyssey: Voices from Scotland's Recent Past* (Edinburgh, 1980)

Odyssey, the Second Collection (Edinburgh, 1982)

Kenefick, William & Arthur McIvor eds., *Roots of Red Clydeside 1910–1914: Labour Unrest and Industrial Relations in West Scotland* (Edinburgh, 1996)

King, Elspeth, *The Scottish Woman's Suffrage Movement* (Glasgow, 1978)

Knox, W. W., *Industrial Nation: Work, Culture and Society in Scotland 1800 to the Present* (Edinburgh, 1999)

Leneman, Leah, *In the Service of Life: The Story of Elsie Inglis and the Scottish Women's Hospitals* (Edinburgh, 1994)

A Guid Cause: The Women's Suffrage Movement in Scotland, rev. ed. (Edinburgh, 1995)

Fit for Heroes? Land Settlement in Scotland after World War One (Edinburgh, 1996)

Lynch, Michael, *Scotland: A New History* (London, 1991)

Macdonald, C. M. M., *The Radical Threat: Political Change in Scotland, Paisley Politics 1885–1924* (East Linton, 2000)

MacDonald, C. M. M. & E. W. McFarland eds, *Scotland and the Great War* (East Linton, 1999)

Macdougall, Ian, ed., *Voices from Home and Work: Personal Recollections on Working Life and Labour Struggles in the Twentieth Century by Scots Men and Women* (Edinburgh, 2000)

McKinlay, A. & R. J. Morris, eds, *The ILP on Clydeside: From Foundation to Disintegration* (Manchester, 1991)

McLaren, Eva Shaw, ed., *A History of the Scottish Women's Hospitals* (London, 1919)

McLean, Iain, *The Legend of Red Clydeside* (Edinburgh, 1983, rev.ed., 1999)

Melling, Joseph, *Rent Strikes: The Peoples' Struggle for Housing in the West of Scotland 1890–1916* (Edinburgh, 1983)

Mileham, P. J. R., *Scottish Regiments* (Tunbridge Wells, 1988)

Milton, Nan, *John MacLean* (London, 1973)

Muir, Edwin, *Scottish Journey* (London, 1935)

Peebles, Hugh, *Warship Building on the Clyde: Naval Orders and the Prosperity of the Clyde Shipbuilding Industry* (Edinburgh, 1987)

Royle, Trevor, ed., *In Flanders Fields: Scottish Poetry and Prose of the First World War* (Edinburgh, 1988)

Glens Folk: Celebrating Life in Angus Glens (Angus, 2000)

Scott, Paul H., ed., *Scotland: A Concise Cultural History* (Edinburgh, 1993)

Scott, W. R. & J. Cunnison, *The Industries of the Clyde Valley during the War* (Oxford, 1924)

Slaven, Anthony, *The Development of the West of Scotland 1750–1960* (London, 1975)

Smout, T. C., *A Century of the Scottish People 1830–1950* (London, 1984)

Smyth, J. J., *Labour in Glasgow 1896–1936* (Edinburgh, 2000)

Wood, Ian S., *John Wheatley* (Manchester, 1990)

First World War

Andrews, I. O., *The Economic Effects of the World War upon Women and Children in Great Britain* (Oxford, 1921)

Aspinall–Oglander, Brig.-Gen. C. F., *Military Operations: Gallipoli, The Official History of the Great War*, 2 vols (London, 1929–32)

Barker, Arthur, *The Neglected War: Mesopotamia 1914–1918* (London, 1967)

Beckett, Ian & Keith Simpson, eds, *A Nation in Arms: A Social Study of the British Army in the First World War* (Manchester, 1985)

Bond, Brian, ed., *The First World War and British Military History* (Oxford, 1991)

Bond, Brian & N. Cave, eds., *Haig: A Re-appraisal 70 Years On* (London, 1999)

Bourke, Joanna, *Dismembering the Male: Men's Bodies, Britain and the Great War* (London, 1996)

Braybon, Gail, *Women Workers in the First World War* (London, 1989)

Brown, Malcolm, ed., *The Imperial War Museum Book of the First World War* (London, 1991)

Buchan, John, *History of the War* (London and Edinburgh, 1915–19)

Cole, Christopher & E. F. Cheeseman, *The Air Defence of Britain 1914–1918* (London, 1984)

Corbett, Julian & Henry Newbolt, *Naval Operations*, 5 vols. (London 1920–31)

De Groot, G. J., *Douglas Haig 1861–1928* (London, 1988)

Edmonds, James E., gen. ed., *History of the Great War, Based on Official Documents: Military Operations, France and Belgium*, 14 vols, (London, 1922–49)

Falls, Cyril, *The First World War* (London, 1960)
Armageddon 1918 (London, 1964)

Ferguson, Niall, *The Pity of War* (London, 1998)

Fussell, Paul, *The Great War and Modern Memory* (Oxford, 1975)

Gordon, Andrew, *The Rules of the Game: Jutland and British Naval Command* (London, 1996)

Grieves, Keith, *The Politics of Manpower* (Manchester, 1988)

Holmes, Richard, *Tommy: The British Soldier on the Western Front 1914–1918* (London, 2004)

James, Lawrence, *Imperial War: The Life and Times of Field Marshal Viscount Allenby* (London, 1993)

James, Robert Rhodes, *Gallipoli* (London, 1965)

Keegan, John, *The First World War* (London, 1998)

Liddle, Peter H., *The Sailor's War 1914–1918* (Poole, 1985)
  Voices of War 1914–1918 (London, 1988)

Macdonald, Lyn, *Somme* (London, 1983)
  1914 (London, 1987)
  Voices and Images of the Great War (London, 1988)
  1915: The End of Innocence (London, 1993)

Marder, Arthur J., *From the Dreadnought to Scapa Flow*, 5 vols (Oxford, 1961–70)

Massie, Robert K., *Castles of Steel: Britain, German and the Winning of the Great War at Sea* (London, 2003)

Middlebrook, Martin, *The First Day on the Somme* (London, 1971)

Middlebrook, Martin & Mary, *The Somme Battlefield* (London, 1991)

Palmer, Alan, *The Gardeners of Salonika* (London, 1965)

Rae, John, *Conscience and Politics: The British Government and the Conscientious Objector to Military Service 1916–1919* (Oxford, 1970)

Raleigh, Walter & H. A. Jones, *The War in the Air,* 6 vols (Oxford 1922–37)

Royle, Trevor, *The Kitchener Enigma* (London, 1985)

Sheffield, Gary, *Forgotten Victory: The First World War – Myths and Realities* (London, 2001)
  & John Bourne, *Douglas Haig: War Diaries and Letters 1914–1918* (London, 2005)

Simkins, Peter, *Kitchener's Army: The Raising of the New Armies 1914–1916* (Manchester, 1986)

Steel, Nigel & Peter Hart, *Defeat at Gallipoli* (London, 1994)

Strachan, Hew, *The First World War: To Arms* (Oxford, 2001)

Taylor, A. J. P., *The First World War: An Illustrated History* (London, 1963)

Terraine, John, *Haig: The Educated Soldier* (London, 1963)
  The Western Front 1914–1918 (London, 1964)
  To Win a War: 1918 (London, 1978)

Travers, Tim, *The Killing Ground* (London, 1987)
  How the War was Won (London, 1992)

Wakefield, Alan & Simon Moody, *Under the Devil's Eye: Britain's Forgotten Army at Salonika 1915–1918* (Stroud, 2004)

Wilson, Trevor, *The Myriad Faces of War: Britain and the Great War 1914–1918* (Oxford, 1986)

Winter, Denis, *Death's Men: Soldiers of the Great War* (London, 1978)
  Haig's Command: A Re-Assessment (London, 1991)

Winter, J. M., *The Great War and the British People* (London, 1986)

Index

Note to index: Names beginning 'Mc' are indexed as if spelt 'Mac'. Where given, a person's rank normally will be the rank they held when they first appear in the text. Individual infantry regiments and battalions are indexed under 'regiments'. *fn* after a page number indicates a footnote on that page; *passim* indicates many separate mentions within a range.

MILITARY RANKS ABBREVIATIONS

1st Lt.	First Lieutenant	L/Cpl.	Lance Corporal
2nd Lt.	Second Lieutenant	Lt.	Lieutenant
Adm.	Admiral	Lt-Col.	Lieutenant-Colonel
Brig-Gen.	Brigadier-General	Lt-Gen.	Lieutenant-General
Capt.	Captain	Maj.	Major
Col.	Colonel	Pipe-Maj.	Pipe-Major
Cpl.	Corporal	Pte.	Private
C/Sgt.	Colour Sergeant	RSM	Regimental Sergeant-Major
CSM	Company Sergeant-Major	Tpr.	Trooper
FM	Field Marshall	Vice-Adm.	Vice-Admiral
Gen.	General		